TYING THE KNOT

The Marriage Act 1836 established the foundations of modern marriage law, allowing couples to marry in register offices and non-Anglican places of worship for the first time. Rebecca Probert draws on an exceptionally wide range of primary sources to provide the first detailed examination of marriage legislation, social practice, and their mutual interplay, from 1836 through to the unanticipated demands of the 2020 coronavirus pandemic. She analyses how and why the law has evolved, closely interrogating the parliamentary and societal debates behind legislation. She demonstrates how people have chosen to marry and how those choices have changed, and evaluates how far the law has been help or hindrance in enabling couples to marry in ways that reflect their beliefs, be they religious or secular. In an era of individual choice and multiculturalism, *Tying the Knot* sign posts possible ways in which future legislators might avoid the pitfalls of the past.

REBECCA PROBERT is a Professor at the School of Law, University of Exeter, and Specialist Consultant to the Law Commission's Weddings Project. She is author of *Marriage Law and Practice in the Long Eighteenth Century: A Reassessment* (2009) and *The Changing Legal Regulation of Cohabitation: From Fornicators to Family, 1600–2010* (2012).

CAMBRIDGE STUDIES IN ENGLISH LEGAL HISTORY

Edited by

J. H. Baker
Fellow of St Catharine's College, Cambridge

Tying the Knot: The Formation of Marriage 1836–2020 Rebecca Probert

Maintenance in Medieval England Jonathan Rose

The Reinvention of Magna Carta 1216–1616 John Baker

Insurance in Elizabethan England: The London Code Guido Rossi

The Law of Contract 1670–1870 Warren Swain

A History of English Tort Law 1900–1950 Paul Mitchell

Sir Edward Coke and the Reformation of the Laws Religion, Politics and Jurisprudence, 1578–1616 David Chan Smith

Medieval English Conveyances John M. Kaye

Marriage Law and Practices in the Long Eighteenth Century: A Reassessment Rebecca Probert

The Rise and Fall of the English Ecclesiastical Courts, 1500–1860 R. B. Outhwaite

Law Courts and Lawyers in the City of London, 1300–1550 Penny Tucker

Legal Foundations of Tribunals in Nineteenth-century England Chantal Stebbings

Pettyfoggers and Vipers of the Commonwealth: The 'Lower Branch' of the Legal Profession in Early Modern England C. W. Brooks

Roman Canon Law in Reformation England R. H. Helmholz

Sir Henry Maine: A Study in Victorian Jurisprudence R. C. J. Cocks

Sir William Scott, *Lord Stowell Judge of the High Court of Admiralty, 1798–1828* Henry J. Bourguignon

The Early History of the Law of Bills and Notes: A Study of the Origins of Anglo-American Commercial Law James Steven Rogers

The Law of Treason in England in the Later Middle Ages J. G. Bellamy

William Sheppard, Cromwell's Law Reformer Nancy L. Matthews

TYING THE KNOT

The Formation of Marriage 1836–2020

REBECCA PROBERT

University of Exeter

CAMBRIDGE
UNIVERSITY PRESS

CAMBRIDGE
UNIVERSITY PRESS

University Printing House, Cambridge CB2 8BS, United Kingdom

One Liberty Plaza, 20th Floor, New York, NY 10006, USA

477 Williamstown Road, Port Melbourne, VIC 3207, Australia

314–321, 3rd Floor, Plot 3, Splendor Forum, Jasola District Centre, New Delhi – 110025, India

103 Penang Road, #05–06/07, Visioncrest Commercial, Singapore 238467

Cambridge University Press is part of the University of Cambridge.

It furthers the University's mission by disseminating knowledge in the pursuit of education, learning, and research at the highest international levels of excellence.

www.cambridge.org
Information on this title: www.cambridge.org/9781316518281
DOI: 10.1017/9781009000109

© Rebecca Probert 2021

First published 2021

A catalogue record for this publication is available from the British Library.

Library of Congress Cataloging-in-Publication Data
Names: Probert, Rebecca, author.
Title: Tying the knot : the formation of marriage, 1836–2020 / Rebecca Probert, University of Exeter.
Description: Cambridge, United Kingdom ; New York, NY : Cambridge University Press, 2021. | Series: Cambridge studies in English legal history | Includes index.
Identifiers: LCCN 2021025062 (print) | LCCN 2021025063 (ebook) | ISBN 9781316518281 (hardback) | ISBN 9781009000109 (ebook)
Subjects: LCSH: Marriage law – England – History. | Husband and wife – England – History. | BISAC: LAW / Legal History
Classification: LCC KD753 .P767 2021 (print) | LCC KD753 (ebook) | DDC 346.42/016–dc23
LC record available at https://lccn.loc.gov/2021025062
LC ebook record available at https://lccn.loc.gov/2021025063

ISBN 978-1-316-51828-1 Hardback

For Mum, who was unable to marry in accordance with her beliefs, in the hope that others will be able to do so.

CONTENTS

PREFACE AND ACKNOWLEDGEMENTS

I have always enjoyed weddings. From the age of nine I sang in the choir of my local village church, and from the front row of the choirstalls I had by far the best view of what was going on. Barely a yard away from the bride and groom, I could see their smiles and their loving glances as they exchanged their vows, while their family and friends could only watch the backs of their heads. When I got married to my husband, Liam, in 2006, we filled the choirstalls with our nearest and dearest so that they too could see and share in that moment.

It was very easy for us to get married. All we had to do was speak to the vicar and to the parish office. The banns were duly called, although as relative newcomers to the parish and the church nobody knew who we were. For other friends and family it was not quite so simple. One friend wanted to marry in the Catholic church she had attended as a child, but, having moved away in the meantime, she had to establish residence in the district in order to be able to do so. Another wanted both an imam and a Lutheran minister to play a part in his wedding, reflecting his and his partner's different faiths, but had to settle for a sequence of ceremonies. These are just two examples of the difficulties that individuals might face in getting married according to their beliefs.

For the past few years I have been closely involved in discussions about how the law might be reformed. In 2015 I was seconded to the Law Commission to work on its scoping study of the law governing how and where people can marry in England and Wales.[1] In 2018 it was announced that the Commission would be asked to undertake a full law reform project in this area,[2] and I was part of the team that began work on this project in 2019. The Commission's consultation paper putting forward provisional proposals for a new marriage law that

---

[1] Law Commission, *Getting Married: A Scoping Paper* (17 December 2015).
[2] The announcement was made by HM Treasury as part of its 2018 Budget: HM Treasury, Budget (29 October 2018), para. 5.52.

would allow for greater choice within a simpler legal structure was published in the autumn of 2020,[3] and its final report will follow later in 2021.

Working with the team at the Law Commission – Nicholas Hopkins, Matt Jolley, Elizabeth Welch, and Sam Hussaini – has been a joy and an inspiration, but I should stress that nothing in the pages that follow draws directly on any of the discussions with them, or with the many religious groups, belief organisations, celebrants, registrars, and policymakers with whom we have consulted. Nonetheless, the experience has inevitably influenced my perception of the past. Hearing how the law does and does not work for different groups has made me curious to find the reasons for these differences, to ascertain whose voices were heard in the earlier debates over how the law should be reformed, and whose were not. Listening to the very different views about what form the law should take, and learning about the different practices that need to be accommodated, has also given me a certain degree of sympathy for past reformers tasked with finding a solution that balanced competing interests and desires, even where that solution was far from perfect. That said, certain earlier solutions were clearly politically motivated, others were accepted because no one could think of anything better, and some supposedly fundamental principles seem to have emerged by accident.

That, however, is to anticipate. Here I just wish to thank all of those who have played a part in the making of this book. First and foremost, I want to thank my husband, Liam, for his superlative research assistance, eagle-eyed reading of drafts, and willingness to be a sounding board for ideas. I would also like to thank my father-in-law, *sean* Liam, who was dragooned into providing research assistance during lockdown, and whose review of websites and construction of spreadsheets was very helpful. I am enormously grateful to Professor Chris Barton for reading the entire manuscript in draft and for his helpful comments. The initial seeds of this book were sown when writing an article on the 150th anniversary of the 1868 Royal Commission on marriage law, and I would like to thank Maebh Harding and Brian Dempsey for their collaboration on that piece. Dr Stephanie Pywell of the Open University invited me to work with her on a number of empirical projects on weddings, and I am hugely grateful for her meticulous approach to the collection and analysis of data. The writing of this book overlapped with

[3] Law Commission, *Getting Married: A Consultation Paper on Weddings Law*, CP No. 247 (3 September 2020).

work on a Nuffield-funded project on non-legally binding marriage ceremonies, and I benefitted from many stimulating conversations with my colleagues on that project, Dr Rajnaara Akhtar, Dr Vishal Vora, Sharon Blake, and Tania Barton. I would also like to thank Daniel Hill for alerting me to many examples of lockdown weddings that I might otherwise have missed, and Lucy-Clare Windle for sharing her dissertation on wedding dresses with me.

Having presented various aspects of the book as it developed, I am also very grateful for the helpful feedback that I received from attendees at the British Legal History Conference in St Andrews, the Oxford Legal History Forum, Edinburgh Law School, Newcastle Law School, the inaugural conference of the Register of Qualified Genealogists, the Devon Family History Society, the Peak District Family History Society, the Odiham U3A (who added some local context to the tale of the Reverend Lush, discussed in Chapter 4), and Professor Mélanie Methot's enthusiastic history students at the University of Alberta.

I also want to thank the many family historians who so generously provided information about their ancestors' weddings. Some of the stories they shared deserved a book in themselves. Special thanks go to Christine Brumbill, Bryan Grimshaw, Susan Donaldson, Margaret French, Jenny Gordon, Wendy Hamilton, Kathy Irvine, Valerie King, Keith Howard McClellan, Elizabeth Parsons, Jenny Paterson, Lesley Plant, Mike Sadler, Joan Smith, Deborah Whitehead, Jill Wright, and Peter Zimmermann for being willing to write up these stories as case studies, to Liz Harris for providing data on almost 700 weddings in Nonconformist chapels in Desborough, and to Gwyneth Wilkie and Ruth Midgely for alerting me to useful sources of information. Peter Calver published the original call for information in his Lost Cousins newsletter, and the Devon Family History Society and Isle of Wight Family History Society also published the call. In addition, helpful information was provided by all of the following: Adrian Abbott, Carol Abbott, Matthew Abel, Dawn Adams, Geoff Allan, Jenepher Allen, Tony Allen, Rosie Ansell, Colleen Armstrong-Thomas, Val Bachelor, Mary Barry, Pam Blackaby, Andrew Braid, Brian Brown, Chris Bourne, John Buchanan, Steve Bumstead, Anne Burns, Mary Butlin, Philip Carnall, Shirley Casey, John Cassidy, Jan Clemenson, Val Clinging, Robyn Coghlan, Barbara Cole, Julie Collins, Madeleine Cook, Judith Cooper, Alan Craxford, Helen Davies, Roger Davies, Sally Davies, Margaret Dennis, Marg Dolen, Norma Doling, Mary-Ann Dunn, M. Duxbury, Victoria Dyke, Teresa Eckford, Brian Ekins, Karen Eldridge,

Lesley Eldridge, Hilary Elliott, Joyce Engmann, Noreen Evans, Karin Fancett, Janet Findlay, Sheila Fleming, Tom Flintham, John Godfrey Francis, Jennifer Fraser, Janet Freeman, Sue Frezza, Alison Galligan, Ann Gardner, Audrey Giacomin, Jon Gilbert, Pauline Gilbertson, Jenny Gordon, Julie Goucher, Pam Griffiths, Judith Gurney, John Hammond, Annette Harris, Sheila Harris (Constantine One Name Study), Kathy Hart, Elaine Hayes, David Heard, Yvonne Herne, Joan Hickey, Guy Hirst, Kate Holloway, Sarah Hughes, Tony Wakefield Hunt, Elaine Huq, Andrew R. Janes, Christine Jemmeson, Jill Johnson, Penny Keens, Elizabeth Kemshead, Rosemary Kennemore, Deborah King, Diana Kirkhope, Denise Langley, Stephen Larkin, Pam Laycock, Barbara Lee, Deirdre Leigh, Bridget Lewis, Jenni Llewellyn, Mike Lofty, Wendy Lynch, Ken Maidens, Beryl Malcolm, Chris Manning, Megan O'Marr, Joan Marshall, Nick Mayne, Anne Mead, Carol Metcalfe, Sara McMahon, Jane Milbourne, Colin Moretti, Alun Morris, Janice Morris, Marion Moverley, Sheila Murray, Roger and Jenny McNae, Tony Newcombe, Pat Nixon, John North, Hilary Oldham, G. W. Oxley, Carol Parker, Sandy Pescod, Barbara Phillips, Pat Phillips, Brenda Powell, Sylvia Precious, Keith Preece, Mary Pringle, Wendy Rakestrow, Mary Ratcliffe, Judith Redfern, Susan Reeve, Dr Edward Reid-Smith, John Reynolds, Barrie Robinson, Diana Robinson, Sandra Robinson, Laura Rouse, Katy Russell-Duff, Ray Rylatt, Sandra Shaw, Ann Simcock, Mary Simpson, Shirley Small, Paul Smallcombe, John Smith, Sue Smith, Jeremy Somerton, Margaret Spiller, Colyn Storer, Janet Stroebel, Mrs Audrey Suthren, David Swidenbank, Carol Tarr, Karen Tayler, Ian Terry, Eileen Thompson, Valerie Thorley, Marilyn Tilley, Kim Tomlinson, Linda Towne, Sandra Vincent, Lorraine Waldron, Angela Ward, Erica Ward, Mary Ward, Annette Watson, Barbara Watts, Jan Webb, Richard West, Irene Wilkinson, John Williams, Kay Winfield, John Wintrip, Peter Wood, Dave Wright, Jane Wright, Josephine Wright, and Mark Young.

Finally, this book is dedicated to my mother, and it is with my parents' wedding in 1971 that we shall start.

ABBREVIATIONS

ER   *English Reports*
GRO   General Register Office
HLMP   *House of Lords Minutes of Proceedings*
JHC   *Journals of the House of Commons*
JHL   *Journals of the House of Lords*
ODNB   *Oxford Dictionary of National Biography*
ONS   Office for National Statistics
PDD   Protestant Dissenting Deputies
PP   Parliamentary Papers
TNA   The National Archives

1

Introduction

On a Saturday morning in December 1971, my parents were married in Coventry register office.[1] My mother wore a long crimson velvet dress; a suitable choice for a cold winter's day, and also a reflection of the fact that those marrying in a register office were advised not to wear white.[2] The register office was located in Cheylesmore Manor, formerly a medieval royal palace, and its stone steps provided an attractive backdrop for the photos. The ceremony itself took place in a small but charming room, in front of a number of guests in addition to their two witnesses. The cost of the entire process was £2.75.[3] Afterwards, they drove to the village where my mother lived for a blessing at her local church. The civil ceremony had clearly taken less time than they expected, as they were too early for the church service and had to go to the pub next door in the meantime. By 12.30 p.m. they were sitting down to a modest lunch with their guests.

This apparently simple example illustrates how far weddings are freighted with history – not just the personal histories of the spouses but also a complex legal, social, and religious history.

The form of the church blessing, and its relationship to the wedding in the register office, was dictated by policy established over a hundred years earlier, in 1856.[4] And the shortness of the earlier civil ceremony reflected the fact that it comprised little more than the repetition of the words that had originally been prescribed by the Marriage Act 1836 when the option of getting married in a register office was first introduced.[5] Fast forward to today, by contrast, and couples marrying in the same room where my parents married can now include their own vows, readings, and music –

---

[1] Barbara Probert, private unpublished diary, 1971.
[2] Betty Owen Williams, *Planning Your Wedding Day from A to Z* (London: W. Foulsham & Co Ltd, 1964).
[3] This comprised 75p for each to give notice and £1.25 for the attendance of the registrar.
[4] Marriage and Registration Act 1856; see further Chapter 4.
[5] See further Chapters 3 and 7.

at a cost.[6] Reclassified as 'approved premises',[7] and renamed 'the Black Prince Room', getting married there on a Saturday morning now costs £511, fifteen times more than an increase based on inflation alone.[8]

How a couple can marry, and what they have to do in order to be married, is thus determined by a combination of laws, some recent, some made decades if not centuries ago. How they choose to marry will often be shaped by the social norms of the day, with the idea of a 'proper' wedding taking different forms over time. It may also be influenced by their religious beliefs, or by their lack of belief. But my parents' wedding is also an example of how we cannot necessarily assume that the way in which a couple choose to marry is a true reflection of their beliefs.

Looking at the statistics, it would be easy to assume that my parents were simply following the growing trend for weddings to be celebrated without religious rites. In 1971, a register office wedding was nothing out of the ordinary, with the number of such weddings being almost equal to the number that were celebrated in churches, chapels, synagogues, mosques, gurdwaras, and temples combined.[9] But my parents were not marrying in the register office out of choice. They were unable to marry in the church where my mother worshipped, on account of the fact that my father had previously been married, and his first wife was still alive. Forty years earlier, however, a couple in their position could not have been denied a church wedding; before 1937, Anglican clergy could only refuse to marry a person who had been divorced on the basis of their adultery, not the person who had obtained the divorce.[10] The mid-twentieth century saw the approach of the Church of England to the remarriage of those who had obtained a divorce becoming more restrictive, with consequences for the numbers marrying according to its rites.[11]

---

[6] www.ceremoniesinsidecoventry.co.uk/cheylesmoremanorceremonysuite.

[7] The concept of 'approved premises' was introduced by the Marriage Act 1994 to enable civil weddings to be celebrated in a wider range of places; on this, and on the reclassification of many former register offices, see further Chapter 9.

[8] This comprises £35 each for giving notice, £430 for the ceremony, and £11 for the certificate: www.ceremoniesinsidecoventry.co.uk/homepage/18/ceremony-fees-from -1-april-2020-31-march-2021, last accessed 10 July 2020. £2.75 in 1971 is roughly equivalent to £37.50 today.

[9] See ONS, 'Marriages in England and Wales 2017' (14 April 2020), table 1: 'Number of marriages by type of ceremony and denomination, 1837 to 2017'; John Haskey, 'Marriage Rites – Trends in Marriages by Manner of Solemnisation and Denomination in England and Wales, 1841–2012' in Joanna Miles, Perveez Mody, and Rebecca Probert (eds.), *Marriage Rites and Rights* (Oxford: Hart, 2015). See further Chapter 8.

[10] See further Chapters 4 and 7.

[11] See further Chapters 6 and 7.

Tying the Knot is about these intertwined legal, social, and religious histories. It has three interconnecting aims. The first is to analyse how the laws governing how couples can marry have evolved, from the 1836 Act that established the basic foundations of much of the current law to the present day. The second is to assess the evidence as to how couples have actually married over that period. And the third is to evaluate how far the law has enabled them to do so in accordance with their beliefs. That phrasing is deliberately broad, intended to encompass not only religious beliefs and non-religious beliefs such as Humanism, but also what might be termed beliefs about marriage itself. A couple's preference for a civil wedding, for example, might be motivated either by a lack of religious belief or by a positive belief that marriage is a civil contract and should be celebrated with civic rites.[12] Alternatively, their choice of a civil wedding may be made independently of their beliefs, on the basis of convenience or a desire for concealment. Or – as in the case of my parents – it might not be a choice at all, but simply the only means of getting married that was available to them in practice.

Looking at these three issues together provides a different perspective from considering each of them in isolation. It is only by looking at how the law was experienced in practice that its limitations become clear. Equally, without a proper understanding of the legal constraints within which they had to operate, we may misinterpret the choices that couples made, and mistakenly attribute certain beliefs to them. How couples married was not necessarily how they would ideally have married had other options been available. The constraints that I will be examining are not just those that affected remarriage after a divorce, but the whole panoply of regulations about where weddings could take place, and who could conduct them. The path to marriage in the past was just as complex as it is today, with many couples having an additional ceremony before or after their legal wedding. The form of those earlier ceremonies may have differed from those that are celebrated today, but whether they are Christian, Jewish, Muslim, Hindu, Sikh, Pagan, Humanist, interfaith, a blend of different traditions, or completely unique to the parties involved,[13] their existence points to the limitations of the law.

---

[12] See, e.g., Ben Rogers, 'White Wedding Blues', *The Guardian*, 29 April 2000.

[13] On the rise of bespoke ceremonies, see Stephanie Pywell, 'The Day of Their Dreams: Celebrant-led Wedding Celebration Ceremonies' (2020) *Child and Family Law Quarterly* 177 and 'Beyond Beliefs: A Proposal to Give Couples in England and Wales a Real Choice of Marriage Officiants' (2020) *Child and Family Law Quarterly* 215.

With reform of the laws regulating weddings under consideration at the time of writing,[14] it is all the more important to understand how those laws evolved, how they were experienced, and the problems that they have generated. In disentangling the knots of the current law and reshaping it for the future, knowing the history of each provision, and the purpose that it was intended to serve, is vital. Otherwise, the fact that a particular provision has endured over the decades may lead to an unwarranted assumption that there must have been a good reason behind its introduction and that it worked well in the past. It is all too easy to retrofit apparently convincing explanations. It is also important to know what has worked in the past and what has not, in order to assess what might be necessary to close the gap between what is permitted in theory and what is available in practice.

In this introductory chapter, I first set the Marriage Act 1836 in context by giving some background regarding the process of getting married prior to its passage, setting out its key terms, and explaining how it forms the foundation of the current law. I then go on to look at how the 1836 Act is generally perceived much more positively than the current law regulating weddings, and suggest some reasons for that difference in perceptions. My use of the term 'weddings' here is deliberate; this is a book about getting married, not about marriage itself, and the third section of the chapter explains the difference. Narrowing the focus to weddings is necessary in order to do justice to the richness of the sources about how couples have married, and the evidence about their beliefs, and in the fourth section I set out the range of material on which I have drawn, before closing with a summary of the book's structure and coverage.

The Foundation of the Modern Law

The Marriage Act 1836 was not the first piece of legislation to regulate the process of getting married in England and Wales – that was the Clandestine Marriages Act 1753, over eighty years earlier. Under its terms the only way of getting married had been according to the rites of the Anglican church. Only Jews and Quakers had been exempted from the need to marry in this way; all other couples had been expected to marry in the Anglican church, regardless of their beliefs or lack of them.

---

[14] Law Commission, *Getting Married: A Scoping Paper* (17 December 2015); *Getting Married: A Consultation Paper on Weddings Law*, CP No. 247 (3 September 2020).

While the 1753 Act was repealed in the 1820s, the Marriage Act 1823 made no change to the options available to couples, merely to the consequences of failing to comply with certain legal requirements.[15]

In my earlier work *Marriage Law and Practice in the Long Eighteenth Century*, I traced the passage of the 1753 Act and how it operated in practice.[16] I showed how other Protestant dissenting denominations, which had not previously developed their own forms of weddings, married in the Church of England without any additional ceremony, while English Catholics tended to navigate the competing requirements of conscience and law by having an Anglican wedding and an additional Catholic ceremony.[17] That background is important to set the scene for the Marriage Act 1836. The passage, terms, and take-up of the 1836 Act cannot be properly understood unless it is appreciated that the previous story of marriage law and practice was overwhelmingly one of conformity with a single set of religious rites.[18]

The story of the 1836 Act is far more complex, as a brief sketch of its provisions will demonstrate. From 1 July 1837, weddings could take place in any certified place of worship that had been duly registered for weddings, or in one of the new register offices. Jewish and Quaker weddings were brought within the framework of the law, rather than simply being exempted from the need to comply with it; they, along with all others marrying other than according to Anglican rites, had to give notice to a new state official, the superintendent registrar. Anglican weddings remained primarily governed by the 1823 Act, but even these could now be preceded by civil preliminaries. And state oversight of marriage was further asserted by stipulating that *all* marriages should be centrally registered. Responsibility for registration was devolved in the case of Anglican, Jewish, and Quaker marriages, but all other marriages had to be attended by a registrar.[19] When combined with the different

---

[15] See further Chapter 2.

[16] Rebecca Probert, *Marriage Law and Practice in the Long Eighteenth Century: A Reassessment* (Cambridge: Cambridge University Press, 2009).

[17] *Ibid.*, ch. 9; see also Rebecca Probert and Liam D'Arcy-Brown, 'Catholics and the Clandestine Marriages Act of 1753' (2008) 80 *Local Population Studies* 78.

[18] A rather different view was previously advanced by John Gillis, *For Better, For Worse: British Marriages 1600 to the Present* (Oxford: Oxford University Press, 1985) and Stephen Parker, *Informal Marriage, Cohabitation and the Law, 1750–1989* (Basingstoke: Macmillan, 1990), both claiming that there was widespread evidence of non-compliance with the 1753 Act. For my rebuttal of such claims see *Marriage Law and Practice*.

[19] See further Chapter 2 for the details of these provisions.

forms of preliminaries that were recognised,[20] there were no fewer than ten different routes to a legally recognised marriage.[21]

Both the 1823 and 1836 Acts were amended before being consolidated in the Marriage Act 1949, and the 1949 Act has been much amended since. In particular, those marrying in a registered place of worship may now do so in the presence of an 'authorised person' appointed by their own religious group,[22] and, as noted earlier, there is now the option of having a civil wedding on a wide range of 'approved premises' rather than just in a register office. Nonetheless, much of what the 1836 Act set in place still forms part of the current law. The distinction between Anglican and civil preliminaries remains. So too does the separate treatment of Anglican, Jewish, and Quaker weddings. The 1836 Act thus forms the logical starting point for any consideration of the current law governing how couples can marry. But as the next section will discuss, how it has been viewed may differ depending on whether it is seen against the backdrop of the earlier restrictions or the diversity of England and Wales today.

Perceptions of Past and Present

While the 1836 Act has attracted surprisingly little commentary,[23] the story told about it has generally been a positive one in that it has been seen as an important liberalising measure that recognised the religious (and irreligious) diversity of nineteenth-century England and Wales.[24]

---

[20] There were four different forms of preliminary to an Anglican wedding, two for weddings in register offices or registered places of worship, and (initially) one for Jewish and Quaker weddings: see further Chapter 3.

[21] Olive Anderson, 'The Incidence of Civil Marriage in Victorian England and Wales' (1975) 69 *Past & Present* 50, put the figure at eight, but this was excluding Jewish and Quaker weddings, presumably on the basis that these options were not available outside those religious groups.

[22] As a result of the Marriage Act 1898; see further Chapter 5.

[23] The best account is that by Stephen Cretney, *Family Law in the Twentieth Century: A History* (Oxford: Oxford University Press, 2003). Joseph Jackson's *The Formation and Annulment of Marriage* (London: Butterworths, 2nd ed. 1969) has a lengthy chapter on the history of marriage law, but the 1836 Act is consigned to a short section listing the provisions of the various Acts passed between 1822 and 1899 (see pp. 67–69). Scot Peterson and Iain McLean devote a few pages to it (*Legally Married: Love and Law in the UK and the US* (Edinburgh: Edinburgh University Press, 2013), pp. 100–02). Stephen Parker provides a little more detail in his *Informal Marriage*, although he dismisses the provisions of the Act as being 'as dry as old bones' (p. 72).

[24] See, e.g., Anderson, 'Civil Marriage', p. 50 ('[i]f the central characteristic of democratic capitalist society is mass choice, then democratic capitalist marriage arrived in England

This, however, stands in stark contrast to the verdict on the current legislation, the Marriage Act 1949; here, the emphasis has been on its limitations and failure to accommodate different beliefs.[25] This difference in perceptions can in part be explained by the fact that the population of England and Wales is far more religiously diverse than it was in 1836, with individuals espousing a far wider range of religious and non-religious beliefs. But there are in addition three other reasons why the 1949 Act is widely regarded less favourably than its predecessor. The first two relate to a tendency in at least some of the scholarship to exaggerate the extent to which the 1836 Act liberalised the law; and to underestimate the extent to which the 1949 Act made provision for different faiths. The third reason, however, is that some of the changes that have been made in the intervening years have in fact *removed* choices; to this extent, the perceptions of the 1836 Act as liberal and the current law as restrictive are entirely justified.

While the full details will be explored in the chapters that follow, it is necessary to say a little more about all three points here, not least because they raise some important issues about terminology. First, the liberalising effects of the 1836 Act have been exaggerated by accounts that imply that it allowed couples to be married in any chapel and by any minister of religion.[26] Had this been the case, the take-up of the new options might

---

on 1 July 1837'); Parker, *Informal Marriage*, p. 49, contrasting it with 'the rigid provisions of Lord Hardwicke's Act'; Cretney, *History*, p. 12, describing the Act as a 'brilliant compromise'; Jennifer Phegley, *Courtship and Marriage in Victorian England* (Santa Barbara: Praeger, 2012), p. 117, noting 'the widening options for legal marriage'. Peterson and McLean, *Legally Married*, are more negative, describing the process of getting married in a register office as 'unpleasant' (p. 102), but they do also suggest that there was 'substantial demand' for the new forms of marriage introduced by the Act (p. 103).

[25] See, e.g., Peter W. Edge and Dominic Corrywright, 'Including Religion: Reflections on Legal, Religious, and Social Implications of the Developing Ceremonial Law of Marriage and Civil Partnership' (2011) 26(1) *Journal of Contemporary Religion* 19; Prakash Shah, 'Judging Muslims' in Robin Griffith-Jones (ed.), *Islam and English Law* (Cambridge: Cambridge University Press, 2013), 144–156, Valentine Le Grice and Vishal Vora, 'Nikah: Principle and Policy' (2017) *Family Affairs* 56; All-Party Parliamentary Humanist Group, '*Any Lawful Impediment?' A Report of the All-Party Parliamentary Humanist Group's Inquiry into the Legal Recognition of Humanist Marriage in England and Wales* (2018).

[26] Gillis, *For Better, For Worse*, p. 219, referring to the 'legalization' of chapel marriage, without setting out the requirements with which places of worship had to comply before legal weddings could be solemnised there; Lawrence Stone, *Road to Divorce: A History of the Making and Breaking of Marriage in England* (Oxford: Oxford University Press, 1995), p. 133, referring to the possibility of marrying in 'a sacred religious ceremony conducted by a minister in holy orders in a church or chapel'; John Witte Jr, *From Sacrament to*

have been far greater,[27] and the law would operate very differently today. In fact, the exacting criteria for places of worship to be registered for weddings meant that many were not,[28] and the 1836 Act conferred no direct authority on ministers at all. Even after 1898, when it was possible for registered places of worship to appoint their own 'authorised persons', their authority derived from their appointment, rather than whether they held a particular ministerial post, and their role was to register the marriage, not necessarily to conduct the wedding.[29] Right through to the present day, many registered places of worship have not appointed their own authorised person and remain dependent on a registrar attending and registering any weddings that take place there.[30] Throughout the book I have therefore used the more precise, if cumbersome, terminology of 'registered place of worship', in preference to the more colloquial 'chapel', to keep the limitations of the law at the forefront of readers' minds.[31]

Second, the tendency to underestimate the extent to which the 1949 Act made provision for different faiths is evident in the way that some commentators have contrasted the rules applicable to Judeo–Christian

---

Contract: Marriage, Religion and Law in the Western Tradition (Louisville: Westminster John Knox Press, 2nd ed. 2012), p. 305, suggesting Catholics, as well as Jews and Quakers, were able to marry 'in accordance with the religious laws and customs of their own communities', and claiming that all that was required was for these marriages to be registered after the fact; Carolyn Lambert, 'Introduction: The Lottery of Marriage' in Carolyn Lambert and Marion Shaw (eds.), *For Better, For Worse: Marriage in Victorian Novels by Women* (London: Routledge, 2018), p. 3, claiming that the 1836 Act 'enabled ministers of churches other than the Church of England to conduct marriages'.

[27] See, e.g., Roderick Floud and Pat Thane, 'The Incidence of Civil Marriage in Victorian England and Wales' (1979) 84 *Past & Present* 146, who rightly highlight the difficulties of marrying in a registered place of worship. The subsequent demolition of their argument that such difficulties might explain the fluctuations in the resort to the register office (see Olive Anderson, 'The Incidence of Civil Marriage in Victorian England and Wales: A rejoinder' (1979) 84 *Past & Present* 155) should not obscure the fact that their basic point holds good: see further Chapter 5.

[28] See further Chapter 2 for the criteria and Chapters 3, 4, and 5 for the proportions of places of worship that were registered.

[29] See further Chapter 5.

[30] Law Commission, *Getting Married: A Consultation Paper on Weddings Law*, para. 5.110, noting that only around 12,000 of approximately 22,500 registered places of worship have their own registers, indicating that an authorised person has been appointed.

[31] The terminology of 'chapel' is in any case problematic, given that there are Anglican chapels as well as non-Anglican ones, that many Christians would refer to their place of worship as a church rather than a chapel, and that adherents of other faiths would tend to use other terms.

groups with those applicable to other faiths.[32] This would be a valid point in relation to the 1836 Act, since under its provisions only certified places of worship could be registered for weddings, and the only places of worship that could be certified as such were Christian ones. But this limitation disappeared in 1855,[33] and ever since then it has, at least in principle, been possible for every religious group in England and Wales to register its place of worship for weddings.[34] It is therefore misleading to suggest that the Marriage Act 1949 does not apply to all faiths.[35] While it does not apply to all faiths *equally*, the dividing line is not between 'Christian' and other faiths. All Christian groups other than Anglicans and Quakers are subject to exactly the same rules as, for example, Muslims, Hindus, and Sikhs as far as the option of marrying in a registered place of worship is concerned; moreover, as we shall see, the differential treatment of Anglican, Jewish, and Quaker weddings has not always been to the benefit of the individuals involved.[36]

The extent to which the statutory scheme – past and present – makes provision for different faiths has also been underestimated by the tendency to describe weddings in registered places of worship as 'civil' ones.[37] But 'civil' is an ambiguous term in this context and may be understood in a number of ways. The 1836 and 1949 Acts did not use the term at all, so there is no statutory definition to which we can turn. For some, 'civil' denotes any marriage that is recognised by the state, whether accompanied by religious rites or not.[38] By that reckoning, Anglican, Jewish, and Quaker weddings are all properly described as 'civil', along with those in registered places of worship or register offices. For others, the dividing line between civil and religious may rest on

---

[32] See, e.g., Ralph Grillo, *Muslim Families, Politics and the Law: A Legal Industry in Multicultural Britain* (Farnham: Ashgate, 2015), p. 45; *Independent Review into the Application of Sharia Law in England and Wales* (Home Office, February 2018), p. 17.

[33] See further Chapter 4.

[34] For the first registration of a mosque under the 1836 Act, see Chapter 7.

[35] See, e.g., Dame Louise Casey, *The Casey Review: A Review into Opportunity and Integration* (London: Department for Communities and Local Government, 2016), para. 8.50, noting that the review had 'heard strong arguments that the Marriage Act should be reformed to apply to all faiths'.

[36] See further Chapters 3, 5, 6, 7, and 8.

[37] See, e.g., Grillo, *Muslim Families*, p. 45.

[38] See, e.g., A. Bradney, *Religions, Rights and Laws* (Leicester: Leicester University Press, 1993), pp. 40, 42; *Integrated Communities Strategy Green Paper* (March 2018), p. 58, which referred to the possibility of a couple entering into 'a legally recognised marriage through a religious ceremony' but went on to refer to 'the requirement that civil marriages are conducted before or at the same time as religious ceremonies'.

whether any contact with the state is required as part of the process.[39] Which weddings are classified as 'civil' according to that understanding would differ depending on whether the focus is on registration (required of all), the presence of a civil registrar (required only of register office weddings and those in registered places of worship without their own authorised person), or civil preliminaries (required for all non-Anglican weddings). And for yet others 'civil' denotes a wedding that is devoid of religious content.[40]

Those applying the term to weddings in registered places of worship seem to have in mind the fact that couples marrying in this way have to repeat the same prescribed declarations and vows as are required of those marrying in a register office. In the words of one scholar, ceremonies in registered places of worship are 'civil' ones since they 'take place outside the normal place for such ceremonies, namely the Register Office'.[41] Yet the fact that the words are the same does not justify regarding the ceremony in a registered place of worship as simply an extension of that in a register office. Legislators in 1836 saw themselves as primarily making provision for those who dissented from the Anglican church to marry according to their own rites; the option of getting married in a register office was intended for that small subcategory of dissenters who regarded marriage as a civil contract.[42] They would therefore have been surprised by this idea of the register office as the 'normal' place for the making of the prescribed vows. Moreover, while the prescribed words may be 'civil' in the sense of being prescribed by the state, they may also be incorporated into a religious service.

For the sake of clarity, the term 'civil' will be used here to denote weddings that are devoid of religious content. On that basis, weddings in a registered place of worship should (generally) be classified as religious rather than civil. That qualification of 'generally' is necessary because there has never been any statutory requirement that religious rites *have* to

---

[39] See, e.g., Parker, *Informal Marriage*, p. 48, suggesting that marriages in registered places of worship should be classified as civil because they had to be preceded by civil preliminaries and (until 1898) could only take place in the presence of a registrar.

[40] See, e.g., General Register Office, *Content of Civil Marriage Ceremonies: A Consultation Document on Proposed Changes to Regulation and Guidance to Registration Officers* (June 2005), para. 4.

[41] Thomas Glyn Watkin, 'Vestiges of Establishment: The Ecclesiastical and Canon Law of the Church in Wales' (1990–92) 2 *Ecclesiastical Law Journal* 110, 111.

[42] Stephanie Pywell and Rebecca Probert, 'Neither Sacred nor Profane: The Permitted Content of Civil Marriage Ceremonies' (2018) 30 *Child and Family Law Quarterly* 415, and see further Chapter 2.

be used as part of a wedding in a registered place of worship. This brings us on to the third point, that the Marriage Act 1836 made provision for some choices that have since been removed. As we shall see, it was intended to cater for a wide range of situations: a wedding in a registered place of worship could consist of no more than the prescribed words, while one in a register office could include hymns and prayers.[43] By this reckoning, even weddings in the register office were not originally 'civil' ones, since they did not have to be secular.

Understanding the detail of what the 1836 Act required and permitted, how the scheme it established changed over time, and how people actually married under its provisions is therefore crucial in evaluating the extent to which couples have been able to marry in accordance with their beliefs. That brings us on to another important point about the scope of this book, and the difference between *weddings* law and *marriage* law.

Weddings Law and Marriage Law

This book is about the laws regulating how people married, how people actually married, and how both changed over time. It is not about *whether* couples married,[44] or what happened before or after.[45] Nor is it about the theological, spiritual, or social significance of getting married. It takes as its basic premise the fact that the state recognises a certain set of relationships as constituting a marriage – with consequences for the rights and responsibilities of those concerned – and that this is likely to continue for the foreseeable future.[46] It does not, therefore, venture into

---

[43] At least until 1857, when the prohibition on religious content accidentally imposed by the Marriage and Registration Act 1856 came into force. See further Chapters 3 and 4, for evidence of the religious ceremonies that accompanied a number of early register office weddings and the unexpected reasons underpinning the prohibition.

[44] On which, see Rebecca Probert (ed.), *Cohabitation and Non-marital Births in England and Wales, 1600–2012* (London: Palgrave Macmillan, 2014) and *The Changing Legal Regulation of Cohabitation: From Fornicators to Family, 1600–2010* (Cambridge: Cambridge University Press, 2012).

[45] For accounts of the process of falling in love and the changing rites of courtship see, e.g., Phegley, *Courtship and Marriage*, and Claire Langhamer, *The English in Love: The Intimate Story of an Emotional Revolution* (Oxford: Oxford University Press, 2013), and for discussion of how expectations and experiences of marriage have changed over time see, e.g., Lucy Delap, Ben Griffin, and Abigail Wills (eds.), *The Politics of Domestic Authority in Britain since 1800* (London: Palgrave Macmillan, 2009) and David Clark (ed.), *Marriage, Domestic Life and Social Change* (London: Routledge, 1991).

[46] These consequences have of course been transformed over the period – on which see R. H. Graveson and F. R. Crane (eds.), *A Century of Family Law* (London: Sweet & Maxwell, 1957); Cretney, *History*; Gillian Douglas, *Obligation and Commitment in Family*

the debates about whether there should be a state-recognised concept of marriage or whether this should be left to religious bodies or to private agreements.[47] It is about getting married, not about marriage itself.[48]

Distinguishing the two is important. I therefore use the term 'wedding' to denote the act of going through a ceremony that results in a legally recognised 'marriage'; in other words, a couple celebrate their wedding, but register their marriage. The term 'marriage' will also be used when discussing issues of validity. Finding an appropriate term for ceremonies that do not result in a legally recognised marriage is more fraught, since many couples will regard their religious ceremony as their wedding, whatever its status in the eyes of the law.[49] I have variously referred to religious-only marriage ceremonies and celebratory marriage ceremonies as the context requires, in order to try to combine legal accuracy with a more positive terminology than appears in the law reports.[50]

Of course, keeping a clear distinction between the laws regulating weddings and those governing marriages is not always easy. Couples' choices as to how they married were often influenced by the fact that they were trying to hide the fact that they were not eligible to do so, or wanted to escape the notice of those who might object to their union. Since the rules on who can marry whom have their own complex history, it is useful to provide an overview of them here, with a brief indication of how they intersect with the story of how couples marry.[51]

Law (Oxford: Hart, 2018) – which in turn may influence whether couples choose to enter into a legally recognised marriage.

[47] For such debates, see Elizabeth Brake, *Minimising Marriage: Marriage, Morality, and the Law* (Oxford: Oxford University Press, 2013); Gary Chartier, *Public Practice, Private Law: An Essay on Love, Marriage and the State* (Cambridge: Cambridge University Press, 2016); Daniel Hill, 'The State and Marriage: Cut the Connection' (2017) 68(1) *Tyndale Bulletin* 95; Julian Rivers, 'Could Marriage Be Disestablished?' (2017) 68(1) *Tyndale Bulletin* 121.

[48] Brief reference is made to civil partnerships below (and see further Chapter 9), but the focus is on getting married rather than formal relationships more generally.

[49] See, e.g., Rajnaara C. Akhtar, 'Religious-Only Marriages and Cohabitation: Deciphering Differences', 69–84, and Rehana Parveen, 'From Regulating Marriage Ceremonies to Recognizing Marriage Ceremonies', 85–101, in Rajnaara C. Akhtar, Patrick Nash, and Rebecca Probert (eds.), *Cohabitation and Religious Marriage: Status, Similarities and Solutions* (Bristol: Bristol University Press, 2020).

[50] See, e.g., the terminology of 'non-qualifying ceremony' adopted by the Court of Appeal in *AG v. Akhtar* [2020] EWCA Civ 122.

[51] The rules as to when a marriage may be *voidable*, by contrast, do not affect how couples marry and so are not considered here.

Minimum Age and Parental Consent

For much of the nineteenth century it was hardly necessary for any checks to be made as to whether those seeking to marry had attained the minimum age at which it was possible to do so. The minimum was set at so low a level – 12 for a girl and 14 for a boy – that virtually no one married under it. Even if they did, the marriage could be ratified once the relevant age had been reached.[52] From the late nineteenth century, this low age was at odds with the measures put in place to protect girls against sexual exploitation,[53] and attracted increasing criticism. But only in 1929 was the minimum age set at 16, and marriages under that age classified as automatically void.[54]

More significant in terms of shaping couples' choices about how they married was the age at which it was possible to marry without parental consent – or, more accurately, without either claiming to have parental consent or running the risk of parental dissent, since a lack of parental consent did not affect the validity of the marriage. Until 1969, this was set at 21, but it was all too easy for individuals to claim to be of age at a time when no documentary evidence of age was required. In 1969, when the age was lowered to 18,[55] it was expressly provided that a superintendent registrar could refuse to issue the necessary authority for the marriage to go ahead 'unless satisfied by the production of written evidence' that the necessary consent had been obtained.[56] Only in 1999, however, were superintendent registrars given the power to require documentary evidence of age,[57] by which time the rising age of first marriage had rendered the issue of parental consent redundant in all but a small number of cases. It was, however, to re-emerge as a focus of policy concern in the twenty-first century, the issue now being the risk of teenagers being forced into unwanted marriages.[58]

---

[52] Cretney, *History*, p. 58.

[53] Laura Lammasniemi, '"Precocious Girls": Age of Consent, Class and Family in Late Nineteenth-Century England' (2020) 38(1) *Law and History Review* 241.

[54] Age of Marriage Act 1929; see now Marriage Act 1949, s. 2; Matrimonial Causes Act 1973, s. 11(a)(ii).

[55] Family Law Reform Act 1969, s. 2(1)(c).

[56] *Ibid.*, s. 2(3).

[57] Immigration Act and Asylum Act 1999, s. 162.

[58] For an overview of whose consent was required at different times, and how it had to be given, see Rebecca Probert, 'Parental Responsibility and Children's Partnership Choices' in Rebecca Probert, Stephen Gilmore, and Jonathan Herring (eds.), *Responsible Parents and Parental Responsibility* (Oxford: Hart, 2009), 237–54.

Prohibited Degrees

Marriages might, however, be void for a range of other reasons. From 31 August 1835, any marriages within the prohibited degrees were void, rather than voidable.[59] Controversially, these prohibitions encompassed not only close blood relatives but also former in-laws. The biblical idea that husband and wife were one flesh meant that the relatives of one were deemed to be the relatives of the other, even after death, so a man was prohibited from marrying the sister of his deceased wife (or the widow of his deceased brother) just as he would have been prohibited from marrying his own sister.[60] Despite these prohibitions, many couples did manage to go through a ceremony of marriage, often choosing a location where they were unknown or marrying in a form that assured them a degree of privacy.[61] Such prohibitions on marriages between those related by 'affinity' were abolished one by one over the course of the twentieth century.[62] All that remains are rules against marrying a small set of close blood relations and anyone who has been a child of the family.[63] Eligibility to marry did not, however, necessarily mean that the couple could marry as they chose; as we shall see, Anglican clergy were given the right to refuse to conduct the marriages of those who were within the formerly prohibited degrees.[64]

Prior Marriage

Throughout the period a marriage might also be void on account of a prior marriage. The significance of this prohibition changed over time

[59] Marriage Act 1835.

[60] For an excellent account of the prohibitions, see Sybil Wolfram, *In-law and Outlaws: Kinship and Marriage in England* (London: Croom Helm, 1987).

[61] For an example of one such wedding, see Jenny Paterson, 'Married in a Register Office – or were they?' (2021) JGFH (forthcoming).

[62] See the self-explanatory Deceased Wife's Sister's Marriage Act 1907 and Deceased Brother's Widow's Marriage Act 1921; the Marriage (Prohibited Degrees of Relationship) Act 1931 (which removed the prohibitions on marrying the niece, nephew, aunt, or uncle of a deceased spouse); the Marriage (Enabling) Act 1960 (which removed the restrictions on marrying such relations where the first marriage had ended in divorce rather than death); the Marriage (Prohibited Degree of Relationship) Act 1986 (which allowed marriages between a former step-parent and step-child, or between a parent-in-law and son- or daughter-in-law, subject to certain conditions) and the Marriage Act 1949 (Remedial Order) 2007 (which removed those conditions insofar as they related to marriages between a former parent-in-law and son- or daughter-in-law).

[63] Marriage Act 1949, s. 1 and sch. 1.

[64] See further Chapter 6. The current exemption applies only to those marriages permitted as a result of the 1986 Act and the 2007 Order: Marriage Act 1949, s. 5A.

as divorce became easier,[65] but this in turn raised a whole set of new issues about how those who had been divorced could remarry.[66] For those who had not obtained a divorce, escaping detection and prosecution for bigamy generally required individuals to put some time and distance between their marriages and thus also shaped how they married. As cohabitation became more common in the 1960s, fewer couples ran this risk. In more recent decades, however, the need to identify intended marriages that may be void on account of a prior marriage has re-emerged in the context of polygamous marriages.[67]

Sex and Gender

The most significant change to the laws governing marriage in the past decade has of course been that allowing same-sex couples to marry.[68] The 1990s saw an increasing number of countries across the world making provision for same-sex couples to enter into a legally recognised relationship, and from 5 December 2005 same-sex couples could enter into a civil partnership in England and Wales too. Despite the common tendency to refer to civil partnerships as 'marriages', the law was clear that the two were not the same.[69] In late 2010, the Equal Love campaign publicly challenged the limitations of the law by sending same-sex couples seeking permission to marry, as well as mixed-sex couples seeking permission to enter into civil partnerships, to their local register offices. The coalition government subsequently announced its support for legalisation of same-sex marriage, the Marriage (Same Sex Couples) Act was passed in 2013, and from March 2014 same-sex couples were able to marry. With civil partnerships becoming available to opposite-sex couples from the

---

[65] On the transformation in the ease of untying the knot, see Roderick Phillips, *Putting Asunder: A History of Divorce in Western Society* (Cambridge: Cambridge University Press, 1988); Stone, *Road to Divorce*; Colin Gibson, *Dissolving Wedlock* (London: Routledge, 1994); Daniel Monk, Joanna Miles, and Rebecca Probert (eds.), *Fifty Years of the Divorce Reform Act 1969* (Oxford: Hart, forthcoming 2022).

[66] See further Chapters 4 and 7.

[67] For discussion of polygamy, see Anthony Bradney, *Law and Faith in a Sceptical Age* (Abingdon: Routledge, 2009), pp. 109–12.

[68] For a helpful overview see Nicola Barker and Daniel Monk, 'From Civil Partnership to Same-Sex Marriage: A Decade in British Legal History' in Nicola Barker and Daniel Monk (eds.), *From Civil Partnership to Same-Sex Marriage: Interdisciplinary Reflections* (Abingdon: Routledge, 2015), 1–26.

[69] The most obvious manifestation of this was the classification of overseas same-sex marriages as civil partnerships: Civil Partnership Act 2004, s. 215; *Wilkinson v. Kitzinger* [2006] EWHC 2022 (Fam).

end of 2019,[70] a person's legal gender no longer determines their ability to marry or enter into a civil partnership.[71] Again, however, this does not mean that all couples can marry as they choose, with most types of religious weddings still being unavailable to same-sex couples.[72]

Sources

As set out earlier, the aim of *Tying the Knot* is to evaluate the relationship between law and practice, with a particular focus on how far the law has enabled couples to marry in accordance with their beliefs. Addressing each of these elements requires a range of different sources to be used.

In terms of understanding the evolution of the law, it is necessary to go beyond the terms of what was eventually enacted. Every Act was preceded by numerous draft bills, and scrutinising them shows what options were being considered, which proposals were unsuccessful, and how the terms of the successful ones had evolved over time. It is also necessary to go beyond the debates recorded in *Hansard*; in the early nineteenth century, it was far from being a verbatim account of what was said in Parliament, being compiled from newspaper reports rather than by a dedicated team of transcribers. In addition to recording what was said in Parliament, national, regional, and even local newspapers also debated how the law should be reformed and recorded reactions to new laws, providing insights into the concerns of the time. Periodicals published by specific religious denominations proved to be a particularly fruitful source of information about what reforms different groups wanted, while the petitions that were presented to Parliament reveal who was calling for reform.

In examining how couples married, essential background information about the number and type of weddings each year is provided by the detailed reports published by the Registrar-General from 1839 onwards, and by the more recent publications of the Office for National Statistics. Depictions of weddings in novels and plays, and, later, in TV shows and films also help to illuminate how different options were perceived. While such sources need to be treated with care, even the most wildly inaccurate

---

[70] Civil Partnerships, Marriages and Deaths (Registration etc) Act 2019; Civil Partnership (Opposite-sex Couples) Regulations 2019, SI 2019/1458.

[71] In addition, the Gender Recognition Act 2004 allowed individuals to obtain legal recognition of the fact that their gender was not as recorded on their birth certificate and marry in their 'reassigned' gender.

[72] See further Chapter 9.

of such depictions has a valuable role to play in illuminating popular misconceptions about the law – and perhaps what people think *should* be possible.

Evaluating whether the way in which couples married reflected their beliefs is inevitably more challenging. There are obvious challenges in talking about what past generations believed, or even how they behaved.[73] That said, much work has been done on the history of religion, and comparing the percentage of the population who could be classified as belonging to a particular religious group with the percentage of weddings taking place according to the rites of that group gives some indication of whether there might have been a mismatch between beliefs and practices. In assessing the beliefs of individual couples, wedding announcements in local newspapers proved to be a particularly fruitful source of information about the content of weddings, and also showed how some couples had an additional ceremony before or after their wedding. From the 1960s, the burgeoning range of wedding magazines provides insights into couples' aspirations and choices. And particularly valuable information about couples' beliefs and choices was provided by almost 200 family historians who replied to my request for information about register office weddings and weddings involving Nonconformist or Catholic ancestors.[74] Between them, they provided data relating to over a thousand weddings across England and Wales that had been celebrated between 1837 and the present day, with examples from 44 counties and 288 registration districts.[75] Many also shared stories about their ancestors and were able to provide information about the religious affiliation of the couples in question, which enabled their choice of wedding to be evaluated.[76]

---

[73] For a helpful discussion of the differences between believing, belonging, and behaviour, and between church attendance, religious allegiance, and formal membership: see Clive Field, *Periodizing Secularization: Religious Allegiance and Attendance in Britain, 1880–1945* (Oxford: Oxford University Press, 2019), ch. 1.

[74] The request for information was issued via the Lost Cousins network and a number of family history societies. Family historians were asked to supply data about ancestors who had married in a register office and about the marriages of any ancestors who were Nonconformist or Catholic. The phrasing of the second question was designed to elicit information about those who had not married in a registered place of worship as well as those who did.

[75] Data were provided about 607 register office weddings, 345 weddings in registered places of worship, and 69 Anglican weddings that had involved parties at least one of whom was Catholic or Nonconformist. A full list of all those who responded is included in the acknowledgements.

[76] Some of these stories will be referred to in the chapters that follow, and a set of them will be published in the *Journal of Genealogy and Family History* (JGFH).

Structure

While each route into marriage has its own history and its own distinct trajectory, analysing each separately would miss the broader connections between them. The structure is therefore chronological rather than thematic, with each chapter telling a set of stories about a specific period of time. This means that the coverage of each route into marriage differs between chapters; at certain times there may be a considerable amount to say about a particular type of wedding, while at others it may fade into the background. Stories about change always need more explanation than ones about continuity.

We begin with the conception, design, and implementation of the 1836 Act. Chapter 2 shows how the way in which demands for reform were framed – the plea to be relieved from compulsory conformity with the rites of the Anglican church when marrying – shaped the solution adopted in 1836. This insight is crucial to understanding the whole subsequent history of marriage law and practices and the problems with which reformers are grappling today. The 1836 Act was based upon the negative principle that no one should be compelled to marry in a form that ran counter to their beliefs, rather than any positive principle that everyone should be able to marry in a form that reflected their beliefs. It gave those campaigning for reform what they had asked for, but not in the form they had wanted, largely because they had no existing practices that could give shape to a possible solution.

The legacy of this is clear from Chapter 3, which analyses the take-up of the new law and how its limitations were quickly revealed. It explains how take-up differed as between Catholics and Protestant Dissenters, and reveals how many of those marrying in a register office had a religious ceremony of some kind before, after, or even during that wedding. Chapter 4 shows how controls over the form of the ceremony were tightened in 1856, almost it seems by accident, thereby removing some of the options that had been available to couples in the early years. It also analyses the proposals of the 1868 Royal Commission; had these been enacted, the subsequent history of weddings would have been very different. In the absence of wider reform, the final decades of the nineteenth century saw a campaign to dispense with the need for registrars to be present at marriages in registered buildings. Chapter 5 explores the divisions within Dissent that made finding a replacement for the registrar so difficult, and shows how the solution that was adopted in 1898 generated protests in turn.

This is a less positive take on the process of reform than that which appears in many other accounts. The 1856 Act has generally been seen as removing many of the practical obstacles that might otherwise have deterred couples from availing themselves of the types of weddings introduced in 1836, and the 1898 Act has been seen as completing the process. But the additional restrictions imposed by the one, and the limitations of the other, are crucial to understanding how constraints on couples' choices continued through the twentieth century and into the twenty-first.

New constraints emerged at the start of the twentieth century as the result of competing conceptions of marriage. As Chapter 6 shows, there were cases in which the law refused to recognise certain religious ceremonies, and also ones in which individuals disdained to recognise weddings as binding on them on account of their religion. Further complexities developed as the century progressed, with a new divergence between the Church of England and the now disestablished Church in Wales; as Chapter 7 analyses, the passage of the Marriage Act 1949 only served to consolidate that complexity rather than making any revisions to the law.

The period between 1950 and 1993 saw the number of civil and religious weddings gradually converging, with civil weddings briefly overtaking religious weddings in the 1970s. As Chapter 8 shows, there was also a limited degree of convergence in the rules applicable to different types of weddings, as well as numerous proposals for reform being advanced. One of the specific proposals was implemented by the Marriage Act 1994, and Chapter 9 analyses how the following years saw a transformation of marriage practices. While couples were making different choices, the rise of the purely 'celebratory' ceremony suggested that the legal options still fell short of ensuring that couples could marry in accordance with their beliefs. The legacy of the choices made in 1836, 1856, and 1898 were still being felt, with renewed concern about religious-only ceremonies. And in 2020, the inflexibility of the law governing weddings, combined with the restrictions necessitated by a global pandemic, meant that many couples could not get married at all.

Throughout the book, readers may see parallels between past concerns and campaigns and those of the present day. I have generally avoided drawing those parallels in the main body of the book, since this is likely to become confusing for those who are reading it as a work of history, rather than for its relevance to current policy debates. But they are nonetheless important, and so *Tying the Knot* closes by drawing together the strands from earlier chapters and reflecting on how the past can inform current policy debates about how the laws regulating weddings should be reformed. It is not my intention to set out a blueprint as to how that should be done, but simply to illuminate the problems that have arisen in the past and which continue to affect the choices of couples getting married today; to inform, rather than advise.

And with that, let us step back two hundred years to where the campaign for reform began.

2

Conception, Design, and Implementation, 1819–1837

In introducing the bill that was to lay the foundations of modern weddings law, the Whig politician Lord John Russell set out his conception of the role that the state should play:

> What interested the State only was, that what was then done should be a ceremony which was considered binding by both parties. If they once ascertained the parties had given due notice for the purpose, and that the marriage was settled, and that the contract was such as would be binding on the consciences of the parties – when they had ascertained this, he thought they had obtained all that it was necessary for the State to know.[1]

It was an attractively simple statement of the relative interests of the state and the parties. It was also a clever way of obscuring what the bill did not do. While it relieved Dissenters[2] from the need to marry according to the rites of the Church of England, it did so by side-stepping some fundamental questions about the form that any alternative would take and the authority of the person conducting the wedding.

Three factors are key to understanding the approach adopted in the 1836 Act: first, how the campaign for reform had been framed; second, how divided Dissenters were on the appropriate solution; and, third, how concerned lawmakers were about creating an alternative route into marriage. As the first section will show, the conception of the 1836 Act has to be understood against the background of the various proposals for reform that were put forward between 1819 and 1835: how Protestant Dissenters were simply seeking to be freed from compulsory conformity with the rites of the Anglican church; why such a wide variety of proposals were put forward; and why such proposals failed. The design

---

[1] Parl. Deb., ser. 2, vol. 31, col. 372, 12 February 1836.
[2] The term was used by some to encompass all Christians who dissented from the Anglican church and by others to designate Protestant Dissenters alone. Here it is used in its wider meaning, with distinctions being drawn between Catholic and Protestant Dissenters where the context so requires.

of the Act, discussed in the second section, sought to balance what Dissenters were asking for with sufficient safeguards to meet the concerns that had been raised during previous attempts. To do so required a whole new set of processes independent of the Established Church. Unfortunately, the administrative structures that were to underpin such processes were so new that they were not in force in most parts of the country at the time the Act was passed, and the final section of the chapter will explore the implications that this had for its implementation.

In order to make sense of both the divisions within Dissent and the concerns of the state, it may be helpful to sketch the religious background of the period and what Dissenters were seeking an alternative to. From a modern perspective, the England and Wales of the early nineteenth century might appear to be religiously homogeneous. The small Jewish community apart,[3] only a minuscule number of people would have defined themselves as anything other than Christian.[4] The vast majority of the population was Protestant, and most at least nominally Anglican.[5] But outside the Established Church there were Methodists, Baptists, Independents (sometimes known as Congregationalists), Presbyterians, Unitarians, and Quakers.[6] And each of these denominations split into even smaller and more specific entities. There were Armenian Methodists and Calvinistic Methodists. The Armenians were represented by the Wesleyan Methodist Original Connexion, the Wesleyan Methodist New Connexion, the Wesleyan Methodist Association, the Primitive Methodists, and the Bible Christians. The Calvinists included a specific group known as the Countess of Huntingdon's Connexion. Baptists could be classified as General, Particular, and Seventh-Day, but also shared with Independents the view that each local church should be a self-governing entity, answerable to God alone.[7] Presbyterianism was

---

[3] Geoffrey Alderman, *Modern British Jewry* (Oxford: Clarendon Press, 1998).

[4] Rozina Visram, *Asians in Britain: 400 Years of History* (London: Pluto Press, 2002), p. 44; Humayun Ansari, *The Infidel Within: Muslims in Britain since 1800* (London: Hurst, 2004); Sophie Gilliat-Ray, *Muslims in Britain* (Cambridge: Cambridge University Press, 2010), p. 24.

[5] Owen Chadwick, *The Victorian Church: Part One, 1829–1859* (London: SCM Press Ltd, 1987, first published 1966); Clive Field, *Periodizing Secularization: Religious Allegiance and Attendance in Britain, 1880–1945* (Oxford: Oxford University Press, 2019).

[6] Michael Watts, *The Dissenters* (Oxford: Oxford University Press, 1995); K. D. M. Snell and Paul S. Ell, *Rival Jerusalems: The Geography of Victorian Religion* (Cambridge: Cambridge University Press, 2000).

[7] The classification of 'Independent' might also denote a local church that did not view itself as part of a wider group, and this label may have been applied to many Welsh churches for ease of classification: Snell and Ell, *Rival Jerusalems*, p. 102.

represented by the Church of Scotland – particularly in the most northern parts of England – but there was also a distinct branch of English Presbyterianism. There were also Swedenborgians and Moravians and a number of foreign Protestant churches, as well as a number of more radical sects.[8]

For the state, the diversity of Dissent posed a problem. If Dissenters were to be provided with an alternative means of marrying, who would be responsible for its oversight? Here we need to remember how tightly weddings were regulated under the existing law. The Clandestine Marriages Act 1753 had given force to the requirements of the Established Church by enshrining them in statute and invalidating marriages that did not comply with them. All weddings, save those of Quakers and Jews, had to be preceded by the calling of banns or by obtaining a licence from the ecclesiastical authorities, be solemnised in an Anglican church or chapel,[9] and be duly recorded in its registers. While the 1810s and early 1820s had seen debate over the precise formalities that should be required and the consequences of non-compliance, matters had been settled by the Marriage Act 1823. This had re-enacted the requirements set out in the 1753 Act but with the reassuring proviso that only a 'knowing and wilful' failure to comply with them would render a marriage void.[10] With these matters so recently resolved, it is unsurprising that Parliament wished to ensure that any new alternative would not be any less tightly regulated,[11] or that there was little appetite for re-opening any of the debates on what the impact of a failure to comply with a particular formality should be. Any proposals for reform of the law had to provide at least the same safeguards against 'clandestine marriages' as the existing processes for getting married in the Church of England. In other words, any new scheme would have to ensure that weddings could not take place in secret and that there would be an opportunity for

---

[8] Snell and Ell, *Rival Jerusalems*; J. F. C. Harrison, *The Second Coming: Popular Millenarianism 1780–1850* (London: Routledge and Kegan Paul, 1979).

[9] Unless authorised by a special licence to take place elsewhere. The church or chapel could be either the parish church or a chapel of ease built to provide additional facilities for worship within the parish; the latter, however, had to be specifically licensed for weddings.

[10] On the Acts of 1753 and 1823 see Rebecca Probert, *Marriage Law and Practice in the Long Eighteenth Century: A Reassessment* (Cambridge: Cambridge University Press, 2009).

[11] It should, however, be noted that views on the adequacy of the Anglican processes also differed: those who supported reform frequently pointed out the ease with which it was possible to marry by banns (see, e.g., the comments of Dr Lushington: Parl. Deb., ser. 2, vol. 32, col. 1097, 15 April 1836).

objections to be made by the parents or guardians of minors, or by anyone who knew of an impediment to the marriage.

No one really disagreed with the need for safeguards.[12] All accepted that there had to be some form of notice, and that marriages should be registered. The only question was who should be responsible for these elements. The challenge was to establish a process that was sufficiently independent of the existing Anglican structures to satisfy Dissenters and sufficiently rigorous to assuage any concerns about a new law being used as a cloak for clandestinity. With these points in mind, we can now turn to how the demand for reform was framed, and how this shaped the conception of the Act.

Conception

some measure, by which the Dissenters might be freed from the necessity of giving utterance, as a mere matter of form, to sentiments which they entertained not at heart[13]

Between 1819 and 1835 no fewer than eleven bills were introduced into Parliament with the aim of expanding the ways in which couples could marry.[14] The motivation and scope of these different bills varied, as did the reforms they suggested. Each, however, served to shape the eventual 1836 Act in different ways, both positive and negative – whether by the way in which each framed the issue, by the evidence of the practices of different groups, or by the solutions that were proposed and found wanting. And had they emerged in a different order, then reform might have taken a very different path. This is not to claim that there was a clear linear progression of ideas. The path to reform was messy, alternating between proposals for general reform and proposals limited to a single group. There was also much reshuffling of who would be responsible for the preliminaries, the ceremony, and the subsequent registration of the marriage. Nonetheless, only by going back to where the campaign began can we understand the negative principle at the heart of the claims for

---

[12] See, e.g., Parl. Deb., ser. 2, vol. 11, col. 75, 2 April 1824 (Marquis of Lansdowne, noting that it was 'the first duty of the legislature, on civil grounds, to provide against the celebration of clandestine marriages').

[13] Parl. Deb., ser. 2, vol. 17, col. 1408, 29 June 1827 (Marquis of Lansdowne).

[14] This section of necessity covers the same debates discussed in the final chapter of Probert, *Marriage Law and Practice*, but the focus here is on how they were to shape the future, rather than what they indicated about earlier practices.

reform, and of the eventual Act: the principle of freeing Dissenters from compulsory conformity.[15]

The Campaign against Compulsory Conformity

It was the Unitarians who began the campaign. From as early as 1817, petitions to be exempted from the requirements of the Marriage Act flooded into Parliament from around the country.[16] Their argument was that being compelled to participate in a marriage ceremony that included 'devotions addressed to the Father, the Son, and the Holy Ghost' was a violation of their religious beliefs. The Unitarian MP William Smith, emphasising the 'absurdity' of requiring Unitarians to observe a ritual at odds with their conscience,[17] accordingly brought forward bills in 1819 and 1822 proposing that the relevant parts of the service could be omitted upon request.[18]

While this proposal might seem very limited – given that it was not seeking to give Unitarians the right to be married in their own chapels[19] – it was, in fact, highly controversial. The idea that couples could request to change the liturgy to reflect their own conscience was one that went to the heart of the identity of the Church of England and its role in the making of marriage. It raised the controversial question as to whether Anglican clergy were performing a religious rite or simply acting on behalf of the state in effecting a marriage that would be legally recognised. If the former, then their own beliefs were also relevant. As Dr Phillimore pointed out, clergy might well have 'conscientious scruples' in

---

[15] *The Eclectic Review* (July–December 1832) noted the negativity of the arguments: 'Fourteen Reasons Why Dissenters should not submit to have their Marriages celebrated at the Altar of a Consecrated Building, before Clergymen belonging to a Church to which they cannot conscientiously conform'.

[16] *JHC*, 8 July 1817, p. 466 (petition from the Unitarians of Kent and Sussex); *JHL*, 27 May 1819, p. 639 and 3 June 1819, p. 497 (petitions from Plymouth, Tenterden, Liverpool, Newport, Exeter, Gloucester, London, Framlingham, Thorne, Bristol, Chichester, Norwich, and Lincoln); Parl. Deb., ser. 2, vol. 6, col. 1460, 17 April 1822 (petition from Kendal).

[17] Parl. Deb., ser. 2, vol. 6, col. 1462, 17 April 1822; *Morning Chronicle*, 18 April 1822.

[18] A Bill to relieve certain Persons dissenting from the Church of England, from some parts of the Ceremony required by Law in the celebration of Marriages (Bill 514), *JHC*, 28 June 1819, p. 587; A Bill to alter and amend certain Parts of ... The Marriage Act, affecting certain Dissenters (Bill 228), 22 April 1822.

[19] Nor is there any evidence that this was happening. The undignified protests against the form of words used in the Anglican rite reported by Dr Lushington confirm that these weddings were taking place in church: Parl. Deb., ser. 2, vol. 12, col. 1241, 25 March 1825.

conducting a ceremony without any reference to the Trinity, or the divinity of Christ.[20] If the latter, then the ceremony was 'degraded into a mere civil ordinance'.[21] It was the inevitable tension between spiritual and social considerations faced by an Established Church, and it was to arise repeatedly as reformers struggled to find a solution that was entirely independent of its processes.[22]

Consideration for the conscientious objections of Anglican clergy led to this particular option for reform being abandoned.[23] But framing the principle at stake as being the right to marry in a way that did not violate one's conscience was to have important consequences. In addition to setting up the clash of beliefs between Unitarian couples and Anglican clergy, it opened up objections to any reform that was sectarian, rather than general, in effect. As was noted, Catholics, as well as other Protestant Dissenters, also objected to compulsory conformity.[24] And most fundamentally of all, it was not the same as a principle that non-Anglican religious groups should be able to conduct weddings.

The Ambiguity of the Existing Exemptions

There were, of course, two groups who were already exempted from the need to marry in the Anglican church. Since the special treatment of Quakers and Jews was regularly invoked by Unitarians in their petitions and by proponents of reform in Parliament,[25] it is necessary to explain why this was an ambiguous and unhelpful precedent for them in particular.

First, the rationale for exempting Quakers and Jews had largely rested on the unlikelihood of either group marrying in the Anglican church.

---

[20] Parl. Deb., ser. 2, vol. 40, col. 1503, 1 July 1819.

[21] *Ibid.*

[22] As one rector grumbled after conducting the wedding of a Methodist, the clergy were reduced to performing 'the mechanical part' of the rites of passage: John Skinner, *Journal of a Somerset Rector, 1803–1834* (Oxford: Oxford University Press, 1971), p. 328.

[23] This, at least, was the tactful (and tactical) suggestion of the Marquis of Lansdowne when advancing a different proposal for reform: Parl. Deb., ser. 2, vol. 13 col. 1027, 3 June 1825.

[24] Lord Castlereagh, then Leader of the House of Commons, had urged Smith not to press his bill on the basis that it gave no relief to Catholics: Parl. Deb., ser. 2, vol. 40, col. 1503, 1 July 1819. Smith himself reported back to the Protestant Dissenting Deputies that many other Dissenters had 'subsequently expressed their wishes to partake of the relaxation requested': *Minutes of the Protestant Dissenting Deputies*, Guildhall MS 03083, 9 August 1822.

[25] See, e.g., the arguments advanced by Smith during the debates on the 1822 bill (Parl. Deb., ser. 2, vol. 6, col. 1461, 17 April 1822) and the petitions cited earlier.

Quakers had not merely been Dissenters but *dissidents*, refusing to engage with the state on a range of issues and conducting their own marriage ceremonies in the face of doubts as to their legal validity, while Jews too had married according to their own rites.[26] Second, the terms of the exemption were ambiguous, giving no clue as to how the legal status of Quaker and Jewish marriages was to be assessed.[27] As Lord Eldon, then Lord Chancellor, commented in 1824, the exemption presumably meant that such marriages were as valid as if the 1753 Act had never been passed 'but what made them valid . . . was not so easy to say'.[28] While it had been resolved that the validity of Jewish marriages was to be determined by the application of Jewish law,[29] this was of little assistance. The Unitarians had no existing rites of their own that could be used as the touchstone for validity, still less anything equivalent to Jewish laws, or to the structures of religious authority within the Jewish community of England and Wales.[30]

Third, it was all too easy for the analogy to backfire. Even when what was being proposed was not an outright exemption but a regulated alternative, opponents of reform spent more time cataloguing the various ways in which Unitarians were fundamentally different from Quakers and Jews than explaining why any particular solution would not work. The key element here was the perceived impossibility of anyone passing themselves as Quaker or Jewish in order to take advantage of the exemption, and the perceived ease with which anyone could claim to be a Unitarian.[31] This underlined how the issue was not merely whether

[26] See further Probert, *Marriage Law and Practice*, chs. 5 and 6.

[27] Clandestine Marriages Act 1753, s. 18; Marriage Act 1823, s. 31.

[28] Parl. Deb., ser. 2, vol. 11, col. 440, 4 May 1824. This was particularly true of Quaker marriages, whose validity had not been tested in court at this stage. Only in 1829, in an action for criminal conversation, did the courts decide that it would be sufficient to prove a marriage according to the forms of the Society of Friends: *Deane* v. *Thomas* (1829) M & M 361; 173 ER 1189, but even then this fell short of a decision on how validity would be tested.

[29] *Lindo* v. *Belisario* (1796) 1 Hag Con (App) 7; 161 ER 636. As this and subsequent cases demonstrated, the application of religious law might result in *non*-recognition of ceremonies where the necessary rites had not been observed; see also *Goldsmid* v. *Bromer* (1798) 1 Hag Con 324; 161 ER 568.

[30] Admittedly, these structures were in the process of evolution and their authority was dependent on the willingness of the community to recognise them, rather than on any formal legal standing (see, e.g., Alderman, *Modern British Jewry*), but they nonetheless played an important role in giving evidence to the ecclesiastical courts as to what was required for a valid marriage.

[31] As Lord Eldon and the Bishop of Chester both highlighted, the existing exemption only applied where both parties were Quakers or Jews. Even Lord Liverpool, more sympathetic to reform, thought that Unitarians should be required to have confirmation 'that they

special provision should be made for the Unitarians:[32] there was also
a need to ensure that any new exemption did not open up a potential
avenue for clandestine marriages.[33] If anything, all that the discussion
about Quaker and Jewish marriages had shown was their own anomalous
and uncertain standing, and the need for at least some regulations to be
extended to them.[34]

The Idea of Permitting Ceremonies in Licensed Places of Worship

The enduring concerns about clandestine marriages meant that any
new options for getting married would have to include proper safeguards. After a Select Committee appointed to review the law of
marriage in 1823 decided against making any recommendations in
relation to the marriages of Dissenters,[35] the initiative was taken up
by a leading Whig statesman, the Marquis of Lansdowne. At first sight,
his proposal that any Dissenters – Protestant or Catholic – should be
able to marry in any licensed place of worship that had been registered
for marriage, according to 'such Rites and Ceremonies' as accorded
with their religious feelings,[36] looks very similar to what was eventually
enacted in 1836. There were, however, a number of concerns that
explain why the 1823 bill failed, and which the 1836 Act had to address
in order to succeed.[37]

First, while the 1823 bill required licensed places of worship to be
registered for marriage, it did not limit what kinds of places could
be registered. The objection that this would mean that 'marriages might

<hr/>

were bona fide Unitarians, and did not assume the character for a temporary purpose':
Parl. Deb., ser. 2, vol. 11, cols. 79–80, 82, 89, 2 April 1824. See also the arguments put
forward by Robert Peel: professing himself willing to give relief 'to sincere Unitarians', he
expressed his concern that 'pretended religious scruples might be professed': Parl. Deb.,
ser. 2, vol. 12, cols. 1242–43, 25 March 1825.

[32] Other analogies were drawn to undermine the argument for special treatment: one MP
suggested that Unitarians were akin to 'Mahometans' in denying the divinity of Christ:
Parl. Deb., ser. 2, vol. 12, col. 1237, 25 March 1825.

[33] Parl. Deb., ser. 2, vol. 12, cols. 1242–43, 25 March 1825.

[34] Parl. Deb., ser. 2, vol. 11, col. 440, 4 May 1824.

[35] The reason given was the sheer diversity in the circumstances and desires of Dissenters:
*Second Report from the Select Committee Appointed to Consider the State of the Marriage
Laws*, 13 May 1823.

[36] A Bill . . . for granting Relief to His Majesty's Subjects, not being members of the Church
of England, in relation to the solemnization of matrimony, 5 June 1823.

[37] While the fact that the Whigs were in opposition obviously did not help the chances of
success, it should be noted that Lansdowne's later bills did make rather more progress.

be contracted in every alehouse'[38] was no mere hyperbole. The long-standing system of licensing places of worship had its roots in suspicion of those who did not conform to the Established Church and a desire to know where they were meeting.[39] Any place where Dissenters met – however humble the building and however small the congregation – had to be licensed, and so many meeting houses might simply be a room in a private dwelling, a barn, or part of an inn.[40]

Second, the bill made no reference to who would conduct the ceremony or whether any official figure would be present at all. This was understandable in the light of the diversity of views on these issues within different Dissenting denominations and the informal role of many ministers and preachers.[41] Yet the diversity of Dissent also allowed opponents of reform to stir up concern about allowing some of the more radical or less well-known groups to conduct marriages. As Eldon protested, Lansdowne's proposal would open up places for the celebration of marriage for the followers of Joanna Southcott, 'together with ranters, jumpers, and various other sects, of whose principles they knew nothing'.[42] Such scaremongering was all the more effective because of

---

[38] Parl. Deb., ser. 2, vol. 9, col. 970, 12 June 1823. It was significant that the objection was made by the Earl of Liverpool, who had previously expressed his support for reform. More predictably, objections were also made by Eldon and Redesdale (cols. 970–71).

[39] Toleration Act 1688, s. 19; Roman Catholic Relief Act 1791, s. 5. For discussion see Wendy Kennett, 'The Place of Worship in Solemnization of a Marriage' (2015) 30(2) *Journal of Law and Religion* 260.

[40] The *Return to an Address ... dated 22 March 1836 for A Return of the Number of Registered Dissenting Meeting-Houses and Roman Catholic Chapels in England and Wales* demonstrates the modesty of many meeting houses. Norwich had 26 certified places of worship that were 'merely Dwelling-houses or Rooms', while 144 private houses and 12 rooms were listed for Somerset. The returns for Norfolk, Ely, and Huntingdon all mentioned barns (pp. 6, 7, 27–28, 39, 42). There is also evidence of Catholics meeting for mass over the stable of the George Inn in Devonport at the start of the nineteenth century, while in Walsall the Dragon Inn had been hired for this purpose: Bernard W. Kelly, *Historical Notes on English Catholic Missions* (London: Kegan Paul, Trench, Trübner & Co., 1907), pp. 315, 410.

[41] On the latter point see B. L. Manning, *The Protestant Dissenting Deputies* (Cambridge: Cambridge University Press, 1952, ed. Greenwood), p. 131; Emma Griffin, *Liberty's Dawn: A People's History of the Industrial Revolution* (New Haven: Yale University Press, 2013, ppbk 2014), pp. 191, 201.

[42] Parl. Deb., ser. 2, vol. 9, col. 968, 12 June 1823. Joanna Southcott, who had died in 1814, had identified herself with the 'woman clothed with the sun' alluded to in Revelations, and had prophesied that she was pregnant with Shiloh (Harrison, *The Second Coming*, p. 94). 'Ranter' was a derogatory term for a Primitive Methodist, while the 'Jumpers' were an evangelical Welsh Methodist movement who took their nickname from their habit of jumping for joy.

the lack of existing practices to provide reassurance about how such groups – or any other Protestant Dissenters – might conduct themselves. Had any Protestant Dissenters been conducting their own marriage ceremonies, then those advocating reform might have been able to adduce evidence of their respectability and reliability. In the absence of such practices, it was all too easy to worry that reform would enable anyone at all to set up their own marriage shop.

Third, the bill envisaged that banns would still have to be called in the parish church, or a licence obtained, in advance of the ceremony taking place, and that the marriage would have to be recorded in the parish registers. This continuing dependency on the Established Church was certain to please neither Dissenters nor Anglicans.[43] Moreover, the fact that there would inevitably be a gap between the ceremony taking place and the marriage being registered generated concern about what would happen if there was no record of the marriage at all.[44]

In two further attempts at reform in 1824 and 1825, Lansdowne did his best to address the concerns that had been voiced.[45] Rather than trying to reform the law for all Dissenters, he reverted to finding a way of relieving the specific grievance of Unitarians. His 1824 bill tightened up the provisions about which places of worship could be registered for marriage,[46] while that debated in 1825 added a stipulation that the officiating Unitarian minister would also have to be registered,[47] and would be responsible for keeping register books.[48] That each bill made a little more progress than its predecessor[49] can be attributed to these

---

[43] As was argued by Eldon and the Earl of Westmorland in relation to a similar clause in a later bill, this would make the Established Church the 'handmaid' of the Unitarians: Parl. Deb., vol. 11, cols. 79, 87, 2 April 1824; col. 440, 4 May 1824.

[44] The bill specified that the couple and their witnesses would have to make an appointment with their local vicar before 7pm on the day of their wedding. If this was prevented by 'Accident, Neglect, Inadvertence, or Wilful Default', there was a back-up provision allowing for registration within the next six months, but only with the authority of the King's Bench.

[45] Bills 'for granting relief to certain Persons dissenting from the Church of England, in relation to the Solemnization of Marriages', 11 March 1824, 23 February 1825.

[46] Only bona fide places of worship that had been used as such for at least a year could be registered for weddings. The 1825 bill added a cap on the number that could be registered.

[47] Ministers would have been required to make an affidavit that their ministry was limited to Unitarian congregations; their names would, for a small fee, be recorded in the Court of the (Arch)bishop.

[48] This last suggestion was a relatively late amendment (see Bill 81, 9 May 1825). Copies of such registers were to be sent to the diocesan registrar on an annual basis.

[49] The 1824 bill, which had been introduced in the Lords, was lost at Committee stage: Parl. Deb., ser. 2, vol. 11, col. 446, 4 May 1824. The 1825 bill was introduced in the Commons

additional safeguards, although some individuals were so opposed to the idea of reform that the actual terms of any proposal hardly mattered.[50] That each ultimately failed suggested that regulating where marriages could take place would not be sufficient if the conduct of the ceremony and its registration were to be left to Dissenting ministers.

The Idea of Marrying before a Magistrate

Such concerns about delegating responsibilities to Dissenters led to an alternative solution being put forward in 1827 – that of allowing Unitarians to marry before a justice of the peace, mayor, or alderman.[51] Given the important role that these individuals played in so many spheres of regulation, they were in many respects an obvious choice to be tasked with conducting marriages.[52] So different a mode of marriage was in many respects less threatening to the Church of England, in that it avoided any implication of religious equality, and it also reflected the view of many Dissenters that marriage was a civil contract.[53]

That is not to suggest that the proposal was an uncontroversial one. Some were unhappy about allowing a non-religious form of marriage, invoking the unpromising precedents of Cromwell's Commonwealth and Revolutionary France,[54] or, more moderately, simply expressing concern about making marriage a 'civil contract' and divesting it of 'the

and passed with relative ease but narrowly failed to achieve a second reading in the Lords: Parl. Deb., ser. 2, vol. 13, col. 1032, 3 June 1825.

[50] Most notably, Eldon was just as vehement in making the case against a reform benefitting the Unitarians alone as he had been in opposing more general reform in 1823, although his volte face did not pass without comment: see Parl. Deb., ser. 2, vol. 11, cols. 79, 94, 2 April 1824.

[51] A Bill . . . for granting Relief to certain Persons dissenting from the Church of England, in respect of the Mode of celebrating Marriages (Bill 160, printed 20 June 1827); Parl. Deb., ser. 2, vol. 17, col. 1343, 19 June 1827.

[52] On their role in local administration, see William Cornish, Stephen Banks, Charles Mitchell, Paul Mitchell, and Rebecca Probert, *Law and Society in England, 1750–1950* (Oxford: Hart, 2nd ed. 2019), pp. 19–20.

[53] This view, it should be noted, was not incompatible with a marriage being celebrated with religious rites: see John Witte Jr, *From Sacrament to Contract: Marriage, Religion and Law in the Western Tradition* (Louisville: Westminster John Knox Press, 2nd ed. 2012), chs. 5 and 6.

[54] Parl. Deb., ser. 2, vol. 17, col. 1343, 19 June 1827; col. 1413, 29 June 1827. Smith's bill did originally envisage that couples would be making their declarations 'in the Presence of God', in a similar vein to the religiously-inspired form of marriage prescribed during the Commonwealth.

solemnities of religion'.[55] Others pointed out that those magistrates who
were also clergymen might be put in a difficult position if their duties as
the former clashed with their conscience as the latter.[56]

Overall, however, the reassurance provided by marriages being conducted before a representative of the state led to this particular option for
reform enjoying a considerable degree of support, despite the fact that it
was still dependent on the Anglican church for preliminaries and registration. It passed the Commons, and its second reading in the Lords, and
might have passed into law had there been sufficient time for its third
reading before the end of the session.[57] And this idea of marriages being
made in the presence of a representative of the state, as we shall see, was
to be a crucial element in securing the eventual passage of the 1836 Act.

Recognising Practices Rather than Principles

In the meantime, a different set of arguments for reform was being
voiced. There had for some time been evidence that immigrant Irish
Catholics were marrying before their own priests.[58] There was also
evidence from overseers of the poor that women who had gone through
such religious-only marriage ceremonies were subsequently being abandoned, along with their children, with no legal status and no legal redress.
Following Catholic emancipation,[59] MPs pressed for such ceremonies to
be recognised as marriages in order to address this problem,[60] with bills
being introduced in 1833 and 1834.

The case for reform was couched in terms of practices rather than
principles. It was bolstered by claims that religious-only marriage ceremonies were taking place in considerable numbers[61] and by the fact that
the cost of supporting the children of these unrecognised unions fell

---

[55] Parl. Deb., ser. 2, vol. 17, col. 1344, 19 June 1827; col. 1418, 29 June 1827.
[56] Parl. Deb., ser. 2, vol. 17, col. 1415, 29 June 1827.
[57] *Ibid.*, col. 1427.
[58] As early as 1823 there had been petitions to enable Catholic priests to solemnise marriages
      (*JHL*, 12 June 1823; Parl. Deb., ser. 2, vol. 9, cols. 965–67, 12 June 1823); a bill was drafted
      (Bill 534, 8 July 1823) but apparently never introduced.
[59] Catholic Relief Act 1829.
[60] Parl. Deb., ser. 2, vol. 18, col. 553, 10 June 1833. John Wilks, Mr O'Connell, and Charles
      Langdale all spoke even more passionately on this issue during the debates on a later bill:
      Parl. Deb., ser. 2, vol. 25, cols. 1026–27, 7 August 1834.
[61] Wilks suggested that there might be more than 20,000 each year (*Morning Chronicle*,
      8 August 1834). Given that Catholic weddings did not reach that level for another
      hundred years, this seems unlikely, but in the absence of any reliable statistical data
      there was no means of knowing this.

upon the parish in which they had been born.[62] The initial proposal was simply to legalise what was already happening in practice, which, it was argued, would only be putting Catholic weddings on the same footing as Quakers and Jews.[63] But while Catholics did have a known ritual,[64] an outright exemption for such a large group was unlikely to find favour with those concerned about clandestine marriages.[65] The subsequent 1834 bill therefore proposed a new framework within which Catholic weddings could take place: under its terms, couples would have their banns called in the Catholic church and give notice of their intention to marry to a magistrate; the wedding would then be conducted by a priest in a licensed place of worship, following which a copy of the marriage register would be sent by the priest to the local clerk of the peace.[66]

With the promise of a more general reform measure being introduced, the 1834 bill was subsequently withdrawn.[67] But it had shown that it was possible to devise alternatives to Anglican preliminaries and registers, and this was to be crucial to the scheme of the 1836 Act.

Translating Principles into Practicalities

By 1834 there was broad agreement that there needed to be alternatives to getting married in the Church of England. In addition to the evidence of hardship caused by the non-recognition of Catholic ceremonies, a number of Protestant Dissenters were now united in calling for change.[68] In response to this evidence of a broader demand for change, two separate government bills were introduced in 1834 and 1835. The

[62] *Royal Commission of Inquiry into Administration and Practical Operation of Poor Laws* (1834), PP 44, p. 99; App. A. pp. 103, 105; *Report on the State of the Irish Poor in Great Britain* (1836), PP 34, pp. 3, 23, 61–62, 87–88.

[63] A Bill to legalize the Marriages of Roman Catholics in England by their own Clergy; Parl. Deb., ser. 2, vol. 18, col. 553, 10 June 1833 (Lord Molyneux).

[64] As reflected in the earlier suggestion by Lord Liverpool that an exemption could easily be made to apply to Catholics: Parl. Deb., ser. 2, vol. 9, col. 969, 12 June 1823.

[65] Tracing the progress of the 1833 bill is something of a challenge in the absence of debate in Hansard and some confusion in the record between it and a different bill relating to Catholic marriages in Ireland, but it did not proceed to a third reading.

[66] A Bill to authorize the Marriages of Roman Catholics in England by their own Clergy, 26 June 1834.

[67] Parl. Deb., ser. 2, vol. 25, col. 1028, 7 August 1834.

[68] The 'United Committee' consisted of three representatives from each of the Protestant Dissenting Deputies, the General Body of the Protestant Dissenting Ministers of the Three Denominations, the Protestant Society, and the United Associate Presbytery of the Secession Church of Scotland: Guildhall Library, MS 03086, *Minute Books of a Committee called the United Committee Appointed to Consider the Grievances under which Dissenters*

fact that they were introduced by governments of very different political hues – the 1834 bill[69] being introduced by Lord John Russell under the Whig administration of Earl Grey, and that in 1835[70] by the Conservative Prime Minister Robert Peel – is significant for two reasons. In the short term, the febrile political situation meant that neither bill had much chance of becoming law.[71] But the fact that both Whig and Conservative administrations had put forward proposals for reform – albeit ones that were almost the exact converse of each other[72] – meant that there was at least broad agreement on the principle that the law should be reformed.

It was clear that any new scheme would need to make provision for a variety of different ways of getting married. Russell's 1834 bill was criticised for failing to provide any option for those who saw marriage as a civil contract. Commentators highlighted how two Birmingham couples had taken the law into their own hands and created their own secular ceremony;[73] Shilohite siblings Charles and Mary Louisa Bradley had exchanged rings and pledges with their respective partners after morning service at the Lawrence St Chapel, these rings being 'stamped with the impression of the "United Rights of Man and Woman"'.[74] It was

Now Labour, Vol. 1. However, the Society of Friends and the Wesleyan Conference had both declined to join.

[69] A Bill for granting relief in relation to the Celebration of Marriages to certain Persons dissenting from the United Church of England and Ireland.

[70] A Bill Concerning the Marriages of Persons not being Members of the United Church of England and Ireland, and objecting to be married according to the Rite thereof.

[71] Earl Grey resigned in July 1834, Lord Melbourne was sacked in November, and the Duke of Wellington acted as caretaker for Peel until the latter returned from holiday; Peel's minority government then fell in April 1835, to be succeeded by a new Whig administration under the premiership of Lord Melbourne.

[72] The 1834 bill proposed religious preliminaries (Anglican, plus notice in the chapel), marriages in Dissenting chapels that had been licensed by a magistrate for the purpose, and registration by the Dissenting minister (with a copy being sent to the diocesan registrar). The 1835 bill involved civil preliminaries, acknowledgement of the marriage before a magistrate, and registration in the parish registers.

[73] *Birmingham Gazette*, 12 May 1834; *British Magazine and Monthly Register of Religious and Ecclesiastical Information, Vol. VI* (1 July 1834), p. 114.

[74] The Shilohites were a successor to the Southcottians: some time after Joanna Southcott's death, John 'Zion' Ward had proclaimed that he was Shiloh, the messiah with whom Joanna had claimed to be pregnant. The Bradley family were strongly associated with Ward and also with radical thinkers such as Richard Carlile: see J. E. M. Latham, 'The Bradleys of Birmingham: The Unorthodox Family of "Michael Field"' (2003) 55 *History Workshop Journal* 189. Their invocation of the 'United Rights of Man and Woman' linked their marriage ceremony to the radical writings of Thomas Paine and Mary Wollstonecraft. While the ceremony was by way of being a publicity stunt, it does seem

claimed that it provided 'an example of the opinions and feelings which are growing up in the country'.[75] The Bradleys were hardly typical, however,[76] and Peel's subsequent proposal for a purely civil procedure was roundly criticised in its turn.[77] As the United Committee had emphasised, Dissenters wanted weddings 'to be performed either by Dissenting Ministers, or by Magistrates, at the option of the Parties'.[78] It was clear that any reform would have to allow Dissenters to celebrate their weddings with either religious rites *or* a secular option – and the Bradleys' secular ceremony in a dissenting chapel indicated that the line between the two might be blurred.

Nonetheless, the elements of a workable scheme were beginning to emerge from these two bills, along with the 1834 bill seeking to authorise Catholic weddings. Peel adopted the latter's idea of giving notice to a justice of the peace as an alternative to the Anglican preliminaries. The idea of making Dissenting ministers responsible for keeping registers of the marriages they conducted – as proposed by Russell in his 1834 bill – having failed to find favour, the focus shifted to the creation of a new system of civil registration.[79] Indeed, the petitions that poured in from Dissenters made it clear that they wanted a uniform civil system

---

to have marked the start of their life together: a daughter, Emma Harris Bradley, was born to Charles and Emma in 1835.

[75] John Stuart Mill, 'Mr William Brougham's Bills for a Registry of Births, Deaths, and Marriages', 14 May 1834, in John M. Robson (ed.), *Essays on England, Ireland, and Empire: Vol. VI* (Toronto: University of Toronto Press, 1982), pp. 231–33.

[76] The very fact that this single case was so widely reported suggests that active resistance, rather than reluctant conformity, was rare: it hardly supports Paul Johnson's claim that '[c]hapel ceremonies were conducted long before Nonconformist marriages became legal in 1837' (*The Birth of the Modern: World Society 1815–1830* (London: Phoenix, 2013), p. 499).

[77] A Bill Concerning the Marriages of Persons not being Members of the United Church of England and Ireland, and objecting to be married according to the Rite thereof, 30 March 1835. It envisaged Dissenters simply going before a magistrate to acknowledge their marriage.

[78] *Minute Books*, Vol. 1, 16 June 1834, recording the deputation sent to Brougham in relation to his projected Marriage Bill. The Congregational Board took the view that Peel's proposal did not meet its 'just expectations' and that a religious ceremony should be an option: *Minute Books*, Vol. 1, 19 May 1835.

[79] The campaign for civil registration of course was far broader than the campaign for reform of the marriage laws. In 1833, a Select Committee had concluded that 'a national civil registration of births, marriages and deaths should be established', and bills to this effect were introduced in 1833 and 1834. For an excellent account of how Dissenters campaigned for civil registration – and of the divisions within Dissent – see M. J. Cullen, 'The Making of the Civil Registration Act of 1836' (1974) 25 *Journal of Ecclesiastical History* 39.

rather than registration being delegated to individual congregations.[80] But it was still unclear how this could be done. The contemporary proposal that responsibility for registration could be devolved to local tax collectors[81] was met with some derision: as John Stuart Mill tartly noted, this illustrated 'the total absence of machinery for the conduct of administrative business'.[82]

Upon the Whigs resuming power in 1835, a new way of achieving a system of civil registration presented itself. The Poor Law Amendment Act 1834 had made provision for parishes to be united into larger districts known as Unions for the purposes of the administration of relief, with each Union having its own workhouse, Board of Guardians, and a number of officers. The first report of the Poor Law Commissioners appointed to administer the new system noted that one of the responsibilities of the master of the workhouse was to keep a register of births and deaths taking place there.[83] They also reported that 2,066 parishes had been formed into 112 unions, and that the results of so doing had been highly beneficial. The reaction of Lord John Russell was that it was 'exactly what he wished to receive'.[84]

Designing the Act

When you know how, you know who[85]

At the opening of Parliament on 4 February 1836, William IV expressed his anxiety for Parliament to consider measures that would both remedy the grievances of Dissenters and be 'of general advantage to the whole body of the community'.[86] Eight days later, Russell introduced two linked bills into

---

[80] The necessity of a system of civil registration was a point made repeatedly in the debates and in the petitions to Parliament: see Parl. Deb., ser. 2, vol. 21, cols. 780, 783, 787, 25 February 1834; col. 994, 3 March 1834; *JHL*, 28 February 1834, p. 35; *JHL*, 11 March 1834, p. 57. It was also highlighted by the United Committee: *Minute Books of a Committee called the United Committee Appointed to Consider the Grievances under which Dissenters Now Labour*, Guildhall MS 03086, Vol. 1, p. 169, 5 March 1834.

[81] A Bill to establish a General Register of Births, Deaths and Marriages in England, printed 14 May 1834.

[82] John Stuart Mill, 'Mr William Brougham's Bills'.

[83] Appendix A, p. 93.

[84] Anthony Brundage, *The Making of the New Poor Law, 1832–1839: The Politics of Inquiry, Enactment and Implementation, 1832–39* (London: Hutchinson, 1978), p. 101, citing PLC Minutes, 9 October 1835.

[85] Dorothy L. Sayers, *Busman's Honeymoon* (London: Gollancz, 1937), ch. 20.

[86] Parl. Deb., ser. 2, vol. 31, col. 4, 4 February 1836.

the House of Commons. The first addressed Dissenters' demands for the civil registration of births, marriages, and deaths, using the Unions created by the Poor Law Amendment Act as the basis for a system of new registration districts. As Russell noted, the existing parish registers were seriously incomplete insofar as they related to baptisms; the marriage register, by contrast 'was filled with the names of Dissenters, as well as those of members of the Church, by the former being absolutely compelled to partake in the ceremony of the communion, to which many of them on principle objected'.[87] The second proposed two ways in which Dissenters could marry independently of Anglican preliminaries, rites, or registration.[88]

The second bill was dependent on the first, as these new ways of marrying were designed backwards from the question of who would be responsible for registration. Since the new civil registrars would be responsible for ensuring that non-Anglican marriages were duly registered, it made sense both to require them to attend the wedding and to receive the initial notice of intention to marry.[89] Weddings would be able to take place either in a registered place of worship or in the office of the new 'superintendent registrar'.[90] Setting aside the detailed regulations as to how places of worship were to be registered, very little else was to be required. There was to be no regulation of who should conduct the wedding, or – apart from the inclusion of certain prescribed words – what form it should take.[91]

---

[87] *Morning Post*, 13 February 1836. A rather different version appears in *Hansard*, reporting him as saying that 'in a country and amongst a people composed of various sects and religions, it was quite obvious that a registration of marriages according to the rites of the established religion alone could never possibly be perfect or complete' (Parl. Deb., ser. 2, vol. 31, col. 369, 12 February 1836). Stephen Parker, *Informal Marriage, Cohabitation and the Law, 1750–1989* (Basingstoke: Macmillan, 1990), p. 70, relied on this to claim that Russell had conceded 'that dissenting marriages were sufficiently prevalent to distort seriously the official statistics', but given that *Hansard* was compiled from newspaper reports it is often more helpful to look at such reports directly. Since the more detailed report in the *Morning Post* fits with the tenor of all the preceding debates, and the lack of any evidence that Dissenters were marrying according to their own rites, it seems clear that this is a more accurate representation of what Russell actually said.

[88] Parl. Deb., ser. 2, vol. 34, col. 492, 13 June 1836.

[89] This was the case under the original draft of the bill, although the responsibility for receiving notices was later transferred to the superintendent registrar: A Bill ... For Marriages in England (hereafter simply 'Marriage Bill'), 17 February 1836, cl. 2.

[90] The superintendent registrar would also have overall oversight of the system in each registration district.

[91] See clause 14. The requirement in clause 16 that 'every entry of such Marriage shall be signed by the Minister or other person by or before whom the Marriage was celebrated' also implied considerable flexibility.

This was, in essence, what became the Marriage Act 1836. Rather than seeking to chart every twist and turn of the debates, this section will focus on how the key components of the new system were seen. It evaluates the role of the civil registrar; the regulation of buildings; the *lack* of regulation of the content of the wedding; the differential treatment of the Church of England; and the new exemptions that were carved out for Quakers and Jews. It closes by examining more closely the reliance on the machinery of the New Poor Law, and why this was more problematic than has previously been appreciated.

The Presence of the Civil Registrar

The proposal that a civil registrar would have to be present at Dissenters' weddings was a clever one. It sidestepped any difficult questions about the status and identity of Dissenting ministers and indeed whether Dissenting weddings needed to be conducted by a minister at all. It provided reassurance to those who were concerned about the risks of any new options being abused: the diversity of Dissent became much less of a threat if there was a known and accountable official present at the wedding. This explains why MPs evinced far less concern about clandestine marriages in the debates on the 1836 bill than they had in relation to earlier proposals that did not offer this safeguard. The presence of the registrar also ensured that marriages would be registered immediately after they had taken place. And it was compatible with the principle that individuals should not be compelled to marry in a way that was inconsistent with their beliefs.

It was not, however, what many Dissenters had wanted. Petitions continued to flood into Parliament asking that 'the solemnization of Marriages amongst Dissenters may at the option of the parties be effected by their own Ministers, or by a Civil Magistrate'.[92] The grievance here was twofold: first, the lack of recognition accorded to Dissenting ministers, and, second, the 'injurious' distinction between Dissenters' marriages and those conducted in the parish church.[93] Even at the time, then, there was an awareness of the limitations of the scheme that was being proposed.

[92] Petitions presented by 129 Independents from Derby (18 February, Second Report of the Select Committee, Appendix, p. 16), 324 Baptists from Nottingham and 4,793 Dissenters from Essex (8 March, Appendix to the Fourth Report, p. 40).

[93] See, e.g., Petition from the General Baptists assembling in Stoney Street Chapel, Nottingham, 8 March 1836, Appendix to the Seventh Report, p. 121.

Regulating Where Weddings Could Take Place

In addition, a number of requirements were included to ensure that these new types of weddings would be taking place only in identified locations. The location of the office of the superintendent registrar for every registration district had to be confirmed to the Registrar-General. Places of worship also had to be specifically registered before weddings could take place there.[94] The conditions for registration – that twenty householders would have to certify that it was their usual place of worship, and had been used as such for a year – were those that had already been accepted as additional safeguards in earlier bills.[95] Such conditions removed the possibility of weddings being conducted under the auspices of very small groups, as well as reducing the risk of 'marriage shops' being set up under the guise of religion.[96] And the new condition that only 'separate' buildings could be registered closed off any possibility of weddings taking place in a room in a private house. All these conditions were clearly intended to ensure that Dissenters did not enjoy more freedom in where they married than those marrying according to Anglican rites.

One limitation that was not explicitly stated in the legislation was that only Christian places of worship could be registered for weddings. This was a corollary of the fact that only Christian places of worship could be licensed in the first place.[97] The limitation did not go entirely unnoticed, since it was suggested at one stage that provision should be made for synagogues to be registered so that Jews could marry in registered places of worship too.[98] But given the tiny number of adherents of other non-Christian faiths, and

---

[94] The returns that were submitted by clerks of the peace would have reinforced the perception that additional regulations were needed, rather than simply permitting marriages to take place in any licensed place of worship. Asked for details of the number of places so licensed, many frankly admitted that they did not know, and had no records: see the *Return* of registered Meeting-Houses and Chapels, and see further above on the origins of the requirement for all places in which Dissenters met to be licensed.

[95] The requirement that the building had been used as a place of worship for at least a year had first appeared in Lansdowne's 1824 bill, while the requirement of 20 householders came from Russell's 1834 bill.

[96] Although a piece in *Blackwood's Magazine*, reprinted in the *Morning Post*, 11 May 1836, opined that 20 householders 'may easily be found in any low quarter in any town ready to give their signature for a license which will bring this trade into their vicinity, with its attendant concourse of carousals' and complained that there was nothing in the law 'to prevent this marriage-house from being a joint-stock speculation . . . a regular appendage to the gin-palace . . . a preliminary to abominations of every description'.

[97] Toleration Act 1688; Roman Catholic Relief Act 1791; Places of Religious Worship Act 1812.

[98] See further below.

their lack of any places of worship that might be registered, it was hardly surprising that no one saw any need to consider any broader provision.

Respecting Beliefs

The need for regulations as to the presence of a registrar and the registration of the building reflected the concerns that had been voiced over the years about the risks inherent in creating a new route into marriage. By contrast, the lack of regulation of the content of the wedding itself – and the absence of any explicit requirement that weddings in registered places of worship be celebrated with religious rites[99] – reflected both the range of views within Dissent and the way in which the campaign for reform had been framed as being about relief from compulsory conformity. The example of the Bradleys had demonstrated that some highly religious couples might want to express their consent to marriage in a non-religious form. In any case, exactly what should be classified as 'religious' might be a matter of debate: as Peel pointed out, '[o]ne party might consider that to be a religious ceremony of which others might take a different view'.[100] The Act gave couples the freedom to decide what form the ceremony should take, rather than requiring their compliance with religious rites.[101] In this sense respect for individual belief was simultaneously absent from and at the heart of the 1836 Act: since nothing was specified, anything was possible. All that the law required was that each party declared that they were free to marry,[102] and consented to marry the other, in a prescribed form of words.

While it was assumed that most weddings in registered places of worship would naturally be celebrated with religious rites, the possibility that they might not be did generate some controversy, especially when it was viewed in conjunction with the new option of marrying in the office

---

[99] Contrast Lansdowne's 1823 bill, which had explicitly stated that marriages should be solemnised 'with such Rites and Ceremonies, as shall accord with the Religious Feelings of the Parties to be married'.

[100] *Morning Post*, 14 June 1836, reporting the previous day's debates in Parliament.

[101] In this it set up a potential clash between the couple and those responsible for the building in which the wedding was to take place, since there was no requirement that the wedding be conducted according to the rites of the denomination who worshipped there: see further Chapters 3 and 4.

[102] This additional requirement had been added following a proposal made by Dr Nicholl at committee stage (*Morning Post*, 14 June 1836) although his original reference to 'holy' matrimony was quietly dropped.

of the superintendent registrar, which it was assumed would not be attended with any religious rites at all.[103] During the various stages of the bill in the Commons, a number of protests were made against the idea of allowing couples to dispense with a religious ceremony.[104] In the Lords, the Bishop of Exeter made an attempt to amend the prescribed words to include at least some references to a deity; in his version, couples would declare that they were making their vows 'in the presence of God' and promise to live together 'according to God's holy ordinance'.[105] The reason given for rejecting this amendment was not the inappropriateness of religious content in the secular setting of the superintendent registrar's office, but rather the undesirability of the registrar presiding over a religious exchange in registered places of worship.[106] The message was clear: weddings could be celebrated with whatever rites the couple might choose – including in the office of the superintendent registrar, there being no prohibition on the use of any religious service there – and the state would not impose any expression of belief that might generate new complaints about compulsory conformity by those who did not share it.

But there was one final, and even more controversial, debate about who would be able to take advantage of these new options. Here again the earlier attempts at reform had left their legacy. The tenor of the campaign against compulsory conformity had by its very nature created an expectation that these new options were intended for those who did not see themselves as members of the Established Church. The five bills proposing alternatives for Unitarians had all required a declaration by the

---

[103] See, e.g., the attack on the bill in *Blackwood's Magazine*, reprinted in the *Morning Post*, 11 May 1836, which sarcastically noted that the law was taking care that the feelings of those marrying there 'shall be shielded from any impertinent intrusion of the most simulated form of homage'.

[104] See e.g. Mr Law's description of it as 'a gratuitous desecration of the marriage rite': Parl. Deb., vol. 34, col. 492, 13 June 1836. This was echoed by others claiming that the change reduced marriage to a mere civil contract: see col. 491(Mr Poulter), col. 492 (Mr Hardy), and col. 494 (Mr Trevor).

[105] Parl. Deb., vol. 35, col. 605, 28 July 1836. This would have made the ceremony more like its religiously motivated seventeenth-century precursor: Philpotts had previously quoted with approval the 'most solemn formula' adopted 'at the time of the Usurpation' (at col. 604) but added in an additional reference to God in his version. His amendment was initially accepted by the Lords, albeit by a very thinly attended House, but was reversed by a convincing majority four days later: Parl. Deb., vol. 35, col. 688, 1 August 1836.

[106] See Melbourne's comment that it would be 'very objectionable, to many parties, to introduce a civil officer into their chapel for the purpose of taking part in the performance of a somewhat religious ceremony': Parl. Deb., vol. 35, col. 688, 1 August 1836.

parties of their religious affiliation, in order to ensure that such alternatives would be limited to those who had a genuine objection to the Anglican rite.[107] The issue was whether the Marriage Bill would be similarly explicit in limiting the new options to Dissenters, and whether couples would have to declare their objections to marrying in the Anglican church.

In the original draft of the bill no such declaration was required. The clause introducing the option of marrying in the office of the superintendent registrar presented this possibility as being for those who objected to marrying in a registered place of worship, but it did not require that such objections be made explicit. A subsequent amendment would have required couples to make a solemn declaration that they had 'conscientious scruples against marrying in any church or chapel, or with any religious ceremony'.[108] It was then further proposed that all couples wishing to marry in the new way should have to make a formal statement of their objection to marrying in the Church of England.[109] This, however, was seen as subjecting Dissenters to a religious test,[110] and Russell had no wish to limit the scope of the new options in this way.[111] The decision was taken that no declaration should be required of anyone, however they were choosing to marry.[112] The phrasing of the original bill was restored,[113] although not without a further and even more heated debate.

That this single issue absorbed so much time and effort, and generated so much bitterness, reflected just how much was at stake. The fact that anyone could take advantage of the new options, without giving any reason as to why they wanted to do so, was declared to be an attack on the Church of England; there were obvious implications for its status and standing if its parishioners chose to marry elsewhere. On the other hand,

---

[107] The heated discussions about the difficulty of defining a Unitarian, discussed above, reflected the concern that accommodating their beliefs might open up new options for those who did not really share them.

[108] See Parl. Deb., ser. 2, vol. 34, col. 1024, 28 June 1836, for Russell's account of how the clause found its way into the bill.

[109] Parl. Deb., ser. 2, vol. 34, col. 1021, 28 June 1836, Mr Goulburn.

[110] Parl. Deb., ser. 2, vol. 34, col. 1022, 28 June 1836, Dr Lushington.

[111] Parl. Deb., ser. 2, vol. 34, col. 1024, 28 June 1836, Lord John Russell.

[112] *Ibid.*, col. 1032.

[113] Marriage Act, s. 21. As Chapter 3 will show, even the reference to marriage in the office of the superintendent registrar being for those who objected to marrying in a registered building was inapt; many of those who married in such offices would have preferred to marry in a registered place of worship but did not have the option of doing so.

had the 1836 Act included a declaration of the kind contemplated, its scope would have been highly limited. Making such a declaration would have posed particular difficulties for the large number of Wesleyan Methodists, many of whom did not define themselves as Dissenters, worshipped in their parish church as well as in their own chapels, and could not conscientiously have claimed to object to the rites of the Anglican church.[114] In requiring no declaration, the Act allowed any couple, in principle, to choose to take advantage of its provisions.

The Differential Treatment of the Church of England

While the Church of England was losing its virtual monopoly over weddings, it was not losing its privileges entirely. It was envisaged that Anglican weddings would continue to be celebrated by Anglican clergy, according to the form set out in the *Book of Common Prayer*, in its own churches. Such weddings would continue to be regulated by the earlier Marriage Act 1823 rather than being included within the scope of the new legislation.

That said, there were some changes. One was the possibility of Anglican weddings being preceded by the new civil preliminaries. This was considerably less radical than Russell's original suggestion that banns should be abolished and that all couples would give notice to the super-intendent registrar.[115] The second, and more significant, change related to how marriages would be registered. Under the accompanying regis-tration legislation, Anglican clergy were to be issued with new registers and required to send copies of entries to the local superintendent registrar.[116] Admittedly, in the light of the criticisms that had been levelled at the existing system of parochial registration, Anglican clergy may have counted themselves fortunate that they were still to be trusted with registering marriages, rather than having to accept the presence of a civil registrar at their weddings. Even so, the fact that they were to be directly answerable to the state was a significant shift in terms of their status.

---

[114] Rupert Davies, A. Raymond George, and Gordon Rupp (eds.), *A History of the Methodist Church in Great Britain: Vol. 2* (London: Epworth Press, 1978).

[115] Excepting, as always, those marrying on the basis of a special licence from the Archbishop of Canterbury. Russell's proposal for the abolition of banns found support in the Commons but was amended in the Lords.

[116] Births and Deaths Registration Act 1836, ss. 30, 31.

Further amendments in the Lords saw the addition of a whole set of provisions enhancing the existing powers of bishops to license Anglican chapels for weddings in addition to the parish church.[117] These additional provisions may have been occasioned by the somewhat embarrassing discovery that two Anglican places of worship had not in fact been licensed; just as the issue of wider reform was being debated, special legislation had to be passed to validate the marriages that had taken place there.[118] The need for there to be an easier process for licensing chapels may also have been motivated by the desire to ensure that the Church of England could compete with the new options envisaged by the Marriage Bill. The programme of building new Anglican places of worship that had begun in the late 1810s had led to many chapels of ease being constructed within existing parishes in large urban areas.[119] Dissent being far stronger in towns and cities than in the countryside,[120] it was all the more important for these new Anglican chapels to be licensed for weddings, so that no one was impelled to marry in a Dissenting chapel or superintendent registrar's office on the basis of convenience alone.

The Exempted Groups

The original draft of the Marriage Bill had made no mention of Quakers or Jews – either by way of provision or, more significantly, exemption. But at Committee stage in the Commons it was specifically provided that Quakers and Jews 'may continue to contract and solemnize marriages' according to their own usages.[121] It was never proposed that a registrar would have to attend such weddings; the accompanying bill on registration had from the outset envisaged devolving responsibility to Quaker and Jewish bodies to certify who would be responsible for registering their marriages.[122] And despite an amendment – later dropped – allowing synagogues to be registered for weddings,[123] it never seems to have been

---

[117] Marriage Act 1836, ss. 26–34.
[118] Marriages in St Anne's Chapel, Wandsworth Act 1836 (a chapel of ease to the parish church); St Clement, Oxford, Marriages Validity Act 1836 (a new church built to accommodate the growing population of the district).
[119] N. J. G. Pounds, *A History of the English Parish* (Cambridge: Cambridge University Press, 2000), pp. 507–08.
[120] Chadwick, *The Victorian Church*, p. 368.
[121] Marriage Bill 1836, 18 April 1836, cl. 2.
[122] A Bill for Registering Births, Deaths and Marriages in England, 17 February 1836 (Bill 33).
[123] *Morning Post*, 14 June 1836; Marriage Bill, 30 June 1836, cl. 16.

envisaged that Quakers and Jews would be subject to the same requirements relating to witnesses, open doors, and prescribed words as every other group.[124]

An ambiguous exemption thus became a specific privilege, at least on the face of the legislation. The new requirements for Quaker and Jewish weddings involved far less state oversight than those applicable to other non-Anglican weddings. This, however, was not the same as a lack of regulation. It is the provisions on how Quaker and Jewish marriages were to be registered that are key to understanding how they were regulated. Within the highly structured Society of Friends, the recording clerk at their central office in London was the obvious person to certify who should be appointed as a registering officer. In the absence of any equivalent figure within the Jewish community, the initial draft of the registration bill identified the secretaries of the two leading synagogues as being jointly responsible for certifying the secretaries of the other synagogues to whom register books would be issued. The final version, by contrast, conferred this power on 'the president for the time being of the London committee of deputies of the British Jews',[125] a relatively new organisation.[126]

The provisions for Quaker and Jewish weddings can thus be seen as the converse of those dealing with weddings in registered places of worship: the explicit recognition of their usages created constraints as well as conferring privileges. In identifying certain bodies as being responsible for deciding who could register a Quaker or Jewish marriage, the 1836 Act effectively gave those bodies the power to decide on matters of religious identity and practice.

In addition to the provisions about registration, the new scheme did still require Quakers and Jews to give notice to the superintendent registrar. And so here we need to turn to the machinery that was to underpin the new processes applicable to all non-Anglican weddings.

The Machinery of the New Poor Law

The new schemes for both the solemnisation and registration of marriages were dependent on the machinery of the New Poor Law. The

---

[124] Marriage Bill, 30 June 1836, cl. 40.

[125] Births and Deaths Registration Act 1836, s. 30.

[126] While it could trace its origins back to 1760, it was only in 1835–36 that it adopted its new name, constitution, and representative basis: see Michael Clark, 'Identity and Equality: The Anglo-Jewish Community in the Post-Emancipation Era, 1858–1887' (DPhil thesis, Oxford, 2005), p. 128.

Boards of Guardians established under the provisions of the Poor Law Amendment Act 1834 were responsible for determining how the Union under their jurisdiction should be divided into registration districts, for appointing the superintendent registrar (who in turn appointed the registrars responsible for registering marriages), and for providing a register office.[127] There was, however, a fundamental problem in this reliance, in that the 1834 Act was not yet in operation in most of the country. This was partly because organising parishes into a Union took time, usually involving careful negotiations with local interests and demands.[128] It was also because the Poor Law Commission had no power to dissolve existing Unions;[129] their composition could only be changed if two-thirds of their guardians agreed.[130] This requirement of local consent, along with the assumption that the new scheme would not apply across the country as a whole, had smoothed the passage of the 1834 Act.[131] But one consequence was that in 1836 large areas of the country were not subject to its provisions, and did not expect to be. In other words, the Marriage Act was dependent on an administrative machinery that did not yet exist.

There was thus more than a degree of optimism in Russell's hope that enough of the country would have been divided into Unions under the 1834 Act for the new systems of registration and marriage to be implemented from March 1837.[132] As the two bills were working their way through Parliament, this was starting to look less likely,[133] and so provision was made for the formation of 'temporary districts' for areas where

---

[127] Births and Deaths Registration Act 1836, ss. 7 and 9; Marriage Act 1836, s. 17.

[128] For examples of negotiation, see Norman McCord, 'The Implementation of the 1834 Poor Law Amendment Act on Tyneside' (1969) 14 *International Review of Social History* 90; Byung Khun Song, 'Continuity and Change in English Rural Society: The Formation of Poor Law Unions in Oxfordshire' (1999) 114 *English Historical Review* 314.

[129] For example, where parishes had been incorporated by local legislation, or had combined together to provide a workhouse under 'Gilbert's Act' ('An Act for the better Relief and Employment of the Poor', 1782). See further Brundage, *The Making of the New Poor Law*, p. 130; Samantha A. Shave, *Pauper Policies: Poor Law Practice in England, 1780–1850* (Manchester: Manchester University Press, 2017), p. 39.

[130] Poor Law Amendment Act 1834, s. 32.

[131] M. E. Rose, 'The Anti-Poor Law Movement in the North of England' (1966) 1(1) *Northern History* 70, 71–72. On the passage of the 1834 Act see Brundage, *The Making of the New Poor Law*, ch. 3.

[132] Parl. Deb., ser. 2, vol. 31, col. 369, 12 February 1836.

[133] Only 228 Unions that had been formed by February 1836, with a further 111 being created between 8 February and 1 August 1836, in sharp contrast to Russell's hope that there would be more than 800.

no Union had been formed.[134] Such temporary districts were, however, only for the purposes of implementing the registration legislation, not for implementing the New Poor Law, and as such had no Board of Guardians.

Had matters been left there, it would have been possible to implement the marriage legislation regardless of whether a Union had been created under the New Poor Law. But a further amendment in the Lords scuppered this possibility. This amendment required all notices of marriage to be read before Boards of Guardians appointed under the 1834 Act[135] – with no fallback for places that had no such Board. The formation of a temporary district was of no assistance in this regard. The upshot was that no notices of marriage could be read – and so no certificates authorising non-Anglican weddings could be issued – in any district where the New Poor Law was not in force.

When the Marriage Bill returned to the Commons there was markedly little enthusiasm for this particular amendment. The Radical MP John Wilks was particularly strident in his protest, noting that it would render the legislation inoperative in two-thirds of the country.[136] His objection was a valid one: while the 330 or so Unions that existed by this time covered over 7,000 parishes, they accounted for only around a third of the population of England and Wales.[137] The general feeling was nonetheless that it would be better to pass the bill and seek to make amendments to the scheme later rather than risk losing the chance of reform altogether.[138]

With this reluctant acquiescence, the Marriage Act finally received Royal Assent on 17 August 1836. It was due to come into force on 1 March 1837, which meant that the authorities had just over seven months to extend the machinery of the New Poor Law to the vast swathes of the south-west, the north of England, and Wales where as yet no Unions had been created at all.[139] What had seemed like the perfect

---

[134] Such districts were to be formed by the Poor Law Commissioners, and their superintendent registrar appointed directly by the Registrar-General: Births and Deaths Registration Act 1836, s. 10. Who was to provide the register office was not mentioned.

[135] The bill as originally introduced had not required that notices of marriage be made public, relying instead on the identity of the parties being verified by some person who was known to the registrar: Marriage Bill, 17 February 1836, cl. 3.

[136] Parl. Deb., ser. 2, vol. 35, col. 1122, 11 August 1836.

[137] Judging from the 1831 census, around 5.6m persons lived in areas that formed part of a Union, as compared to a total population of 16.5m for England and Wales as a whole.

[138] Parl. Deb., ser. 2, vol. 35, cols. 1122–31, 11 August 1836.

[139] At this stage there were no Unions in Cornwall, Yorkshire, Lancashire, Northumberland, or Durham, and only one in each of Cumberland, Cheshire, and Westmorland, and

solution to the long-standing question of how to provide a framework within which Dissenters could marry was about to give rise to a whole new set of problems.

Implementation

the principle is good, and the only good thing about it. It cannot be worked as it now stands; and we are positive that if tried it will be found any thing but satisfactory[140]

The second half of 1836, and the first few months of 1837, saw the newly created General Register Office busying itself with how the Marriage Act would be implemented.[141] Register books in a new standard format had to be distributed to those responsible for registering marriages under the new scheme.[142] It was an enormous task. As the new Registrar-General[143] subsequently reported, books had been sent to 11,694 Anglican clergy, 817 registrars, 90 Quaker registering officers, and 36 secretaries of Jewish synagogues.[144] Guidance was also issued on the registration of places of worship,[145] the provision of register offices,[146] and the appointment of superintendent registrars and registrars of marriage.[147]

Where a Union was in place, the clerk to the Board of Guardians was to be offered the role of superintendent registrar as a matter of course; only if he refused it or was disqualified from acting would the guardians need

(excepting Monmouthshire) Wales; overall, two-thirds of the population fell outside the scope of the 1834 Act.

[140] *Manchester Times*, 4 March 1837.

[141] Its actions, and the guidance it issued, are set out in the *First Annual Report of the Registrar-General of Births, Deaths and Marriages in England* (London: HMSO, 1839).

[142] Births and Deaths Registration Act 1836, s. 30. The standard form made no concessions to the varying size of parishes: *The Standard*, 2 March 1837, wryly reported that one country clergyman, who had conducted just seven weddings in his tiny parish since 1800, had calculated that the new register book would last for the next 4,286 years.

[143] The first holder of the post was Thomas Henry Lister, a novelist who had been involved in various official commissions. It was perhaps not a coincidence that he was the brother-in-law of Lord John Russell: see Donald Hawes, 'Thomas Henry Lister', *ODNB*, 24 May 2012.

[144] *First Annual Report*, p. 4.

[145] 'Notice to Persons Desirous of Registering Buildings for the Solemnization of Marriages', issued 26 January 1837, *First Annual Report*, Appendix I.

[146] Circular from the GRO to Boards of Guardians, 8 October 1836, *First Annual Report*, Appendix B.

[147] Circular from the GRO to the Clerks of the Boards of Guardians, 10 October 1836, Appendix C; Circular from the GRO to Superintendent Registrars, 23 January 1837, *First Annual Report*, Appendix F.

to seek another suitably qualified person.[148] Opponents sniped that clerks might not be fit persons to be superintendent registrars, who, in the view of the *Bradford Observer*, should have 'gentlemanly manners and address'.[149] Questions of suitability – this time in terms of religious compatibility rather than social standing – also arose in relation to the new registrars of marriage. The Registrar-General asked superintendent registrars to bear in mind that the duties of such registrars would almost exclusively relate to Dissenters,[150] and there was a strong feeling that only registrars who were themselves Dissenters should be present at marriages in registered places of worship.[151]

The chief challenge, of course, was the creation of Unions in the first place. The need to have the machinery of the New Poor Law in place in order to implement the Marriage Act meant that the focus was on speed rather than careful negotiation.[152] The predictable consequence was that both became more controversial. In Yorkshire, there was active resistance to the creation of Unions, and newspapers reported one Assistant Commissioner having to beat a hasty retreat when meetings turned fractious.[153] The marriage and registration legislation was contemptuously described as a 'stalking-horse' for the imposition of the 1834 Act, registration being seen as 'a strange matter to put into the hands of the Commissioners and Guardians'.[154] And in South Wales, a group of Unitarians met to declare that they would continue to marry in the parish church, since marrying 'through the functionaries of the New Poor Law Amendment Act . . . would seem to countenance that most oppressive and cruel Act'.[155]

---

[148] Births and Deaths Registration Act 1836, s. 7. January 1837 saw the advertisements pages of local newspapers filled with hopeful candidates – generally solicitors – offering themselves as candidates for vacant posts: *Leeds Mercury*, 21 January 1837; *Bradford Observer*, 26 January 1837. For the view that they should have been appointed centrally, see *Manchester Times*, 4 March 1837.

[149] *Bradford Observer*, 12 January 1837. See further Chapter 3 on some of the spurious reports that circulated about superintendent registrars.

[150] *First Annual Report*, Appendix F.

[151] *Bradford Observer*, 23 February 1837.

[152] Brundage, *The Making of the New Poor Law*, p. 152; Rose, 'The Anti-Poor Law Movement'.

[153] *The Standard*, 14 January 1837, reporting the reaction in Bury, where walls were 'covered with placards, calling on the rate-payers "to meet and resist the introduction of the Whig Starvation Act"'; *Leeds Times*, 25 January 1837, reporting how the coat of Power, the Assistant Commissioner in question, was ripped from his back when he tried to escape.

[154] *The Champion and Weekly Herald*, 21 January 1837.

[155] *Hull Packet*, 3 February 1837; *Woolmer's Exeter and Plymouth Gazette*, 4 February 1837; *Essex Standard*, 17 February 1837.

So rather than the implementation of the Marriage Act being facilitated by the machinery of the New Poor Law, it was the requirements of
the Marriage Act that transformed the New Poor Law into a more-or-less
compulsory national system to ensure that the machinery was in place. In
this respect, the Marriage Act was at least indirectly responsible for the
riots and civil disturbances that broke out in response to the attempts of
the Poor Law Commissioners to impose their scheme.

By February 1837, it was clear that there was no chance of the Marriage
Act being brought into force in March.[156] The timely publication of the
first instalment of *Oliver Twist*, with the instantly memorable scene in
which the half-starved child pleaded for more gruel from the parish
beadle and overseer of the workhouse, was hardly calculated to assuage
fears about the effect of implementing the New Poor Law.[157] With
potential work-arounds having been ruled out,[158] Parliament agreed to
a delay of four months.[159]

Even with this extra time it seemed unlikely that the harried Assistant
Commissioners would manage to divide all of the country into Poor Law
Unions.[160] In both Yorkshire and Lancashire, the Poor Law
Commissioners had to make extensive use of their power to form tem-
porary districts.[161] Such powers ensured that the new system of registra-
tion could be implemented, but specific revisions had to be made to the
Marriage Act to enable it to operate independently of the New Poor
Law.[162] In the absence of a Board of Guardians, notices of marriage were

[156] Parl. Deb., ser. 2, vol. 36, col. 84, 2 February 1837.

[157] The first instalment appeared in *Bentley's Miscellany* on 1 February 1837. It proved
immediately popular, and 1,000 additional copies of the next issue had to be printed:
Claire Tomalin, *Charles Dickens: A Life* (London: Viking, 2011), p. 75.

[158] The King's Bench held that Commissioners could not require pre-1834 Unions to elect
Guardians under the 1834 Act: Brundage, *The Making of the New Poor Law*, p. 156.

[159] Registration and Marriage Acts Suspension Act 1837.

[160] Petitions against the New Poor Law – bearing 26,000 signatures – were presented by the
MP John Fielden: Parl. Deb., ser. 2, vol. 38, col. 455, 2 May 1837. See also '"Working" of
the Poor Law System', *The Champion*, 5 May 1837; *The Times*, 17 May 1837. Efforts to
implement the New Poor Law slackened: while 83 new Unions had been created in
January and February alone, covering another 2,076 parishes, the following four months
saw only a further 40 coming into existence.

[161] Under the Births and Deaths Registration Act 1836, s. 10. By 1 July 1837 they had
formed 1,152 parishes and places into 270 temporary districts, which had in turn been
formed into 71 registration districts by the Registrar-General: see *Third Report of the
Poor Law Commissioners* (London: Charles Knight & Co, 1836–37), p. 19; *First
Annual Report*, p. 6.

[162] The passage of what was then termed the Marriages and Registration Acts Amendment
Bill has for the most part to be traced through newspaper reports, the record in *Hansard*

to be displayed in the office of the superintendent registrar.[163] Despite some grumblings that this would not provide sufficient publicity, it was accepted as a necessary stopgap.[164] The need for there to be an office for the notices to be displayed in was addressed by allowing superintendent registrars to 'appropriate some fit Room or Rooms'.[165] Even where Unions had been created, some of the new Boards were proving recalcitrant, necessitating back-up provisions as to who could exercise their powers where they had failed to do so.[166] As the basis for a new system of local administration, it was all rather makeshift.

It was also done in something of a rush. The provisions of the amending legislation had to be in place before 1 July 1837, when the marriage and registration legislation was due to come into force. To delay any further would have exposed the government to further criticism. The bill finally had its third reading in the Commons on 16 June, and was sent up to the Lords three days later.[167] The very next day, on 20 June 1837, William IV suddenly died, and discussion of the amending legislation had to yield priority to more pressing constitutional matters. The Lords just managed to scramble through the necessary stages, and the amending legislation received Royal Assent on 30 June, one of the first Acts to be signed by the new Queen. The scene was finally set for the new marriage law to take effect. But with the 1,329 parishes that still lay outside the operation of the New Poor Law being subject to

---

being particularly sketchy. The short title later given to it – the Births and Deaths Registration Act 1837 – rather obscured its important role in revising the law regulating weddings.

[163] Births and Deaths Registration Act 1837, s. 24. As noted above, provision had already been made for the appointment of superintendent registrars by the Registrar-General where no 1834 Union had been created.

[164] The alternative of defining 'guardians' to include those elected under local or general acts – as suggested by Sir Samuel Whalley, a long-standing opponent of the New Poor Law – was rejected: *The Times*, 12 June 1837. The government clearly had no intention of providing a permanent alternative to the New Poor Law.

[165] Births and Deaths Registration Act 1837, s. 21.

[166] The Births and Deaths Registration Act 1837 empowered the Poor Law Commissioners to divide a Union into registration districts (s. 13), the Registrar-General to appoint a superintendent registrar (s. 14), and the Commissioners of the Treasury to provide a register office (s. 20). The Registrar-General was also given the power to allocate parishes to Unions (s. 9), to divide or unite existing districts and Unions (s. 10), and, when uniting them, to decide which Board of Guardians should have the power of appointing a superintendent registrar (s. 11).

[167] Parl. Deb., ser. 2, vol. 38, col. 1500, 16 June 1837; col. 1674, 28 June 1837.

a different set of requirements, it was not the most promising of starts.[168]

Conclusion

It is understandable why those campaigning for reform sought to argue that no one should have to marry in a way that ran counter to their beliefs. It was a principle that they could argue had already been accepted in relation to Quakers and Jews. It was also in accordance with a broader – if gradual – move towards religious toleration and the shift in authority from church to state.[169] Yet the existing exemptions were at best ambiguous and at worst positively unhelpful. The principle also pointed to a need for general reform, thereby precluding measures that benefitted a single group. Most fundamentally of all, the principle was essentially a negative one, offering no guidance on how it was to be achieved. Protestant Dissenters were seeking the right not to have to marry in the Church of England rather than to be able to marry in a specific form, were divided on what form any alternative should take, and had no existing practices that could shape any solution.

Viewed as a matter of principle, the Marriage Act 1836 gave campaigners what they were asking for – an alternative to being married according to Anglican rites. But it did so in a way that made it clear that this alternative was different from, and not equal to, such rites, and not all Dissenters were happy with the result. Moreover, the attempt to minimise the differences between the different types of non-Anglican weddings had succeeded only to a limited extent. Dissenters were to return to these differences in due course, challenging the nature of the preliminaries required in the 1850s, and the necessity of the registrar being present at their weddings – but not at those of Jews and Quakers – in the 1880s and 1890s.[170]

Viewed as a matter of politics, the 1836 Act was masterly both in assuaging the concerns that had been voiced in relation to earlier

[168] *First Annual Report*, p. 6. It has been estimated that around 10 per cent of the population of the West Riding 'remained outside the geography of the New Poor Law for another decade': Rose, 'The Anti-Poor Law Movement', pp. 89–90.

[169] It was somewhat odd that jurisdiction over marriages – in terms of their validity and the availability of remedies such as orders for separation and restitution of conjugal rights – remained with the church courts until 1857, a situation which was to attract growing criticism: see S. M. Waddams, 'English Matrimonial Law on the Eve of Reform (1828–57)' (2000) 21 *Journal of Legal History* 59.

[170] See further chapters 4 and 5.

measures and in advancing other agendas. The link with civil registration was calculated to please the many Dissenters who had campaigned for such a system. And the need for there to be an administrative system in place that could take responsibility for such registration provided a reason to press ahead with the introduction of the New Poor Law. But the linkage of marriage law with the Poor Law was to prove problematic, not only in relation to the practical implementation of the 1836 Act but also at an ideological level. It was to be some time before the 'taint' of the workhouse was to be removed from marriage law entirely.

That, however, is to anticipate. In July 1837 many of these problems were some way in the future, and the question was whether the new options would prove popular. As the next chapter will show, the fears of opponents that the 1836 Act would transform the way in which couples married were not to be realised – at least not in the short term.

3

Reactions to the Act, 1837–1854

The first year of the Marriage Act 1836 being in force saw fewer marriages being registered than had been expected. As the Registrar-General explained, a number of couples, labouring under a misapprehension as to the effect of the Act, had rushed to marry in the Anglican church before it came into force, 'thus causing a deficiency in the Returns for the ensuing year'.[1] Nor, indeed, did the numbers taking advantage of the new options provided by the Act suggest any huge pent-up demand for non-church or even non-Anglican weddings: in its first year, just 1,093 couples married in a register office[2] and 2,976 in a registered place of worship, as compared to 107,201 in the Church of England.[3] Various anti-Whig newspapers gleefully pointed out how few couples were marrying according to the new forms,[4] and underlined the exceptionalism of those who did by distinguishing those 'united' or 'coupled' under the new Act from those 'married' according to the old form.[5]

Admittedly, the particularly low figures in the first year can in part be explained by the continuing issues with the implementation of the Act. In some areas, as we shall see, the necessary machinery was not in place for some time after 1 July 1837. But even once these initial teething problems were resolved, the take-up of the Act was still relatively slow.

---

[1] *First Annual Report of the Registrar-General* (London: HMSO, 1839), p. 12 and Appendix O.

[2] While the Marriage Act 1836 had referred to couples marrying 'in the office of the superintendent registrar', the accompanying legislation on registration adopted the more convenient terminology of 'register office' (Births and Deaths Registration Act 1836, s. 9) and the latter term will be used here. As we shall see, however, the office was not always in a purpose-built building and could just be the premises occupied by whoever happened to be superintendent registrar at the time.

[3] *First Annual Report*, p. 17.

[4] *The Times*, 2 September 1837; *Woolmer's*, 10 February 1838.

[5] *Westmorland Gazette*, 27 January 1838; *Ipswich Journal*, 20 January 1838; *Southampton Herald*, 2 June 1838, 3 October 1840.

In exploring the varying reactions to the 1836 Act in its early years, the key issue to be considered is how far it had enabled couples to marry in accordance with their beliefs. It has been estimated that in 1840 around 23 per cent of the population could be classified as non-Anglican.[6] Yet in that year under 5 per cent of marriages took place in a registered place of worship, and well under 2 per cent before a superintendent registrar.[7] And in 1851, when the number of attendances in non-Anglican places of worship was not far behind that in the Church of England,[8] the figures were 10.4 per cent and 4.4 per cent, respectively.[9] There does therefore appear to be a clear disjunction between how people worshipped and how they married, even taking into account the large numbers who were nominally Anglican and married in their parish church without being regular worshippers there.[10] And this sense of disjunction is supported by the data from family historians, many of whom supplied examples of couples getting married in one church or chapel but worshipping else-where, or marrying in a register office despite having very firm religious beliefs.[11]

In seeking to understand the choices that couples were making about how to marry, this chapter looks first at what the new forms of marriage had in common – that is, the requirement of giving notice to the superintendent registrar – in order to ascertain whether that particular requirement was responsible for discouraging couples from marrying under the 1836 Act. It goes on to explore how take-up differed markedly between different religious groups, with Catholics being more likely to register their buildings than Protestant Dissenters, and how many of those who married in a register office might have preferred to marry in their own place of worship had this option been available to them. And it concludes by showing that even Quakers and Jews were not free from constraints, and by considering the impact on Anglican weddings. In short, the reactions to the 1836 Act were just as diverse and complicated as the campaign for reform had been.

---

[6] Clive Field, *Periodizing Secularization: Religious Allegiance and Attendance in Britain, 1880–1945* (Oxford: Oxford University Press, 2019), table 2.1.

[7] *Fourth Annual Report of the Registrar-General* (London: HMSO, 1842), recording marriage from 1 July 1840 to 31 June 1841.

[8] For a detailed analysis of the figures, see K. D. M. Snell and Paul S. Ell, *Rival Jerusalems: The Geography of Victorian Religion* (Cambridge: Cambridge University Press, 2000).

[9] *Fourteenth Annual Report of the Registrar-General* (London: HMSO, 1853), p. 4.

[10] On nominalism within Anglicanism, see Field, *Periodizing Secularization*.

[11] See further Rebecca Probert, 'Interpreting Choices' (2021) JGFH (forthcoming).

The New Preliminaries

more expensive, more dilatory, and less decent[12]

Scholars have been divided as to whether the new preliminaries – the process of giving notice to a superintendent registrar and being issued with a certificate authorising the wedding to go ahead, with, if one paid more, a licence – would have encouraged or deterred the take-up of the new options.[13] Some imply that these new processes were quicker, cheaper, and more private than their Anglican counterparts of banns and ecclesiastical licence.[14] Others suggest that they were designed to be unattractive.[15] It is therefore necessary to look at the requirements in a little more detail to assess their impact on those getting married under the 1836 Act.

The new options were not necessarily any cheaper, and were certainly no quicker, than marrying in the Anglican Church. The period of residence required before notice could be given was no shorter for those using the new preliminaries.[16] The sheer size of the new registration districts – consisting of an amalgamation of numerous parishes – meant that most individuals would have to travel further to the register office to give notice than they would in going to their parish church.[17] And an individual's ability to give notice might depend on whether the superintendent registrar was actually in his office – which he often was not, given that those who held this role almost invariably had other jobs to do as

[12] *Yorkshire Gazette*, 1 July 1837.

[13] It should be borne in mind that the new preliminaries were required before *all* non-Anglican marriages and could also precede Anglican ones if the parties so chose.

[14] Lawrence Stone, *Road to Divorce: A History of the Making and Breaking of Marriage in England* (Oxford: Oxford University Press, 1995), p. 133; Jennifer Phegley, *Courtship and Marriage in Victorian England* (Santa Barbara: Praeger, 2012), p. 115.

[15] Scot Peterson and Iain McLean, *Legally Married: Love and Law in the UK and the US* (Edinburgh: Edinburgh University Press, 2013), p. 102.

[16] A period of seven days' residence was required before notice could be given to the superintendent registrar: Marriage Act 1836, s. 4. By contrast, banns were to be called in the parishes where the parties dwelt, with no minimum period being stated; clergy could require seven days' notice if they so wished (Marriage Act 1823, s. 7) but this was thought to be something of a dead letter (*Morning Post*, 14 June 1836). Fifteen days' prior residence was required where the marriage was to be by licence, whether an ecclesiastical licence issued by the bishop or a civil one issued by the superintendent registrar: Marriage Act 1823, s. 10; Marriage Act 1836, s. 12.

[17] Although the 1836 Act did not actually specify that notice had to be given in person, and it was later suggested that it could be given by post before 1857: *Report from the Select Committee on Nonconformist Marriages (Attendance of Registrars)* (London: HMSO, 1893), p. 128.

well. One groom indignantly reported that he 'had to call six times in one day, and twice on the following', before he could give his notice of intention to marry.[18]

Once notice had been given, a wait of twenty-one days was required before the superintendent registrar's certificate authorising the marriage could be issued.[19] The cost of the process was two shillings – one for notice to be given and one for the certificate.[20] The calling of banns, by contrast, could be both quicker (as little as fifteen days between the first calling and the marriage taking place[21]) and cheaper (as little as a shilling[22]). Paying extra for a licence from the superintendent registrar cut the waiting period to seven days,[23] but a common licence was generally no more expensive,[24] and, as the *Yorkshire Gazette* reminded its readers, 'may be obtained after supper, if you sup early, and the parties may be married before breakfast next morning'.[25]

Nor did the new preliminaries necessarily offer any greater privacy. After all, it was easy for couples who wished to escape notice to have their banns called in a parish where they were unknown.[26] In large towns and cities, the inclusion of one's name in a long list of others would have pretty much guaranteed anonymity. Marriage notice books were open to inspection by the public, whether the marriage was to be by licence or by certificate, and the entries therein were on occasion reported in the local press.[27] And where the marriage was by certificate, the additional requirement that the notice of the intended wedding be read at three successive meetings of the Board of Guardians of the Poor Law Union

---

[18] 'Tory Perversion of the Dissenters Marriage Act', *Leicestershire Mercury*, 30 December 1837.

[19] Marriage Act 1836, s. 14.

[20] Marriage Act 1836, ss. 5 and 7. This would equate to around £11 today.

[21] If the marriage took place immediately after the third calling of the banns: for examples of this happening see *Report of the Royal Commission on the Laws of Marriage 1867–8* [4059], App. 1, p. 48.

[22] *The Ipswich Journal*, January 14, 1837.

[23] Marriage Act 1836, s. 7.

[24] The cost of a civil licence was fixed at £3 plus stamp duty (Marriage Act 1836, s. 11); the cost of an ecclesiastical licence varied between dioceses but a survey towards the end of the period reported that the average was £2 7s 2¾d (Hull Terrell, *A History of the Dissenters' Marriages Bill of 1855* (London: Robert Theobold, 1855), p. 19). £3 in 1837 would equate to around £340 today.

[25] *Yorkshire Gazette*, 1 July 1837.

[26] See Parl. Deb., ser. 2, vol. 32, col. 1097, 15 April 1836 (Dr Lushington).

[27] The *Yorkshire Gazette* took it upon itself to publish notices of marriage, in order, as it claimed, to better fulfil the intentions of the Marriage Act: *Yorkshire Gazette*, 1 July 1837, although its enthusiasm seems to have waned quite quickly.

was hardly calculated to assist those who wanted to avoid awkward questions about their eligibility to marry. Boards were composed of representatives from the parishes covered by the Union, and there were often around forty persons present.

Equally, it is unlikely that couples would have been deterred from using the new preliminaries out of fear that the Board might actually *prevent* them from marrying. There is nothing to support the speculation[28] that the requirement that notices be read before the Board of Guardians had been intended to allow improvident marriages to be stopped.[29] The men appointed to these Boards were not directly involved with the day-to-day distribution of relief but consisted of individuals of a certain standing within the community.[30] They could of course raise concerns where they were aware of an impediment,[31] and had to refuse to accept a notice where the parties were not resident in the district.[32] But they had no legal power to prevent a wedding going ahead simply because it was improvident.

In any case, having one's marital intentions announced to the Board of Guardians had little impact on the experience of getting married, since couples were not required to appear before the Board in person. Despite the opposition of certain MPs during the debates prior to the passage of the Act[33] and the campaign against the process that began in the 1850s,[34] this particular requirement does not seem to have attracted much adverse comment in the intervening period. It is also worth noting that some couples actively chose the civil preliminaries when marrying in the Anglican church.[35]

[28] Stephen Parker, *Informal Marriage, Cohabitation and the Law, 1750–1989* (Basingstoke: Macmillan, 1990), p. 73; Peterson and McLean, *Legally Married*, p. 102.

[29] See Chapter 2 for the circumstances surrounding the introduction of this particular requirement.

[30] On the aristocratic leadership of many Boards, the social standing of their members, and their perceived role as a new form of local government see generally William C. Lubenow, *The Politics of Government Growth: Early Victorian Attitudes Towards State Intervention, 1833–1848* (Newton Abbot: David & Charles Ltd, 1971); Anthony Brundage, *The Making of the New Poor Law, 1832–1839: The Politics of Inquiry, Enactment and Implementation, 1832–39* (London: Hutchinson, 1978).

[31] For an example of a guardian doing so, see *CP*, 24 March 1840.

[32] Marriage notice books recorded occasional teething problems with issues about when notices had to be read and where notice could be given: see, e.g., *Chipping Norton, Faringdon, Witney and Woodstock Registration Districts: Marriage Notices 1837–1851* (High Wycombe: The Eureka Partnership, 2003), p. 9.

[33] See Chapter 2.

[34] See further Chapter 4.

[35] By 1854 2.8 per cent of Anglican weddings were preceded by civil preliminaries, and couples getting married in the Anglican church accounted for 12.9 per cent of those

In short, it is unlikely that anyone was drawn to use the new options on the basis of the cost or speed of the civil preliminaries, although the greater privacy that could be obtained in non-Union areas may have proved attractive to some. Equally, there is no reason to believe that the new processes were unduly off-putting. We need to look elsewhere to understand the low and variable take-up of the Act.

Catholic Marriages: When Two Become One

Roman Catholic marriages are such as they have ever been, and are uniformly celebrated in Catholic places of worship, and with rites peculiar to the faith[36]

The response to the 1836 Act among Catholics was immediate and enthusiastic. Nearly 200 Catholic chapels were registered for weddings in the first year alone,[37] and by 1851 weddings could take place in around 65 per cent of the buildings in which Catholics met for public worship.[38] Even more significantly, the number of weddings celebrated in each of these chapels was far higher than in registered buildings generally.[39] The result was that Catholics accounted for just over a quarter of weddings in registered places of worship in 1844,[40] despite constituting only around one-tenth of non-Anglicans.[41]

---

giving notice to the superintendent registrar: *Seventeenth Annual Report of the Registrar-General* (London: HMSO, 1856), p. 7.

[36] 'Our Wedding Day!', *The Family Treasury*, Vol. 1 (London: Houlston and Stoneman, 1854), p. 21.

[37] *First Annual Report*, p. 6. By 1840 22 of London's 27 Catholic chapels were registered.

[38] The percentage is calculated from the number of registered buildings at the end of 1850 (*Thirteenth Annual Report of the Registrar-General* (London: HMSO, 1852), Table VII) and the number of Catholic chapels recorded at the time of the 1851 Census of Religious Worship (Snell and Ell, *Rival Jerusalems*, p. 423). The latter of course excludes those chapels that were solely for the use of a particular family.

[39] This can be calculated from 1844, when the figures for Catholic weddings were first published separately. In that year there were eight weddings for every registered Catholic chapel, compared to three for every Nonconformist one (see the table of registered places of worship in the *Sixth Annual Report of the Registrar-General* (London: HMSO, 1844), p. xiv and the number of marriages in *Seventh Annual Report*, p. x). By 1850 the respective figures were 15 and 3.5 (*Thirteenth Annual Report of the Registrar-General* (London: HMSO, 1846), Table VII and p. 4).

[40] *Seventh Annual Report*, p. x. As might be expected, there was considerable variation by region, with almost half of all Catholic weddings that year taking place in Lancashire (p. xi).

[41] Catholics accounted for around 2.7 per cent of the population in 1840, and Nonconformists for around 20 per cent: Field, *Periodizing Secularization*, table 2.1.

This enthusiasm reflects the fact that Catholics had long had ceremonies in their own chapels in addition to a wedding in the Anglican church: from 1837 it was simply a matter of the two – the religious and the legal – becoming one. The high proportion of Catholic chapels being registered may also have owed something to a specific provision that applied to them alone. After the GRO had issued its guidance as to what constituted a 'separate' place of worship capable of being registered for weddings,[42] the Earl of Shrewsbury successfully moved an amendment allowing Catholic chapels to be registered even if they were part of another building.[43] While his claim that Catholics would otherwise be 'entirely' excluded from the operation of the Act – on the basis that their chapels tended to be attached to schools, colleges, and mansions[44] – was something of an overstatement,[45] the amendment did enable a number of Catholic chapels to be registered for weddings that would not otherwise have been.[46]

The amendment also marked the start of a new phase for Catholics in terms of their willingness both to seek special treatment for their weddings and to campaign for change more broadly. It was the Catholics, for example, who were involved in the first case to test the interpretation of the 1836 Act. The issue was whether a certificate could be granted to authorise a wedding in a district in which neither of the couple was resident, the Act having failed to specify this either way.[47] Given that

[42] Its 'Notice to Persons desirous of Registering Buildings for the Solemnization of Marriages', issued 26 January 1837 (First Annual Report, Appendix I), had confirmed that, in order to be registered, a building had to be 'distinct and complete ... in itself, and not merely a room or part of a dwelling-house or other building'.

[43] Births and Deaths Registration Act 1837, s. 35. The willingness of the House of Lords to agree to specific provision for Catholic places of worship may have owed something to the grandeur of the chapels that graced the homes of rich Catholic landowners. It may also have been simply because there was no time for debate. The amendment was agreed on 29 June, two days before the legislation had to be in force: see further Chapter 2.

[44] Parl. Deb., ser. 2, vol. 38, col. 1674, 28 June 1837.

[45] For a helpful summary of how Catholic places of worship had evolved – from being hidden while there was a prohibition on Catholics meeting for worship, through the discreet styles adopted immediately after the Catholic Relief Act 1791, to the more confident construction of churches in the 1810s onwards – see Historic England, 19th- and 20th-Century Roman Catholic Churches: Introductions to Heritage Assets (Historic England, 2017).

[46] Including his own chapel at Alton Abbey – now better known as Alton Towers – which then consisted merely of a room inside the house. Other chapels that were registered for marriage included that at Coughton Court, where many marriages had been celebrated in the eighteenth century: see Rebecca Probert and Liam D'Arcy-Brown, 'Catholics and the Clandestine Marriages Act of 1753' (2008) 80 Local Population Studies 78.

[47] Notice had to be given in the district of residence – by just one of the couple if both were resident in the same district, or by both if they lived in different districts: Marriage Act

some registration districts still had no registered places of worship, and many had only ones belonging to a single denomination, there was a distinct risk that not being able to marry in a different restriction district would leave many couples unable to marry under the new Act at all.[48] Nonetheless, in the summer of 1839, a Catholic couple were denied a certificate in exactly this scenario[49] – the official assumption apparently being that anything that was not expressly permitted by the Act must perforce be prohibited. The Catholic Institute reacted quickly, supporting a second couple in a similar situation – Thomas Brady and Mary Hetherington – to challenge this restrictive interpretation of the legislation in court.[50] While the judge refused to order that a certificate should be issued,[51] the case did at least highlight the deficiencies in the terms of the Act,[52] and the need for further reform.[53]

A few months later, a bill was introduced by the Catholic MP Charles Langdale to address the issue. It attracted relatively little opposition, and passed onto the statute books in August 1840.[54] Under its terms, if a couple declared that they belonged to a religious group that had no registered place of worship within their own registration districts, they could be authorised to marry in the nearest place of worship outside the district that had been so registered.[55] While this was far from giving couples a free choice as to where they could marry, it did at least mean that the lack of local provision was not an insuperable obstacle to marrying according to one's own religious rites. Its impact was perhaps greatest among Catholics, since their smaller overall numbers and

---

1836, s. 4. That notice had to state the building in which the marriage was to take place. It was clear that a superintendent registrar could not grant a *licence* for a marriage to take place in a registered place of worship that was not within his district (s. 11), but the Act made no mention of any such restriction on the grant of a *certificate*.

[48] Unless they established residence in the district where they wished to marry, or simply lied.

[49] TNA, HO39/5.

[50] Rebecca Probert, 'A Catholic Couple in the Register Office' (2021) JGFH (forthcoming).

[51] *Ex p Brady* (1840) 8 Dowl. 332.

[52] The Law Officers clearly took the view that the issue was not clear-cut, noting that 'the Act is so obscure on this point that it is absolutely necessary to have the difficulty removed by Act of Parliament': TNA, HO39/5, letter dated 11 January 1840.

[53] As the Catholic Institute noted, the narrow interpretation of the Act rendered it 'of comparatively little or no benefit to thousands of our Catholic fellow countrymen, who reside in districts in which there happens to be no Catholic chapel', adding that 'such districts are unfortunately too numerous': *The Tablet*, 3 May 1840.

[54] For accounts of the debates see *The Tablet*, 3 May 1840, 6 June 1840; *The Times*, 30 May 1840, 16 July 1840, 27 July 1840, 6 August 1840.

[55] For the declarations that had to be made, see Marriage Act 1840, sch. 1.

concentration in certain areas meant that it was less likely that there would be a Catholic chapel in every district. The unevenness of provision – and the benefit of being able to marry in a different district – was demonstrated by the wild variations in the average number of weddings per registered place of worship across different counties. The highest averages were found not in those places that had the largest number of Catholics, but in those that had the fewest places where they could marry: seventy-seven couples married in Gloucestershire's one registered Catholic chapel in 1850 alone.[56]

Even so, there were still many Catholics across England – and more especially across Wales – for whom marrying in a Catholic chapel that had been registered for weddings would have entailed a long and arduous journey. For such couples, a religious-only marriage ceremony in their local but unregistered Catholic chapel and a wedding in the Anglican church would have been the only realistic option. *The Tablet* complained that an 'extremely large' number of Catholics were still getting married in the Anglican church,[57] although many announcements of double weddings in fact involved ceremonies that could both have been legal.[58] Overall, when viewed as a percentage of the *total* number of weddings, Catholic weddings were still less common than might have been expected from the size of the Catholic population.

There were also ongoing grumbles about the operation of the 1836 Act. Efforts had been made to mitigate the impact of the requirement that a registrar be present by emphasising the need for those appointed to be acceptable to those whose marriages they were registering.[59] Some

---

[56] The figures are calculated from the data in the *Thirteenth Annual Report*, which is the first to provide a breakdown by county of both the number of Catholic weddings and the number of Catholic places of worship registered for marriage. South Wales, with 137 weddings across three chapels, or 44 per chapel, was a distant second, followed by Surrey, with 184 weddings in six chapels, or 31 per chapel. Slightly lower averages were recorded in those counties in which Catholicism was strong enough to have a greater number of registered places of worship: the average was 28 in Lancashire and Middlesex, 24 in Cheshire, 14 in Staffordshire and Warwickshire, and 13 in Yorkshire and Durham.

[57] *The Tablet*, 21 January 1854. There were also couples who married in the register office after a Catholic ceremony in an unregistered chapel: see further below.

[58] See, e.g., *Newcastle Journal*, 2 September 1837; *Yorkshire Gazette*, 30 September 1837; *Devizes and Wiltshire Gazette*, 6 August 1840; *Newcastle Courant*, 30 October 1840; *York Herald*, 22 January 1842; *Cheltenham Looker-on*, 6 June 1846; *Southampton Herald*, 14 April 1849; *Blackburn Standard*, 16 May 1849; *Birmingham Gazette*, 2 December 1850.

[59] See Appendix F of the *First Annual Report*, noted in Chapter 2, on the criteria governing the appointment of registrars.

registrars were themselves Catholics, appointed primarily to register marriages in Catholic places of worship.[60] In many areas, however, this was not the case. The late 1840s saw letters in *The Tablet* passionately arguing that Catholics should seek to campaign for further reform: the requirement that a registrar be present was regarded as humiliating; the imposition of requirements additional to those of Catholic canon law as iniquitous; and the possibility that a priest might be prosecuted for flouting the requirements of the Act as persecution.[61] There was a sense that the time might be right to press for further change.

In 1850, however, the likelihood of Catholics being given greater rights to conduct their own weddings rapidly receded in the wake of the furore created by the decision of Pope Pius IX to change the way in which the Catholic church operated in England and Wales. For the first time since the seventeenth century there were to be Catholic dioceses and Catholic bishops, a move which *The Times* labelled as 'the Papal Aggression'. The grandiloquent announcement by the newly appointed Cardinal-Archbishop of Westminster, Cardinal Wiseman, that he would hence-forth be responsible for governing Middlesex, Hertford, and Essex further fuelled the fear that Catholicism posed a threat to the nation.[62]

It is unlikely to be a coincidence that there was a hardening of official attitudes towards Catholic weddings at this time. In 1851, the GRO wrote to one priest to ask why he had conducted a ceremony without a superintendent registrar's certificate or licence, and in the absence of a registrar. After initially denying that such a ceremony had taken place,[63] the priest acknowledged his ignorance 'as to the extent of the liabilities incurred in the solemnisation of marriage, and as to the probability of the law being enforced in all cases',[64] and claimed that such ignorance was widely shared among his fellow priests. The new clamp-down even extended to religious-only marriage ceremonies that were part of the process of getting married. The Registrar-General informed Cardinal Wiseman that he had received new legal advice overturning his earlier

---

[60] *The Tablet*, 8 January 1848, noting the appointment of a Catholic registrar in Wigan. The registrar in question was William Halliwell, a schoolteacher, recorded in *Slater's Directory for Lancashire* (1855) as 'Registrar of Marriages (for Catholics)'. See also the letter in *The Tablet*, 14 July 1848 noting the communication from the 'Catholic Registrar of Marriages for N' in the Eastern Counties.

[61] *The Tablet*, 26 February 1848, 7 April 1849, 14 July 1849.

[62] See Walter Ralls, 'The Papal Aggression of 1850: A Study in Victorian Anti-Catholicism' (1974) 43(2) *Church History* 242.

[63] HO45/3707, letter dated 28 February 1851.

[64] HO45/3707, letter to the Home Secretary, Sir George Grey, dated 10 March 1851.

assumption that the Catholic ceremony 'might be regarded merely as an inchoate proceeding, ancillary to the subsequent legal marriage'.[65] The official line was now that a priest would be guilty of a felony in such cases, even if the couple went through a legal wedding on the same day.

Whether this was accurate was another matter. The issue of exactly when a felony might be committed was put to the test in 1854, when a Catholic priest, Thomas Tierney Ferguson, was prosecuted for the way in which he had conducted the marriage ceremony of Thomas Coatley and Hannah Steele. Hannah, who was a servant, a Protestant, and heavily pregnant, had given notice of her intention to marry Thomas, her Irish Catholic lover, at Holland-street Chapel. Thomas, however, had other intentions, and insisted on the ceremony taking place at a different Catholic church, St Thomas'. Ferguson, the priest at St Thomas', seems to have been a willing accomplice, telling Hannah – despite her protest-ations – that she did not need a different certificate in order for the wedding to go ahead. The ceremony was conducted in the vestry where no one would see them, with only Coatley's father as a witness. Thomas abandoned Hannah a few days later, and her father turned her away from his home on the basis that the certificate of her marriage was not a real one.[66]

At his trial at the Old Bailey, Ferguson was found guilty on the basis that he had solemnised a marriage in a place other than that stated in the certificate.[67] It was a reminder of the importance of complying with the law. But it was also a reminder that the offences underpinning the new system were highly specific. A further charge of conducting a marriage in a registered building in the absence of a registrar was not pursued, apparently, it seems, on account of doubts as to whether the vestry where the ceremony had taken place counted as a registered building.[68] This in turn suggests that a priest would not be guilty of an offence in conducting a marriage in a building that had not been registered for weddings at all.[69] Nonetheless, the GRO welcomed the verdict, express-ing the hope that 'such unlawful proceedings' would cease and circulating

[65] *The Tablet*, 5 April 1851.

[66] *Morning Chronicle*, 2 September 1854.

[67] *Proceedings of the Old Bailey*, 27 November 1854.

[68] St Thomas' had been registered for marriages in 1849 (*London Gazette*, 20 July 1849), but at the time of Ferguson's committal the magistrate had asked whether this would include the vestry and noted that it would be necessary to have evidence that marriages were usually performed there.

[69] Section 39 had enacted that it would be an offence to 'knowingly and wilfully' solemnise a marriage in any place other than 'the registered Building or Office specified in the Notice

a caution against them,[70] and the Law Officers continued to maintain that any marriage that did not comply with the requirements of the Act would be void, and that any priest conducting a religious-only marriage ceremony would be guilty of a felony, whether it was conducted before, after, or instead of a legally binding marriage.[71]

Even if this was incorrect, there were indications that matters had not necessarily improved for women and children. There continued to be reports of women going through a religious-only Catholic ceremony only to find – as before – that their supposed husbands had no obligation to support them.[72] It was not a promising time for the Catholic community to press the argument that they could be entrusted with conducting their own weddings in the absence of a registrar.

For Catholics, then, the story was primarily one of continuity, in terms of both compliance and non-compliance. While compliance could now often be achieved by having a wedding in a registered place of worship in the presence of a registrar, not all Catholics had this option, and so many continued to have two ceremonies. Others, whether by accident or design, married outside the framework of the Act.[73] As the next section will show, the pattern of take-up among Protestant Dissenters was markedly different.

The Novelty of Dissenting Weddings

As this is the first Dissenting marriage in the parish, it has made a little stir; indeed, nothing else is talked about[74]

Weddings in the chapels of Protestant Dissenters, unlike Catholic ones, were a novelty. Throughout the second half of 1837 and 1838, announcements in local papers drew attention to weddings that were the first in a particular chapel.[75] Some lucky couples were presented with a Bible or prayer book – or in one case 'a handsome set of china' – in recognition of

and Certificate'. It had not made it an offence to solemnise a marriage in a place other than a registered place of worship or register office.

[70] TNA, RG29/1, letter dated 15 December 1854.

[71] TNA, TS25/873.

[72] See, e.g., the case of John Ryan, reported in *The Londonderry Standard*, 24 January 1856. I am grateful to Gwyneth Wilkie for this reference.

[73] The uncertainty as to what consequences would follow for the priest and the parties was one that would continue over the decades: see further Chapter 4.

[74] 'New Marriage Act', *Bradford Observer*, 17 August 1837.

[75] *Leicester Chronicle*, 29 July 1837; *Western Times*, 6 October 1837; *Manchester Times*, 28 October 1837; *Liverpool Mercury*, 22 December 1837; *York Herald*, 23 December 1837;

the fact.[76] How these weddings were conducted was also telling; since most denominations lacked any liturgy or established rites, those conducting these early weddings had to extemporise.[77] One Methodist minister was reported as taking the Anglican marriage service as 'his ground work' while 'introducing some alterations'.[78] And the wedding that apparently made so much 'stir' was reported as consisting simply of the prescribed words, a couple of Bible readings, and a prayer, and lasted less than a quarter of an hour.[79] The 1836 Act was bringing a whole new social practice into existence – if rather more slowly than had been expected.

Unsurprisingly, many of the early adopters had particularly close connections with Dissent.[80] Numerous ministers or preachers, or their families, featured among these early weddings.[81] The very first bride at the Presbyterian Meeting House in Stourbridge – itself the first place to

---

Western Times, 6 January 1838; *North Wales Chronicle*, 9 January 1838; *Western Times*, 5 April 1838; *Southampton Herald*, 2 June 1838.

[76] *Manchester Times*, 28 October 1837; *York Herald*, 23 December 1837; *Westmorland Gazette*, 27 January 1837.

[77] See, e.g., *Woolmer's*, 10 February 1838, referring to a couple planning to pass through 'the new and undefined ordeal of "Marriage Rite"' at the Independent Meeting House in Wellington; *The Times*, 27 September 1843, reporting proposals for a suitable form of marriage ceremony; 'Our Wedding Day!', *Family Treasury*, p. 21, noting that '[w]hen marriages take place in chapels, the national form is generally preferred to any other, with a few immaterial omissions or substitutions'.

[78] *Woolmer's*, 9 September 1837. Wesley's 'Form of Solemnisation of Matrimony' (published in 1784, in the service book intended for use in North America), had similarly been modelled on the Anglican service: David M. Chapman, *Born in Song: Methodist Worship in Britain* (Warrington: Church in the Market Place Publications, 2006), ch. 8.

[79] 'New Marriage Act', *Bradford Observer*, 17 August 1837. This particular source is, it should be noted, open to some suspicion: it is a letter purporting to be written by an unnamed young lady about her sister's wedding in an unnamed village in a chapel whose denomination is unspecified. It may simply have been an invention by the editors to counter some of the more negative depictions of the new options. But if that is the case, then it acquires new interest as reflecting what supporters of the new options wanted people to think about them.

[80] See further Probert, 'Interpreting Choices'; Joan Smith, 'Susan Darke: A Puzzling Chapel Marriage' (2021) JGFH (forthcoming).

[81] *Leicestershire Mercury*, 12 August 1837 (Rev. James Simmons, Baptist minister of Charles St Chapel in Leicester, at the Baptist Chapel in Coventry); *Trewman's Exeter Flying Post*, 12 September 1839 (marriage of a Wesleyan Methodist minister in a Wesleyan Methodist Chapel); *Worcestershire Chronicle*, 28 April 1841(Rev. Henry Solly, Unitarian minister). A little later, Susanna Walter, an itinerant preacher for the Bible Christians, was the first bride to marry in their newly registered Providence Chapel in Northlew in 1850 (information kindly supplied by Andrew R. Janes of the Devon Family History Society).

be registered for weddings under the Act[82] – shared a surname with the minister conducting the ceremony.[83] There was, however, a marked disparity between the extent of Dissent and the popularity of marrying in a Dissenting place of worship, which stood in sharp contrast to the take-up among Catholics.

Later commentators have tended to assume that this was a matter of choice on the part of Protestant Dissenters. The author of one late-nineteenth-century textbook suggested that possessing 'the liberty of marrying in their own chapels appeared to satisfy them without largely exercising it'.[84] However, in order to assess whether individual couples did indeed possess that 'liberty', it is necessary to look a little more closely at how the system was working in practice.

It is possible that Protestant Dissenters, with no tradition of marrying in their own chapels, were deterred from beginning to do so on account of the cost, complexity, and the fact that a civil registrar had to be present.[85] Yet these obstacles applied equally to Catholics, and in any case should not be overstated. While a fee of five shillings had to be paid to the registrar for attending the wedding, this was the same as was paid for marrying in a register office and was generally no more expensive than marrying in church.[86] The complexity of organising a wedding lay solely in ensuring that the registrar could attend on the same day as the minister. And while complaints had been made during the passage of the Act about the requirement that a registrar be present – and were to be made again with even more passion towards the end of the century[87] – in practice the system seems to have worked well. As with the Catholics, some efforts seem to have been made to ensure that registrars were in

---

[82] *London Gazette*, 26 May 1837.

[83] *Worcestershire Chronicle*, 27 September 1838, reporting that Miss Louisa Savage was married by the Rev. John Savage.

[84] James T. Hammick, *The Marriage Law of England: A Practical Treatise on the Legal Incidents Connected with the Law of Constitution of the Matrimonial Contract* (London: Shaw & Sons, 1887), p. 17.

[85] These are suggestions offered by Roderick Floud and Pat Thane in the context of marriage patterns in the late nineteenth century ('Debate: The Incidence of Civil Marriage in Victorian England and Wales' (1979) 84 *Past & Present* 146, 154); see also the robust rejection of these suggestions by Olive Anderson ('The Incidence of Civil Marriage in Victorian England and Wales: A Rejoinder' (1979) 84 *Past & Present* 155).

[86] And the poor might not pay at all: the register of Fairland Chapel, an Independent Chapel in Wymondham, Norfolk, noted that one young couple 'came without money in their purse and never paid the registrar his fee'. I am grateful to Matthew Abel for providing this example.

[87] See further Chapter 5.

sympathy with those whose weddings they were recording. Some weddings were even recorded as taking place 'by' (rather than 'before') registrars who belonged to the same denomination, suggesting that some were not performing a purely civil function.[88] *The Times* might harrumph that 'the distinction between being "married in church" and "superintended at chapel" is generally viewed as involving an indignity which Dissenters are fain to eschew',[89] but this was a gibe from a newspaper that was notoriously hostile to the Marriage Act.

The most significant obstacle to taking advantage of the new provisions was whether one's place of worship had actually been registered for weddings in the first place.[90] This varied significantly by denomination. The older dissenting groups – the Independents, Baptists, Unitarians, and Presbyterians – accounted for roughly three-quarters of all registrations,[91] despite their smaller overall numbers.[92] But even among these groups the majority of places of worship remained unregistered. Only the Presbyterians – very much a minority denomination[93] – had registered the majority of their buildings by 1851.[94] The Unitarians had registered well under half of their buildings by this point, despite having campaigned so hard for change, and the percentage was still lower among Independents and Baptists.

Among the Methodists – who accounted for around 10 per cent of the total population[95] – it was lower still. This was understandable given that Methodists did not generally align themselves with the older dissenting groups and had not joined in the campaign for reform.[96] If we were to discount all Methodists, then the disparity between the number of Dissenters and marriages in Dissenting places of worship would be lessened, though it would not disappear altogether. But attitudes varied

---

[88] See Deborah Whitehead, 'The Four Marriages of John Allwright, 1826–1915' (2021) JGFH (forthcoming).

[89] *The Times*, 2 September 1837.

[90] This factor is rightly emphasised by Floud and Thane ('Debate') in relation to the later nineteenth century, and was even more of an issue in the early years of the Act.

[91] *First Annual Report*, p. 6.

[92] According to Field, *Periodizing Secularization*, table 2.1, these older dissenting groups accounted for only around two-fifths of Nonconformists in 1840.

[93] On their numbers and geographical distribution, see Snell and Ell, *Rival Jerusalems*, pp. 95–98.

[94] Presbyterian denominations were recorded as having 160 places of worship (Snell and Ell, *Rival Jerusalems*, Appendix A), and 132 places of worship registered for marriage (*Thirteenth Annual Report*, Table VII).

[95] Field, *Periodizing Secularization*, table 2.1.

[96] See Chapter 2.

within different strands of Methodism, and even within the same strand. Not all Wesleyan Methodists agreed with the advice of their 1837 Conference that chapels should not be registered for marriage;[97] nor, after Conference changed its mind in 1845, did the number of registrations increase dramatically. Even by 1851 fewer than 5 per cent of the 11,500 Methodist places of worship had been registered for marriage.[98]

Among smaller denominations, the availability of a registered place of worship in any given registration district would often have been a matter of chance. The Registrar-General's reports provide a reminder of both the sheer variety of dissenting churches and the extent of Dissent even within Dissent. In the first tranche of registrations, the United Secession Church accounted for thirteen buildings, the Swedenborgians for six,[99] and the Relief Church for three; the Independent Seceders and the Church of England Independents each had two, while the Moravians, the Swiss Protestants, the German Lutherans, the Berean Universalists, the Israelites, the Arians, the Bible Christians, the Freethinking Christians, the Cowardites, the Baptist Seceders, and the Lady Huntingdon's Seceders had just one each.[100] Some of these groups were so specific that the chapel that was registered was the only place where they met.[101] Others, however, had a significant number of adherents with little opportunity of marrying in their own place of worship.[102]

The disparity between the number of places of worship that existed and the number that were registered for weddings should not come as a surprise. After all, the criteria for registration had been specifically designed to preclude weddings being conducted in the rooms, private houses, and barns where many Nonconformists still met.[103] Even some

---

[97] *First Annual Report*, p. 6, reports that Methodists accounted for 82 of the 1,257 buildings registered by the end of 1838. The Countess of Huntingdon's Connexion registered another 11.

[98] Snell and Ell, *Rival Jerusalems*, Appendix A; *Thirteenth Annual Report*, Table VII.

[99] Including one designated as 'the New Jerusalem Church'.

[100] *First Annual Report*, p. 17.

[101] This was the case for the short-lived breakaway group from the Countess of Huntingdon's Connexion. The Northampton Tabernacle was built in 1835 by 'Lady Huntingdon's Seceders', registered for weddings in August 1837, and sold off in 1846 after the seceders fell out with their minister: 'The Chapels Society', *Newsletter*, No. 57 (September 2014), p. 9; *London Gazette*, 15 August 1837, 30 December 1845.

[102] The Bible Christians, founded in North Devon in 1815, had a significant presence across the West Country: Snell and Ell, *Rival Jerusalems*, p. 150.

[103] In 1847 'the Ranters used twice as many rented rooms as permanent chapels for worship': Michael Watts, *The Dissenters* (Oxford: Oxford University Press, 1995), p. 604. See also Emma Griffin, *Liberty's Dawn: A People's History of the Industrial*

purpose-built chapels did not necessarily have sufficient householders in attendance to certify that it was their usual place of worship. This underlines the necessity of considering the availability of the new options from the perspective of individual couples. For them, the overall number of places of worship that were registered for weddings mattered less than the local picture. In 1842 there were still eighty-one registration districts – around 13 per cent of the total – with no registered places of worship at all.[104] The ability to marry in a registered place of worship in a different district would have helped, but only for those willing and able to travel some distance.

For those who had no place of worship of their own denomination sufficiently close to make marrying there a realistic proposition, there were three options – get married in a place of worship registered to a different denomination, in the Church of England, or in the register office. As regards the first of these, there are some examples of couples from one denomination marrying in a place of worship registered to a different denomination in the early years of the Act. Louisa Smedley, a Methodist, married in a Baptist chapel in 1845; as her marriage certificate recorded, the ceremony took place according to the rites of the *parties*, rather than according to the rites of the Baptist church.[105] The *North Devon Journal* similarly recorded a Bible Christian minister conducting the marriage of a fellow minister at a Baptist Chapel in Bideford in 1850.[106] Such flexibility was facilitated by the Act, which as we have seen had made no stipulation as to how weddings were to be conducted.[107]

Most Methodists, however, continued to marry in the Anglican church, as is reflected by newspaper announcements of the weddings of Methodist ministers[108] and by examples of couples with strong

---

Revolution (New Haven: Yale University Press, 2013, ppbk 2014), p. 189 for examples of prayer meetings being held in barns.

[104] *Lists of Chapels Belonging to the Church of England From Returns; of Places of Public Worship Registered for Solemnization of Marriages under the Provisions of the Acts of 6 and & William IV, c. 85 and 1 Victoria, c. 22; also of all Superintendent Registrars and Registrars* (London: W. Clowes and Sons, 1842).

[105] Probert, 'Interpreting Choices'. I am grateful to Mary Ratcliffe for this example.

[106] *North Devon Journal*, 25 July 1850. See also *Liverpool Mail*, 15 April 1848, noting the marriage of a Baptist minister at the Wesleyan Chapel at Fenny-bridges (with thanks to Joan Smith of the Devon Family History Society for this example).

[107] See further Chapter 2.

[108] *Gloucester Journal*, 29 July 1837; *Bristol Mercury*, 12 August 1837; *Devizes and Wiltshire Gazette*, 6 August 1840.

connections to Methodism marrying in the parish church.[109] Given the different views within Methodism, it is not possible to say whether this was a matter of choice or constraint in individual cases, but in general terms Methodists did not regard a wedding in the Anglican church as being incompatible with their beliefs.

Overall, then, it seems fair to conclude that a combination of legal limitations on what could be registered, and the decisions made by different religious groups as to whether to register operated as a significant constraint on the choices available to individual Dissenters under the 1836 Act. Many continued to marry in the Anglican church. But those who disliked the idea did at least now had the option of marrying in a register office. In order to understand the significance of choosing the latter course, we should now turn to how this newest of the new options operated in practice.

The Misnomer of 'Civil' Marriages

The very idol-worshippers and cannibals of the dreariest wastes in Heathen lands have more moral, more religious modes of marriage[110]

The novel possibility of marrying with no religious rites attracted much negative comment. A diatribe against such marriages in the *Halifax Guardian* claimed that any man who would be willing to accept public money to preside over such a 'tackling' was 'an infidel in his deeds', and any man asking a woman to marry in this way 'is a beast in his heart'.[111] Newspapers dubbed the 1836 Act the 'Broomstick Marriage Act'[112] – the adjective 'broomstick' at that time denoting something ersatz or lacking authenticity in some way.[113] And once the first set of statistics was

---

[109] Probert, 'Interpreting Choices'.

[110] *Halifax Guardian*, reprinted in the *Morning Post*, 14 September 1838.

[111] *Ibid.* The word 'beast' evoked the injunction in the marriage service of the *Book of Common Prayer* that marriage was not to be undertaken 'unadvisedly, lightly, or wantonly, to satisfy men's carnal lusts and appetites, like brute beasts that have no understanding'.

[112] *Essex Standard*, 8 March 1839; *Jackson's Oxford Journal*, 12 September 1840; 'Saint Valentine: or, Thoughts on the Evil of Love in Mercantile Community: The Galanti Show' (1843) 13 *Bentley's Miscellany* 151. Even a decade later, register office marriages were still being referred to as 'broomstick' marriages: see *Berrow's Worcester Journal*, 5 April 1849.

[113] On this meaning of the term 'broomstick', see Rebecca Probert, *Marriage Law and Practice in the Long Eighteenth Century: A Reassessment* (Cambridge: Cambridge University Press, 2009).

published, commentators rejoiced in the fact that the number marrying in the register office was so low – around one in a hundred – and congratulated 'all who reverence religion and good order'.[114] But, as this section will show, many of those who married in a register office did in fact have strong religious beliefs and were able to include religious content in their wedding.

Evidence of the religiosity of those marrying in the register office comes from a variety of sources. In some cases, we know (or can infer) the beliefs of specific couples. Among the very first to be married in a register office were the Shilohite Bradleys, whose earlier unofficial declaration of self-marriage in their chapel had attracted so much attention in 1834:[115] their (second) double wedding took place by licence at the Birmingham register office on 9 July 1837.[116] Another early adopter was Augustus De Morgan, Professor of Mathematics at the resolutely non-denominational University College London, who had Unitarian leanings but called himself a 'Christian unattached' and was committed to the principle of religious neutrality.[117] Marriage notices also recorded a number of Dissenting ministers marrying in a register office.[118] And the details provided by family historians of couples marrying in the register office in this period showed that at least a third had some link to Dissent, as evidenced by where they or their children were baptised, by later marriages, or by their known attendance at religious services.[119]

In other cases, the religious beliefs of the couple can be inferred from their choice of an additional religious ceremony. After Francis Green married in the register office in Northleach in July 1837, 'the party proceeded to Wharf-road Chapel, Cirencester, where the Reverend John Burder ... performed a religious service appropriate to the occasion'.[120] Green was the pastor of Chedworth's Congregational Church, but neither it nor the Cirencester chapel were registered for

---

[114] 'First Annual Report of the Registrar-General', *The Monthly Law Magazine and Political Review*, October 1839–January 1840, Vol. 6. p. 49.

[115] See Chapter 2.

[116] *Birmingham Gazette*, 10 July 1837.

[117] 'Augustus De Morgan', *ODNB*. De Morgan married Sophia Frend at the St Pancras register office on 3 August 1837: *Leicestershire Mercury*, 12 August 1837.

[118] *Western Times*, 5 April 1838 (Rev. John Corser, Baptist Minister); *Leeds Mercury*, 26 August 1837 (Rev. John Dyer, Secretary of the Baptist Missionary Society); *Manchester Times*, 4 November 1837 (Rev. William Howe, Independent Minister of Hindley).

[119] See further Probert, 'Interpreting choices'.

[120] *Gloucester Journal*, 22 July 1837.

weddings at this time. The *Stamford Mercury* reported how another couple were married first at the register office and afterwards in a private house, by a Baptist minister.[121] There were also announcements of Catholics having had a religious-only ceremony before going to the register office.[122]

Perhaps most surprisingly of all, some couples even had a religious wedding in the register office itself. The 1836 Act had merely specified the declarations and vows that had to be included; it had said nothing about whether religious content should be excluded. The marriage of Thomas Brady and Mary Hetherington – the Catholic couple whose test case had led to the passage of the 1840 Act – took place in the Salford register office 'according to the rites and ceremonies of the parties', suggesting that some kind of Catholic ceremony took place.[123] Announcements of weddings in the local papers mention that Dissenting ministers were present to give 'a suitable address', read passages from scripture, and conclude the proceedings with a prayer.[124] Indeed, when Commander Poyntz RN married a Miss Brinn in 1837, it was thought worthy of note that it was 'a purely civil contract',[125] while the option of marrying in the register office 'with or without any religious ceremony' was sufficiently well-known to be included in an 1852 guide to wedding etiquette.[126]

This evidence of religiosity in the register office is important for three reasons. First, it reinforces the fact that not everyone could marry in their own place of worship: most couples who married in a register office would no doubt have preferred to marry in their own place of worship if they could have done so. Second, it underlines how the new law was intended to be flexible: there was no rigid divide between religious and secular at this stage.[127] And third, it shows that marrying in a register office cannot be interpreted as evidence of a demand for a 'civil' form of

---

[121] *Stamford Mercury* 25 Aug 1837. See also *Royal Cornwall Gazette*, 29 December 1837, reporting a couple who were married at the Camelford register office 'and subsequently by the Rev. W. Patteson, of the Wesleyan Association'.

[122] *Yorkshire Gazette*, 30 September 1837; *The Tablet*, 8 August 1840 ('Married ... at the Bavarian Ambassador's Chapel, Warwick St, and afterwards at the Registrar's Office, Surrey-street').

[123] GRO, Certified copy of an entry of marriage, 1 March 1840, Salford registration district.

[124] See, e.g., 'Marriages', *Western Times*, 6 October 1837; *Trewman's Exeter Flying Post*, 7 September 1837.

[125] 'Marriages', *Western Times*, 6 October 1837.

[126] Anon, *The Etiquette of Courtship and Matrimony: With a Complete Guide to the Forms of a Wedding* (London: David Bogue, 1852), p. 61.

[127] See further Chapter 2.

marriage. Only a tiny number married there because they wanted a non-religious wedding.

This lack of demand for civil marriage merits a little more discussion in the light of the very different view taken by other scholars.[128] It is worth reiterating just how few couples married in a register office in the early years of the Act.[129] The absolute numbers are more important than either their relative increase[130] or the proportion in individual districts.[131] In Salford, for example, almost a fifth of all weddings were celebrated in the register office in 1841, far more than in any other registration district, but this figure represented just six weddings.[132]

Nor can the low take-up be attributed to structural factors. While in some places it had taken a few months to put the necessary facilities in place,[133] accounting for the particularly low number of register office marriages in the first quarter, by the end of 1837 every registration district had its own register office. The preliminaries required before a register office wedding were the same as for all non-Anglican weddings, and the fee to the registrar was the same as when the ceremony took place in a registered place of worship. And contrary to what has been claimed,[134] the register office was not invariably located in the workhouse. Some were, but many of the original offices consisted simply of the premises occupied by the person who happened to be superintendent registrar at that

---

[128] See, e.g., Olive Anderson, 'The Incidence of Civil Marriage in Victorian England and Wales' (1975) 69 *Past & Present* 50; Peterson and McLean, *Legally Married*, p. 103.

[129] ONS, 'Marriages in England and Wales 2017' (14 April 2020), table 1: 'Number of marriages by type of ceremony and denomination, 1837 to 2017'.

[130] Peterson and McLean argue that one should look at the relative increase rather than the absolute number (*Legally Married*, p. 103). The flaw in this argument is that the low figures for 1838, which they use as their baseline, magnify the extent of the modest increase that followed.

[131] C.f. Anderson, 'The Incidence of Civil Marriage', who focuses on the proportion of civil marriages.

[132] *Fifth Annual Report of the Registrar-General* (London: HMSO, 1843). In the same year the 12 non-Anglican weddings in Berwick-upon-Tweed accounted for 35.2 per cent of the total, underlining how easily percentages can be skewed when the base numbers are small.

[133] In York, for example, no registrar of marriages was appointed, and no register office provided, until September, and the first notices of marriage 'after the new mode' were only published at the end of that month: *Yorkshire Gazette*, 16 September 1837, 23 September 1837, 30 September 1837.

[134] See, e.g., Peterson and McLean, *Legally Married*, p. 102, who assert, without any supporting evidence, that the register office was 'a room in the poor-house'.

time.[135] Others were part of new, purpose-built buildings that exuded a sense of civic pride. At Chorlton-on-Medlock in Manchester, the office was part of the new Town Hall, while that in Totnes was a handsome construction whose front elevation evoked a classical temple.[136]

The variations in take-up in different registration districts are better viewed as reflecting the unavailability, unattractiveness, or inconvenience of the various options in different localities rather than by any regional differences in the demand for a secular form of marriage. The potential impact of local factors is well illustrated by the differing take-up across the city of Exeter, which was split between two registration districts, Exeter and St Thomas. In Exeter, register office weddings were three to four times as popular as across England and Wales as a whole; whereas in St Thomas, the percentage of such weddings was almost identical to the national average.[137] Marrying in the Exeter register office entailed a degree of privacy; as a pre-1834 Union, it had no Board of Guardians before whom notices had to be read, and such notices of marriage were therefore simply posted up in the office of the superintendent registrar, a local solicitor.[138] By contrast, those who married in the St Thomas register office had to have their notices read before its Board of Guardians, and the office itself lay within the curtilage of the workhouse. The higher percentage of weddings in the Exeter register office is more likely to reflect these practical differences than differing attitudes towards 'civil' marriage on either side of the Exe.

Finally, we can see from the reactions to register office weddings just how alien non-religious weddings seemed at the time. One superintendent registrar was reported as saying that he had 'seen women go away with tears in their eyes at what appeared to them so imperfect a ceremony'.[139] A number of men accused of bigamy pleaded their innocence on the basis that they had not thought their register office weddings were

---

[135] See further Rebecca Probert and Liam D'Arcy-Brown, 'Workhouse Weddings? A Case Study of Register Office Ceremonies in Devon, 1837–1856' (in preparation).

[136] The building still survives, although it is now in private hands and named 'Haytor'. A plaque records its early history.

[137] *Fourth Annual Report of the Registrar-General of Births, Deaths and Marriages in England for 1841* (London: HMSO, 1842).

[138] As required by the Births and Deaths Registration Act 1837, discussed in Chapter 2.

[139] *Royal Cornwall Gazette, Falmouth Packet, and General Advertiser*, 11 April 1856. The *Westmorland Gazette*, reporting the first wedding in the superintendent's office in Chorley, noted that the ceremony lasted just three minutes: 'Coupled under the New Act', *Westmorland Gazette*, 21 October 1837.

legal.[140] George Stiffell, for example, objected that 'they merely went into an office, where fees were paid and some words read, without any intervention of parson or church ceremony'.[141] Patrick Fitzgerald similarly argued that his second wedding 'was no marriage at all, as it niver tuk place in church or chapel, or upon the Holy Book'.[142] While these particular individuals were no doubt trying to escape or mitigate their punishment, there would have been no point in making such arguments unless they were likely to resonate with judge and jury. And occasional comments by judges suggested that they did not regard a register office wedding as wholly equivalent to one celebrated in church. Sentencing Thomas Meanly in 1849, one judge commented that '[p]erhaps if you had been obliged to go into a church, that might have brought to your recollection that it was a solemn ceremony to be performed in the presence of Almighty God. But you went to a register-office. I am sorry for it.'[143]

From the low take-up of the new options, let us now turn to how those groups who had always married according to their own rites navigated the new formalities.

The Exempted Groups: Freedoms and Restrictions

both of these are rarities – the comets of the matrimonial system[144]

As before the 1836 Act, Quaker and Jewish weddings stood on a different footing. While couples marrying according to the usages of these groups now had to give notice to the civil authorities, and processes were in place for their marriages to be centrally registered, what happened in between was left unregulated by the statute. Yet this does not mean that individual Quakers and Jews were exempt from controls. As this section will show, the references to 'usages' meant that there was far less flexibility in how Quaker and Jewish weddings were conducted than was the case for other non-Anglican religious groups.

---

[140] See, e.g., Thomas Matthews, who 'said he did not think the first marriage a legal one, not having heard the service read' (*The Northern Star and National Trades' Journal*, 22 March 1851), and Adolphus Maddock, who objected to its legality on the basis that the ceremony took place in a room and not in a church (*Proceedings of the Old Bailey*, 7 April 1851).

[141] *Morning Post*, 1 June 1850.

[142] *Manchester Courier etc*, 25 August 1849.

[143] *Liverpool Mercury*, 27 March 1849.

[144] *Leamington Spa Courier*, 21 January 1837.

Moreover, the power of their governing authorities to decide who could register a marriage could be used as a tool to ensure religious orthodoxy.

The Society of Friends

The lack of external regulation of Quaker weddings was more than made up for by the regulations imposed by the Society of Friends itself. A rigorous process of approval was required before a wedding could take place, by comparison with which the formal notification to the superintendent registrar would have appeared simplicity itself. Contemporary accounts of Quaker weddings indicate that the Society's stipulation that weddings were to take place only in meeting houses in which meetings for worship were held was closely observed.[145] Witnesses may not have been required by the 1836 Act, but there was no question of a Quaker wedding taking place without them, and, while no third party was required to be present to conduct the wedding or take any formal role, there was still a convention that a member of the Society would stand up and explain the processes that had been observed, and invite those present to sign the wedding certificate.[146] Similarly, although Quaker weddings did not have to include the words prescribed by law for weddings in registered buildings, every such wedding did include exactly the same vows prescribed by the Society.

One legal restriction was, however, proving increasingly onerous. The fact that a Quaker wedding could only be conducted where both parties were Quakers was consistent with the opposition expressed by the Society of Friends to marrying out.[147] But at a time of declining membership, endogamy was starting to pose something of a problem.[148] From their heyday in the late seventeenth century, the number of Quaker marriages had been steadily falling,[149] and the number of weddings was small even in proportion to the Society's number of

---

[145] *Woolmer's*, 9 March 1850; *Standard*, 30 August 1851.

[146] See, e.g., *The Standard*, 30 August 1851.

[147] Elizabeth Isichei, *Victorian Quakers* (Oxford: Oxford University Press, 1970), p. 115, notes that the Society 'unfailingly expelled every member who married a non-Quaker – perhaps between a quarter and a third of all who married at all'.

[148] On the decline in membership, see Snell and Ell, *Rival Jerusalems*, p. 111.

[149] The 1820s saw 864 Quaker marriages; by the 1840s this had dropped to 666: J. S. Rowntree, *The Friends' Register of Births, Deaths and Marriages, 1650-1900* (Leominster, 1902), p. 14.

adherents.[150] So although Quakers were able to marry in accordance with their beliefs in terms of how they married, they had to limit their preferences as to who they married, and look beyond their locality, in order to do so.[151] George Graham, in his annual report as Registrar-General, commented on the 'unusual reluctance to marry among the male or female members of this remarkable sect', predicting that, unless it was to win new recruits, it would 'eventually decline in England'.[152] It was a warning that the Quakers were to take to heart.[153]

Jewish Weddings

Jewish law was equally clear as to how weddings were to be solemnised. The core element was the placing of a ring on the bride's finger by the bridegroom while pronouncing the words, 'Thou art wedded unto me according to the law of Moses and Israel'.[154] This exchange had to take place before witnesses, who had themselves to be Jewish, and was generally accompanied by a range of other rituals – the erection of a canopy, or *chuppah*, blessings from the rabbi, the bride and groom drinking from the same glass of wine, and the smashing of a glass.[155]

Jewish couples availed themselves of their relative freedom from regulation in a way that Quakers did not. Free from any requirement to marry during prescribed hours, Jewish weddings often took place after afternoon prayers.[156] Often such weddings were celebrated in private homes, rather than in the synagogue under whose auspices they were

---

[150] In 1851, 22,478 attendances were recorded at 371 Quaker meeting houses on Census Sunday (Snell and Ell, *Rival Jerusalems*, Appendix A), but only 65 couples married in a Quaker ceremony that year (*Fourteenth Annual Report*, p. 4).

[151] See, e.g., Pamela Richardson, 'The West Country Fox Family: A Study of Provincial English Quakerism, 1840–1920' (unpublished Ph.D. thesis, University of Exeter, 2007), pp. 38, 65, 175 on the marriages that did not take place, at least in part because of religious differences, and on the variety of locations from which suitable spouses were drawn. The average distance travelled by grooms marrying in the meeting house at Falmouth was close on two hundred miles: Falmouth Society of Friends, *Register of Marriages, 1839–94*.

[152] *Thirteenth Annual Report*, p. iv.

[153] For the changing rules on who could marry in a Quaker ceremony, see Chapter 4.

[154] See the evidence given by the Chief Rabbi to the 1868 Royal Commission: *Report*, App. 1, p. 45.

[155] For contemporary accounts of Jewish weddings, see *Westmorland Gazette*, 8 September 1838; *Hampshire Advertiser*, 8 December 1849.

[156] *Hampshire Advertiser*, 8 December 1849.

conducted.[157] In Plymouth, none of the marriages registered by the town's synagogue in this period took place in the synagogue itself.[158] In these respects Jewish weddings were very different from all others.

Crucially, however, not all synagogues were able to register weddings, but only those whose secretaries had been duly certified to do so by the body named in the legislation.[159] The new constitution of the London Committee of Deputies of the British Jews[160] made certification dependent on the relevant ecclesiastical authorities confirming that the synagogue could indeed be described as 'Jewish'.[161] In effect, the Marriage Act 1836 gave the Committee a powerful tool to require the growing number of Jewish communities to remain orthodox in their practices.[162]

This power was very soon being put to the test. On 15 April 1840, a breakaway group of twenty-four leading figures announced that they intended to set up a new synagogue, 'where a revised service may be performed ... in a manner more calculated to inspire feelings of devotion'.[163] Meeting first at the Bedford Hotel in Southampton Row, the West London Congregation of British Jews was formally established on 27 January 1842 in a former dissenting chapel just off the Euston Road.[164] But when the President of the London Committee refused to certify its secretary, it had no way of conducting weddings.[165] Members of the congregation thus faced a stark choice: marry in a register office, in

[157] Bernard Susser, *The Jews of South-West England: The Rise and Decline of their Medieval and Modern Communities* (Exeter: University of Exeter Press, 1993), p. 185; *Northampton Mercury*, 14 August 1841, describing the marriage of Jacob Joseph and Elizabeth Samuel 'at his residence'.

[158] Susser, *The Jews of South-West England*, p. 185.

[159] See further Chapter 2.

[160] Its more familiar name, the Board of Deputies, will be used, although it was not adopted until much later.

[161] On the constitution of the Board see H. S. Q. Henriques, *Jewish Marriages and the English Law* (Oxford: Hart, 1909). The relevant ecclesiastical authorities were either the Haham or other designated official of the Sephardim, or the Chief Rabbi: Geoffrey Alderman, *Modern British Jewry* (Oxford: Clarendon Press, 1998), p. 40.

[162] Michael Clark, 'Identity and Equality: The Anglo-Jewish Community in the Post-Emancipation Era, 1858–1887' (DPhil thesis, Oxford, 2005), pp. 46–47; Alderman, *Modern British Jewry*, pp. 31, 44, 47.

[163] Quoted by David S. Katz, *The Jews in the History of England 1485–1850* (Oxford: Oxford University Press, 1994), pp. 335–36.

[164] *Ibid.*, p. 342.

[165] David Feldman, *Englishmen and Jews: Social Relations and Political Culture, 1840–1914* (New Haven: Yale University Press, 1994), p. 24; Clark, 'Identity and Equality', p. 50. As only Christian places of worship could be certified as such, it did not even have the option of being registered as a place of worship and conducting marriages there with a registrar present, although this was to change in the 1850s, as Chapter 4 will show.

the Anglican church, or in a non-legally recognised religious ceremony. As Mr Alderman Salomon later noted, 'we were compelled to submit to a gross humiliation'.[166]

It is clear, then, that the 1836 Act did not leave Quaker and Jewish weddings untouched. It should be seen as having adopted a different model of regulation for these two groups, rather than no regulation at all – one based on regulation by an overarching organisation rather than on regulation of the place of marriage. The privileges that the Act conferred were no doubt appreciated by the bodies named in the legislation, and by many Quaker and Jewish couples. And any Quakers who chafed against the restrictions of the Society had a plethora of other Dissenting churches from which to choose, or even the option of setting up their own place of worship and registering it for weddings.[167] But for some Jewish groups – and couples – the restrictions would have seemed much more obvious than the freedoms.

Anglican Rites, Registration, and Resistance

They are married, and have signed their names in one of the old sneezy registers[168]

Across England and Wales, the vast majority of weddings were still taking place according to Anglican rites.[169] Novelists continued to unite their heroes and heroines in church as if no other options were available, even when the weddings were modest affairs, secret, or bigamous.[170] The main change for Anglican clergy was the need to submit returns of the marriages they registered to the GRO. Despite

---

[166] *Report of the Royal Commission on the Laws of Marriage 1867–8* [4059], Evidence given by Mr Alderman Salomon, 7 March 1866, noting that his niece had married in the register office before having an additional ceremony conducted by one of the ministers of the new synagogue.

[167] One group did just this: the 'Evangelical Friends' split from the Society and registered their own place of worship in Chorlton-on-Medlock in 1839 (*London Gazette*, 9 January 1839). The group was, however, short-lived: see John Punshon, *Portrait in Grey: A Short History of the Quakers* (London: Quaker Home Service, 1984), p. 189.

[168] Charles Dickens, *Dombey and Son* (London: Bradbury & Evans, 1848), ch. 57.

[169] The percentage was higher in England than in Nonconformist Wales, but even in the latter around two-thirds of couples still married in their parish church in the early 1850s: *Fourteenth Annual Report*, p. 4.

[170] The classic example is of course Mr Rochester's frustrated first attempt to marry Jane Eyre; their eventual (legal) marriage takes place with little fanfare: Charlotte Brontë, *Jane Eyre* (London: Smith, Elder & Co, 1847).

occasional problems, this aspect of the new scheme does not seem to have caused too much difficulty. Reporting on his correspondence with members of the clergy about the certified copies that they were now required to submit, the Registrar-General acknowledged 'the civility and alacrity with which the Clergy, with only very rare exceptions give me their assistance in rectifying accidental errors which they may have committed'.[171]

In other respects, Anglican weddings continued much as they had done before the Act. A few more chapels within parishes were licensed for weddings[172] and duly celebrated the first couples to tie the knot there.[173] A few were not, but conducted ceremonies anyway, necessitating the passage of special legislation to confirm their validity.[174] Occasional cases came to court where it transpired that the banns had been called in the wrong names, often as a means of concealing a marriage of which parents and guardians were likely to disapprove.[175] Overall, though, such problems affected only a minuscule percentage of weddings in the Church of England.

However, one change that began to impinge on an increasing number of clergy was the possibility of an Anglican wedding taking place after civil rather than ecclesiastical preliminaries. Under an 1837 amendment to the Marriage Act, they were obliged to marry couples who had obtained a superintendent registrar's certificate.[176] In the early years of the Act's operation there were occasional examples of clergy refusing to do so,[177] although others contented themselves with a snide reference to

---

[171] *Sixth Annual Report,* p. xi. For a less positive assessment of the system of registration, see Michael Whitfield Foster, 'A *Comedy of Errors': The Marriage Records of England and Wales, 1837–1899* (Wellington, privately printed, 1998).

[172] See Chapter 2 on the inclusion of provisions in the Marriage Act enabling this to be done.

[173] *Leeds Intelligencer,* 2 September 1837, reporting the first marriages at Christ Church in the parish of Bradford, and Lockwood in the parish of Almondbury.

[174] See, e.g., Upton cum Chalvey Marriages Validity Act 1850; Marriages, Holy Trinity Church, Hulme, Validity Act 1853; Christ Church (Todmorden) Marriages Validity Act 1855. While creating a chapel of ease within a growing parish was easier – and so more common – than creating a wholly new parish from part of it (A. Jones, *A Thousand Years of the English Parish* (London: Cassell & Com, 2002), p. 263), the risk was that the need for it to be licensed as well as consecrated was overlooked.

[175] *Brealy* v. *Reed* (1841) 163 ER 601; *Tooth* v. *Barrow* (1854) 164 ER 214; c.f. *Wright* v. *Elwood, falsely calling herself Wright* (1837) 1 Curt. 662; 163 ER 231; *Orme* v. *Holloway* (1847) 5 Notes of Cas. 267.

[176] Births and Deaths Registration Act 1837, s. 36.

[177] TNA, HO39/5, HO107/2409 (noting that the Reverend John Armstrong of Wallsend had been given a warning).

'workhouse banns'.[178] As the number of couples opting for civil preliminaries increased,[179] there were more opportunities for problems to arise,
and the GRO found itself embroiled in correspondence with both indig-
nant officials and irate ecclesiastics.[180]

In 1849, John Hayes, the superintendent registrar of Leigh in
Lancashire, found himself on a collision course with various clergymen
in his district. One, the Reverend Irvine, insisted that it was contrary to
the rubric of the Church of England to marry other than after banns or
licence,[181] and flatly refused to do so.[182] Another, the Reverend James,
also refused to accept the superintendent registrar's certificate,[183] despite
Hayes accompanying the groom on two separate occasions.[184] His osten-
sible objection was to the fact that the man in question, one Henry Fisher,
had not been confirmed, but this was seen as a mere pretext. With the
bishop apparently stating that he had no power to compel a clergyman to
solemnise such a marriage, and the Board of Guardians declining to fund
an action for an order of mandamus in the Court of Queen's Bench,
resort was had to the criminal law and the Reverend James found himself
on trial at the Liverpool Assizes.[185] His acquittal – on the technical basis
that as the parties had not presented themselves to be married, he had not
actually refused to marry them – left the central question of whether
a clergyman could refuse to accept the civil preliminaries unresolved, at
least for the moment.[186]

Viewed from the perspective of couples who worshipped and married in their local parish church, the 1836 Act had made no difference

---

[178] Marriage register of St Andrew, Rugby. I am grateful to Roger and Jenny McNae for
drawing my attention to this example.
[179] While the numbers were modest, the increase was still noticeable. In 1838, 493 Anglican
marriages (0.5 per cent) had been preceded by civil preliminaries but by 1850 it was 3,136
(2.4 per cent): see *Thirteenth Annual Report*, p. 4. There might be a range of reasons for
a couple to use the civil preliminaries: see, e.g., Liam D'Arcy-Brown and Lesley Plant, 'A
"Catholic" Marriage in the Parish Church?' (2021) JGFH (forthcoming) for an example.
[180] See TNA, HO45/1947, recording an incident in 1847 when a Reverend Scott refused to
accept the certificate. His bishop, the Bishop of Exeter, reacted angrily to Graham's
enquiry about this incident, asking 'under what authority you, as Registrar General, are
justified in catechising me!' and denying any knowledge of Scott's actions.
[181] TNA, HO45/2989.
[182] *Ibid.*, letter dated 12 February 1849. Irvine had also refused to conduct the marriage of
John Greenough, telling him he had to be confirmed and have taken the sacrament.
[183] *Ibid.*, letter dated 31 July 1849.
[184] *Ibid.*, letter dated 2 August 1849.
[185] *R v. Moorhouse James* (1850) 2 Den 1; 169 ER 393.
[186] See further Chapter 4.

at all. Viewed from the perspective of Anglican clergy, it had imposed new administrative requirements relating to the registration of marriages, and generated a new set of challenges to the conscience of those who saw the civil preliminaries as incompatible with the canon law. And viewed from the perspective of the Church of England as an institution, the early reactions to the Act had provided reassurance that relieving Dissenters from compulsory conformity would not result in a massive exodus from church to chapel. But the question of what role an Established Church should play in conducting weddings once multiple ways of getting married were recognised had not gone away.

Conclusion

The early reactions to the Marriage Act 1836 were shaped by what had gone before. Catholics continued to marry according to their own rites, the main differences being the possibility of such rites being accorded legal recognition, the availability of the register office as an alternative to the Anglican church where no registered Catholic chapel was available, and the risk of prosecution where priests conducted ceremonies in such registered chapels otherwise than in accordance with the law. Protestant Dissenters had to create new marriage ceremonies and were proportionately far less likely to register their places of worship for marriage, or to marry there. In this respect, the choices available to any given couple to marry in accordance with their beliefs depended on their religious affiliation and which registered places of worship were accessible to them. It was at least open to all couples in England and Wales to marry in their local register office, though, and the inclusion of prayers and Bible readings underlines how this particular option was intended to complement that of marrying in a registered place of worship. For some, however, the nature and location of the register office meant that it was not a particularly attractive option.

The low uptake of the new forms introduced by the Marriage Act 1836 should be evaluated in the light of its limitations. Some of the initial teething problems – those that were the result of poor drafting or oversights that were then narrowly construed by those tasked with implementing the law – were relatively easily solved. And despite some of the unattractive features of the new civil preliminaries, it seems unlikely that these were responsible for discouraging couples from marrying under the 1836 Act. But the restrictions on which places of worship could be registered meant that not everyone was able to marry where they worshipped.

The different reactions to the Act also signalled some of the problems that lay ahead. The coherence of the exemptions for Quakers and Jews was already beginning to unravel. Only a tiny minority of those marrying in the Anglican church were opting to give notice to the superintendent registrar, and risked being refused by Anglican clergy if they did so. Russell's original ambition of putting all religious groups on more or less the same footing, with the same preliminaries required for all, was looking ever more unlikely to be realised.

Some of the specific grievances with the way that the Act operated were to become the subject of a new campaign for reform in the 1850s, with various amendments being enacted. And – as the next chapter will also show – the more fundamental policy decisions underpinning the Act were to come under review as early as the 1860s, with some far-reaching reforms being proposed.

4

Amendments Enacted and Reform Deferred, 1855–1872

The law regulating weddings was the target of a renewed campaign for change in the 1850s. This time it was the Protestant Dissenting Deputies – the representatives of 'old' Dissent – who led the way.[1] The tone of their petitions was very different from those that had flooded into Parliament two decades earlier. The focus was very much on the practicalities of getting married and the need to remove certain 'unnecessary obstacles and inconveniences' that stood in the way of non-Anglican weddings. Bills were introduced in 1854 and 1855,[2] and a further attempt in 1856 eventually proved successful. The resulting Marriage and Registration Act 1856 addressed all of the points that the Deputies had raised. Unfortunately, but perhaps inevitably, it also made some changes which individual Nonconformists may not have welcomed, and some that the Deputies had not asked for at all, and in so doing subtly recalibrated the roles of the state and the church in the making of marriage.

The changes that the 1856 Act made to the preliminaries merit some discussion because they were linked to the question of the relative ease or difficulty of the different routes into marriage. In his annual report as Registrar-General, George Graham made a direct link between these changes and the ability of couples to marry in accordance with their beliefs, rejoicing that '[n]o one has now any just ground of complaint' and that the remaining weddings in the Church of England 'were performed by no unwilling conformists to her rites'.[3] But of still

---

[1] Petition of the Deputies of the Three Denominations of Protestant Dissenters, Presbyterian, Independent, and Baptist, in and within twelves miles of London, appointed to protect their civil rights (29 June 1854, *Fiftieth Report of the Select Committee*, Appendix to Reports of the Committee on Public Petitions, p. 636).

[2] For a history of the 1854 and 1855 initiatives, see Hull Terrell, *A History of the Dissenters' Marriages Bill of 1855* (London: Robert Theobold, 1855).

[3] *Twentieth Annual Report of the Registrar-General of Births, Deaths and Marriages in England* (London: HMSO, 1859), p. iv.

greater significance to the relationship between belief and mode of marriage were two further changes made by the 1856 Act that have generally been overlooked: a new right for religious groups to control who married in their places of worship, and a new prohibition on any religious content in a register office wedding.[4] Between them, these changes removed much of the flexibility that the 1836 Act had permitted, and so require a more detailed discussion.

The 1850s also saw the passage of two pieces of legislation that were to have an impact on how and where couples could marry. The Places of Worship Registration Act 1855 made it possible for non-Christian places of worship to be certified as such, while the Matrimonial Causes Act 1857, which introduced judicial divorce, exempted Anglican clergy from having to conduct the remarriages of those who had been divorced on the basis of their adultery. The implications of these for Jewish and Anglican weddings will be considered in turn, along with other changes in the 1856 Act that affected such weddings, and the legislation passed in 1860 and 1872 that allowed a wider range of persons to marry according to the usages of the Society of Friends.

All of these changes show how the coherence of the scheme enacted in 1836 was beginning to fragment. There was, however, a moment at which the possibility of more wide-ranging reform – and a more coherent scheme – seemed possible. The Royal Commission on the Laws of Marriage that was set up in 1865 was tasked with creating a uniform law of marriage for the United Kingdom.[5] Much of the evidence it received underlined the deficiencies of the existing laws in their domestic application, and its proposed scheme would have had the added benefit of creating a uniform law governing weddings within England and Wales.[6] The chapter closes, however, with the downbeat debates in which it was made clear that reform would not be forthcoming.

---

[4] Paul Johnson and Robert M. Vanderbeck, 'Sacred Spaces, Sacred Words: Religion and Same-Sex Marriage in England and Wales' (2017) 44(2) *Journal of Law and Society* 228, 234, briefly note the introduction of the prohibition, but do not offer any explanation as to why it was introduced.

[5] *Report of the Royal Commission on the Laws of Marriage* (London: HMSO, 1868), Cm 4059 (hereafter *RC Report*).

[6] Rebecca Probert, Maebh Harding, and Brian Dempsey, 'A Uniform Law of Marriage? The 1868 Royal Commission Reconsidered' (2018) *Child and Family Law Quarterly* 217.

Removing Obstacles and Inconveniences?

The acts of Parliament which have been passed, with the intention of giving
facilities for the celebration of marriage to parties who were dissatisfied with the
laws and canons of the Established Church, have been found to be attended
with many inconveniences, which lessened their utility[7]

The list of grievances presented by the Dissenting Deputies in 1854 was surprisingly short.[8] All but one of their complaints related to the preliminaries required before a wedding. While they closed with the request that 'Dissenters may have the same facilities for marrying in the mode in which they prefer as are enjoyed by members of the Established Church', this was very far from being a demand for complete equality. Indeed, it seems that their demands were not merely motivated by their position vis-à-vis the Church of England but by the relative weakness of 'old' Dissent versus 'new' Nonconformity. As we shall see, their final – almost entirely overlooked – request about who could get married in their chapels may well hold the key to why grievances about the preliminaries were suddenly being aired almost twenty years after the Marriage Act 1836 had established these requirements, and why certain restrictions were not being challenged.

The complaint heading the list of grievances was the requirement for notices of marriage to be read before Boards of Guardians. This requirement was roundly criticised both in the press and in Parliament,[9] and no one seemed keen to retain it.[10] Finding an alternative that would be both acceptable and effective was, however, something of a challenge. The proposal made by the Dissenting Deputies – that those wishing to marry should simply have to make a declaration that they were free to do so[11] – was adopted as an *additional* requirement,[12] rather than being treated as sufficient in itself. Delegating oversight of the preliminaries to individual

---

[7] Terrell, *History*, p. 3.

[8] Petition of 29 June 1854, above. A virtually identical list was presented the following year (24 April 1855, *Twenty-Seventh Report of the Select Committee*, Appendix to Reports of the Committee on Public Petitions, p. 239).

[9] See, respectively, *Leeds Mercury*, 10 July 1855; Parl. Deb., ser. 3, vol. 138, col. 716, 17 May 1855 (Mr Cheetham); vol. 139, col. 1335, 24 July 1855 (Lord Brougham); vol. 142, col. 939 (Mr Apsley Pellatt).

[10] The Registrar-General had spoken in favour of reform some years earlier: *The Times*, 19 March 1850. See also Terrell, *History*, p. 13, noting that the 'universal testimony' of guardians was 'against the usefulness of such a formality as a means of publicity'.

[11] See their petitions of 1854 and 1855, above.

[12] Marriage and Registration Act 1856, s. 2.

congregations was not seen as an option by either Nonconformists or the state.[13] Even the suggestion of displaying a list of intended marriages at the doors of non-Anglican churches and chapels failed to find favour.[14] In the absence of any other solution, legislators fell back upon the same temporary expedient that had been devised in 1837 for districts without a Board of Guardians – that of displaying notices 'in some conspicuous place' in the register office.[15] No one, however, attempted to suggest that this had worked well or that any advantage would accrue from adopting it more widely.[16] The best that anyone managed to say was that even if this new procedure 'would not give better security than now existed … it would not give worse'.[17] There was also a telling shift in the language used in the debates. While some MPs concerned about the change still referred to the need for *publicity*,[18] the new solution was described in terms of *publication*.[19] There was a difference, as all concerned would have been well aware. The notices would be there in the register office to be seen, but whether anyone would see them was another matter.

The second set of complaints identified by the Deputies related to the process for obtaining a licence from the superintendent registrar – the grievance here being that it was more difficult than obtaining a licence from a bishop.[20] The amendments enacted made it possible for just one party to give notice,[21] cut the waiting period to just

---

[13] See, e.g., Parl. Deb., ser. 3, vol. 138, col. 716, 17 May 1855 (Mr Cheetham explaining that ministers 'would not be willing to take upon themselves the functions of a civil officer by proclaiming the banns').

[14] A clause to this effect was inserted into the 1855 bill during its Committee stages. The *Leeds Mercury*, 10 July 1855, claimed that this would be even worse than reading notices before the Board, as it might attract unwelcome comment. The clause was removed during the third reading of the bill: *Daily News*, 17 July 1855; Terrell, *History*, p. 11.

[15] Marriage and Registration Act 1856, s. 4. On the original reasons for this expedient being adopted, see Chapter 2. Terrell, *History*, p. 13, suggests that there were still around 300 places that had no Board of Guardians under the New Poor Law and which were therefore still following this procedure.

[16] As the *Bury and Norwich Post*, 5 March 1856, bluntly noted: '[e]xperience has proved that "publication" in the registrar's office is equivalent to no publication at all'.

[17] Parl. Deb., ser. 3, vol. 142, col. 940, 4 June 1856 (Mr Henley). The suggestion that notices could be displayed *outside* the register office was rejected after a heated debate, with publicity being recast as 'exposure' by its opponents: cols. 942 (Sir Andrew Agnew) and 945 (Mr E. Ball).

[18] Parl. Deb., ser. 3, vol. 142, col. 939, 4 June 1856 (Mr Hardy, Sir William Heathcote).

[19] Parl. Deb., ser. 3, vol. 142, col. 939, 4 June 1856 (Mr Pellatt).

[20] See further Chapter 3.

[21] Marriage and Registration Act 1856, s. 6. Notice was to be given in the district where they had resided for the previous 15 days (MRA 1856, s. 2) but the wedding itself could take place in a different district.

one day,[22] and slashed the cost.[23] The result was in fact to tip the advantage in the opposite direction: while civil licences were no quicker than ecclesiastical ones, and no cheaper than marrying by banns, they did now usually offer the cheapest way to have a quick wedding.[24]

The impact of all these changes was immediate: in 1857, weddings in registered places of worship increased by 10 per cent over the previous year, and those in the register office by almost 20 per cent.[25] As the Registrar-General emphasised, this did not imply 'any change of creed in any considerable part of the population'.[26] In particular, the sudden rise in the number of register office weddings suggests that it should not be assumed that the couples who married there were motivated by any rejection of religion. Convenience clearly played a role in shaping couples' choices.[27] Some who might otherwise have married in church were clearly attracted by the greater privacy now afforded by civil preliminaries. After 1856, a growing number of register office weddings involved those seeking to avoid attention for one reason or another – pregnant brides, older couples marrying for a second time, younger ones lying about their age, couples within the prohibited degrees of marriage, and bigamists.[28] The connotations of marrying in a register office began to shift accordingly.

The increase in the number of marriages in registered places of worship might have been still higher had it not been for one further change. The final complaint of the Dissenting Deputies had been 'that marriages are sometimes celebrated by the registrars in Dissenting chapels between parties not connected with such chapels ... without the permission of the parties interested in such chapels', and they had asked 'that Dissenting Chapels licensed for marriage may be protected against the intrusion of

---

[22] Marriage and Registration Act 1856, s. 9.

[23] *Ibid.*, s. 10. The new cost was £1 10s (plus stamp duty) rather than £3.

[24] This was not necessarily the case everywhere, as the cost of obtaining an ecclesiastical licence varied across dioceses: see Terrell, *History*, p. 19.

[25] *Twentieth Annual Report*, pp. iii–iv.

[26] *Ibid.*, p. iv.

[27] For an example of how the 1856 changes brought licences within the reach of couples of more modest means, see Elizabeth Parsons, 'A Simple Register Office Wedding' (2021) JGFH (forthcoming).

[28] See Elizabeth Parsons, 'A Bigamous Marriage in the Register Office' (2021) JGFH (forthcoming). Judging from reports of trials, twice as many bigamous marriages took place in a register office than was the case across the population as a whole: Rebecca Probert, *Divorced, Bigamist, Bereaved? The Family Historian's Guide to Marital Breakdown, Separation, Widowhood, and Remarriage* (Kenilworth: Takeaway, 2015).

improper parties and at inconvenient hours'.[29] They were clearly averse to couples whose own denomination had not registered its places of worship using the registered chapel of a different denomination to marry according to their own rites.[30] The 1855 bill proposed that if any religious service were used in a registered building, it would have to be 'in accordance with the usages' of the religious body by whom the building in question had been registered.[31] While the 1856 Act did not go this far, it did require couples to obtain permission from the relevant authority before marrying in a registered place of worship.[32] It would, therefore, have been possible for those in authority to require that any couples wishing to marry in a particular place of worship conform to its particular usages.

It was significant that this change was instigated by the representatives of the older Dissenting groups – which had, as we have seen, already registered many of their places of worship for marriage.[33] Its effect would primarily have been felt by newer groups, and in particular by the Methodists, far fewer of whose places of worship had been registered.[34] It is unlikely to be a coincidence that the Dissenting Deputies were pressing for this change in the wake of the 1851 Census of Religious Worship, which had provided statistical evidence of the dominance of Methodism.[35] Independents, Baptists, and Presbyterians may well have wished to reclaim their territory by closing their doors to non-members. The fact that they had invested in registering their buildings – and that this gave them an advantage over other groups – may also explain why they made no complaint about the need for registration.

---

[29] See their petitions of 1854 and 1855, above.
[30] Terrell, *History*, p. 23. For examples of such weddings taking place, see Chapter 3.
[31] Dissenters' Marriages Bill 1855, cl. 9.
[32] Marriage and Registration Act 1856, s. 11. Exactly whose permission was required varied; for Roman Catholic chapels it was the priest officiating at the wedding; for other registered buildings it could be the minister or one of the trustees, owners, deacons, or managers of the registered building.
[33] On the differential rates of registration across different denominations, see Chapter 3.
[34] Its impact would have been slightly mitigated by a further amendment allowing a wedding to take place in the parties' usual place of worship even if the building in question was located outside their district of residence: Marriage and Registration Act 1856, s. 14. This option could only be used if the building was no further than two miles from the limits of the district, and was of course no use at all if that building had not been registered either.
[35] K. D. M. Snell and Paul S. Ell, *Rival Jerusalems: The Geography of Victorian Religion* (Cambridge: Cambridge University Press, 2000).

By the mid-1860s, marriages in registered places of worship still only accounted for 14 per cent of the total, well below the percentage of the population who worshipped in non-Anglican chapels. Most places of worship remained unregistered,[36] and the new need for permission to marry in any given place of worship removed certain choices from couples seeking to marry according to their own rites. No longer were marriages conducted according to the rites 'of the parties' or 'by the registrar' in registered places of worship;[37] after 1856, marriage certificates almost invariably record that the marriage was conducted according to the rites of the denomination that had registered the building.[38] Couples whose own place of worship was not registered, and who did not have easy access to an alternative belonging to their own denomination that was registered,[39] therefore had to choose between the Anglican church and the register office. The latter option, however, had also become less flexible. As we have seen, couples marrying in the register office in the early years of the 1836 Act had been able to include some religious content. After 1856 that was no longer possible, as the next section will explain.

Religious Rites – After, During, or Before?

Persons desirous may add the Religious Ceremony ordained by the Church[40]

In order to understand how the prohibition on any religious content in a register office ceremony came about, we need to backtrack a little and begin with something that might seem at first to have no connection with this at all. It should be said at the outset that, in the absence of any explicit debate, much necessarily rests on inference. Nonetheless, the sequence of events provides an explanation both for the inclusion of this particular

---

[36] See, e.g., *Twenty-eighth Annual Report of the Registrar-General of Births, Deaths and Marriages in England* (London: HMSO, 1867), p. viii, noting that at the close of 1865 5,352 places of worship were registered for weddings, as compared to 16,819 certified places of religious worship. Registration varied by region as well as religion: Welsh Calvinistic Methodists were far more likely than their English counterparts to register their buildings for weddings (Table 8).

[37] For earlier examples, and their significance, see Chapter 3.

[38] Rebecca Probert, 'Interpreting Choices' (2021) JGFH (forthcoming). I am grateful to the many family historians who provided copies of marriage certificates.

[39] As before, it was possible to marry in the nearest place of worship of one's particular denomination if there was no registered building of that denomination within the district: Marriage Act 1840, s. 2; Marriage and Registration Act 1856, s. 13.

[40] Marriage and Registration Act 1856, s. 12.

prohibition and for the significance of the somewhat opaque provision of which it was part, which stated that a register office wedding could be followed by a religious ceremony if the parties so wished.[41]

The early 1850s had seen a particular controversy emerging regarding clergymen who 'remarried' couples who had already been married in a register office or chapel. What made these ceremonies particularly contentious at this time was their link to a particular strand of High Anglicanism that had originated with the Oxford Movement in the 1830s: sometimes dubbed 'Newmanites', 'Puseyites', or 'Tractarians',[42] a number of churchmen were attempting to evoke an earlier age in which the church had more power and reinstating rituals that had not been seen since the Reformation. Suspicions of their Catholic leanings – which were reinforced by some high-profile conversions to Rome – had made them a target for criticism at the time of the so-called Papal Aggression in 1850.[43] One particularly controversial figure was the Reverend Bennett, whose 'Romanizing' tendencies had led to his church in London being attacked and whose subsequent appointment as incumbent of Frome in Somerset prompted questions in Parliament.[44] In his view, couples who married otherwise than in church were 'living in a state of fornication'. In 1854, such a couple were persuaded to remarry in Frome parish church,[45] sparking outrage.

[41] *Ibid*: 'If the Parties to any Marriage contracted at the Registry Office . . . shall desire to add the Religious Ceremony ordained or used by the Church or Persuasion of which such Parties shall be Members to the Marriage so contracted, it shall be competent for them to present themselves for that Purpose to a Clergyman or Minister of the Church or Persuasion of which such Parties shall be Members, . . . but nothing in the Reading or Celebration of such Service shall be held to supersede or invalidate any Marriage so previously contracted, nor shall such Reading or Celebration be entered as a Marriage among the Marriages in the Parish Register: Provided also, that at no Marriage solem-nized at the Registry Office of any District shall any Religious Service be used at such Registry Office.'

[42] These being allusions to John Henry Newman, whose conversion to Rome in 1845 reinforced fears that those within the Movement were crypto-Catholics, Edward Bouverie Pusey, Professor of Hebrew at Oxford, and the Movement's publication of *Tracts for our Times* in the 1830s: see Owen Chadwick, *The Victorian Church: Part One, 1829–1859* (London: SCM Press Ltd, 1987; first published 1966), p. 168.

[43] See Chapter 3.

[44] See Walter Ralls, 'The Papal Aggression of 1850: A Study in Victorian Anti-Catholicism' (1974) 43(2) *Church History* 242, 251, for an account of the controversy occasioned by Bennett's adoption of certain High Church rituals at the church of St Barnabas in the parish of St Paul's Knightsbridge. For the debates on Bennett's appointment, see Parl. Deb., ser. 3, vol. 120, cols. 895–941, 20 April 1852.

[45] The (re)marriage was that of William and Elizabeth Dimmocks, who had previously married at the Zion Chapel in Frome, and was conducted by Bennett's curate. Bennett

A Dissenting minister at Frome complained to George Graham, who in turn asked Palmerston, as Prime Minister, to make representations to Bennett's bishop.[46] The difficulty for the authorities was that Bennett did not appear to have flouted any law. There was nothing in the statute prohibiting a clergyman from conducting a ceremony where the couple was already married, and Bennett had adhered to all of the regulations governing Anglican weddings. Banns had been called and the 'remarriage' was included in the official returns and registered accordingly. But the correspondence behind the scenes gives the strong impression that Graham was now on the lookout for any infraction of the law that might found the basis of a prosecution.

In 1856 he found just such a case. Richard Meux Benson, the vicar of Cowley, had conducted an Anglican ceremony for a couple who had been married in Oxford register office – but he had done so without banns or licence. This, it was noted, 'would be a fit case for prosecution'.[47] The Protesting Dissenting Deputies also appear to have been keen to take action,[48] and alighted upon another clergyman – Alfred Lush, the curate of Greywell in Hampshire – who had similarly performed an Anglican ceremony for a couple who had married in an Independent chapel. Both Benson and Lush found themselves facing prosecutions for conducting marriages without any preliminaries.[49]

It is hard to escape the suspicion that Lush and Benson were paying the price for the views expressed by Bennett.[50] According to Lush, the couple he had married, Francis and Sarah Freeman, had asked to be remarried in church following doubts expressed by neighbours about the validity of

---

had conducted a similar ceremony the previous year for William and Caroline Burton, who had previously married at Badcox Meeting House. In each case the earlier marriage was grudgingly acknowledged in the Anglican marriage register by recording where the parties had been 'previously united': Somerset Heritage Service, D\P\fr.jo/2/1/25.

[46] TNA, HO45/5549. See also 'Puseyite Re-Marriages at Frome', *Bristol Mercury*, 27 May 1854.

[47] TNA, HO45/OS6357.

[48] *Daily News*, 8 February 1856.

[49] Lush's subsequent appearance at the petty sessions in Odiham was reported in the *Morning Post*, 13 February 1856. A true bill was returned against him at the Hampshire Spring Assizes but the trial was removed to the Queen's Bench by a writ of certiorari: *Berkshire Chronicle*, 8 March 1856. Benson, meanwhile, was committed for trial at the Oxford Assizes: *Morning Post*, 25 February 1856.

[50] Benson, while influenced by Pusey, does not seem to have been as controversial a figure as Bennett; accounts of his life and work suggest that he was a deeply spiritual figure and committed parish priest: see Martin L. Smith (ed.), *Benson of Cowley* (Oxford: Oxford University Press, 1980).

their marriage.[51] They were, moreover, both regular communicants and had only married in the Independent chapel to escape the notice of 19-year-old Sarah's parents. In Cowley, meanwhile, Sarah Carey had asked Benson to perform the ritual of 'churching' her – a blessing and thanks-giving for her recovery after giving birth. While Benson was willing to acknowledge the legality of her marriage to Richard Carey at the Oxford register office, he told her that she would also need to be married in the sight of God before he would church her. In other words, these particular clergymen were not imposing Anglicanism on unwilling Dissenters, but rather performing such services for members of their flock who had happened to marry by other means.

There was nothing in the original drafts of any of the bills that led up to the 1856 Act about remarriages of this kind, and no complaint had been made in the original petitions of the Protestant Dissenting Deputies. But on the third reading of the 1856 bill, a clause was added that seemed to have the cases of Lush and Benson in mind. It provided that the parties 'to any Marriage contracted before the Registrar' could, if they so wished, have a religious ceremony after-wards but that 'nothing in the Reading or Celebration of such Service shall be held to supersede or invalidate any Marriages previously contracted'.[52] The reference to weddings before the registrar covered those in registered places of worship as well as those in the register office. While couched in permissive terms, it was clearly intended – and seen – as a rebuke to individuals such as Bennett, Benson, and Lush.[53] The message was that clergy should not cast any doubt on the validity of marriages that had been duly solemnised under the Marriage Act 1836.

Given that the bill was not considered until after midnight,[54] it is understandable, if unfortunate, that no report appeared in the news-papers, and no debate was recorded in *Hansard*. The clause must have been added in the early hours of the morning of 1 July 1856, since it appears for the first time in the version that was sent to the House of Lords later that day.[55] But it is unlikely to be a coincidence that, on that very same day, Lush sat down and penned an apology for his

---

[51] 'The Re-Marriage Case at Greywell', *Berkshire Chronicle,* 1 December 1855.

[52] Marriage and Registration Acts Amendment Bill, 1 July 1856 (No. 205), cl. 12.

[53] See, e.g., the *Bradford Observer,* 28 August 1856, discussed below.

[54] *JHC,* vol. 111, p. 310.

[55] Marriage and Registration Acts Amendment Bill, 1 July 1856 (No. 205).

actions.[56] It was later reported that the charge against him had been withdrawn.[57]

Ten days later, on the afternoon of 11 July 1856, the Select Committee appointed to consider the bill met. Again, no report of any debate appears to exist, so the story has to be followed through the Minutes of the House of Lords and the various drafts of the bill. The Committee revised the clause so that it referred only to the possibility of having a religious ceremony after a wedding in the register office, rather than after *any* wedding before a registrar.[58] The former possibility, of course, was the point at issue in Benson's trial, which had still to take place.

By coincidence, Benson's trial began only an hour or so after the Select Committee had revised the clause. It was clear from the start that the judge had little sympathy with the case against Benson. The key difficulty facing the prosecution was the mismatch between the offence as set out in the statute – which was designed to deter clergy from conducting clandestine marriages without banns or licence – and the harm that was said to have been committed by Benson having conducted a ceremony for a couple who were already married. Counsel for the prosecution rather desperately sought to argue that matters of property might be at stake if clergy conducted such ceremonies without the proper preliminaries and it then transpired that the earlier wedding before the registrar had been invalid as well, which was hardly the issue at hand. Nor did the argument that Benson's actions were 'calculated to throw doubt' on the validity of marriages conducted under the 1836 Act or to 'create misgivings' in the minds of those who had married in this way have much chance of success, given Sarah Carey's evidence that Benson had told her the register office wedding was perfectly legal, and the fact that the entry he had made in the marriage register explicitly noted that the couple were 'married previously at the registrar's-office'.[59] The judge took the view that no offence had been committed, on the basis that the ceremony

[56] A letter posted in London on the morning of 1 July would have reached Greywell by the afternoon; alternatively, a telegram could have been sent via Odiham Post Office.

[57] The letter was subsequently reprinted in the *Berkshire Chronicle*, 23 August 1856.

[58] The Select Committee sat at 1pm: *HLMP*, 11 July 1856, p. 853. For the version of the bill as amended by the Select Committee, see Marriage and Registration Acts Amendment Bill (No. 236). While the Committee included both the Archbishop of Canterbury, John Bird Sumner, and Benson's own bishop, Samuel Wilberforce, Bishop of Oxford, neither of them were likely to be sympathetic to the High Church view and it seems unlikely that the clause was intended to exculpate Benson.

[59] The significance of the difference between referring to the parties as 'married' rather than 'united' at the register office is clear from earlier discussions: see Chapter 2.

performed by Benson had effected no change in the status of the parties, and directed the jury to acquit. As he joked, if Benson had read the ballad of *Chevy Chase* to them, 'it would have had the same legal effect, though the effect upon their consciences would have been different'.[60]

Had the provision in the 1856 bill merely been intended to allow clergy to conduct a religious ceremony after a wedding in the register office, the outcome in Benson's case would have shown that it was unnecessary. Once it is understood as a rebuke to the hubris of the higher elements of the Anglican church, however, it clearly still had a role to play, and a further amendment clarified that any subsequent religious ceremony should not be entered in the marriage register. That the provision was seen as prohibitory as well as permissive is clear from the reaction in the Liberal *Bradford Observer*, which exulted that it put 'an effectual stop . . . to the re-marriages by which the Tractarian clergy have striven to cast a slur upon the civil contract and upon marriages lawfully solemnized in registered buildings'.[61]

There was, however, a further twist in the tale. The explicit statement that a religious ceremony could be performed after a wedding in the register office could be taken as implying that such a ceremony could *not* be performed after the couple had been married before the registrar in a registered place of worship.[62] It was logical, then, for a further addition to be made to the clause, stipulating that 'at no Marriage solemnized at the Register Office of any District shall any Religious Service be used'. After all, it would be odd if a clergyman was prohibited from remarrying a couple who had married in a registered place of worship, but not where a couple had had the exact same form of ceremony in a register office. But with a single stroke this recast marriage in the register office as a purely secular rite.[63]

No longer was it possible for a wedding to be celebrated in the register office with prayers or readings from scripture, or even, in the view of one vicar, with a 'God bless you' from the registrar.[64] Yet there was no

[60] *The Times*, 12 July 1856. The comparison was an odd one, since *Chevy Chase* was about hunting; presumably the judge's point was that it had absolutely no connection with marriage.
[61] *Bradford Observer*, 28 August 1856.
[62] This was certainly the assumption made in *The Justice of the Peace, and County, Borough, Poor Law Union, and Parish Law Recorder*, Vol. 21 (1857), p. 90, 7 February 1857.
[63] No debate on this fundamental change was recorded in *Hansard*, or in any of the newspaper reports.
[64] Samuel Wilks argued that for a registrar to say 'God bless you' would be 'a violation of the statute, as it is a prayer, and there may be persons who do not believe that there is a God': *RC Report*, Appendix, p. 20.

attempt to fill the gap that was left by devising any form of state-sanctioned ritual.[65] Register office weddings were now defined by their lack of content, as graphically illustrated by the black line drawn through the printed phrase 'according to the rites and ceremonies' in all subsequent marriage certificates. The change also led to a shift in the way that such weddings were conceptualised, as reflected by the formal adoption of the terminology of 'civil marriage' in the Registrar-General's annual reports from this point on.[66] In 1836, marrying in the office of the superintendent registrar had been provided for Dissenters who viewed marriage as a civil contract; from 1857, 'civil' marriages were provided by the state as a purely secular ceremony.

The significance of this change has never been appreciated, partly because of the lack of awareness of the extent to which religious content was included in register office weddings before 1856, and partly because register office weddings increased immediately afterwards for other reasons. Some of those getting married in the register office would have given little thought to the form of the ceremony. But given that many chapels remained unregistered, there would also have been many Dissenters who were unable to marry in their own place of worship but were opposed to the idea of marrying in the Anglican church. The effect of the new prohibition on religious content was simply to prevent them from having a wedding in the register office that reflected their beliefs.

Somewhat ironically, given how the prohibition on religious rites during a register office wedding had come about, there was still considerable uncertainty regarding what *was* permissible before or after a legal wedding. This was of particular significance for Catholics, as the group who had been most likely to have dual ceremonies.[67] It was clear that it was permissible to have a religious ceremony after a register office wedding. And it was assumed that it was not possible to have a religious ceremony after a religious wedding. But from announcements in the newspapers it is clear that dual

---

[65] Contrast the more detailed stipulations surrounding civil weddings in France, which included the officer responsible for celebrating the wedding reading out the relevant parts of the Civil Code setting out the parties' respective rights and duties within marriage: Mary Ann Glendon, *State, Law and Family: Family Law in Transition in the United States and Western Europe* (Amsterdam: North-Holland Publishing Company, 1977), pp. 56–57.

[66] *Twentieth Annual Report*, p. iv.

[67] See further Chapter 3.

ceremonies continued,[68] and while the sample is small and biased towards a certain section of society, it displays a very clear pattern. If the Anglican wedding came first, the later ceremony was not registered. If the Anglican ceremony came second, both were registered.[69] It seems that the message that Anglican clergy had taken from Benson's case was that 'remarriages' should be conducted with the proper preliminaries and duly registered, rather than that they should not take place at all.

That these dual ceremonies were not seen as a cause of concern may reflect the fact that the individuals involved tended to be particularly well connected, even by the standards of whose weddings were reported in the newspapers.[70] It may also have been because no one was quite sure what the 1856 Act meant. When the Baptist MP Sir Morton Peto asked the government whether they would take action against a clergyman who had remarried a couple in church eight days after they had married in an Independent chapel, the response was that no offence had been committed in this case.[71] If such a remarriage *was* permissible – which some commentators did question[72] – then the very premise on which the prohibition of religious content in the register office had been based was flawed. But given that no one was willing to bear the costs of a prosecution where the chances of success were so uncertain, the point was never resolved. It also remained unclear whether it was permissible for a couple to have a religious ceremony *before* their wedding, and whether this differed according to whether the wedding was in the register office or celebrated according to religious rites.[73]

---

[68] See, e.g., *Morning Chronicle*, 13 December 1859; *Leeds Times*, 16 July 1864; *Manchester Courier*, 19 May 1865; those involved included a French count, a baronet, and the daughter of an MP.

[69] Rebecca Probert, 'After the Act: Dual Marriage Ceremonies, 1837–1887' (in preparation).

[70] It would, for example, have been rather embarrassing to raise questions about the marriage of the daughter of M. de Smirnoff, senator and privy councilor at St Petersburg, who went through ceremonies in both the Anglican and Greek Orthodox Church (*Manchester Courier*, 5 August 1865).

[71] Parl. Deb., ser. 3, vol. 172, cols. 1465–66, 27 July 1863.

[72] 'The St Briavel's Re-Marriage Case', *Daily News*, 30 July 1863, suggesting that the Reverend Horatio Walmesley, who had conducted the Anglican ceremony, was guilty of a crime.

[73] A prohibition on a religious-only marriage ceremony taking place before a register office wedding could arguably be implied from the provision in s. 12 that such a ceremony could take place afterwards, upon the parties presenting the certificate of their earlier wedding to the minister. There was, however, no equivalent provision from which a prohibition on a religious-only marriage ceremony taking place before a religious wedding could be

It is hard to escape the suspicion that the claimed illegitimacy of certain practices was motivated by the anti-Catholicism of mid-Victorian England, and that had it not been for the Romanising tendencies of a handful of Anglican clergymen the question of what happened after a legally binding marriage would never have become an issue, no one would ever have questioned the legality of conducting a second religious ceremony, and no one would have thought of prohibiting the inclusion of religious content in register office ceremonies.

The Exemption from the Universal

words to give to clergymen the same privileges in this respect as to dissenting ministers[74]

While the 1856 Act sent a clear message that Anglican clergy were to accept the validity of weddings in the register office, or in registered buildings, it also allowed them to refuse to accept the validity of civil preliminaries. Thereafter, couples could only marry by superintendent registrar's certificate in the Established Church with the consent of the incumbent.[75] It was a further step back from Russell's original intention that all weddings should be preceded by civil preliminaries.

From one perspective this might indicate that the state had backed down in the face of the obduracy of a handful of clergy. But it was in fact entirely consistent with the way in which the 1856 Act sharpened the distinctions between different routes into marriage. With those in charge of registered places of worship able to decide who married there,[76] it was declared to be a grievance that Anglican clergy could not at least insist on compliance with the regular canonical forms on

---

implied. Of course, if it had been an offence to conduct a wedding outside the framework of the Act, then this would have applied equally to any religious-only marriage ceremony, whatever followed it; however, as we have seen in Chapter 3, the offences set out in the 1836 Act were very specific in their terms and conducting a wedding without a certificate or licence from the superintendent registrar was not one of those listed, in contrast to the clear provision in the 1823 Act that an Anglican clergyman who conducted a ceremony without banns being called or a licence obtained would be guilty of a felony (Marriage Act 1823, s. 21).

[74] Parl. Deb., ser. 3, vol. 140, col. 1929, 5 March 1856 (Mr Henley).

[75] Marriage and Registration Act 1856, s. 11.

[76] See earlier. It was also noted that Nonconformist ministers were under no obligation to marry a couple who presented themselves to be married: Parl. Deb., ser. 3, vol. 140, col. 1929, 5 March 1856.

the part of those exercising their right to be married in the parish church.[77]

Underpinning this debate was the far bigger issue of whether the Church of England was an Established Church whose laws were the law of the land, a national church whose clergy were obligated to conduct the weddings of any of their parishioners regardless of their faith or lack thereof, or a denomination with its own requirements and preferences.[78] This issue was to arise in an even starker form during debates over reforms to the law of divorce. The Matrimonial Causes Act 1857 made provision for divorces to be granted by a court,[79] rather than, as previously, only by private Act of Parliament. The new basis for granting divorces was hardly more generous than earlier practices: only adultery was to justify the ending of a marriage and wives would have to show 'aggravated' adultery.[80] Anglican bishops were divided on whether divorce, even for adultery, should be allowed at all, whether the divorced should be able to remarry, and, if so, whether they should be permitted to remarry in church.[81] For present purposes our interest lies with the last of these; after much debate, a new exemption was created, providing that no Anglican clergyman could be compelled to solemnise the remarriage of any person who had been divorced on the basis of their adultery.[82]

It is worth emphasising that there was no outright prohibition either from Parliament or the Anglican establishment on the divorced – whether adulterous or not – remarrying in church,[83] and the number who were prevented from doing so was probably very small.[84] But the exemption was nonetheless highly significant. As with the right to refuse

---

[77] Parl. Deb., ser. 3, vol. 138, cols. 714–15, 17 May 1855 (Mr Henley).

[78] For discussion of the status of ecclesiastical law in this context, see Bruce S. Bennett, 'The Church of England and the Law of Divorce since 1857: Marriage Discipline, Ecclesiastical Law and the Establishment' (1994) 45 *Journal of Ecclesiastical History* 625.

[79] The newly created Court for Divorce and Matrimonial Causes was given jurisdiction to determine the validity of disputed marriages, a task previously performed by the church courts: for discussion of this, see R. B. Outhwaite, *The Rise and Fall of the English Ecclesiastical Courts, 1500–1860* (Cambridge: Cambridge University Press, 2010).

[80] Matrimonial Causes Act 1857, s. 27.

[81] Bennett, 'The Church of England'; Chadwick, *Victorian Church: Part One*, pp. 482–83. The remarriages of those divorced by private Act of Parliament had almost invariably taken place in church.

[82] Matrimonial Causes Act 1857, s. 57.

[83] Any other clergyman entitled to officiate within the diocese could conduct the wedding in the church of the incumbent who had refused to conduct it.

[84] Partly because the number of divorces and remarriages remained low, and partly because it was very easy to lie: Probert, *Divorced, Bigamist, Bereaved?*

civil preliminaries, the exemption reflected the tension between what was permitted by the law of the land and the consciences of the clergy. The debate over divorce and remarriage went deeper, however, since what was at issue was not just the rubric's specifications about banns and licences but rival interpretations of scripture and divine law. And the exemption was also to set the tone for the future. Getting married according to Anglican rites was no longer the near-universal practice it had once been, and more than one member of the clergy took the view that it should be reserved to those who regarded it as a religious rite.[85]

From these exemptions to the once-universal entitlement to marry in the Anglican Church, we turn to the two groups who were largely exempted from most of the requirements of the 1836 Act, and how the terms of their exemption were beginning to fragment in different ways in the 1850s.

The Exemption to the Exemption

patchwork legislation to provide for the wants of a solitary synagogue[86]

The legitimacy of vesting the regulation of Jewish marriages in the Board of Deputies had been challenged by its refusal to recognise the reformist West London synagogue in the 1840s. Two different ways of addressing such non-recognition were proposed during the debates over reforms to marriage law in 1855. The first, which would have allowed any synagogue to be registered for weddings in the same way as any other place of worship, met with opposition from the Board.[87] The second, by way of compromise, limited recognition to the West London synagogue alone.[88]

The passage of the Places of Worship Registration Act 1855 then allowed *any* place of worship to be certified as such, without the previous

---

[85] See, e.g., the view of the Dean of Chichester that it would be 'conducive to the cause of true religion and virtue' if all weddings had to take place before government officials, since this would enable the Church to 'confine the administration of the ordinance to those who approach it with a religious intent, and with that spiritual preparation which is required to render efficacious any rite or ceremony of our holy religion' (*RC Report*, Appendix, p. 12).

[86] Terrell, *History*, p. 32.

[87] Its President described the proposed change as 'unnecessary and injurious', placing in peril 'the due observance of those usages of the Jews relating to marriage which have always been permitted to them', and expressed the fear that it 'would subject the Jewish community to consequences, respecting the validity of its marriages, which might seriously affect the welfare of future generations' (12 July 1855: *Fifty-fourth Report of the Select Committee*, Appendix, 1124, 9156).

[88] *Standard*, 17 July 1855; Terrell, *History*, pp. 32–33.

limitation that it had to be Christian.[89] Since there was nothing in the Marriage Act 1836 stipulating that only Christian places of worship could be registered for weddings, this opened up a means for the West London synagogue to conduct its own weddings, and it was quick to avail itself of the option.[90] Admittedly, this meant that its weddings were subject to the same restrictions as those in any other registered place of worship – they had to take place in the building that had been registered, in the presence of a civil registrar, and include the words prescribed by statute. But it did at least provide a means of sidestepping the veto of the Board of Deputies.

The possibility of non-Christian places of worship being certified as such and registered for weddings did, however, raise a more fundamental question: if Jewish marriages could now be regulated in this way, was any special treatment still needed? A logical solution would have been to abolish the specific exemption for Jewish weddings and leave all synagogues to follow the same process as the West London synagogue. What in fact happened was exactly the reverse, with an exemption to the exemption being carved out. The 1856 Act gave the West London synagogue the power to certify not only its own secretaries but also those belonging to other synagogues.[91] This enabled it to act as an umbrella organisation for reformist synagogues in the same way that the Board did for orthodox ones, although the terms on which it was permitted to do so were closer to those governing registered places of worship.[92]

---

[89] The 1855 Act was part of a wider reshaping of the process – and purpose – of certifying places of worship. The Protestant Dissenters Act 1852 had required places of worship to be certified to the Registrar-General, replacing the former somewhat haphazard reporting to either the ecclesiastical authorities or justices of the peace. The 1855 Act had then made the process a voluntary one so far as meeting for worship was concerned.

[90] It was registered for weddings in February 1856: *London Gazette*, 8 March 1867.

[91] The clause had something of a chequered progress through Parliament: see *The Times*, 5 June 1856.

[92] The identity of the synagogue's secretary had to be certified to the Registrar-General by 'twenty householders professing the Jewish religion' who were members of the West London synagogue: MRA 1856, s. 22. That secretary could in turn certify to the Registrar-General that a particular person was the secretary of another synagogue connected with the West London synagogue, as long as that synagogue consisted of 'not less than twenty householders professing the Jewish religion' and had 'been established for not less than one year'. In practice, it was not the secretary but the Council that exercised this power: H. S. Q. Henriques, *Jewish Marriages and the English Law* (Oxford: Hart, 1909), p. 39.

Since this change was in addition to that effected by the Places of Worship Registration Act 1855, synagogues now had three different routes to recognition. They could have their secretaries certified by the Board of Deputies, as the 1836 legislation had envisaged, or by the West London synagogue, as the 1856 amendment allowed, or they could be certified as a place of worship and apply to the Registrar-General to be registered for weddings, thereby being independent of either. It says much for the influence of the Board of Deputies and the cohesion of Anglo-Jewry that virtually no synagogues opted for either of the latter routes during the 1850s and 1860s.[93] But the options were there.

For individuals, rather than institutions, Cupid might throw in an additional complicating factor. The special provisions for synagogues under the auspices of the Board of Deputies or the West London synagogue applied only where both parties were Jewish. Synagogues that were registered as places of worship could conduct the weddings of whomsoever they chose, and how they chose. But these being few and far between, and subject to the rules on residence and location, most marriages between Jews and non-Jews had to be conducted in register offices, churches, or the registered places of worship of other denominations. While attitudes to marrying outside the Jewish community were softening,[94] no changes to the way in which such marriages were conducted seem to have been contemplated. As the next section will show, it was otherwise with the Society of Friends.

The Opening up of the Exemption

the gradual conformity of 'Friends' to the usages of the rest of the world[95]

There had been concern within Quaker circles for some time about the decline in their numbers.

---

[93] One Reform congregation was founded in Manchester and its secretary certified by the West London synagogue: *RC Report*, Appendix, p. 45. However, changes within orthodox Judaism meant that 'an institutionally distinct Reform Judaism was a feeble affair': David Feldman, *Englishmen and Jews: Social Relations and Political Culture, 1840–1914* (New Haven: Yale University Press, 1994), p. 66.

[94] Outmarriage was no longer a reason for exclusion from the Jewish community, and those who married according to non-Jewish rites were able to continue worshipping with their congregation: Michael Clark, 'Identity and Equality: The Anglo-Jewish Community in the Post-Emancipation Era, 1858–1887' (DPhil thesis, Oxford, 2005), p. 246.

[95] *Berkshire Chronicle*, 6 September 1856.

In 1858, an influential analysis identified their rules against marrying out as 'the most influential proximate cause' of this decline.[96] Following this, the Society decided that it would no longer disown those who married non-Quakers.[97] The Quaker MP John Bright was instrumental in bringing forward a bill to amend the Marriage Act 1836, and the ensuing Marriage (Society of Friends) Act 1860 allowed those who 'professed with' or were 'of the persuasion of' the Society to marry according to its usages;[98] this, it was explained, would encompass 'persons holding the same views' who were not formally members of the Society.[99] Twelve years later the need for even this looser form of allegiance was removed, and legislation enabled the Society to permit non-members to marry according to its usages.[100]

These changes obviated the need for discussion about what it meant to be a Quaker at a time when that was a matter of some debate.[101] Quakers were becoming more like everyone else in a number of respects.[102] The most visible change was in their attire as the Society's traditional strictures about simplicity in dress were relaxed.[103] The late 1850s and 1860s saw a noticeable change in the reporting of Quaker weddings, with an increasing focus on style over substance. This new generation of Quaker brides was richly and fashionably attired, generally in white, and attended by a number of bridesmaids in 'gorgeous array'.[104] The celebrations that followed were

---

[96] J. S. Rowntree, *Quakerism Past and Present: An Inquiry into the Causes of its Decline in Great Britain and Ireland* (London: Smith Elder and Co, 1859), p. 153.

[97] The change was agreed at the 1859 Yearly Meeting: John Punshon, *Portrait in Grey: A Short History of the Quakers* (London: Quaker Home Service, 1984), p. 191.

[98] Marriage (Society of Friends) Act 1860, s. 1.

[99] Parl. Deb., ser. 3, vol. 156, col. 631, 7 February 1860 (Mr Mellor).

[100] Marriage (Society of Friends) Act 1872, s. 1. It was made a precondition that they produce a certificate from the registering officer at the time of giving notice, to assuage any concern about the potential for this liberalization to be abused: Parl. Deb., ser. 3, vol. 210, col. 233.

[101] On contemporary divisions within the Society, see Thomas C. Kennedy, 'Heresy-Hunting among Victorian Quakers: The Manchester Difficulty, 1861–83' (1991) 34 *Victorian Studies* 227; Punshon, *Portrait in Grey*, pp. 189–90.

[102] Elizabeth Allo Isichei, 'From Sect to Denomination in English Quakerism, with Special Reference to the Nineteenth Century' (1964) 15(3) *British Journal of Sociology* 207; for contemporary comment, see *Berkshire Chronicle*, 6 September 1856; *Liverpool Mercury*, 24 September 1867.

[103] The Society changed its rules on dress in 1859: Punshon, *Portrait in Grey*, p. 191.

[104] *Berkshire Chronicle*, 6 September 1856; *Newcastle Journal*, 2 July 1859 (bride in *moire antique*); 'Grand Quaker Wedding', *Salisbury and Winchester Journal*, 14 July 1860; *Manchester Courier*, 26 August 1865 (bride 'attired in a rich white silk grenadine'); 'A

similarly elegant and costly: at one, the bill of fare for the wedding breakfast had been printed on satin *cartes* at a cost of three guineas, was in French, 'and showed no trace of the peculiar homeliness once appertaining to the Society of Friends'.[105]

Quaker endogamy, and their distinctive attire, had been two of the justifications offered for their special treatment in the 1820s and 1830s.[106] The changes within the Society might have prompted questions as to whether such special treatment was still justified, especially since there was nothing in the process laid down by the Marriage Act that was incompatible with their beliefs and practices.[107] Quakers married in meeting houses within the hours prescribed by law, and their belief that it was God, rather than any third person, who made the marriage was perfectly compatible with an exchange of consent before a registrar whose role was simply to record it. It should also be noted that the extension of the right to marry according to Quaker usages was not a necessary consequence of the abandonment of endogamy; after all, there was nothing to prevent Quakers from marrying non-Quakers according to *other* forms.

Fears that allowing non-Quakers to marry according to Quaker usages would lead to abuse were unfounded.[108] The Society continued to exercise close control over who married according to its usages, and the number doing so barely changed.[109] Viewed in the context of the law as a whole, however, the change meant their special position was even harder to justify. From the 1860s onwards, attempts were made to devise a single framework that could encompass, rather than exempt, Quakers and Jews.

Fashionable Quakers' Wedding', *Liverpool Mercury*, 24 September 1867 (bride 'elegantly attired in a rich train of white corded silk').

[105] *Cheshire Observer*, 20 May 1865; see also *Salisbury and Winchester Journal*, 14 July 1860.

[106] See Chapter 2.

[107] See Elizabeth Isichei, *Victorian Quakers* (Oxford: Oxford University Press, 1970), p. 162, noting that '[i]t was generally accepted that the original reasons behind the ... marriage rules had lost their validity'.

[108] Parl. Deb., vol. 210, col. 1471, 18 April 1872 (Duke of Marlborough).

[109] *Thirty-fourth Annual Report of the Registrar-General of Births, Deaths and Marriages in England* (London: HMSO, 1873), p. lxii. However, an increasing number of Quakers married non-Quakers (see, e.g., Pamela Richardson, 'The West Country Fox Family: A Study of Provincial English Quakerism, 1840–1920' (unpublished Ph.D. thesis, University of Exeter, 2007), p. 109) and membership of the Society itself begin to increase again from the mid-1860s (Isichei, 'From Sect to Denomination', p. 219).

The Prospect of Wider Reform

*it must be universally conceded, that, if it be possible to reduce them to one
uniform system, such an object is in the highest degree desirable*[110]

The focus of the Marriage and Registration Act 1856 had been on
resolving specific issues that had arisen with the 1836 Act. It was amending rather than reforming legislation. But a decade later the possibility of
more wide-ranging reform was on the agenda. Differences in the marriage laws of England, Wales, Scotland, and Ireland had been highlighted
by a high-profile dispute between Major Yelverton and Theresa
Longworth as to whether they were legally married; with one ceremony
having taken place in Ireland, and another alleged to have taken place in
Scotland, the case was fought out in different courts, with each taking
a different approach to the question.[111] Understandably, the emergence
of these differences generated a considerable hullabaloo,[112] and in 1865
a Royal Commission was set up with the remit of creating a uniform
marriage law for all four countries of the United Kingdom.[113]

It was a challenging task, and one that was perhaps always doomed to fail
given how far the marriage laws of each jurisdiction diverged and the dissent
within the Commission as to the best means of ensuring consistency.[114] For
present purposes, two aspects of its work are of particular interest: first, how
the evidence submitted to the Commission illuminates the discrepancies in
the law governing different types of weddings *within* England and Wales,
and, second, how its wide-ranging proposals would have transformed
the law.

The picture of law and practice was somewhat skewed by the fact that
most of the evidence came from the Anglican establishment.[115] There

---

[110] *RC Report*, p. xxiv.

[111] Since the litigation turned on the laws governing weddings in Ireland and Scotland, it lies
outside the scope of the present chapter; for discussion, see Probert, Harding, and
Dempsey, 'A Uniform Law of Marriage?'

[112] For discussion, see Rebecca Gill, 'Imperial Anxieties of a Nineteenth Century Bigamy
Case' (2004) 57 *History Workshop Journal* 58; Helena Kelleher Kahn, 'The Yelverton
Affair: A Nineteenth Century Sensation' (2005) 13 *History Ireland* 21; Chloe Schama,
Wild Romance: The True Story of a Victorian Scandal (London: Bloomsbury, 2011).

[113] The Commission consisted of Lord Chelmsford, Lord Naas, Baron Lyveden, William
Monsell, John Inglis, Thomas O'Hagan, Sir James Plaisted Wilde, Spencer Horatio
Walpole, Page Wood VC, Sir Roundell Palmer, Sir Hugh McCalmont Cairns, George
Young, Travers Twiss, and Alexander Murray Dunlop.

[114] For an account of the divisions within the Commission and its ultimate failure, see
Probert, Harding, and Dempsey, 'A Uniform Law of Marriage?'

[115] This was perhaps inevitable: the circular letter sent by the Commissioners in June 1865
was directed to 'all Bishops', along with a selection of clergy 'and other individuals

was a single submission from the Roman Catholic Church in England, evidence from the Chief Rabbi and a Jewish MP, and a number of communications from the Registrar-General. But not one Protestant Dissenting minister, or even denomination, submitted evidence of practice in England and Wales.

The evidence that was submitted is nonetheless telling. It is clear that the Anglican establishment was concerned about the rise in the number of weddings celebrated outside its churches. While none of the submissions expressed any concern about those taking place in Catholic or Nonconformist chapels, a number were highly critical of the location and conduct of register office weddings.[116] The differences in the preliminaries attracted even more discussion, with many claiming that the lack of inquiry or publicity involved in giving notice at the register office was an incentive to couples to marry there.[117] Yet many admitted that the system of banns was not working either, with clergy unable to verify whether those presenting themselves to be married in large urban parishes were resident there, let alone whether they were free to marry.[118] The solutions proffered by the churchmen who gave evidence to the Commission varied considerably. Some believed that there should be no incentive to choose one form of wedding over another on the basis of cost or privacy, and that it should therefore be made easier for a couple to marry in their parish church with *no* publicity.[119] Others, by contrast, thought that the calling of banns should be made more rigorous,[120]

suggested as likely to give important practical information on the subject of the inquiry'. Written responses from bishops or their representatives, diocesan registrars, archdeacons, deans, rural deans, and individual clergy accounted for 21 of the 26 written responses relating to the law of England and Wales in the lengthy Appendix. Oral evidence was also subsequently given by the Bishop of Oxford and the Archdeacon of Gloucester: *RC Report*, Minutes of Evidence, 21 February and 27 June 1866.

[116] *RC Report*, Appendix, pp. 13, 35.

[117] *RC Report*, Appendix, pp. 1–2, 8, 13, 15, 35–36, 38–39. There was also a particularly arid debate on precisely when during divine service banns had to be read: 'The Law of Marriage by Banns' (7 July 1866) 41 *The Law Times* 613.

[118] The Bishop of Ely argued that '[i]n large parishes it is almost impossible for the clergyman to make personal inquiries concerning parties who may take up a temporary residence for the purpose of having the banns published in the parish church' (*RC Report*, Appendix, p. 1; see also pp. 2, 8, 15, 53).

[119] To this end a number proposed making licences cheaper (*RC Report*, Appendix, pp. 1, 2, 8, 13, 16, 53); a more radical suggestion was that those who wished to marry without banns should be able to give notice to the incumbent of their parish church, with the details of the intended marriage being entered into a publicly accessible notice book but not otherwise published: *RC Report*, Minutes of Evidence, 27 June 1866, p. 166.

[120] A particularly detailed submission was received from the Reverent Samuel Wilks – the Rector of Nursling and the author of *Banns: a Railroad to Clandestine Marriages* –

perhaps to head off any further proposals for universal civil preliminaries.[121]

The distinctive treatment of Jewish weddings also came in for criticism – not because of the freedoms it conferred, but because of the way in which it was being used to ensure religious conformity. In the view of Mr Alderman Salomon MP, the power of the Board of Deputies to certify secretaries had become 'an element of religious discipline' and a means 'of sustaining Jewish ecclesiastical authority by the assumed power and action of Parliament'.[122] By way of example, he noted that the Board had refused to certify the secretary of a new synagogue in Bayswater 'on some technical point'.[123] He also anticipated that other breakaway groups would follow the West London synagogue in challenging religious orthodoxy, and that the law might have to recognise further divisions within Judaism, 'multiplying religious names in Acts of Parliament'.[124]

The fact that the Commission was looking at practices across the United Kingdom provided an opportunity for the Catholic Archbishop and Bishops of England to press their case for Catholic priests to be 'the legal witnesses of the marriages celebrated by them', as was the case in Ireland.[125] They drew attention to the challenges of registering newly created places of worship for weddings, to the 'ludicrous' effect of repeating to the registrar words already spoken in the service, and to the financial burden for couples of paying fees to both priest and registrar.[126]

Having reviewed the laws in operation in the different parts of the United Kingdom, the Commission concluded that having one uniform system would be both desirable and feasible.[127] Since none of the systems

---

arguing that the procedure followed at the register office was far more exacting and proposing that clergy should be required to collect similar details as to the condition, age, dwelling place, and parish of the parties, their length of residence there, whether any necessary parental consent had been given, and whether there were any impediments to the marriage (*RC Report*, Appendix, p. 19).

[121] The Registrar-General had drawn attention to the problems with the calling of banns in his evidence, citing one curate who had published the banns of 99 couples one Sunday morning (*RC Report*, Appendix, p. 40) and noting that hundreds of names were called in the Cathedral Church at Manchester in early December in preparation for marriages over the Christmas period (p. 51).

[122] *RC Report*, Appendix, p. 11.

[123] *Ibid.*

[124] *Ibid.*, Minutes of Evidence, 7 March 1866.

[125] *Ibid.*, Appendix, p. 44.

[126] *Ibid.*, pp. 44–45.

[127] The description of the Commission's recommendations draws on Probert, Harding, and Dempsey, 'A Uniform Law of Marriage?'

in operation were regarded as ideal, reform could not be achieved simply by extending the laws of England and Ireland to Scotland, or vice versa. Universal civil marriage – which had been adopted elsewhere as a means of unifying newly created states – was not seen as an option.[128] Instead, the Commission noted their conviction that it was important 'to interfere no further with the general sentiments and habits of the people ... than is absolutely necessary for the purpose of constructing a safe and consistent marriage code'.[129] This meant, in their view, that the State should 'associate its legislation ... with the religious habits and sentiments of the people, and ... obtain, as far as possible, the religious sanction for the marriage contract'.[130]

With this in mind, the Commission set out the principles that it thought should underpin a 'sound marriage law'. First, the law should be both as simple and as certain as possible. Second, the State 'should be absolutely impartial and indifferent as between the members of different religious denominations'.[131] Third, while 'every proper and reasonable facility' should be given for celebrating weddings, the state also had a duty 'to discourage, and place obstacles in the way of sudden and clandestine marriages',[132] in order to ensure that the parties were both eligible and suitable.

To achieve this, the Commission proposed a new system focused on the authorisation of persons rather than places. Under its scheme, all priests and ministers, whatever their religious affiliation, would in principle have been able to conduct and register weddings, with no need for a civil registrar to be present.[133] While it referred to weddings being conducted by a 'duly authorised' celebrant, the Commission did not attempt to establish any particular process of authorisation, merely recommending that the role be limited to 'such ministers of religion as are in the active exercise of official duties in their several churches or

---

[128] This was understandable: while universal civil marriage had been introduced in some nations that had no history of civil marriage at all, there had always been some reason for doing so beyond the desire for uniformity, whether to proclaim a definite break with the past, to signal the unity and independence of a new nation, or to assert the primacy of the nation-state over transnational influences: see Rebecca Probert, 'State and Law' in Paul Puschmann (ed.), *A Cultural History of Marriage in the Age of Empires* (London: Bloomsbury, 2020), 59–75.

[129] *RC Report*, p. xlv.

[130] *Ibid.*, p. xxv.

[131] *Ibid.*

[132] *Ibid.*

[133] 'When the duty of registrars *quoad hoc* is performed by the officiating ministers or other official witnesses of any religious denomination ... the further security of the attendance of the civil registrar does not seem to be important, still less to be a condition upon which it can be necessary to make the validity of a marriage depend' (*Ibid.*, p. xxxvii).

denominations, and occupy positions which make them amenable to public responsibility, and to the censure and discipline of their own religious communities'.[134] This need for a link to a church or community meant that places of worship would still need to be certified and registered,[135] but the validity of a marriage would not depend on it being solemnised in any particular place. All that would be required was for the couples to give notice of their intention to marry to their authorised celebrant,[136] and then to exchange their consent to marry in the presence of that person and two witnesses.[137] The marriage would then be registered by the celebrant.

The proposed move away from the regulation of buildings was clearly motivated by the need to devise a scheme that would work for the whole of the United Kingdom and the fact that both Scotland and Ireland had a long tradition of solemnising marriages at home as well as in places of worship. But it would also have addressed the problems that the regulation of buildings had created in England and Wales. A decade earlier, when the laws governing the licensing of places of worship were changed, Lord Brougham had claimed that all existing and future licences had accidentally been nullified, and that thousands of marriages had thereby been invalidated.[138] Whether or not this was true,[139] the status of a ceremony in a place of worship that not registered for weddings remained doubtful. The view of the Law Officers had been that it would be void,[140] but this was not expressly stated in the 1836 Act. The

---

[134] *RC Report*, p. xxxv.

[135] *Ibid.* Exactly who would have authority to certify the church or chapel would depend on the nature of the religious denomination: the episcopal would be registered under the certificates of their bishops, Presbyterians under the certificates of their presbyteries, and other Nonconformist places of worship under the certificates of the officiating minister for the time being and not less than 10 householders, defined as 'members of the congregation who have frequented the place in question, as their ordinary place of worship, for the period of one year next before the date of the certificate' (p. xxxvi).

[136] *RC Report*, p. xliii. A twin-track process was envisaged, with a waiting period of 15 days if the bride and groom were both personally known to the officer or minister, and both professed themselves to be of the same religious persuasion, and 21 days in other cases.

[137] *RC Report*, p. xxxvi.

[138] On the basis that if a building was not licensed for worship, it was not eligible to be registered for weddings either: Parl. Deb., ser. 3, vol. 139, col. 658, 10 July 1855.

[139] The Lord Chancellor doubted Brougham's construction, but it was nonetheless thought advisable to include a provision that in future the validity of a marriage could not be challenged on the basis that the place of worship in which it took place had never been certified as such: Places of Worship Registration Act 1855, s. 13.

[140] TNA TS25/873, and Brougham, in introducing the amending legislation, took the same view.

Act only referred to a marriage being void if the parties knowingly and wilfully married in a registered place of worship other than that specified in the notice of marriage, and made no mention of the consequences if the place was not registered at all.[141] The cases that came before the courts offered little assistance on this point; in none of them was the validity of the marriage directly in issue, and the willingness of judges to presume that the place of worship had been registered did not answer the question of what the result would be if there was evidence that it was not.[142] For Anglican weddings, by contrast, the consequences of non-compliance were clearer,[143] and there was a constant stream of Acts validating marriages celebrated in places where they should not have been.[144]

The proposed reforms would also have achieved parity among different religious groups. Anglican places of worship would have had to be registered in the same way as others. Quaker weddings would have continued much as before; the Commission noting that their registering officers, 'although not celebrating marriages as ministers of religion, fulfil ... functions practically equivalent',[145] and recommending that weddings conducted in their presence should continue to be recognised.[146] And Jewish weddings, it suggested, would be liberated rather than restricted by the new scheme; the control of the Board of Deputies would end, with no more questions about whether a wedding had been conducted according to Jewish 'usages'. The view of the Commission was very similar to that expressed by Lord John Russell in

---

[141] Marriage Act 1836, s. 42.

[142] See, e.g., the couverture case of *Sichel* v. *Lambert* (1864) 15 CB Rep (NS) 781; 143 ER 992. The reliance on the presumption in such cases was somewhat odd given that the Registrar-General had a list of all registered places of worship.

[143] Marriage Act 1823, s. 22 provided that a marriage would be void if the parties 'knowingly and wilfully' married 'in any other Place than a Church, or such Public Chapel wherein Banns may be lawfully published'.

[144] Rebecca Probert, 'The Validation of Marriages by Subsequent Legislation' (in preparation). Examples included new churches that had neither been designated as a chapel of ease nor assigned a district (Coatham Marriages Validity Act 1856; Christ Church (West Hartlepool) Act 1857), and newly consecrated but unlicensed chapels of ease (see, e.g., Frampton Mansel Marriage Act 1868).

[145] *RC Report*, p. xxxvi.

[146] The Quaker belief that it was God, rather than any third person, who made the marriage was reflected in the use of the term 'witness' as an alternative to 'celebrant'. The requirement that the wedding be conducted in their presence would have entailed a minor change to the law, which did not specifically require the registering officer to be present, but not to the Society's practices.

1836;[147] the state, it noted, 'ought not in any case to take notice of or enforce compliance with [any] ceremonies or usages, as necessary to the validity of any marriage, in other respects duly solemnized'.[148]

The possibility of a non-religious form of wedding would have remained, with those choosing this option giving notice to a civil registrar and exchanging consent before either a superintendent registrar or registrar. But overall the role of the state in the making of marriage would have diminished. Any attempt to publicise intended weddings was abandoned, the Commission describing the existing processes as 'nugatory' and the mooted alternative of displaying them on church or chapel doors 'offensive'.[149] Additionally, the Commission proposed that neither a failure to comply with the preliminaries nor the lack of authorisation of the person conducting the ceremony should invalidate a marriage.

The Commission's report, eventually published in September 1868, met with a favourable reaction from the press, both in terms of the thoroughness of the investigation and the substantive proposals. As *The Morning Post* noted, 'nothing previously published on this important subject has succeeded in showing with such distinctness how varied in method, how complex and multiplied in particulars, how anomalous in application, and how inefficient and unsatisfactory are our present marriage laws'.[150] Most commentators took the view that the laws of all parts of the United Kingdom were in need of reform, but *The Standard* noted with unjustified smugness its 'satisfaction at finding that the law of England, on the whole, comes pretty near to the ideal'.[151] The pages of evidence in the Appendices showed how inaccurate that was. But the perception that the Commission's proposals were essentially assimilating the marriage laws of Ireland and Scotland to those of England and Wales was to prove the death-knell to hopes of a uniform marriage law for the whole of the United Kingdom.[152]

This would not have prevented the Commission's proposals being enacted for England and Wales alone,[153] but it did take away the point

---

[147] See Chapter 2.

[148] *RC Report*, p. xxxvii.

[149] *Ibid.*, p. xli. It did, however, envisage that notices of marriage would be kept in a book that would be available for public inspection.

[150] *The Morning Post*, 10 September 1868. See also *The Huddersfield Chronicle*, 3 October 1868.

[151] *The Standard*, 9 September 1868.

[152] See Probert, Harding, and Dempsey, 'A Uniform Law of Marriage?'

[153] *The Times*, 25 August 1868, praised the fact that under the Commission's scheme marriages would be less at risk of being annulled for failure to comply with the

of doing so. Nor was there sufficient enthusiasm for the Commission's proposals to make their enactment politically advantageous. While the Catholics were certainly in favour of vesting authority in their priests, not all Dissenters took the same view.[154] Many within the Jewish community were dismayed by the idea that they would no longer be treated differently and by the removal of the Board's powers; indeed, synagogues reacted to the Commission's recommendations by actively affiliating themselves to the Board, thereby endorsing it as a representative body for British Jewry.[155] And the Registrar-General, George Graham, had expressed his opposition to any change,[156] which would also have made the task of implementing the Commission's recommendations more challenging; having held the post for over twenty years, his views would have carried considerable weight.

It is unsurprising, then, that no move was made to legislate the fundamental reforms proposed by the Commission. Five years after the publication of the Report, the Commission's chair asked Selbourne, the new Lord Chancellor,[157] whether there was any likelihood of the government introducing reform, noting the eminence of those who had served on the Commission, the number of persons who had given evidence or information, and the fact that Selbourne himself had been responsible for the 'able and carefully prepared' Report.[158] While agreeing that the issue was an important one that he hoped would 'one day' be embodied in law, Selbourne refused to give any pledge 'as to the time or manner in which the government would deal with this subject, if indeed during their tenure of office, it would be possible to deal with it at all'.[159] Reform of marriage law was clearly off the agenda.

Conclusion

Unlike the Marriage Act 1836, the Marriage and Registration Act 1856 was not trying to put forward a coherent new scheme, but attempting to

formalities, and suggested that its reforms should be acceptable in England and Wales even if they were not acceptable in Scotland.

[154] On the divisions within Dissent on this point – which were to prove so challenging even in achieving more limited reform – see further Chapter 5.

[155] Clark, 'Identity and Equality', p. 167.

[156] *RC Report*, Appendix, pp. 40–41, 50–51.

[157] Roundell Palmer, one of the members of the Royal Commission, had been created Baron Selbourne upon being appointed as Lord Chancellor in October 1872.

[158] Parl. Deb., ser. 3, vol. 216, col. 1699, 3 July 1873.

[159] *Ibid.*, col. 1700.

respond to very specific grievances, address anomalies that had been identified, and defuse tensions. Its terms, passage, and impact provide an illustration of the difference between amendments designed to remove a problem and reforms designed to improve the law. They demonstrate how easily an unsatisfactory stopgap can become a permanent fixture, and how attempts to respond to a specific issue can have profound consequences.[160]

The prohibition on the inclusion of a religious service in the register office was part of a general sharpening of the distinctions between different routes into marriage that took place in this period. Anglican clergy could no longer be compelled to marry a couple after civil preliminaries, or any person who had been divorced on the basis of their adultery, and the owners of registered places of worship had greater control over who married there. At the same time there was a blurring of distinctions between the weddings of the exempted groups and the rest of the population – in terms of the fact that synagogues could now be registered for weddings, and that Quaker weddings were open to non-Quakers – raising the question as to whether such exemptions were still needed. The coherence of the scheme established in 1836 was rapidly fragmenting. More positively, the removal of the restriction that only Christian places of worship could be registered for weddings did at least ensure that the law was capable of accommodating different religious faiths, even if it was to be some time before any groups other than Jews sought to avail themselves of this.

Had the recommendations of the 1868 Royal Commission been enacted, the subsequent history of marriage law would have been very different. While its recommendation that the preliminaries could be delegated to religious groups would have reversed one of the key elements of the 1836 Act, it would also have led to far greater equality among such groups. In the absence of wide-ranging reform, however, these ideas of responsibility and equality were to coalesce around a much more specific demand, as the next chapter will show.

---

[160] Both the requirement that notices were to be displayed in the office of the superintendent registrar and the prohibition on religious content have remained part of the law to the present day.

5

Differences, Divisions, and Dispensing
with the Registrar, 1873–1899

On 20 March 1878, Archibald Primrose, the 5th Earl of Rosebery and future prime minister, married Hannah de Rothschild. Their different faiths, and the implications that this had for the way in which their wedding could be celebrated, meant that this event attracted even more attention than might be expected of a union between a handsome young aristocrat and an heiress of 'almost fabulous wealth'.[1] Early reports that they would marry according to both Christian and Jewish rites having proved to be mere speculation,[2] the wedding took place at a register office, albeit one specially authorised for the occasion and with more guests than was usual at such events. Later that morning, the couple went through a second ceremony at an Anglican church, in the presence of an even more glittering array of guests, including the then Prime Minister, Disraeli, the Prince of Wales, and his younger brother the Duke of Cambridge.[3] All of the latter signed as witnesses to the marriage – despite the fact that this second ceremony should not have been registered at all, as 'A Nonconformist' pointed out in a letter published in *The Times* the following day.[4] The bride's relatives, however, were noticeably absent, and it was subsequently reported that Hannah had been 'read out' of the Jewish community.[5] The *Church Times* seemed equally unhappy about the ceremony that had taken place in church, muttering darkly about the 'invasion' of the church by the unbaptised.[6]

We will return to various aspects of this particular wedding over the course of the chapter, since it reflected some of the key issues that emerged or became more apparent in the final quarter of the nineteenth

[1] 'The Rosebery-Rothschild Marriage', Sheffield Independent, 21 March 1878.
[2] 'London Correspondence', *Nottinghamshire Guardian*, 18 January 1878.
[3] 'Marriage of Lord Rosebery', *The Times*, 21 March 1878.
[4] 'Lord Rosebery's Marriage', *The Times*, 22 March 1878.
[5] 'A Few Notes about Two Recent London Weddings', *Worcestershire Chronicle*, 30 March 1878.
[6] *Church Times*, 29 March 1878.

century. For one thing, it illustrates the differences in the way that civil and religious weddings were celebrated, and how the relationship between them was still a matter of some uncertainty. It also underlines how a civil wedding might often be the only option for those of different faiths. As the first section will show, there was also a sharpening of differences between different types of religious weddings. The Catholic hierarchy placed an increasing emphasis on being married according to Catholic rites; the Jewish authorities struggled with the issue of religious-only marriage ceremonies among recent immigrants outside the established structures; and the first cases of marriage ceremonies being conducted according to Muslim rites were recorded. These developments have not gone unremarked, but discussion of them has generally been limited to the literature on different religious groups.[7] By bringing them together we can see how they formed the backdrop to wider debates about reform to the laws governing weddings.

The reactions to the Rosebery–Rothschild marriage also hint at deeper divisions between different religious groups. The quickness of 'Nonconformist'[8] to point out how the Anglican ceremony had flouted the law reflected wider tensions that were to escalate over the period. There was an increasing sense of division between the Wesleyan Methodists and the Anglican church, reflected in increasing numbers of Methodist chapels being registered for weddings. And the ability of Anglican clergy – but not their Nonconformist counterparts – to register the marriages that they conducted was a significant element in the campaign to dispense with the presence of the registrar at weddings in such registered places of worship. Many Nonconformists – and Catholics – were demanding equality with the Established church in this and other respects.

All of this is essential to understanding both the passage and terms of the Marriage Act 1898 – which eventually allowed each registered place of

---

[7] See, e.g., David Feldman, *Englishmen and Jews: Social Relations and Political Culture, 1840–1914* (New Haven: Yale University Press, 1994); Geoffrey Alderman, *Modern British Jewry* (Oxford: Clarendon Press, 1998), p. 144; Rainer Liedtke, *Jewish Welfare in Hamburg and Manchester, c. 1850–1914* (Oxford: Oxford University Press, 1998), p. 155; Michael Clark, 'Identity and Equality: The Anglo-Jewish Community in the Post-Emancipation Era, 1858–1887 (DPhil thesis, Oxford, 2005); Rozina Visram, *Asians in Britain: 400 Years of History* (Pluto Press, 2002), p. 104; Humayun Ansari, *The Infidel Within: Muslims in Britain since 1800* (London: Hurst, 2004), p. 134.

[8] The term had been in use for some years as an alternative term for Protestant Dissenters; by this period it tended to be used in preference to the older term, and this chapter will follow the usage of the time.

worship to appoint its own 'authorised person' to register marriages that were celebrated there – and its limitations. The differences and divisions of the 1870s and 1880s show both why the demand to dispense with the registrar was made with such vigour and why it was so hard to achieve. They also help to explain why the solution adopted in the 1898 Act was so limited. Despite the fact that it was to be the last of the major reforms to the laws regulating weddings in registered places of worship, it did not, as most commentators have assumed, sweep away the last of the problems affecting such weddings.[9] As we shall see, concerns about becoming authorised meant that take-up was limited and registrars continued to attend the majority of weddings in registered places of worship.

Differences

The existing law is not based on the idea of religious equality[10]

The glamour of the Rosebery–Rothschild register office wedding was very much the exception rather than the norm. As the *Daily News* reported, there had never been a civil wedding 'of equal brilliancy'.[11] The usual office having been deemed unsuitable, the Registrar-General held that the larger room next to it could be included within the register office for the day. The 'cartloads of rhododendrons, azaleas, fan palms, tree ferns, trumpet lilies, and other decorative shrubs and flowers' that arrived the day before the wedding helped to transform 'the dull, magisterial air of the apartment'.[12] Hannah's white silk dress would have been the envy of most register office brides, and members of the aristocracy were present to witness the wedding. Yet, the guest list at the subsequent church ceremony – for which Hannah donned full bridal attire[13] – was

---

[9] Commentary on the 1898 Act has been somewhat sparse but the overall tone has been positive. Roderick Floud and Pat Thane briefly refer to it as ending the cost and complexity of 'chapel' marriage ('Debate: The Incidence of Civil Marriage in Victorian England and Wales' (1979) 84 *Past & Present* 146, 147). Stephen Cretney similarly suggested that the Act should be seen 'as completing the reforms of the law begun . . . 60 years before' (*Family Law in the Twentieth Century: A History* (Oxford: Oxford University Press, 2003), p. 21), while Satvinder Juss, 'Church of England Marriages: Historical Particularity or Anomaly' (2009) 9(1) *Kings Law Journal* 643, 653 refers to it as enabling priests and ministers to officiate at weddings.

[10] *Daily News*, 27 March 1886.

[11] 'The Rosebery-Rothschild Marriage', *Daily News*, 20 March 1878.

[12] *Ibid.*

[13] *The Times* describes her as wearing a 'a white embroidered morning dress' in the register office and one of 'white satin with a brocaded train', together with 'a veil of Brussels lace

even more eminent. Even this most sumptuous of register office weddings was not quite the same as a wedding in church.

Literary depictions of register office weddings similarly conveyed a message that such weddings were different from ones in church in terms of everything from the status of the parties to their sartorial choices. For novelists, a register office wedding provided a convenient shorthand to convey the unsuitability, undue speed, or secrecy of the match (and sometimes all three).[14] In Gissing's *The Nether World*, which depicted the lives of the slum dwellers of Clerkenwell, it was the novel's anti-heroine, Clementina Peckover, who elected to marry in a register office. Both her motives and her justification speak volumes about how such weddings were seen: her motive was to ensure that no one learned of it in advance, but she attempted to disarm any suspicions her husband-to-be might have by giving the justification that it would require no expense in terms of dress.[15]

Of course, novelists were making a particular point by locating these weddings in a register office. But their ability to do so depended on their readers sharing certain assumptions about the implications of a register office wedding, and these depictions did have some basis in reality.

Setting apart a few early feminists who married in the register office because it did not have the same patriarchal connotations as a church wedding,[16] the evidence suggests that most couples who married in register offices in this period did so for practical reasons rather than out of preference. For some it was a means to evade scrutiny,[17] while for

---

with orange blossoms' ('Marriage of Lord Rosebery', *The Times*, 21 March 1878). The *Buckinghamshire Herald* added that she also wore a grey cashmere cloak and a bonnet to the earlier ceremony: 'Marriage of the Earl of Rosebery and Miss Hannah De Rothschild', *Buckinghamshire Herald*, 23 March 1878.

[14] An impulsive couple is united at the register office in Mrs Oliphant's *Hester* (1883), while Conan Doyle features an unsuitable wedding in 'The Boscombe Valley Mystery' in *The Adventures of Sherlock Holmes* (1891) ('what does the idiot do but get into the clutches of a barmaid in Bristol, and marry her at a registry office?'). Similarly, among the couples marrying in the register office in Thomas Hardy's *Jude the Obscure* (1895) are a pregnant bride with a black eye and a groom who is just out of prison.

[15] George Gissing, *The Nether World* (1889).

[16] See, e.g., Philippa Levine, *Feminist Lives in Victorian England: Private Roles and Public Commitment* (Oxford: Basil Blackwell, 1990), p. 37

[17] See, e.g., the case studies by Jenny Paterson, 'Married in a register office – or were they?'; Bryan Grimshaw, 'A just-in-time marriage in the register office'; Wendy Hamilton, 'A pregnancy and a register office wedding'; Valerie King, 'Sex, lies and register office weddings'; Susan Donaldson, 'A puzzling register office marriage – and its prequel' (2021) JGFH (forthcoming).

others it was a way of getting married without spending too much money.[18]

There were still a few Nonconformists who married in the register office in preference to the Anglican church where no other option was available to them.[19] But the evidence from family historians suggests that it was increasingly couples from different faiths or denominations who married in the register office, as in the case of the Rosebery–Rothschild wedding.[20] Sometimes this was because the separate faiths or denominations had particular rules on intermarriage. Marrying according to the usages of the Jews remained restricted to Jews alone as a matter of law,[21] while the Catholic church certainly did not favour the idea of Catholics marrying Protestants. Other religious groups set preconditions that one or other of the parties might be unable to meet. The parish church was in principle open to all save the small number of those who had been divorced, but marriages between Anglicans and Jews did generate objections,[22] and some clergy refused to conduct the weddings of those who had not been baptised in the Anglican church.[23] The possibility of marrying according to Quaker usages was no longer restricted as a matter of law, but non-members had to have permission from the Society and the few who chose this route tended to have close connections to Quakerism.[24] Marrying in a registered place of worship similarly required the permission of the governing authority of the

---

[18] The issue here was not so much the *legal* costs of different routes into marriage – marrying in the register office was not necessarily any cheaper than a church wedding – as the different expectations of how each should look. On the increasing emphasis on the wedding dress as a special (if not distinctive) dress, and the expectation that for a church wedding one's dress should be new, and ideally white, see Lucy-Clare Windle, 'Forever and a Day: The Life of the English Wedding Dress 1860–1906' (MA dissertation, University of Southampton, 2005).

[19] And some, it should be noted, did so as a matter of principle: see, e.g., Jill Wright, 'The Plymouth Brethren and register office weddings' (2021) JGFH (forthcoming).

[20] Rebecca Probert, 'Interpreting choices' (2021) JGFH (forthcoming).

[21] Marriage Act 1836, s. 2.

[22] Five years prior to the Rosebery–Rothschild wedding, a caveat was entered against the proposed marriage of the Hon. Elliott Yorke (a descendant of the Lord Hardwicke responsible for the passage of the Clandestine Marriages Act 1753) to Annie De Rothschild: *Fife Herald*, 13 February 1873. The marriage was in fact celebrated at a register office, with the Anglican service following afterwards; *The Tablet*, 15 February 1873.

[23] See, e.g., TNA, HO45/9979/X53527.

[24] The first Quaker wedding to take place between non-members was that of the suffragist Laura Pochin and the future Liberal MP Charles McLaren: *Morning Post*, 8 March 1877. Charles was the nephew of the Quaker MP John Bright.

building.[25] And some mixed-faith couples may simply have preferred the neutrality of the register office even if it was possible to marry in the church or chapel that one of them attended, especially given the uncertainties about the legality of having two religious ceremonies.[26]

The Rosebery–Rothschild wedding also raised the still unresolved issue about the relationship between a civil wedding and any subsequent religious ceremony. The Registrar-General was quick to counter any suggestion of wrongdoing in the registration of the couple's Anglican ceremony. According to a letter published in the *Manchester Examiner*, his view was that since both ceremonies took place on the same morning, they 'would be held to constitute one marriage', and so 'the officiating minister did nothing illegal in registering the marriage in the usual way'.[27] Yet, this explanation was impossible to reconcile either with the terms of the statute or with the previous advice given by the Law Officers. The 1856 Act had been perfectly clear that any subsequent religious ceremony should not be registered, even if it had been entirely unclear on what the consequences of such registration should be.[28] Registration was clearly 'illegal' in the sense of not being permitted by law, even if no criminal penalty attached to it. One suspects that the Registrar-General's approach to the registration of the Rosebery–Rothschild Anglican ceremony was heavily influenced by the status of the men who signed the marriage certificate; after all, the Law Officers had suggested that Catholic priests might be guilty of a felony in conducting religious-only marriage ceremonies even when these took place on the same day as the register office or Anglican wedding.[29]

The Catholic church had, however, changed its approach to non-Catholic weddings. In a pastoral letter of 1873, the Archbishop of Westminster made it clear that marrying in a register office, or in the Anglican church, was now strongly discouraged, even where one of the couple was Protestant. With a non-Catholic wedding now being seen as 'sacrilege', the blessing of the Catholic church was to be withheld. This meant that a priest would not conduct a ceremony after the couple had married in a different form or, if he knew of the couple's intentions to

---

[25] Marriage and Registration Act 1856, s. 11; see Chapter 4.

[26] On which see Chapter 4.

[27] 'Church News', *The Graphic*, 6 April 1878.

[28] Marriage and Registration Act 1856, s. 12; on the ambiguities of this provision, see Chapter 4.

[29] For the suggestion by the Law Officers that this might constitute a felony, see Chapter 3.

marry elsewhere, before.[30] By way of consolation, the Catholic authorities pointed out that they did at least recognise marriages conducted
according to other forms as valid, which, had the Council of Trent[31] been
in force in England, they would not have done.[32]

There was, however, something of a difference between the wishes of
the Catholic hierarchy and the practices of ordinary Catholics. The
vehemence with which the authorities insisted that couples should not
marry before anyone other than a Catholic priest was undoubtedly
underpinned by fears that many were doing just that. Catholic weddings
continued to account for a little over 4 per cent of the total: while this was
only a fraction less than the 5–6 per cent of the population who might be
considered to be Catholic,[33] viewed from within the Catholic community
it assumed more significant proportions.[34] One letter to *The Tablet*
complained that there were actually fewer Catholic weddings in
Liverpool in 1878 than in 1857, despite an increase both in communicants and in churches where weddings could be celebrated.[35] The suggested reason was that couples were marrying before the registrar
'through false representations, which would be detected if they were
made to a priest'.[36]

In a similar vein, Nathan Adler, the Chief Rabbi, identified the rigour
of the preliminary inquiries that he carried out as one of the reasons for
the growing number of ceremonies being conducted according to Jewish
usages outside the formal legal structures. As he noted, it was his practice
to 'require satisfactory proof, in the case of foreigners, either that they are

---

[30] *The Tablet*, 20 September 1873. See also James T. Hammick, *The Marriage Law of England:
A Practical Treatise on the Legal Incidents Connected with the Law of Constitution of the
Matrimonial Contract* (London: Shaw & Sons, 1887), pp. 148–9, noting 'that the Roman
Catholic clergy now decline to celebrate marriage between a Protestant and a Roman
Catholic unless the parties first solemnly promise that no ceremony shall be performed in
a Protestant church'.

[31] In 1563, the Council of Trent had issued a decree (*Tametsi*) stipulating that marriages
were to be celebrated by a Catholic priest in the presence of two witnesses and that other
forms of marriage would not be recognised as valid. The decree had not been promulgated in England and Wales, and there had been explicit recognition of the need to
comply with the requirements of the civil law: John Bossy, 'Challoner and the Marriage
Act' in E. Duffy (ed.), *Challoner and His Church: A Catholic Bishop in Georgian England*
(London: Darton, Longman & Todd, 1981), p. 132.

[32] *The Tablet*, 21 November 1874. As we shall see, this was to change in the early twentieth
century: see Chapter 6.

[33] Field, *Periodizing Secularization*, pp. 52–3.

[34] *The Tablet*, 8 November 1879.

[35] *The Tablet*, 6 December 1879.

[36] *Ibid.*

single or that their wife is dead, or that a legal divorce has taken place', with the result that those who were not eligible to marry went elsewhere to do so. There were also, he suggested, 'foreigners who, unfortunately, believe that they are not bound by the law of the land, and wish to avoid the trouble and expense of civil and religious registration', while a few were unable to bear the cost of getting married in a synagogue.[37]

Adler's insistence that the problem of these irregular ceremonies was generated by 'foreigners' reflected how the Jewish community was changing at this time. During the 1860s and 1870s around 19,000 Jews arrived in England and Wales from Germany, Holland, Poland, and Russia, taking the total Jewish population to 60,000 by 1880.[38] It also underlined just how challenging the issue was for the Jewish author-ities and for Anglo-Jewry as a whole.[39] In the view of the Committee appointed to investigate the issue, such ceremonies brought 'disgrace' on the community.[40] With the Registrar-General asking 'whether some measure for checking the evil could not be adopted',[41] the authority of the Board and its ability to exercise control over marriage practices across the entire Jewish community were in question.[42] And with legal disabilities affecting the Jewish community having only just been removed,[43] Jews were unlikely to welcome any reminder of their original status as aliens. The Rosebery–Rothschild marriage was a sign of how far Jews were now integrated into English society,[44] but the comment that it had attracted underlined how new, and potentially precarious, this was.[45] If English-born Jews did not want to be seen as different from the rest of English society, they had to take steps to encourage their foreign-born co-religionists to comply with the law of the land.

---

[37] *Jewish Chronicle,* 15 June 1877.

[38] Alderman, *Modern British Jewry*, p. 74; Field, *Periodizing Secularization*, p. 67.

[39] See, e.g., David Englander, '*Stille Huppah* (Quiet Marriage) among Jewish Immigrants in Britain' (1992) 34 *Jewish Journal of Sociology* 85.

[40] *Jewish Chronicle,* 15 June 1877.

[41] *Jewish Chronicle,* 28 January 1876.

[42] Feldman, *Englishmen and Jews*, p. 295; Liedtke, *Jewish Welfare*, pp. 155–6.

[43] On the erasure of the political and civil disadvantages to which Jews had previously been subject, see Feldman, *Englishmen and Jews.*

[44] See, e.g., 'The Jewish Peeress', *Sheffield Daily Telegraph*, 26 March 1878, noting that this was the first time that a Jewess had become a peeress.

[45] 'A Mixed Marriage', *Reynold's*, 24 March 1878; 'The Jews and the Rosebery Rothschild Marriage', *Edinburgh Evening News*, 2 April 1878; 'Church News', *The Graphic*, 6 April 1878.

Efforts were accordingly made to raise awareness of what was required for a legally recognised wedding.[46] The United Synagogue[47] introduced a cheaper way of getting married,[48] and many thousands of weddings took place under its auspices in the years that followed.[49] Despite this, concerns were still expressed about ceremonies taking place without the necessary formalities,[50] fuelled by the even larger wave of immigration from eastern Europe that took place in this period.[51] Newly arrived rabbis – 'scholars of high repute, trained in the yeshivot of Russia, Lithuania and Poland'[52] – were used to authorising weddings and divorces themselves and were not keen to accept the authority of the Board of Deputies.

By the 1890s, the Board of Deputies was contemplating the advisability of making it an offence to conduct a marriage ceremony according to Jewish usages outside the legal framework.[53] Under the Marriage Act 1836, the only offence capable of applying to Jewish weddings was that making it an offence for any person to conduct a wedding before the waiting period for the licence or certificate had elapsed, or after the authority to marry had lapsed.[54] The Act said nothing about it being an offence to marry without any authority having been issued at all, and Jews were specifically exempted from the provision making it an offence to marry in any place other than that specified in the notice.[55] A bill was drafted by its

---

[46] See e.g. *Manchester Courier*, 14 August 1877, reporting a sermon delivered in Yiddish and noting that a 'series of addresses in the minor synagogues' were being delivered to raise awareness of the legal requirements. See also the renewed effort at awareness-raising in 1896: *Jewish Chronicle*, 20 November 1896.

[47] The United Synagogue had been established in 1870 as a means of amalgamating Ashkenazi synagogues in the City of London: Alderman, *Modern British Jewry*, p. 85; Jewish United Synagogues Act 1870.

[48] *Manchester Courier*, 14 August 1877, noting that the cost was to be just half a guinea, and that no fee would be required from the poorest. The cost had previously been £3 10s: *Jewish Chronicle*, 13 April 1877.

[49] The solution adopted posed its own problems, with questions being raised about the validity of marriages performed at a synagogue where the registering secretary was not the secretary of that synagogue: *Jewish Chronicle*, 21 November 1890. While the Registrar-General decided not to dispute their validity, the correspondence was a reminder of the complexity of the legal framework governing Jewish marriages.

[50] *Jewish Chronicle*, 8 April 1892.

[51] By 1899, it was estimated that around 120,000 Jews were living in the East End of London alone, and regional communities had also expanded: Alderman, *Modern British Jewry*, p. 118; Field, *Periodizing Secularization*, p. 67.

[52] Alderman, *Modern British Jewry*, p. 144.

[53] Liedtke, *Jewish Welfare*, p. 156.

[54] Marriage Act 1836, s. 39.

[55] *Ibid.*

Committee for Law, Parliamentary, and General Purposes making it an offence to 'knowingly and wilfully solemnise any marriage between persons professing the Jewish religion, in the absence of the secretary of the synagogue lawfully authorised to register such marriage'.[56] While the phrasing was modelled on that applicable to those conducting weddings in registered places of worship,[57] the fact that Jewish weddings were not limited to taking place in synagogues meant that it was very different in its scope. Under the 1836 Act, a Catholic priest was not committing a crime by conducting a religious-only marriage ceremony,[58] but under the proposed bill a rabbi would be. What the proposed offence did not address was what the position would be if the parties did not belong to a synagogue at all. In the event, however, the bill was never introduced into Parliament, although the possibility of a new criminal offence continued to be discussed for some time.[59]

It is of course difficult to know just how many ceremonies were taking place outside the formal legal structures, since by definition they were not recorded in the usual marriage registers.[60] Complaints by the Jewish authorities also need to be read with a certain degree of caution, given their tendency to label any wedding that was not conducted under their auspices as 'irregular', even it was legally valid.[61] That said, the cases coming before the courts in which evidence was given of ceremonies conducted outside the legal framework were sufficient to generate concern, especially when the relationship between the parties had subsequently broken down and women found themselves unable to claim maintenance.[62]

---

[56] Clark, 'Identity and Equality', p. 19.

[57] Marriage Act 1836, s. 39 ('every Person who in any such registered Building or Office shall knowingly and wilfully solemnize any Marriage in the Absence of a Registrar of the District in which such registered Building or Office is situated shall be guilty of Felony').

[58] Assuming that it was not in a registered place of worship: see Chapter 3.

[59] See further Chapter 6.

[60] Englander, 'Stille Huppah', notes that the extent 'is difficult to gauge' (pp. 93–4). It would have been possible, if laborious, to assemble a cohort of Jewish couples and check whether they had married in England and Wales, but it would have been almost impossible to ascertain whether those who had not had married informally and invalidly in England and Wales or perfectly validly overseas.

[61] See, e.g., Jewish Chronicle, 20 April 1888, reporting a meeting of the Board of Deputies at which a 'recent irregular marriage at Manchester' was noted; the marriage in question 'having been performed in the presence of the District Registrar, was legal as a civil one' but 'it was not a marriage according to the usages of the Jews'.

[62] Rosa Frankel, for example, summoned her husband Barnett for desertion and failure to maintain, but the case was dismissed when the magistrate ascertained that no notice had been given to the registrar: Evening Telegraph and Star, 14 November 1894; Morning Post,

Such cases suggested that the status of a Jewish marriage ceremony that had not been conducted in accordance with the formalities required by law was no different from that of any other ceremony celebrated outside the legal framework. This, however, was contested in a case of 1899 in which it was suggested that the annulling clause in the Marriage Act 1836 had no application to Jewish marriages at all. The suggestion was rejected by the judge, but his decision that the wife had not 'knowingly and wilfully' failed to give notice meant that legal effect was given to the ceremony anyway.[63] Of course, given that a Jewish wedding did not have to be celebrated in a particular location, or in the presence of the secretary tasked with registering it, and since other marriages had been upheld even where the necessary preliminaries had not been observed,[64] it is difficult to see how the case could have been decided differently. The context of the case was also important; the issue was one of entitlement to inheritance, and in such cases the courts tended to be far more generous in presuming in favour of validity, especially where the couple had been regarded as husband and wife for a lengthy period of time.[65] Nonetheless, it underlined how the combination of rules that applied to Jewish weddings could result in legal recognition even where none of the legal requirements had been observed.[66]

The 1890s also saw reports of the first Muslim marriage ceremony in England.[67] Of course, whether it was truly the first we cannot know, but given that the number of Muslims in England and Wales was tiny,[68] that the overwhelming majority of them were male and only resident

---

21 November 1894; 'A Jewish Marriage Turns to be No Legal Marriage At All', *Leeds Times*, 1 December 1894. In the same year Rose Silverstein succeeded in obtaining damages of £150 from Morris Schaffner for breach of promise of marriage, but this only served to confirm that the ceremony they had gone through was not legally recognised as a marriage: *Yorkshire Evening Post*, 3 August 1894; 4 August 1894.

[63] *Nathan* v. *Woolf* (1899) 15 TLR 250.

[64] See, e.g., *Greaves* v. *Greaves* (1872) LR 2 P & D 423, where the licence had been obtained the day after the wedding.

[65] Considerable reliance was placed on the evidence of 'reputation': *Daily News*, 10 March 1899. Other contemporary cases show how cohabitation and reputation was becoming a reason for giving effect to a ceremony, rather than, as previously, being treated purely as evidence of the likelihood of a valid marriage having taken place, on which see Rebecca Probert, 'The Presumptions in Favour of Marriage' (2018) 77(2) *Cambridge Law Journal* 375.

[66] This has to be expressed with a degree of caution: as Chapter 6 will show, the courts continued to refuse to recognise Jewish religious-only marriage ceremonies in other contexts.

[67] *The Standard*, 20 April 1891.

[68] Field, *Periodizing Secularization*, p. 68.

temporarily,[69] and that some of those who stayed converted to Christianity,[70] it is unlikely that there were many earlier ones. It was in the final decades of the nineteenth century that there was an increase in students from India and Africa coming to study in England and a growing interest in other faiths.[71] An Oriental Institute was founded at Woking in the early 1880s, and the Shah Jahan Mosque was opened nearby in 1889.[72] Abdul Karim – Queen Victoria's 'munshi'[73] – worshipped there, as did several other of her Muslim servants.[74] There were also a number of conversions to Islam, among them being William Quilliam, a Liverpool solicitor, who opened the Liverpool Muslim Institute in a converted house on Christmas Day 1889.[75]

It was the Liverpool Muslim Institute that began to conduct Muslim marriage ceremonies. Reports of the first of these, in 1891, displayed both a sense of excitement at this novelty and a desire to normalise it.[76] It perhaps helped that the couple in question – a London barrister named Mohammed Ahmad and his English bride, Charlotte Fitch – had already gone through a legal wedding.[77] There was therefore no risk that their Muslim ceremony would raise the same problems as had been generated by irregular Jewish ones. While the detailed reports of the ceremony dwelt on the elements that would be unfamiliar to English readers,[78] and

---

[69] Sophie Gilliat-Ray, *Muslims in Britain* (Cambridge: Cambridge University Press, 2010), p. 28.

[70] See, e.g., Joseph Salter, *The Asiatic in England: Sketches of Sixteen Years' Work Among Orientals* (London: Seeley, Jackson and Halliday, 1873), pp. 182, 232–33; Ansari, *The Infidel Within*, p. 112.

[71] G. Beckerlegge, 'Followers of "Mohammed, Kalee and Dada Nanuk": The Presence of Islam and South Asian Religions in Victorian Britain' in John Wolfe (ed.) *Religion in Victorian Britain: Vol V, Culture and Empire* (Manchester: Manchester University Press, 1997).

[72] Ansari, *The Infidel Within*; Sarah Brown, 'The Shah Jahan Mosque, Woking: an unexpected gem', 46 (Autumn) *Conservation Bulletin* 32. The Institute and mosque were sufficiently well-known to feature briefly in chapter 9 of H. G. Wells' *The War of the Worlds* (1897), if only as one of the casualties of the Martian attack.

[73] Literally, writer or secretary; Karim taught the Queen Hindustani.

[74] 'The first mosque in Britain', *Illustrated London News*, 9 November 1889; *Dover Express*, 31 March 1899.

[75] S. M. Siddiq, 'Islam in England' (1934) 22 *Islamic Review* 14, 15; Beckerlegge, 'Followers'; Steven Horton, 'Britain's First Mosque', http://liverpoolhiddenhistory.co.uk/britains-first-mosque/.

[76] *The Standard*, 20 April 1891; *Liverpool Mercury*, 20 April 1891; *Birmingham Daily Post*, 20 April 1891; *Hull Daily Mail*, 20 April 1891.

[77] The wedding had taken place in the bride's parish church of St Giles, Camberwell, that morning: London Metropolitan Archives, p73/gis/044. The couple had then taken the train up to Liverpool for the second ceremony.

[78] The *Liverpool Mercury*, 20 April 1891 noted that the ceremony was 'marked by the severest simplicity, according to Oriental custom' and that 'the customary formula

highlighted some of its more colourful aspects,[79] they also provided reassurance that it was, in essence, not that different from any other wedding service. One even claimed that it 'bore much resemblance' to that used in the Church of England, and even the exceptions that it noted – the recital of the promises 'my sorrow shall be thy sorrow; my happiness shall be thy happiness' and 'she will be a true and constant wife, and shall stand faithful by thy side whether in sickness or in health, whether in prosperity or adversity' – would have resonated with audiences used to the *Book of Common Prayer*.[80] In 1893, *The Crescent* grandly proclaimed that it had 'become almost adopted as a fundamental principle' that any Muslims in England wishing to be married should make a 'pilgrimage' to the Liverpool Mosque,[81] although given that it had conducted only seven marriages by this time it was perhaps a trifle premature for it to compare itself to Mecca.

Even though these ceremonies did not have any legal effect in themselves, they were important as an expression of belief. And it is also important to note that their lack of legal effect was not because of any prohibition on weddings being conducted according to Muslim rites. The non-registration of the Institute was almost certainly determined by the fact that it performed a combination of functions and so would not have qualified as a separate building for these purposes. While one contemporary textbook writer confidently asserted that 'a Musssulman mosque or a pagan temple could not be registered for marriages',[82] there had, since the Places of Worship Registration Act 1855, been no legal obstacle to any non-Christian place of worship being duly certified as a place of worship and registered for marriages.[83] In this respect at least, no difference was drawn between different faiths and denominations.

observed by the followers of the Prophet was used', the Koran not specifying any form of marriage. Other reports explained that the person officiating at it – in this case the vice-president of the Moslem Institute – had to know Arabic, and bore the title of the moulvie, 'no priest-hood being recognised' (*Hull Daily Mail*, 20 April 1891).

[79] The 'long red silken robe', 'tunic of embroidered black velvet', 'gold belt', and 'high white turban' of the moulvie (*Birmingham Daily Post*, 20 April 1891; *Hull Daily Mail*, 20 April 1891), got more attention than the grey dress of the bride (*Liverpool Mercury*, 20 April 1891).

[80] *Birmingham Daily Post*, 20 April 1891; *Liverpool Mercury*, 20 April 1891.

[81] *The Crescent*, 7 June 1893. This may well have been true, given that the Woking mosque had decided not to conduct weddings (*The Crescent*, 9 December 1893).

[82] W. N. M. Geary, *The Law of Marriage and Family Relations: A Manual of Practical Law* (London: Adam and Charles Black, 1892), p. 89.

[83] As noted in Chapter 4, the initial restriction limiting such certification and registration to Christian places of worship had vanished with the Places of Worship Registration Act 1855. In due course the mosque at Woking was to be registered: see Chapter 6.

We will return in due course to the significance of these differences, but now turn to divisions between the Church of England and other religious groups that led to renewed calls for marriage law reform, to divisions between Nonconformists and Catholics on the scope of such reform, and to divisions within Nonconformity as to how reform should be effected.

Divisions

unjust to Nonconformists that marriage privileges given to the Established Church should be withheld from their Christian brethren[84]

The final decades of the nineteenth century were to see various challenges to the status and privileges of the Church of England. While bills for it to be disestablished attracted little support, it had nevertheless undeniably lost many of its powers.[85] And although the majority of marriages were still conducted in the Anglican church, the percentage was falling.[86] There had been a marked increase in the number of places of worship registered for marriage, from 3,811 in 1856 to 7,136 in 1873 and 10,553 by 1890.[87] This increase was most noticeable among Wesleyan Methodists, who now saw themselves as part of a broad Nonconformist community rather than seeing themselves as occupying 'a distinctive position midway between Anglicanism and Dissent'.[88] As the largest denomination in England and Wales after the Church of England, this shift was a significant one.[89] And as the denomination whose ministers most closely resembled Anglican clergy,[90] it was unsurprising that they were the ones who felt the difference in status most keenly.

Against this backdrop it was inevitable that there should be a renewed focus on the different rules that applied to Anglican marriages and

---

[84] *Bristol Mercury*, 8 January 1886.
[85] Owen Chadwick, *The Victorian Church: Part Two* (London: SCM Press Ltd, 1987, first published 1970), ch. VIII.
[86] Anglican weddings accounted for 75% of the total in 1873, 70% in 1887, and 68% in 1899: ONS, 'Marriages in England and Wales 2017' (14 April 2020), table 1.
[87] *Nineteenth Annual Report of the Registrar-General* (London: HMSO, 1858), table VI; *Thirty-Sixth Annual Report of the Registrar-General* (London: HMSO, 1875), table 9; *Fifty-Third Annual Report of the Registrar-General* (London: HMSO, 1890–1891), table 9.
[88] Henry D. Rack, 'Wesleyan Methodism 1849-1902', ch. 2 in Rupert Davies, A. Raymond George, and Gordon Ruff (eds.), *A History of the Methodist Church in Great Britain: Vol. 3* (London: Epworth Press, 1983), p. 119.
[89] Timothy Larsen, 'A Nonconformist Conscience? Free Churchmen in Parliament in Nineteen-Century England' (2005) 24(1) *Parliamentary History* 107.
[90] Chadwick, *The Victorian Church: Part Two*, p. 254.

discussion of whether other religious groups should similarly be able to conduct marriages without the involvement of the state.[91] There were calls among Catholics for wholesale reform – suggesting that civil notice was unnecessary in the light of the existing practice of calling banns within the Catholic church,[92] arguing for the removal of the declarations and contracting words prescribed by law,[93] and seeking the authorisation of priests to conduct marriages without a civil registrar being present. In the view of a Committee appointed by the Catholic Union to consider proposals for reform, no reform could be considered satisfactory unless it put Catholic clergy on 'precisely the same footing' as their Anglican counterparts.[94] From time to time allusion was made to the 1868 Royal Commission, which had addressed all of these points, but hope that its recommendations might yet be implemented was clearly fading.[95] Nonconformists, by contrast, were not seeking to introduce their own preliminaries[96] and made no protest against the prescribed words.[97] It was only the presence of the registrar to which they objected.

A desire for wider reform would not have precluded Catholics from making common cause with Nonconformists on the specific issue of dispensing with the presence of the registrar. But while there were

---

[91] See, e.g., *Bristol Mercury*, 8 January 1886 ('unjust to Nonconformists that marriage privileges given to the Established Church should be withheld from their Christian brethren'); *North-East Daily Gazette*, 29 January 1886 ('The Dissenting minister claims the same rights as his Established Brother').

[92] *The Tablet*, 8 November 1879, 29 May 1880, 10 March 1888.

[93] The complaint about the prescribed words – and in particular how the practice of repeating them separately in the presence of the registrar, after the Catholic ceremony had already taken place, implied 'insufficiency in the Sacramental form' (*The Tablet*, 14 March 1891) was not a new one, but was given additional force by the development of Catholic devotional practices in the later nineteenth century. See also *The Tablet*, 25 October 1879 ('a gratuitous . . . slur'), 21 April 1888 ('an indignity to Catholics'), 21 March 1891 ('a superfluous insult'). Nonconformists, by contrast, generally had no objection to the prescribed words, which had generally been incorporated into Nonconformist wedding services and did not need to be said separately: see *Liverpool Mercury*, 6 January 1886, 13 March 1886.

[94] *The Tablet*, 14 March 1891, noting the views expressed on the 1887 bill (on which see further below).

[95] *The Tablet*, 21 June 1879, 8 November 1879.

[96] That is not to say that there was satisfaction with the existing preliminaries among Nonconformists, but their proposals for reform tended to focus on the need for the process to be made easier and cheaper rather than arguing for its replacement entirely: see, e.g., the proposals advanced by the Liberation Society (*Birmingham Daily Post*, 13 April 1881) and note Sir Richard Webster's comments on the strong feelings among Nonconformists against the extension of banns to their weddings (*Pall Mall Gazette*, 24 March 1886).

[97] *Liverpool Mercury* 13 March 1886.

occasional examples of Catholics commending reforms proposed by
Nonconformists, there was also a strong emphasis on what divided
them. The failure of the latter to campaign for reform of the preliminaries
was attributed to the fact that 'they have no alternative to present. They
do not publish banns'.[98] When it came to who would be able to keep
records, it was suggested that a dividing line could be drawn between
those groups which had a permanent ministry and those that did not; this
was reasonable enough, but the contemptuous reference to ministers
who were 'caught for a season from behind the tail of a plough, or from
behind a counter' was unnecessarily divisive. That particular editorial
concluded by noting that since there was 'no reason why in this matter
Catholics should not stand on the same footing as members of the
Establishment', the potential exclusion of other religious groups was
'not our concern'.[99]

Had Catholics been more willing to engage in the campaign to dispense with the presence of the registrar, they would have added their
weight to the view that the aim of reform was to recognise the authority of
a priest or minister rather than simply to find a substitute for the
registrar. This was something on which Nonconformists were deeply
divided, reflecting the relative weight attached to equality versus independence within different traditions.[100] There were those – chiefly
the Wesleyan Methodists – who prioritised equality with the
Established Church. For them, the issue was one of status, and their
ideal solution was for all their ministers to be automatically entitled to
solemnise marriages just as Anglican clergy were.[101] But there were also
those – primarily Baptists and Congregationalists – who rejected, on
theological grounds, the idea of centralised control, had no ordained
ministry,[102] and saw legal recognition as tantamount to becoming agents

---

[98] *The Tablet*, 10 March 1888.
[99] *The Tablet*, 7 March 1891. See also 'Catholics and the Marriage Laws', *The Tablet*,
      26 March 1898, which managed to position Catholic priests as simultaneously different
      from the Nonconformist minister in 'constant dread of appearing to be socially or
      ecclesiastically the inferior of the parson', the 'foolish and unnecessary' registrar, and
      the Anglican parson to whom he was no more likely to be compared 'than to a policeman
      or a member of the local fire brigade'.
[100] On the centrality of these ideas within Nonconformity, see Timothy Larsen, *Contested
      Christianity: The Political and Social Contexts of Victorian Theology* (Baylor University
      Press, 2003), pp. 5–6.
[101] This was reflected in the terms of the Marriages of Nonconformists (Attendance of
      Registrars) Bill 1891, see later.
[102] See, e.g., Chadwick, *Victorian Church: Part Two*, pp. 254–5, on the way in which
      Congregationalist and Baptist ministers 'became more like laymen' in this period.

of the state.[103] In prioritising freedom, their preferences were as varied as their practices. Some were happy with the status quo,[104] some agreed with the Wesleyans that reform was necessary but thought legal recognition of ministers should be optional, and some favoured a model of reform that would enable marriages to be conducted in their chapels without a registrar being present but which did not depend on the authorisation of a specific minister. It was, in other words, something of a challenge to find a model that would work for all Nonconformists, since none of these solutions would leave them both equal *and* free.

Indeed, a few Nonconformists – again, primarily Baptists and Congregationalists – favoured requiring a register to attend *all* marriages, including those conducted in the Church of England. This, after all, would have had the benefit of achieving equality without compromising their freedom. This preference was shared – albeit for somewhat different reasons – by a number of those who were responsible for registration. In 1886, George Graham, by now retired from his role as Registrar-General, reiterated what he had said to the 1868 Royal Commission about the desirability of civil registrars attending all weddings,[105] and a number of individual registration officials echoed his remarks.[106] For them, considerations of equality were perhaps less important than their desire to ensure better record-keeping, the deficiencies of Anglican clergy in this regard being a perennial complaint.

There were even some Nonconformists who argued in favour of universal civil marriage. In 1881, the Liberation Society contemplated the idea that all marriages should be civil ones, with any religious service that the parties wanted being added afterwards.[107] The Congregationalist

---

[103] For expressions of this view see *Portsmouth Evening News*, 10 April 1886 (reporting the 'most earnest protest' of the Hants Congregational Union 'against any proposal to make Nonconformist ministers State officials by thrusting upon them the duties of responsible registration'); *Manchester Times*, 5 March 1887 (Congregational ministers 'cannot consistently become servants of the State in a religious function'); Parl. Deb., ser. 3, vol. 350, col. 1555, 24 February 1891 (Mr Halley Stewart noting that Baptist and Congregationalist ministers 'do not wish to be constituted State servants, amenable to the State as registrars, and punishable by the State if they neglect their duty').

[104] The presence of the registrar was a benefit in the view of one correspondent, since it 'relieved the officiating minister from all responsibility as to the regularity and validity of the marriage at which he conducted the religious service' (*Daily News*, 27 March 1886).

[105] *Morning Post*, 21 April 1886; and see Chapter 4 for his evidence to the 1868 Commission.

[106] See the views of a superintendent registrar at the Liverpool Committee of the Liberation Society: *Liverpool Mercury*, 1 March 1887.

[107] Its full title – the Society for the Liberation of Religion from State Patronage and Control – left its agenda in no doubt. On its views on civil weddings, see *Birmingham Daily Post*, 13 April 1881.

MP Alfred Illingworth similarly questioned why the state should concern itself with religious ceremonies when all the safeguards it required would be secured by civil marriage.[108] With an increasing number of countries across the globe removing the possibility of marrying according to religious rites, this was not as fantastical a suggestion as it would have been a few years earlier. While proponents (and opponents) of universal civil marriage still generally invoked the example of France, they could also have pointed to its adoption in Italy, Germany, Switzerland, and Hungary, as well as in a number of former Spanish colonies in South America.[109]

While even ardent advocates of universal civil marriage recognised that it was unlikely to be enacted,[110] some of the arguments put forward in its favour highlighted existing problems in the law of marriage and made the task of those seeking authorisation for their ministers more challenging. As one writer argued, the number of cases 'in which persons imagined that they were married when they were not' could be seen as a reason to make 'a simple legal formality, gone through in the presence of the registrar or some other public official, the sole test of a legal marriage' and leaving any religious ceremony 'to the option of the parties'.[111] The cases involving irregular Jewish ceremonies had exposed the gulf that might exist between religious and legal conceptions of marriage. The 1880s also saw evidence of earlier non-compliance emerging, with the Greek Marriages Act 1884 being passed to validate ceremonies that had been conducted at the two (unregistered) Greek Orthodox churches in London and by Greek Orthodox priests in the homes of the contracting parties.[112] Since a belief in the validity of one's

---

[108] Parl. Deb., ser. 3, vol. 303, col. 1453, 19 March 1886; see also vol. 350, col. 1545, 24 February 1891.

[109] For an overview of universal civil marriage, see Rebecca Probert, 'State and Law' in Paul Puschmann (ed.) *A Cultural History of Marriage in the Age of Empires* (London: Bloomsbury, 2020).

[110] See, e.g., *Birmingham Daily Post*, 13 April 1881, noting the alternative suggestions for reform made by the Liberation Society on the basis that proposals for universal civil marriage were 'not likely to receive general sanction'.

[111] A. B. Basset, 'Our Marriage Laws a Mass of Anomalies', in H. Quilter (ed.), *Is Marriage a Failure?* (London: Swan Sonnenschein & Co, 1888), p. 20.

[112] The churches in question were the Chapel of the Greek Community in Finsbury Circus and the Greek Church of the Saviour, in London Wall: *London Gazette*, 30 November 1883. The preamble to the Greek Marriages Act 1884 referred to ceremonies having taken place there between 1837 and 1857, while the register submitted to the Principal Probate Registry covered the period up to 1865. The Act permitted any party to the marriage, and child or grandchild, or any person interested in the validity of

marriage did not make it so,[113] and the presumptions in favour of marriage offered no assistance in cases of known non-compliance,[114] those who had gone through a religious-only marriage ceremony were left vulnerable.

Nor were misunderstandings confined to ceremonies that took place entirely outside the legal framework. At the same time that the Greek Marriages Bill 1884 was being debated, Parliament was also being asked to pass legislation to validate marriages that had taken place in a Congregational church that had been certified as a place of worship but only belatedly registered for marriages.[115] And as ever, marriages in the Anglican church were even more susceptible to problems. In addition to the perennial issue of the celebration of marriages in unlicensed chapels of ease[116] and new churches,[117] instances had arisen in which ceremonies were

such a marriage, to apply for a decree that such marriages were valid. There were three preconditions to recognition: that it should have been solemnised according to the rites of the Greek Orthodox Church; that it should have been believed to be a valid marriage; and that it should have been entered in the register book by the priest who had conducted the ceremony. If the marriage had already been declared to be invalid, or either of the parties had married a third person, then no such decree could be sought.

[113] It is important here to draw a distinction between belief and reputation. Where the courts were faced with questions as to whether a wedding had taken place many years earlier, evidence that the couple had lived together as husband and wife, and been accepted by the community as such, generated a presumption that there had been a marriage: Probert, 'Presumptions'. The reason why reliance was placed on cohabitation and reputation was generally that one or both of the parties were dead and unable to provide proof of their wedding, the cases being concerned with the issue of who was entitled to inherit from them (see, e.g., *Collins* v. *Bishop* (1878) 48 LJ Ch 31; *Murray* v. *Milner* (1879) 12 Ch D. 845; 'Habit and Repute in England' (1881) *The Law Times* 352; *Re Ivory* (1886) 2 TLR 468; c.f. *Andrewes* v. *Uthwatt* (1886) 2 TLR 895, where the evidence that the parties were reputed to be husband and wife was not sufficiently convincing).

[114] Where there was evidence that the couple had gone through a ceremony of marriage of the kind envisaged by English law, the courts would, in the absence of other evidence, presume that everything needful had been done: Probert, 'Presumptions'.

[115] Wood Green Congregational Church Marriage Legalization Act 1884.

[116] This might occur if an existing chapel of ease had been pulled down and rebuilt without being reconsecrated (Marriages Confirmation (Fulford Chapel) Act 1873; Marriages Confirmation (Gretton Chapel) Act 1873; Cove Chapel, Tiverton, Marriages Legalization Act 1873), or if one had been consecrated but not licensed (Marriages Confirmation (Eton) Act 1873; Marriages Confirmation (Pooley Bridge) Act 1874; Marriages Confirmation (Bentley) Act 1874; Marriages (St James' Chapel of Ease) Buxton 1876 Act; Marriages Legalisation, St Peters' Almondsbury Act 1877; District of St John Cowley Act 1885).

[117] Stopsley Marriage Legalization Act 1884 validated marriages celebrated in the District Church of Stopsley, the Ecclesiastical Commissioners having failed to give the necessary approval for the district to be deemed as a separate parish.

conducted by persons who were not in Holy Orders.[118] The passage
of legislation to declare that such marriages were valid was intended
to provide reassurance rather than to imply that they would otherwise
have been void; as the Attorney-General noted when introducing the
Marriages Legalization Bill 1884, '[h]is own opinion was that those
marriages were valid; but it was important not to have any question
about them'.[119] Nonetheless, against this backdrop of failures by
religious bodies, it is unsurprising that there were concerns about
any proposal to delegate more power to religious groups.

Such concerns were only exacerbated by the division between what
might be termed 'new' and 'newer' Nonconformity. The Salvation
Army, initially founded in the 1860s as the East London Christian
Mission, had accrued around 25,000 members by 1880 and was growing fast.[120] It had no clergy, but a band of 'officers' who were given
a few weeks' training and then dispatched to lead a 'campaign of
salvation' among the poorest and most dispossessed.[121] Another new,
albeit much smaller group were the Christadelphians,[122] who similarly
lacked any concept of a clergy. Since such groups were beginning to
register their places of worship for marriage, any reforms would need
to apply to them as well as to the more established Nonconformist
groups. It was easy to make a case for dispensing with the presence of
the registrar. As the next section will show, it was far harder to decide
who would replace him.

[118] The Marriages Legalization Bill 1884 was introduced to deal with the difficulty that had
arisen 'through a person who was not in Holy Orders having represented himself as
a clergyman and obtained a position as a licensed curate' and having solemnised 'a
considerable number of marriages'. Four years later the Marriages Validation Act 1888
dealt with the 'validity of certain marriages performed by a person who pretended to be
a clergyman, who professed that he had taken Orders in the Church of Rome, and who
was in consequence received into the English Church'.
[119] Parl. Deb., ser. 3, vol. 287, col. 1295, 5 May 1884.
[120] Field, *Periodizing Secularisation*, p. 60. It adopted the name 'Salvation Army' in
1878.
[121] Rosman, *Evolution of the English Churches*, p. 212. The earliest reference to a Salvation
Army building being registered for weddings is that in the *London Gazette*, 16 June 1876,
noting that the Christian Mission Hall in St Johns Street, Wellingborough, had been
registered on 24 May.
[122] Field, *Periodizing Secularisation*, Table 3.5. The *Belfast Newsletter*, 1 April 1867, referred
to there being a 'Christadelphian Synagogue' at Halifax, and in 1888 its meeting room
there was registered for weddings (*London Gazette*, 21 February 1888).

Dispensing with the Registrar

complaints have been made that Religious Bodies do not desire to have present
at their services persons who are not in sympathy with the religious ceremony
which is being performed[123]

The campaign to dispense with the presence of the registrar at marriages in registered places of worship began with little fanfare. Bills were introduced in 1880 and 1881 but failed to make any progress[124] and attracted virtually no attention outside Parliament. From the mid-1880s, however, the campaign intensified as the Wesleyans threw their weight behind it. Certain sections of the press were particularly active in championing the Nonconformist cause. The need for a registrar to be present was lambasted as inconvenient for all concerned,[125] needlessly expensive,[126] and a slur on Nonconformity.[127] There was no hint in the debates of the former policy of appointing registrars who would be in sympathy with the congregations whose marriages they were attending; instead, commentators highlighted how these 'Government officials'[128] were all too 'ready to give a snub whenever they could to the Nonconformist ministry'.[129]

While it was a single-issue campaign,[130] it was far from simple. The issue was not just who would be responsible for registering the marriage – although this, given the divisions within Nonconformity, was challenging enough – but *how* they would do so. Registered places of worship were not issued with their own register books; the registrar brought the official

---

[123] Parl. Deb., ser. 3, vol. 304, cols. 210–8, 29 March 1886 (Sir Richard Webster).

[124] Marriages Registration Bill 1880, introduced 21 May 1880 (*JHC*, vol. 135, p. 143, Bill No. 140); Marriages Registration Bill 1881, introduced 28 February 1881 (*JHC*, vol. 136, p. 99, Bill No. 97); Marriages Registration (No. 2) Bill 1881, introduced 20 August 1881 (*JHC*, vol. 136, p. 481, Bill No. 254).

[125] *Northern Echo*, 16 March 1886.

[126] *Liverpool Mercury*, 6 January 1886; see also the letters in the *Daily News*, 27 March 1886, putting the cost of marrying in a Nonconformist chapel at 13s, as compared to 7s in the Church of England (on the basis that 5s would be paid to the minister as well as to the registrar).

[127] *Liverpool Mercury*, 6 January 1886, 13 March 1886 ('a brand on nonconformity'); *North-East Daily Gazette*, 29 January 1886 ('an interference'); *Daily News*, 27 March 1886 ('a slur on the whole service'); *Manchester Times*, 5 March 1887 ('a badge of inferiority').

[128] *Liverpool Mercury*, 6 January 1886, 13 March 1886.

[129] *Liverpool Mercury*, 1 March 1887, reporting the comments at a conference promoted by the Liverpool Committee of the Liberation Society.

[130] There were, it should be noted, occasional proposals for wider reform: see e.g. 'The Marriage Laws of England', *The Times*, 15 August 1879; *JHC*, vol. 135, p. 11, 6 February 1880.

register with him, and took it away again. In broad terms, proposals for reform adopted one of two strategies. One was to issue register books to specific authorised ministers who would conduct and register marriages. The other was to require the person officiating at the marriage, whoever this might be, to complete certain prescribed documentation confirming that the marriage had taken place and return it to the superintendent registrar.

The latter neatly sidestepped the question of the status of the person officiating, and obviated the need for new register books to be issued. The risk, however, was that it would leave marriage entirely unregulated. While the expectation underpinning the proposal was that marriages would still have to be celebrated in a registered place of worship, there was nothing in it to prevent marriages being conducted by anyone, or anywhere. The clutch of bills that came before Parliament in 1884 provided a powerful reminder of how often mistakes were made regarding where weddings could take place, and how some religious groups might not marry in a place of worship at all.[131] With these recent examples of non-compliance fresh in their minds, it was unlikely that MPs would be willing to accept a solution that simply removed the registrar without any attempt to provide a substitute who was equally knowable, traceable, and accountable.

To provide an alternative means of dealing with some of the practical problems that had arisen, in 1886 the Protestant Dissenting Deputies promoted a bill to extend the hours within which weddings could take place.[132] This addressed the fact that many of the complaints relating to registrars focused on the difficulty of securing their attendance within the four hours permitted by law: for some, there was the inconvenience of marrying at 8am, for others, there was tension as the clock ticked towards noon with no sign of him arriving.[133] The MP introducing the bill, Carvell Williams, suggested that if the permitted hours were extended, 'the difficulty would be so minimised as almost to disappear'.[134] This

---

[131] See the Stopsley Marriage Legalization Act 1884, the Wood Green Congregational Church Marriage Legalization Act 1884, and the Greek Marriages Act 1884, discussed above.

[132] On their opposition to more wide-ranging reform, see B.L. Manning, *The Protestant Dissenting Deputies* (Cambridge: Cambridge University Press, 1952, ed. Greenwood), p. 283.

[133] See e.g. *Liverpool Mercury*, 6 January 1886, 13 March 1886; *Daily News*, 27 March 1886.

[134] *Manchester Times*, 23 January 1886, reporting his letter to *The Nonconformist*; see also Parl. Deb., ser. 3, vol. 303, col. 1448, 19 March 1886.

consideration was not the only motivating factor for the proposed extension,[135] but it was certainly a major one, and the bill passed with relative ease.[136]

While its passage did not dampen the enthusiasm for dispensing with the registrar altogether, the various measures that were proposed failed to make any progress. Political as well as religious allegiances played a part in this, as was illustrated by the opposition of Liberal Nonconformists to the bill put forward by the new Conservative government in 1887.[137] Admittedly, its provisions were particularly restrictive; while nominated ministers would have been allowed to register marriages, the ability to make such nominations would have been limited to those religious groups that had a central organisation capable of 'maintaining discipline ... by censure and removal' and ensuring that its ministers observed the requirements of the law.[138] This, as many pointed out, would pose particular problems for Congregationalists and Baptists, for whom independence from any such control was fundamental, as well as excluding Methodist lay preachers.[139] Faced with vitriolic comments about the deficiencies of the bill and his lack of understanding of Nonconformists,[140] it was small wonder that Sir Richard Webster chose to withdraw it, commenting tartly on 'the persistent opposition with which the Bill has been met by those who are unwilling that any grievance should be removed'.[141]

---

[135] Parl. Deb., ser. 3, vol. 303, cols. 1448–54, 19 March 1886.

[136] Marriage Act 1886.

[137] Marriages (Attendance of Registrars) Bill 1887. For the equally hostile reaction to the Marriages (Attendance of Registrars) Bill 1886, introduced by the Conservative Sir Richard Webster while in opposition, see Parl. Deb., ser. 3, vol. 304, cols. 215 and 218 (Mr Illingworth and Mr Carvell Williams), 29 March 1886. On the alignment between Nonconformity and Liberalism see Timothy Larsen, 'A Nonconformist Conscience? Free Churchmen in Parliament in Nineteenth-Century England' (2005) 24(1) *Parliamentary History* 107.

[138] Marriages (Attendance of Registrars) Bill 1887, cl. 2.

[139] *Manchester Times*, 5 March 1887; *Leeds Mercury*, 5 April 1887. See also the *North Wales Chronicle*, 12 March 1887, which estimated that 'about one-half of the total body of Nonconformists will be left outside the operation of the Attorney-General's Bill'.

[140] The bill was variously described as a 'bungling piece of work' (*Manchester Times*, 5 March 1887), 'full to the brim of vexatious anomalies, annoying inequalities, and perfectly impossible conditions' (*Leeds Mercury*, 18 March 1887), and 'ill-advised, futile and objectionable' (*North Devon Journal*, 24 March 1887), while a local branch of the Liberation Society regretted that it was 'hopelessly spoiled by want of knowledge of Nonconformist organisations' (*Manchester Courier*, 30 March 1887).

[141] Parl. Deb., ser. 3, vol. 317, col. 2006, 25 July 1887.

In the light of the difficulties of legislating for Nonconformists as a whole,[142] and the even more heated debates occasioned by an attempt to legislate for the Wesleyan Methodist Society alone,[143] matters were referred to a Select Committee.[144] Having heard from representatives of a variety of Nonconformist bodies,[145] as well as from the Registrar-General and others involved in the operation of the law, the Committee's report claimed that there was 'widespread dissatisfaction' among Nonconformists as to the operation of the 1836 Act.[146] The Committee was particularly keen to disabuse readers of any impression that the compulsory presence of the registrar was primarily a grievance felt by ministers about their ecclesiastical status. Its conclusion was that this particular requirement 'prevents large numbers of Nonconformists who would otherwise be married by their own ministers in their places of worship from being so married',[147] and it recommended that this hardship should be removed.

It was certainly true that the percentage of weddings in Nonconformist places of worship was much lower than one might have expected. Throughout the period, weddings in Nonconformist places of worship

[142] Not for want of trying: see the Nonconformist Marriages (Attendance of Registrars) Bill 1888, introduced 29 February 1888; Marriages of Nonconformists (Attendance of Registrars) (No. 2) Bill 1888, introduced 12 April 1888; Nonconformist Marriages (Registrars' Attendance) Bill 1889, introduced 22 February 1889; Registrars' (Marriages Attendance) Bill 1893, introduced 1 February 1893. None secured a second reading.

[143] The Marriages of Nonconformists (Attendance of Registrars) Bill 1891 proposed that it should be lawful 'for all ministers of the Wesleyan Methodist Society, under the direction of the Wesleyan Methodist Conference' to conduct marriages in registered places of worship without a registrar being present (Bill No. 144, as printed 2 December 1891). It envisaged that the minister would be responsible for certifying that the ceremony had taken place, and that a failure to do so within seven days would result in a fine of 40 shillings. It did at least make it to Committee, but feelings were running so high that its sponsor, Henry Farmer-Atkinson, complained in Parliament of being libelled in the press: Parl. Deb., ser. 3, vol. 351, col. 266, 5 March 1891.

[144] Parl. Deb., ser. 4, vol. 10, col. 831, 22 March 1893.

[145] The Committee heard from 10 witnesses representing the Wesleyan Methodist Conference, the London Methodist Council, the Wesleyan Methodist Lay Preachers' Association, the Free Methodist Church, the Conference of the Primitive Methodist Church, the Dissenting Deputies, the General Committee of the Congregational Union, the General Baptist Association, the Southern Baptist Association, Independent Churches in Lancashire, and the Society of Friends. The Catholic Church was invited to give evidence but chose not to do so, simply drawing the Committee's attention to the evidence given by the Catholic Bishops to the Royal Commission of 1868.

[146] *Report from the Select Committee on Nonconformist Marriages (Attendance of Registrars)* (London: HMSO, 1893), p. iv.

[147] *Ibid*, p. viii.

only accounted for around 11–12 per cent of the total,[148] at a time when over a quarter of the population regularly attended a Nonconformist place of worship.[149] But the 'striking contrast' that the Committee identified between the relative number of weddings celebrated in the Established and Nonconformist churches and their respective places of worship was not quite as striking when it was taken into account that over half of Nonconformist places of worship were not registered for weddings in the first place.[150]

Committed Nonconformists might be willing to travel some distance to the nearest chapel of their denomination that *had* been registered, but this would not always have been a viable option. Other committed Nonconformists without access to a registered chapel preferred to marry in the register office. Some of those who could have married in their local chapel, and might have done so in other circumstances, may have been swayed by considerations of cost and convenience. A number of witnesses had suggested that many Nonconformists chose to get married in the parish church because it was easier and cheaper than doing so in their own place of worship.[151] But the reasons they gave related primarily to the process of giving notice at the register office before the wedding rather than to the presence of the registrar.[152]

This brings us back to the claim of the Committee that it was the requirement that a registrar be present that was deterring couples from marrying in chapel. The Committee's foregrounding of the registrar as the problem was undoubtedly motivated by concerns about the relative

---

[148] ONS, *Dataset: Marriages in England and Wales 2017* (14 April 2020), table 1.

[149] Field, *Periodizing Secularization*, Table 9.2. C.f. Floud and Thane, who rely on the fact that there were 'roughly as many Nonconformist chapel-goers as Anglican church-goers' on Census Sunday and ask why Nonconformist marriages never approached 50% ('Debate', p. 147); and Olive Anderson, who claims that the 12% of marriages in Nonconformist chapels is 'very much the level one would have expected' ('A Rejoinder' (1979) 84 *Past and Present* 155, p. 161). Admittedly, only 13–14% of the population were *members* of a Nonconformist church, but there is no indication that Nonconformist churches limited weddings in their churches to members.

[150] The Committee specifically referred to Nonconformist places of worship, relying on figures from 1882. In that year the Registrar-General reported that there was a total of 22,070 certified places of worship, of which 9,005 (41%) were registered for weddings: *Forty-Fifth Annual Report of the Registrar-General* (London: HMSO, 1884), p. x.

[151] *Report from the Select Committee on Nonconformist Marriages*, pp. 51, 57.

[152] *Ibid*, pp. 14, 45, 122, 128, 134, The Reverend James Guinness Rogers, a Congregationalist minister, did tell the Committee that there were members of his congregation 'who would not be married at the chapel . . . because the presence of the registrar is obnoxious to them', but he rather undermined this by adding that he had no desire to be a registrar and thought that registrars should be present at all weddings.

status of Nonconformist ministers as compared to Anglican clergy.[153] That the Committee sought to show that this had an impact on couples was clearly tactical, intended to bolster the case for reform. The fact that it also made additional proposals for reform – such as increasing the facilities for giving notice and reducing the fee charged for a building to be registered – indicated that it was aware that the presence of the registrar was not the only obstacle to marrying in a registered place of worship.[154] But the fact that these proposals came some way down a long list meant that the focus remained on the issue of how to dispense with the registrar.

There was nothing in the terms of the bill that was introduced in February 1898 to suggest that it would enjoy any more success than its predecessors in achieving this.[155] When it reached Committee stage, however, Sir Richard Webster – who was back in post as Attorney-General – took a hand. His proposal was that each Nonconformist church should be issued with its own register – as the Established Church was – once a person had been authorised to take responsibility for the custody of that register, the registration of marriages, and the making of returns.[156] Authorisation would be the responsibility of the governing body of the registered building.[157] And his new terminology of 'authorised person' seemed a graceful compromise between the competing concepts of 'authorised minister' and 'person officiating'. Despite some blatantly partisan attempts by one Wesleyan Methodist MP, Robert Perks, to press the case for all Wesleyan Methodist ministers to be authorised en bloc,[158] there was broad acceptance that Webster's proposals would work for all Nonconformists.[159] Some clearly thought that the need for

[153] For a particularly critical take on the Committee see Anderson, 'Rejoinder', pp. 155–7.
[154] *Ibid*, pp. viii–ix.
[155] *JHC*, vol. 153, p. 19. Like many of its predecessors, the Nonconformist Marriages (Attendance of Registrars) Bill, as printed on 11 February 1898, simply required the person officiating to return the paperwork.
[156] Parl. Deb., ser. 4, vol. 59, cols. 334, 350.
[157] Parl. Deb., ser. 4, vol. 59, col. 337.
[158] See his suggestion that the official list of the 1,700 or so ministers of the Wesleyan Methodist Church should be sent to the Registrar-General each year and that each of them would be authorised to conduct weddings: Parl. Deb., ser. 4, vol. 59, col. 338. Perks had been a member of the 1893 Committee and had been responsible for drafting its report (although the rest of the Committee had removed a particularly self-congratulatory paragraph reporting the favourable responses to the bill that Perks himself had put forward).
[159] The Congregationalist MP for Dewsbury, Mark Oldroyd, noted that the proposed mode of appointing authorised persons would 'work admirably well so far as the

an authorised person to be appointed by a specific place of worship was mitigated by the provision that any person so authorised could officiate at any other registered building.[160] There were inevitably some grumbles about the transitional arrangements requiring a fee to be paid to displaced registrars, but this was accepted as necessary to secure reform.

But amid the flurry of minor textual amendments made to the bill during its final stages in the House of Commons there was one in particular that fundamentally changed what it meant to be authorised. The removal of any references to an authorised person 'officiating at' or 'solemnising' a wedding made their role an essentially passive one.[161] A further amendment limited their sphere of operation to the registration district of the place of worship that had appointed them,[162] removing the flexibility that had been praised at Committee stage. Perhaps no one spotted the significance of these changes, dazzled by the prospect of reform finally becoming a reality. Certainly no one queried it. With only a few days left before the end of the session, debate in the House of Lords was limited, and the Act finally received Royal Assent on 12 August 1898.

Viewed from one perspective, the Marriage Act 1898 was a success. It finally provided a means whereby Nonconformist ministers and Catholic priests could conduct weddings in registered buildings without a registrar being present. And it did so in a way that sidestepped any difficult question that might arise about who was to be authorised: an authorised person did not have to be a minister at all, or play any role in conducting the ceremony. Like a registrar, they just had to be there. Yet this compromise meant that it fell far short of what many of those campaigning for reform had wanted.

The true implications of the 1898 Act only became clear when the Registrar-General issued a detailed set of regulations setting out the role of authorised persons and the safekeeping of marriage registers.[163] One new precondition was that a registered building must have an iron safe in

---

Congregational body is concerned', and thought that it would work for the Baptists as well: Parl. Deb., ser. 4, vol. 59, col. 339.

[160] Parl. Deb., ser. 4, vol. 59, cols. 347–8.

[161] Parl. Deb., ser. 4, vol. 63, cols. 1106–7, 3 August 1898.

[162] *Ibid.*

[163] The 1898 Act had conferred power on the Registrar-General, subject to the approval of the Local Government Board, to make rules 'with respect to the forms to be used for the purposes of this Act; the custody of documents required for the purposes of this Act; the duties of registrars, superintendent registrars, and authorised persons under this Act;

which registers could be kept.[164] In vain was it protested that this would pose an obstacle for smaller and poorer groups and that no such security was required in Anglican churches.[165] There were also vociferous complaints regarding 'red-tape and troublesome requirements',[166] with a number of commentators drawing attention to the fact that the new regulations filled at least thirty pages.[167] The detail of the regulations was particularly off-putting when viewed alongside the threateningly vague provision that a failure to comply with any of those regulations, or any other requirement under the Act, would constitute an offence.[168] The specified penalties were £10, £50, or imprisonment for two years with hard labour, but the Act did not specify which applied to which aspects of noncompliance. Nor was the letter sent to authorised persons along with the book of rules and regulations calculated to provide reassurance: individuals were told that 'in your own interests, as well as in those of the persons to be married by you, and also in view of the legal consequences involved, it is of the utmost importance that you should make yourself thoroughly acquainted with the Rules and Regulations in order that nothing may be done or left undone by you in your official capacity which is contrary to any of them'.[169]

Almost as worrying were the suggestions that marriages might be invalidated if the person officiating had not been properly authorised. It was suggested that the trustees required to make the appointment

---

any matter which may under this Act be prescribed; and generally for carrying into effect the provisions of this Act'. (Marriage Act 1898, s. 16).

[164] This was more specific than the provision in the 1898 Act allowing the Registrar-General to refuse to allow an authorised person to be appointed if he was not satisfied that sufficient security existed for the registration of marriages and the safe custody of the register books (s. 7(4)).

[165] *Leeds Mercury*, 20 March 1899; 'Marriage Made Easier: A New Act for the First of April', *Daily News*, 31 March 1899; 'The New Marriage Law', *Western Daily Press*, 1 April 1899; 'The New Nonconformist Marriage Act: How it is Likely to Work in Leeds', *Leeds Mercury*, 1 April 1899; *Sheffield Independent*, 6 April 1899, 8 April 1899; *Hampshire Telegraph*, 8 April 1899. See also *Leeds Mercury*, 15 June 1899, reporting the resolution of the Manchester Conference of the Methodist New Connexion that 'the Registrar-General has needlessly added to the difficulties of adopting and carrying out the Act by the requirements and instructions he has issued'.

[166] *Sheffield Independent*, 6 April 1899.

[167] 'Marriage Made Easier: A New Act for the First of April', *Daily News*, 31 March 1899 noted the '32 closely-printed octavo pages of small type'; *Western Times*, 1 April 1899 commented on the 'tedious regulation' of 'so minute and complicated a character that they occupy over thirty pages of printed matter'.

[168] Marriage Act 1898, s. 12.

[169] Devon Heritage Centre: 5385D/5.

would need to have some legal interest in the registered building.[170] The view of the Attorney-General was that the Act required no particular mode of selection but that a marriage solemnised in the presence of a person who was not authorised would not be valid.[171] When such worries were combined with the lack of any formal provision for authorised persons to be remunerated,[172] the role was hardly an attractive one.[173] As one of the more temperate commentaries noted, 'the responsibilities and emoluments of the office may be regarded as disproportionate'.[174]

Moreover, under the Act authorisation was not an acknowledgement of the status of those who held a particular role but simply permission to act as a replacement registrar.[175] It was very far from giving Nonconformist ministers the same status as Anglican clergy.[176] The new register books that were issued to registered buildings upon an authorised person being appointed seem to have been designed to press this point home. According to the printed form, a wedding was conducted 'in the presence of' an authorised person. This was the same phrase that was used in relation to the witnesses. It was a small but significant change from the word 'by' that had appeared in the marriage registers issued under the 1836 Act. 'By' implied an active role, 'in the presence of', a purely passive one.

---

[170] *Cheshire Observer*, 25 March 1899.

[171] Parl. Deb., ser. 4, vol. 70, col. 388, 24 April 1899. The somewhat convoluted amendment to the 1836 Act setting out when a marriage would be void was ambiguous on this point; see further Chapter 7.

[172] They were to be paid sixpence by the Superintendent Registrar for every entry in the certified copy of the marriage register that they were required to submit every quarter. This sum came out of the fee paid by couples but there was no statutory fee payable by couples to the authorised person for officiating at the wedding.

[173] 'The Humour of the New Marriage Act', *Dover Express*, 24 February 1899. A number of newspapers quoted the case of the Rev. J. Britton, who had besought the prayers of his brethren on becoming an authorised person: *Leeds Mercury*, 1 April 1899; *Yorkshire Evening Post*, 1 April 1899; *Newcastle Courant*, 8 April 1899.

[174] *Sheffield Evening Telegraph*, 10 April 1899. See also the Cardiff registrar who noted that 'the regulations are very strict and the penalties heavy': *Western Mail*, 1 April 1899.

[175] For examples of authorised persons being described in this way see 'The New Marriage Law', *Western Daily Press*, 1 April 1899 ('amateur registrars'); *Western Mail*, 1 April 1899; *Sheffield Independent*, 6 April 1899.

[176] For complaints about the continuing lack of equality see *Leeds Mercury*, 8 April 1899, 15 June 1899; *Sheffield Independent*, 8 April 1899; *Leeds Times*, 8 April 1899; 'New Marriage Act: Yorkshire Presbyterians' Opinion', *Hull Daily Mail*, 9 May 1899; *Liverpool Mercury*, 16 November 1899.

While this change might seem to follow naturally from the fact that the legislation only required the presence of the authorised person, it was in fact entirely unnecessary. The GRO clearly expected that most authorised persons would be ministers of some kind.[177] Even if they were not, there was no reason why the marriage should not be recorded in the same way as before, with the authorised person signing after the minister by whom the ceremony had been conducted, just as registrars had always done.[178] And in those rare cases of a lay authorised person officiating at a wedding with no minister present, it would have been perfectly simple just to cross out 'by' and substitute 'before' – again, just as registrars had done in this situation.[179] The new wording meant that whenever a marriage was recorded by an authorised person, his role as minister – or the role of any other minister conducting the service – was simply irrelevant. It might in retrospect seem like a small point, but it went to the heart of questions about the status of those conducting non-Anglican weddings.

Some religious groups were happy with the 1898 Act, or at least willing to adopt it.[180] But given that it did not give Nonconformist ministers the status that many had hoped for, it is unsurprising that take-up was more limited than the campaign for reform might have suggested would be the case. Only a minority of registered buildings took the step of appointing their own authorised persons; as the Registrar-General reported, by the end of 1900 only 1,495 out of 12,861 had done so. The Wesleyan Methodists accounted for around half of these, and other Methodist denominations for a further one-sixth; just over one-quarter were Congregational and Baptist, and the remainder were drawn from

---

[177] Their standard printed letter to newly appointed authorised persons began with the words 'Reverend Sir', with 'Reverend' being crossed out when they wrote to lay persons: see the letter confirming Thomas Saunders as the duly authorised person for the Gospel Hall in Kingsbridge (Devon Heritage Centre: 5385D/5).

[178] Indeed, authorised persons were instructed that if a separate minister conducted the ceremony, then both of them should sign the entry in the register.

[179] As the instructions given to authorised persons made clear, they would have to adapt the printed form in this scenario in any case, by crossing out the printed words 'according to the Rites and Ceremonies'.

[180] *Sheffield Independent*, 8 April 1899 (letter to the editor from JW Flint noting the adoption of the Act among Congregational churches); *York Herald*, 8 May 1899 (report of the Leeds and York Primitive Methodist district meeting and the recommendation that trustees avail themselves of the Act); *Sunderland Daily Echo*, 10 July 1899 (letter from the Rev. William Spensley testifying to the 'workableness' of the new Act and arguing that being able to avoid the 'humiliation' of the registrar's presence was worth the small amount of trouble involved); *Western Times*, 9 August 1899, noting the first marriage in Southernhay Wesleyan Chapel in Exeter 'under the new and improved arrangements'.

a range of other denominations, or were classified as unsectarian.[181] Catholics, however, were noticeably absent from the list, largely because of an additional provision requiring episcopal sanction for their appointment.[182]

It is also unsurprising that there was no dramatic change in how couples married in the wake of the 1898 Act. After all, the Act had done nothing to address the suggestion that it should be made easier to give notice, or to make it easier to register a building for weddings. There was a small increase in the number and proportion of weddings in registered places of worship, and places that had appointed their own authorised person had, on average, slightly more weddings than those that had not.[183] But it may have been the case that more popular chapels were more likely to appoint an authorised person, rather than that chapels with an authorised person were more popular. Overall, most weddings in registered buildings continued to take place before a registrar, and the 1898 Act was regarded as neither a satisfactory nor a final resolution of the issues.[184]

Conclusion

The differences and divisions of the late nineteenth century explain why the campaign for reform coalesced around the single issue of dispensing with the registrar and why the 1898 Act took the form that it did. No government had any appetite for pressing ahead with the more radical approach proposed by the 1868 Royal Commission, or even with the other proposals for wider reform that were made from time to time. With the emergence of new and more informally organised Nonconformist groups, the evidence of noncompliance within the Greek Orthodox community and among Jewish immigrants, and the first recorded Muslim marriage ceremonies, it was clear that delegating control over weddings to religious groups would result in considerable uncertainty about marital status. Divisions between Catholics and Nonconformists, and among different Nonconformists, meant that even the more limited

---

[181] *Sixty-Third Annual Report of the Registrar-General* (London: HMSO, 1902), pp. vi-viii.

[182] Marriage Act 1898, s. 1(3); on the slowness of the Catholic bishops to sanction the appointment of authorised persons, see Chapter 6.

[183] In 1900 the average number of weddings celebrated in each registered building with an authorised person was 3.8, as compared to 2.3 for registered buildings without an authorised person: *Sixty-Third Annual Report*, p. viii and Table 6.

[184] 'The New Marriage Law', *Western Daily Press*, 1 April 1899; *Leeds Times*, 8 April 1899.

issue of dispensing with the registrar could not be resolved simply by conferring authority on priests and ministers.

Yet while the solution adopted in the 1898 Act was perhaps inevitable in the light of these differences and divisions, the removal from the bill of any reference to authorised persons 'solemnising' marriages, the regulations governing their appointment and actions, and the form of the new registers dispatched to them all served to undermine their status and make the role less attractive. The 1898 Act also added a yet further layer of complexity to the law governing weddings. For the future, how marriages were to be registered depended on whether they were conducted in the presence of a registrar or an authorised person, and the means by which authorised persons could be appointed depended on whether they were Catholic or Protestant. And in terms of the ability of individuals to marry in accordance with their beliefs, little had changed as a result of the 1898 Act.

Indeed, one new division had been introduced. Only Christian places of worship could appoint an authorised person at all.[185] That particular limitation was not made explicit at the time, and so went unnoticed. But it was to acquire much more significance in the following decades, as the next chapter will show.

---

[185] This was not made explicit on the face of the Act, but was implicit in the definition of a registered building as 'any building registered for solemnising marriages therein under the Marriage Act, 1836'. The original version of the bill had defined it as any building that had been registered for religious worship and certified under the Places of Worship Registration Act 1855, which would have included non-Christian places of worship.

6

Competing Conceptions of Marriage, 1900–1919

The first two decades of the twentieth century were to see new challenges to the laws governing both marriage and weddings emerging on all sides. At the heart of these different challenges – which variously involved Anglican, Catholic, Jewish, Sikh, Hindu, and Muslim conceptions of marriage – lay the question of the relationship between the law as set out in statute and the law of an individual's own religion. Whenever this issue came before the courts, the judges were clear that there was one single conception of marriage in England and Wales, and that this was the same regardless of the religion of the parties or how they had married. As Cozens Hardy, the Master of the Rolls, declared, the contract of marriage was 'one and the same thing' whether it was made 'in church with religious vows superadded ... in a Nonconformist chapel with religious ceremonies ... or before a registrar, without any religious ceremonies'.[1]

The absences from this list were telling. There were separate controversies surrounding the relationship between the Roman Catholic church's laws on marriage and those of the state, and about Jewish religious-only ceremonies. The lack of any mention of the possibility of marrying in a mosque, temple, or gurdwara was also unsurprising: at the time he spoke these words, the existing mosques had fallen into abeyance,[2] no temples had been built, and the only gurdwara was inconspicuously located in a house in Shepherd's Bush.[3] While there was nothing to prevent any religious group registering its place of worship

---

[1] *R v. Dibdin* [1910] P 57, p. 109.

[2] The Woking mosque had fallen into disuse after 1900 and was not reopened until 1913 (see Sarah Brown, 'The Shah Jahan Mosque, Woking: an unexpected gem', 46 (Autumn) *Conservation Bulletin* 32, p. 34; 'Khwaja Kamal-ud-Din – the torch-bearer of Islam' (1922) 10 *Islamic Review* 8, p. 9), while the Muslim Institute in Liverpool had ceased to exist in 1908.

[3] At 79 Sinclair Road: see Rozina Visram, *Asians in Britain: 400 Years of History* (London: Pluto Press, 2002), p. 104. It was not registered for weddings until the 1960s: see further Chapter 8.

for weddings,[4] only Christian denominations had the option of appointing an authorised person to oversee weddings there.[5] While the contract of marriage might be the same for all, *how* couples could marry was not.

The competing conceptions of marriage explored in this chapter are linked to the questions of how couples could marry, and how they chose to marry, in various different ways. In some cases the conception of marriage held by a particular religious group determined whether a particular couple could, or should, marry according to its rites. This was the case for the Church of England, whose clergy were exempted from conducting a widening range of weddings, and whose leaders adopted an increasingly restrictive attitude to the remarriages of those whose first spouses were still alive. It was also the case, for different reasons, for the Catholic church, which now insisted that Catholics should be married only by a priest, and that other weddings would not be recognised. A particular conception of marriage might also influence how a religious group navigated the rules on the registration of buildings and appointment of authorised persons, as was the case with ultra-Orthodox Jews and within a new strand of Liberal Judaism. And individuals might also invoke a particular conception of marriage to justify their actions and claim (or disclaim) legal status for their marriages; many foreign-born Jews continued to marry outside the legal framework altogether, generating debates about how the law should treat such ceremonies, and there was a succession of cases featuring Sikh, Hindu, and Muslim men arguing that their capacity to marry was governed by their own personal law. To complete the picture of practice in this period, the chapter will close with a brief consideration of weddings in Nonconformist chapels and register offices and how these were affected by the controversies surrounding other routes into marriage.

The Established Church and the Law of the Land

*the boundaries of the respective domains of Church and State in England have
neither been very strictly defined nor very consistently maintained*[6]

Most weddings continued to take place in the Anglican church, although the trend was very definitely downwards.[7] Some clergy still saw it as their

---

[4] The Woking mosque was to be registered in 1920: see further Chapter 7.
[5] See Chapter 5.
[6] *Banister* v. *Thompson* [1908] P 362.
[7] ONS, 'Marriages in England and Wales 2017' (14 April 2020), table 1.

mission to marry as many couples as possible, making marriage in church as cheap as possible and marrying couples in batches.[8] But it was the marriages that the church would not permit that attracted far more attention.

The repeal of the long-standing and long-contested prohibition on a man marrying his deceased wife's sister sparked particular controversy over clashing conceptions of marriage. The Deceased Wife's Sister's Marriage Act 1907 declared that any such marriages were not to be deemed void or voidable 'as a civil contract', and that the passage of the Act would not make any Anglican clergyman liable for 'anything done or omitted to be done by him in the performance of his duties'.[9] It was clear from the context that this envisaged a new exemption to the clergy's general duty to conduct the weddings of their parishioners and that no clergyman would be liable to any civil or ecclesiastical penalties for either conducting or failing to conduct such a marriage. It was less clear whether it enabled them to refuse to recognise such marriages at all.

This was very quickly put to the test. Shortly after the 1907 Act came into force, a Norfolk vicar, the Reverend Henry Thompson, refused to administer Holy Communion to two of his parishioners on the basis that they were 'open and notorious evil livers'.[10] The marriage of the couple in question, Alan and Emily Banister, was one that had been retrospectively validated by the 1907 Act.[11] Their decision to challenge Thompson's refusal – and his subsequent challenge to being admonished for that refusal – required successive courts to grapple with the question of whether there was a difference between ecclesiastical law and statute law

---

[8] Alexander Paterson, *Across the Bridges, or, Life by the South London River-side* (London: Edward Arnold, 1911), p. 200; Michael Collins, *The Likes of Us: A Biography of the White Working Class* (London: Granta Books, 2004), p. 41.

[9] Deceased Wife's Sister's Marriage Act 1907, s. 1.

[10] The administration of the sacrament had been regulated by law since the Reformation. The first Act passed under the reign of the Protestant boy-king Edward VI established that a clergyman could not deny the sacrament to 'any person that will devoutly and humbly desire it' without a 'lawful cause': 1&2 Edw. 6. C. 1, s. 8. The *Book of Common Prayer* set out a process to be followed where a member of the clergy believed that a person ought not to be admitted to Communion by reason of some 'grave and open sin'.

[11] Emily was the sister of Alan's first wife, who had died some years earlier. The couple had married in Canada (which had legalised such marriages in 1906) on 12 August 1907; while this marriage would have been void on account of their domicile being in England, it was validated when the Deceased Wife's Sister's Marriage Act 1907 came into force nine days later.

as regards the status of a marriage between a man and his deceased wife's sister. The case was initially heard in the ecclesiastical Court of Arches under the Clergy Discipline Act 1840,[12] where Sir Lewis Dibdin noted the difficulty of the question but took the view that at the very least a couple who had been 'lawfully married according to the law of the land' could not by any stretch of the imagination be described as 'open and notorious evil livers' for living together as husband and wife.[13] Thompson then challenged Dibdin's decision in the civil courts,[14] but the King's Bench Division, Court of Appeal, and House of Lords all agreed with Dibdin's view. While individual clergy could refuse to conduct marriages within the formerly prohibited degrees, they could not deny their validity. The case made it clear that as far as the courts were concerned, English law recognised only one contract of marriage, however that contract was made.[15] As Lord Ashbourne commented, the words 'as a civil contract' used in the 1907 Act could not 'diminish or lessen the status or the rights of those who come within its terms ... whether married in church or registrar's office' or 'make duality in marriage'.[16]

Coincidentally, Dibdin was also to be indirectly involved in the other controversy about which weddings the Church of England should conduct. He was a member of the Royal Commission that was appointed to inquire into the laws governing divorce in 1909, and one of the three who refused to accede to its proposal for the expansion of the grounds of divorce beyond adultery.[17] His 1912 treatise on the history of divorce law emphasised that the law of the Church of England as to the indissolubility of marriage had 'remained unchanged' at the Reformation.[18]

---

[12] The Court of Arches was the appeal court for all the ecclesiastical courts in the Province of Canterbury but could also hear cases by letters of request, as was the case here.

[13] *Banister* v. *Thompson* [1908] P 362, p. 391.

[14] Specifically, he sought a writ of prohibition to restrain the Court of Arches from proceeding further in the matter of monition, the Court's decision having been that he was liable to be admonished for repelling the parties from Holy Communion and was admonished to refrain from similar acts in the future.

[15] See in particular the comments of Cozens Hardy MR in the Court of Appeal, quoted at the start of the chapter (*R* v. *Dibdin* [1910] P 57). Fletcher Moulton LJ made a similar point about the law recognising 'only one contract of marriage' (p. 114) however it had been formed, while Farwell LJ rejected the possibility of any 'duality' in marriage (p. 134).

[16] *Thompson* v. *Dibdin* [1912] AC 533, p. 543.

[17] The others were Cosmo Lang, then Archbishop of York and later Archbishop of Canterbury, and the conservative law don Sir William Anson. On the Commission more generally, see William Cornish, Stephen Banks, Charles Mitchell, Paul Mitchell, and Rebecca Probert, *Law and Society in England, 1750–1950* (Oxford: Hart, 2nd ed., 2019), pp. 372–3.

[18] Sir Lewis Dibdin, *English Church Law and Divorce, Part I: Notes on the Reformatio Legum Ecclesiasticarum* (London: John Murray, 1912), p. 78.

The 1916 Archbishops' Committee on Church and State subsequently asserted that the Church of England had 'never varied from its ancient refusal to admit the possibility of divorce'.[19] Of course, the fact that the church courts had not *granted* divorces did not mean that the Church of England had not *recognised* divorces, as was evident from the remarriages that had been solemnised by Anglican clergy.

In the event, there was no change to the law governing either divorce or remarriage after divorce in this period. It remained the case that clergy could only refuse to conduct the remarriages of those who had been divorced on the basis of their adultery.[20] The statute left this to the discretion of the individual. Nor did the Church of England require its clergy to refuse to conduct such remarriages. But as Archbishop of Canterbury, Randall Davidson's personal advice was that clergy *should* refuse to conduct such marriages, and should also discourage the 'innocent' party from marrying for a second time in church.[21] With an increasing number of divorces, particularly after the First World War,[22] there was a growing cohort of individuals who looked elsewhere to marry.

The Catholic Church and the Non-Recognition of Non-Catholic Marriages

The Roman Catholic Church never has been nor ever will be the ... handmaid of the State ... she insists on the necessity of her autonomy[23]

On 19 April 1908 – Easter Sunday – the decree of *Ne Temere* came into effect. Issued by Pope Pius X, it was intended to create uniformity for Catholic marriages worldwide.[24] In setting out precisely what formalities

---

[19] Bruce S. Bennett, 'The Church of England and the Law of Divorce since 1857: Marriage Discipline, Ecclesiastical Law and the Establishment' (1994) 45 *Journal of Ecclesiastical History* 625, p. 628.

[20] Matrimonial Causes Act 1857, s. 57; see further Chapter 4.

[21] See Bennett, 'The Church of England', p. 628, citing correspondence from Davidson in 1903 and 1912.

[22] The number of divorces increased from 577 in 1913 to 1,654 in 1919: ONS, 'Divorces in England and Wales: 2019' (17 November 2020), table 1, number of couples divorcing, by party petitioning and decree granted, 1858 to 2019.

[23] 'The Roman Catholic Church and Marriage', *Manchester Guardian*, 14 September 1907 (letter from Rev. C. Wierz).

[24] 'Decree concerning Sponsalia and Matrimony, issued by the Sacred Congregation of the Council by the Order and with the Authority of our Holy Father Pope Pius X', 2 August 1907. For discussion of the background to the decree see Eoin de Bhaldraithe, 'Mixed Marriages and Irish Politics: The Effect of "Ne Temere"' (1988) 77 *Studies: An*

would be required in order for the Catholic church to regard a marriage as valid, it sought to complete the attempt to outlaw clandestine marriages begun by the Council of Trent in the sixteenth century.[25] In doing so, however, it created a clash between the law of the Catholic church and the law of England and Wales, since it declared that, for a Catholic,[26] the only valid marriage was one conducted before a Catholic priest. This meant that in the eyes of the Catholic church, any Catholic who married in a register office, or in any non-Catholic place of worship, was not validly married.

It should be acknowledged that the new processes adopted for Catholic marriages were considerably more rigorous than the civil requirements in terms of the ability of priests to check whether either of the couple had been previously married. The provision that the baptismal records of each spouse should be annotated with details of the marriage[27] provided a way of checking marital status when any subsequent marriage was contemplated.[28] Such checks served to prevent bigamous marriages more effectively than the process of posting notices in the office of the superintendent registrar.[29]

Nonetheless, the suggestion that the Catholic church would regard non-Catholic marriages as void understandably aroused a considerable degree of disquiet. One priest suggested that it would convert the 'poor lukewarm Catholics' who did not marry in the Catholic church – estimated to be

---

Irish Quarterly Review 284. Special regulations were in place in Germany and the Austro-Hungarian Empire.

[25] The 1563 Council of Trent requiring marriages to be celebrated by a priest in the presence of two witnesses had been widely promulgated in countries in which Catholics were in the majority (including in Ireland), but had had no application in England, Wales, or Scotland.

[26] The decree was to apply to all who had been baptised in the Catholic church or who had converted to Catholicism, even if they had 'fallen away afterwards from the Church', 'Decree concerning Sponsalia and Matrimony', XI(i).

[27] 'Decree concerning Sponsalia and Matrimony', IX(ii); 'Instruction of the Archbishop and Bishops of England and Wales', Report of the Royal Commission on Divorce and Matrimonial Causes, P.P. 1912–13 [Cd. 6478], Appendix XIV.

[28] If each of the couple had to supply a copy of their entry in the baptism register before they married, neither would be able to remarry in a Catholic church without evidence that the other had died in the meantime: Jim Lancaster, 'Marriage – Catholic and Civil' (2020) 38 (3) *Lancashire Family History & Heraldry Society* 24, p. 27.

[29] That said, there were still occasional cases where an individual was acquitted of bigamy because the first ceremony was conducted according to Catholic rites alone: see, e.g., 'Marriage certificates given by priests', *The Tablet*, 2 August 1902, reporting the acquittal of Thomas Lindsay at the Staffordshire Assizes. While the comment that the evidence of the first marriage 'was one of those certificates which were kept voluntarily' implied that the issue was one of evidence, the fact that the marriage was not registered suggests that it was not conducted in the presence of the registrar.

around one-fifth of Catholic couples – 'into bitter unrelenting enemies'.[30] There was some heated correspondence in the *Manchester Guardian* on whether the new law would enable unscrupulous Catholic husbands to evade their obligations by abandoning marriages that were legally valid but which they claimed were not binding on them for religious reasons.[31] When the matter was (somewhat belatedly) discussed in Parliament in 1911,[32] nobody disputed the idea that, although the civil law could not be overridden, and that a marriage entered into in England and Wales had the same consequences regardless of the religious affiliation of the parties, religious groups had a right to set their own expectations of their followers. It was, however, recognised that different conceptions of marriage gave rise to certain dangers. Since individuals might not appreciate that the state had a different conception of marriage from that held by their religion, it was emphasised that 'a very grave responsibility rests upon the priests or ministers of any religion, who lead people to believe that they are not married in the religious sense, to make clear to them at the same time what their civil position is and what are the duties which the law imposes'.[33]

Ne Temere itself does not seem to have altered the marriage patterns of Catholic couples in England and Wales.[34] There was certainly no immediate increase in the number of weddings celebrated in Catholic registered places of worship. Correspondence in *The Tablet* bemoaned the continuing propensity of Catholic couples to marry in the register

---

[30] 'The Decree on Marriage', *The Tablet*, 7 December 1907.

[31] See 'The Roman Church and Marriage', *Manchester Guardian*, 9 September 1907 (letter suggesting that the new regulations might lead Catholics 'into very false and painful positions'); 'The Roman Catholic Church and Marriage', *Manchester Guardian*, 16 September 1907 (letter suggesting that obedience to Catholic law was the answer); 'The Roman Church and Marriage', *Manchester Guardian*, 18 September 1907 (letter asking how the Catholic church could sanction any man or woman 'of honourable principles' breaking the contract entered into before the registrar or in a Protestant church); 'The Roman Church and Marriage', *Manchester Guardian*, 20 September 1907 (reply arguing that 'as no contract is effected, no contract can be broken').

[32] The debate was sparked by the case of an Irish couple, Alexander and Agnes McCann, who had married in a Presbyterian ceremony some years before *Ne Temere*; Alexander, a Catholic, was subsequently advised that this marriage was void in the eyes of the Catholic church and deserted Agnes (for discussion of the case, see Raymond Lee, 'Intermarriage, Conflict and Social Control in Ireland: The Decree *Ne Temere*' (1985) 17(1) *Economic & Social Review* 11.

[33] *Hansard*, HL Deb., vol. 7 col. 206, 28 February 1911.

[34] For an example of one Catholic bride who married in a register office and then had a further ceremony in the Anglican church, see Margaret French, 'Married or Not? A Catholic Bride's Two Ceremonies' (2021) JGFH (forthcoming).

office[35] and suggested that it was time for Catholic churches to avail themselves of the provisions of the Marriage Act 1898 and for priests to be appointed as authorised persons.[36] Since there was no longer any necessity for a fee to be paid to the civil registrar when a wedding took place before an authorised person in a registered place of worship,[37] it was pointed out that it would be possible to offer weddings in the Catholic church more cheaply than in the register office.[38] In other words, financial considerations might succeed where the threat of non-recognition had failed.

The 1898 Act had, however, explicitly provided that the 'trustees or governing body' by whom an authorised person would be appointed would, in the case of Catholics, include the Bishop of the diocese, or the Vicar-General, his principal deputy.[39] The result was that individual Catholic churches did not have the same liberty as their Nonconformist counterparts to appoint an authorised person and had to wait for the Catholic authorities to hold that the Act could be adopted. This finally happened in 1911.[40] Even then it seems that few priests chose to avail themselves of it. The Registrar-General's report for 1919 recorded that only around one in every fifty weddings registered as having taken place in a Catholic church were before an authorised person.[41] Nonetheless, the period after 1911 saw a modest uplift in both the number and percentage of weddings in Catholic places of worship,[42] and one priest

---

[35] See, e.g., 'Marriage Law and Easter Communion: A Defaulters' List?', *The Tablet*, 27 March 1909 (a priest proposing to publish a list of his 'poor black sheep' who had failed to marry in the Catholic church, whom he described as 'unmarried couples').

[36] 'The Marriages of the Poor and the Decree *Ne Temere*', *The Tablet*, 16 June 1910; 'The Marriage Acts of 1898 and 1909', *The Tablet*, 1 April 1911, 8 April 1911.

[37] The requirement for a fee to be paid to the registrar who would have been responsible for registering the marriage had an authorised person not been appointed was a transitional one, ending in 1909.

[38] 'The Marriages of the Poor and the Decree *Ne Temere*', *The Tablet*, 16 June 1910. Weddings in a registered place of worship would still need to be preceded by notice, for which a fee was payable, but those marrying in the register office had to pay 5s to the registrar, whereas Catholic priests would often conduct the wedding for free.

[39] Marriage Act 1898, s. 1(3).

[40] 'Instruction of the Archbishop and Bishops of England and Wales on the Marriage Act of 1898'.

[41] *Eighty-Second Annual Report of the Registrar-General of Births, Deaths and Marriages in England* (London: HMSO, 1920), Table XII.

[42] ONS, 'Marriages in England and Wales 2017' (14 April 2020), table 1. Where such weddings involved a non-Catholic, priests could require conversion as a prerequisite to it going ahead, or at least a promise that any children of the marriage would be brought up as Catholics: on which see Margaret H. Turnham, *Catholic Faith and Practice in England,*

proudly announced that since he had become authorised, '[n]ot one single marriage has taken place from my parish at the Registrar's office'.[43]

In the meantime, as the next section will discuss, the validity of some register office weddings was being challenged by individuals from other faiths on the basis that their religion did not permit the type of marriage that they had contracted.

Civil Weddings and Religious Capacity

the status which the English law gives to a Christian wife, whether married in a register office or in a cathedral church[44]

In March 1903, Maria Caroline de Albuquerque Birch went through a ceremony of marriage with a Sikh law student, Kehr Singh Grewal, at the Hendon register office. Grewal was described on the marriage certificate as a widower, but after the wedding he returned to India and was reunited with his first wife, whom he had married around 1888.[45] Maria accordingly sought a decree of nullity on the ground that the marriage was void, and the court had no hesitation in granting it on the basis 'that the respondent had committed a fraud upon the petitioner by going through a form of marriage in England with her when his lawful wife was alive'.[46] The alternative argument advanced by Grewal – that as a Sikh he was prohibited from marrying a Christian, or indeed outside his caste, and that this invalidated the marriage – was not accepted. But the argument that an individual's religion might determine their capacity to marry – and unmarry – was to surface in a number of other cases in this period, as an increasing number of Indian men who had come to England to work or study formed relationships with English women.[47]

1779-1992: The Role of Revivalism and Renewal (Woodbridge: Boydell Press, 2015), p. 104; Doreen Rosman, *The Evolution of the English Churches, 1500-2000* (Cambridge: Cambridge University Press, 2003), p. 307.

[43] 'Registrar?', *The Tablet*, 18 August 1915.

[44] [1917] 1 KB 634, at 646, per Darling J.

[45] TNA, Divorce and Matrimonial Causes Files, J 77/869/6401.

[46] *Grewal* v. *Grewal*, *The Times*, 1 August 1907.

[47] Official statistics put the number of Indian students in the United Kingdom in 1910 at somewhere between 700 and 1,200: Visram, *Asians in Britain*, p. 88. For contemporary discussion, see Sir EJ Trevelyan, 'Marriages between English Women and Natives of British India' (1917) 17 *Journal of Comparative Legislation and International Law* 223; Sir Frederick Robertson, 'The Relations between the English Law and the Personal Law of Indians in England with Special Reference to the Marriage Law' (1918) 18 *Journal of Comparative Legislation and International Law* 242. For a discussion of the variety of

The issue arose again in 1909, when Louie Venugopal Chetti, nee Taylor, sought a judicial separation from her husband on the basis of his desertion. His response was to deny the legality of the marriage, on the basis that 'according to Hindu law and religion which is the law of his domicile and is his personal law he cannot lawfully marry one who is not a Hindoo by religion'.[48] The President of the Probate, Divorce and Admiralty Division, Sir Gorell Barnes, indignantly rejected the idea that this could invalidate the marriage, denouncing the concept of personal law as 'medieval' and asking:

> Ought he to be allowed to do so? Ought a foreigner domiciled abroad, who comes to this country and here marries in due form according to English law another person domiciled in England, to be allowed to assert that he carries about with him, while here, the burden of an incapacity imposed by the laws of the foreign domicil to do that which he has done voluntarily and in due form according to the laws of England, or to repudiate his marriage on the ground that he is incapable of doing what he has done, and ought our Courts to support such an assertion and repudiation, with the consequent effects on the position of the wife and legitimacy of the child? To my mind the answer should be 'No'.[49]

The idea was perhaps not as unthinkable as this might suggest, given the long-standing rule that an individual's capacity to marry was governed by the law of their domicile,[50] at least where it was the laws governing capacity under English law that had been flouted.[51]

This sense of a clash between different conceptions of marriage was even more pronounced in the long-drawn-out litigation following the wedding of Dr Mir-Anwaruddin, a Muslim law student, to Ruby Pauline Hudd at Wandsworth register office in 1913.[52] The marriage lasted less

---

disputes that were generated, see Mitra Sharafi, 'The Marital Patchwork of Colonial South Asia: Forum Shopping from Britain to Baroda' (2010) 28(4) *Law and History Review* 979.

[48] TNA, Court for Divorce and Matrimonial Causes: Divorce and Matrimonial Causes Files, J 77/856/6006. Their wedding had taken place in the Paddington register office in 1890.

[49] *Chetti* v. *Chetti* [1909] P 67, p. 87.

[50] A.V. Dicey, '*Chetti* v. *Chetti*' (1909) 25 LQR 202.

[51] The description of the willingness of the English courts to disregard the rules governing capacity in other jurisdictions as a 'qualification' to the general rule (Robertson, 'Personal Law', p. 244) was somewhat disingenuous. On attitudes to inter-racial marriages in this period see Shompa Lahiri, *Indians in Britain: Anglo-Indian Encounters, Race and Identity, 1880–1930* (London: Frank Cass, 1999), p. 122.

[52] For a detailed account of the case, see Gail Savage, 'More than One Mrs Mir Anwaruddin: Islamic Divorce and Christian Marriage in Early Twentieth-Century London' (2008) 47 *Journal of British Studies* 348.

than two months. The subsequent litigation lasted several years,[53] but for present purposes the interest of the case lies in Mir-Anwaruddin's attempts to *remarry*. He had ample justification for thinking that he was entitled to do so. Having pronounced a *talaq*,[54] he sought a decree declaring that his marriage had therefore been dissolved, or, in the alternative, for the dissolution of his marriage on the basis of his wife's adultery. While his petition was rejected on the basis of jurisdiction – as he was not domiciled in England and Wales, the court could not grant him a decree – on appeal the judge, Bargrave Deane J, gave an additional ground for the refusal of a decree. This was that Mir-Anwaruddin had satisfied that there was 'no subsisting marriage' in relation to which a decree could be granted, 'that which did take place having been dissolved by law by the parties'.[55] Following this, Mir-Anwaruddin gave notice to the superintendent registrar of Hammersmith of his intention to marry again, together with a full account of his marital history. Upon the superintendent registrar refusing to issue the necessary authorisation, Mir-Anwaruddin sought a writ of mandamus to compel him to do so.[56]

All but one of the six judgments that were delivered, when first the Divisional Court and then the Court of Appeal refused the writ of mandamus,[57] were suffused with references to *Christian* marriage.[58]

---

[53] She sought and obtained an order for separation and maintenance, which he successfully appealed; he sought and obtained a decree for restitution of conjugal rights in the City Civil Court of Madras, which she ignored; she sought a judicial separation in England, which he opposed on the basis of his being domiciled in India and which she subsequently abandoned.

[54] Islamic law permits a husband to divorce his wife unilaterally by repeating words of divorcement, or *talaq*, three times.

[55] Savage, 'More than One Mrs Mir Anwaruddin'.

[56] The newspaper coverage reflected the sense of a clash between competing conceptions of marriage: 'Mohammedan Doctor Wants To Marry Second Time, But the Registrar Objects', *Dundee Evening Telegraph*, 21 September 1916; 'Mohammedan Divorce: Question of its Legality Under English Law', *Western Times*, 22 September 1916; 'Mohammedan and His Wives: Important Court Decision To-Day', *Dundee Evening Telegraph*, 10 November 1916; 'Effect of Marriage Between a Mahomedan and an Englishwoman', *The Times*, 11 November 1916; 'Marriage Laws: Mahommedan Doctor's Desire to Wed a Second English Lady', *Western Times*, 11 November 1916; 'A Mahomedan's Marriage with a Christian', *The Times*, 24 November 1916.

[57] *R v. The Superintendent Registrar of Marriages, Hammersmith* [1917] 1 KB 634.

[58] The only judge not to use the word 'Christian' was A.T. Lawrence J, but as he gave only a short concurring judgment this is hardly surprising. The Jewish Lord Chief Justice, Viscount Reading, was just as insistent as his fellow judges that marriage in England had to be 'Christian': [1917] 1 KB 634, at 640.

The word 'Christian', or variations thereof, appeared over fifty times. Ruby was claimed as a 'Christian' wife, as was any woman married under English law, whatever her beliefs, and whether married 'in a register office or in a cathedral church'.[59] The claim was obviously inapposite, in that it disregarded what such women actually believed.[60] Moreover, if a woman's Christianity derived solely from her getting married under English law, then as a matter of logic her husband should also be described as Christian, regardless of *his* beliefs. But the judgments in the case were stronger on rhetoric than on logic.

The use of the term cannot be explained or excused simply on the basis that by 'Christian' the judges meant 'monogamous'. Their reiteration of the word was clearly deliberate, and served to signal Mir-Anwaruddin's outsider status. This was further reinforced by their choice of quotations from earlier cases; while they might have hesitated before using the term 'infidel' directly, they had no such qualms about quoting Lord Brougham on how English law held 'the infidel marriage to be something different from the Christian'.[61] Their invocation of Lord Penzance's dictum from *Hyde* v. *Hyde and Woodmansee*[62] was equally telling; his defence of what constituted a marriage as 'understood in Christendom' had itself been generated in response to a potentially polygamous marriage.[63]

In the eyes of the court, Mir-Anwaruddin's claimed right to remarry was even more threatening to the idea that marriage should be entered into for life, between one man and one woman, than Hyde's Mormon marriage had been. If the *talaq* had not brought the first marriage to an end, then Mir-Anwaruddin was seeking to take a second wife. If it had, then any second marriage would equally be at risk of such termination. The superintendent registrar's refusal was therefore regarded as entirely justified both because Mir-Anwaruddin was still married and because, if he was not, he was making an application for a 'Mahomedan marriage'

---

[59] [1917] 1 KB 634, at 646, per Darling J.

[60] For examples of women adopting the religion of their husband: see, e.g., 'Decree Against a Bigamist', *The Times*, 5 April 1917, reporting how the second wife of Abdul Hamid converted to Islam before their register office wedding and was sworn on the Koran when giving evidence in his first wife's divorce case. See also Mike Sadler, 'From Jenny Witney to Noliny R Gupta: a mixed marriage in the register office' (2021) JGFH (forthcoming), noting how the wife described herself as 'Hindu by nationality'.

[61] *Warrender* v. *Warrender* (1835) 2 Cl & Fin 488.

[62] (1866) LR 1 P&D 130.

[63] Although it had not as then acquired the status that was later to be attributed to it: Rebecca Probert, '*Hyde v Hyde*: Defining or Defending Marriage? [2007] 19 *Child and Family Law Quarterly* 322.

determinable at will, not a Christian one. The technical question of whether English law could recognise a divorce that had not been granted by a court – and what Mir-Anwaruddin was meant to do if it could not – rather faded into the background against this challenge to the conception of marriage under English law.

While these three cases all raise complex issues of capacity, domicile, and divorce,[64] they also form an important part of the story about the evolution of the laws governing weddings. At the most basic level, the fact that Grewal, Chetti, and Mir-Anwaruddin all married in register offices reflects the lack of any Sikh, Hindu, or Muslim places of worship in which weddings could be celebrated at this time.[65] It also reflects their desire to be legally married; the alternative, after all, would have been a religious-only ceremony with no standing under English law. The indignation generated by their subsequent attempts to argue that their marriages were governed by their personal law and therefore either not binding on them (as in the case of Grewal and Chetti) or terminable by a religious divorce (Mir-Anwaruddin) was not dissimilar to that sparked by Catholic husbands repudiating non-Catholic weddings,[66] or by Jewish husbands relying on the invalidity of religious-only marriages.[67] Nonetheless, the emphasis on marriage in England as 'Christian' set a less than encouraging tone for future interactions between English law and its increasingly diverse population. And the assumption that a Muslim marriage was intrinsically different from a Christian one because of the ease with which it could be terminated and its potentially polygamous nature was to resurface again in subsequent decades as Muslim religious-only marriage ceremonies came to judicial notice.[68]

Moreover, as the next section will discuss, a new line was being drawn between Christian and non-Christian groups in terms of how their weddings were regulated.

---

[64] For contemporary discussion of these wider issues, see Trevelyan, 'Marriages', and Robertson, 'Personal Law'.

[65] There are examples of Muslims marrying in Christian places of worship: see, e.g., 'Walden Bigamist Sentenced: "Doubtful Privilege" of Four Wives', *Cambridge Independent Press*, 26 May 1916, noting Abdul Hamid's wedding in Ilford parish church in 1911 and subsequent conviction for bigamy after he remarried in Hampstead register office.

[66] See, e.g., the reactions to the McCann case in Ireland: *Hansard*, HL Deb., vol. 7 col. 206, 28 February 1911.

[67] See, e.g., the magistrate's criticism of one such husband: *Evening Telegraph and Star*, 14 November 1894.

[68] See the discussion of R v. *Bham* in Chapter 8.

Non-Christian Faiths, Registered Buildings, and Authorised Persons

The Committee are looking into the question of the legal facilities for the solemnisation of marriage in the new synagogue, and it is hoped these may be obtainable in due course[69]

On the face of it, the Marriage Act 1898 had seemed to offer the potential for all faiths and denominations to conduct marriages without the presence of a civil registrar. There was nothing in it that limited the option of appointing an authorised person to certain denominations, despite the fact that the debates had largely focused on Nonconformists. However, the Act's definition of a registered building as 'any building registered for solemnising marriages therein under the Marriage Act 1836'[70] applied only to buildings that could have been registered for marriage at the time of the 1836 Act. In other words, only *Christian* places of worship could appoint an authorised person, despite the fact that other places of worship could be registered for marriage.

This had consequences for Jewish weddings in particular. There were congregations that did not accept the authority of the Chief Rabbi and which chose to register their places of worship so as to be able to conduct weddings independently of the Board of Deputies, even if this meant accepting the presence of the registrar. There were also congregations that were refused recognition. London's Adass Yisroel synagogue[71] was one such, registering itself for weddings in 1913; its disagreement with the authorities was not insuperable, however, and six years later its secretary was duly certified by the Board of Deputies.[72]

The emergence of a new conception of Judaism raised more fundamental challenges. The Jewish Religious Union for the Advancement of Liberal Judaism was established on 16 February 1902. By 1909, it was looking for a building where meetings could be held and the Liberal Jewish Synagogue began to function in 1911, holding its services in a former chapel in Hill Street in Marylebone.[73] Its non-recognition went deeper than the issues about individual authority raised by the

---

[69] 'The Jewish Religious Union: Its Principles and Its Future', *Jewish Chronicle*, 15 October 1909.

[70] Marriage Act 1898, s. 1(2).

[71] For the history of this particular synagogue, see Geoffrey Alderman, *Modern British Jewry* (Oxford: Clarendon Press, 1998), p. 142.

[72] *London Gazette*, 17 January 1913 (Adass Jisroel Synagogue, rear of 124–126 Green Lanes, Stoke Newington); Alderman, *Modern British Jewry*, p. 353.

[73] Alderman, *Modern British Jewry*, pp. 206–8.

occasional ultra-Orthodox synagogue: Liberal Jews were deemed to differ so markedly from those of their Orthodox or Reform counterparts that they were not recognised as persons professing the Jewish religion at all. There was no question of their secretary being certified by either the Board of Deputies or the West London synagogue. Instead, the synagogue was registered for marriages,[74] and a few weddings were celebrated there over the next decade.[75] This route of course meant that Liberal Jews did not enjoy the same freedoms as their Orthodox and Reform counterparts, since they were limited to marrying in the synagogue itself, in the presence of a civil registrar, and had to include the words prescribed by statute.

Whether Liberal Judaism could be accommodated within the existing provision for marriages according to Jewish usages, whether the law on appointing an authorised person should be changed, or whether special provision was needed were all to become a source of controversy in the coming decades.[76] The fact that only places of worship registered by Christian denominations could appoint an authorised person had little impact on other non-Christian faiths at this time, largely because the few places of worship that had been established were not registered for marriage at all. However, some had been conducting non-legally binding marriage ceremonies, to which we now turn.

Non-Christian Faiths and Religious-Only Marriage Ceremonies

There were several forms of ceremony which might be used, and yet be valid as civil marriages; but there must be registration[77]

'MOORISH MARRIAGE: SALFORD GIRL AT TANGIER', pronounced the *Manchester Courier* in May 1905.[78] Clara Casey, a seventeen-year-old dancer, had met Mohammed Ben-Bellkassem[79] when he was performing with a troupe of acrobats at the Empire Theatre in Ardwick, Manchester.

---

[74] *London Gazette*, 29 October 1912.

[75] S. J. Prais and Marlena Schmool, 'Statistics of Jewish Marriage in Great Britain: 1901-1965' (1967) 9 *Jewish Journal of Sociology* 151, Appendix 2, Table I.

[76] See further Chapters 7 and 8.

[77] 'Under the Canopy: Jewish Marriage Practices', *Derby Daily Telegraph*, 3 August 1904.

[78] *Manchester Courier*, 29 May 1905.

[79] His name was variously reported in the newspapers as Mahomed Ben Kasem, Mohammed Ben Bulkhassan, Mahomet Ben Bellkassem, and was also shortened to 'Cassem'. The variation used in the text is that which appears in different civil registers, so is presumably the one he gave to officials.

Two months later – Clara having converted to Islam – they went through a ceremony of marriage at the Liverpool Institute,[80] apparently with the consent of her parents.[81] Afterwards the couple travelled to Ben-Bellkassem's home country of Morocco, from where Clara wrote home to her parents complaining of her husband's violence and expressing her desire to return home. The British Consular authorities then got involved, and the press were quick to follow up on the story.

At the time, it was the dramatic sequel to the wedding that accounted for the column inches devoted to it.[82] For our purposes the significance of the case lies in the fact that it was one of the first reported examples of a marriage ceremony conducted according to Muslim rites without any accompanying legal ceremony.[83] Whether Clara actually understood that the ceremony in the Liverpool Institute had no legal status is difficult to ascertain. In a subsequent statement she claimed that the wife of Quilliam – the founder of the Institute, who had conducted the ceremony – had told her that the marriage was 'perfectly valid'.[84] After her return to England, both she and Ben-Bellkassem reportedly declared their intention to return to each other when they could, and to remarry according to English law.[85] There was, however, the small matter that Ben-Bellkassem was already married, as Clara apparently knew full well.[86] He had married Elizabeth Maud Smith at a register office in Lancashire in 1901,[87] the pair having met in her native Glasgow and, in a reversal of the usual direction of travel, had eloped to England to marry because of opposition from her strict Presbyterian parents.

---

[80] On the role of the Liverpool Institute in conducting Muslim religious-only marriage ceremonies, see Chapter 5.

[81] 'The Mock Marriage: English Girl Interviewed', *Nottingham Evening Post*, 27 May 1905; 'The Mosque Marriage: Clara Casey Tells Her Story', *Manchester Courier*, 29 May 1905.

[82] The sequel got even more dramatic when Clara and Ben-Bellkassem were ordered to attend the Consulate, where, as Clara later told reporters, 'my husband suddenly pulled out a revolver, and pointed it in a threatening manner, with the idea of frightening the official': 'Chorus Girl and Moor: Return of the Bride from Morocco: Miss Casey Interviewed', *Derby Daily Telegraph*, 12 June 1905.

[83] For examples of dual ceremonies, see Chapter 5.

[84] 'The Mosque Marriage: Clara Casey Tells Her Story', *Manchester Courier*, 29 May 1905.

[85] 'Chorus Girl and Moor: Return of the Bride from Morocco: Miss Casey Interviewed', *Derby Daily Telegraph*, 12 June 1905; 'Salford Girl's Romance: The Moorish Marriage', *Manchester Courier*, 12 June 1905.

[86] 'Moor's Two Wives: Married to Scottish and English Girls', *Evening Telegraph* (Dundee), 13 June 1905; 'The Mosque Marriage: Clara Casey Tells Her Story', *Manchester Courier*, 29 May 1905.

[87] BMD, Lancaster, Q3 1901.

The contemporary coverage of Clara and Ben-Bellkassem's marriage is illuminating. Nowhere was it suggested that women needed to be protected from these non-legally binding ceremonies. The *Manchester Courier* reported that the marriage laws and customs of the Islamic authorities in England 'would certainly seem stringent enough in the case of mixed marriages to reduce misunderstanding to a minimum', and explained the oaths that had to be sworn by each party, the practice of explaining the consequence and meaning of the marriage contract to the woman, and the presence of the clause in the contract making it clear that the ceremony would not create a marriage under English law.[88] Of course, in this particular case non-recognition could be equated with freedom from a violent husband, which may explain why this was not seen as a concern.

The Home Office sought the view of the Director of Public Prosecutions as to whether Quilliam had committed any offence in conducting the ceremony. The advice was that he had not, since the statute did not apply to private ceremonies of this kind.[89] It was equally doubtful whether Ben-Bellkassem was guilty of the offence of bigamy in going through a ceremony of marriage with Clara while already married.[90] Yet the non-recognition of a marriage in an unregistered mosque did provide a way for individuals to marry in accordance with their own religious rites and religious laws. While the Liverpool Institute ceased to function in 1908, the Woking mosque was revived in 1913 and began to conduct marriage ceremonies.[91] As one of the judges later commented in the Mir-Anwaruddin case, it would have been possible

---

[88] It noted that the marriage contract would contain a provision stating that '[n]othing herein contained is to be construed in any manner or form to be otherwise than a marriage according to Islamic law, but not, according to either Christian or English law' and that each would 'thrice swear that without qualification or mental reservation of any kind whatsoever they each of his or her own free and unfettered will and accord agree and consent to intermarry one with the other according to the holy laws and undying faith of Islam': 'Moorish Marriage: Salford Girl at Tangier', *Manchester Courier*, 29 May 1905.

[89] David Englander, '*Stille Huppah* (Quiet Marriage) among Jewish Immigrants in Britain' (1992) 34 *Jewish Journal of Sociology* 85, p. 95.

[90] Robertson, considering the issues in 1918, thought that it was arguable that if a second 'Mohammedan' ceremony of marriage took place after a first legal one, the crime of bigamy had been committed ('Personal Law', pp. 255–6), but the cases cited concerned second marriages that would have been void for lack of capacity rather than form.

[91] See, e.g., 'A Muslim Wedding Sermon in the Mosque, Woking', *The Islamic Review* (August 1914) 310. The couple in question also went through a separate legal wedding.

for Mir-Anwaruddin to have 'contracted a marriage in the Mahomedan form and sense' in the mosque at Woking if he so wished.[92]

It was, however, Jewish religious-only marriages, rather than Muslim ones, that were occupying the courts at this time. Magistrates emphasised that no maintenance could be ordered if the wife could not show a legal marriage.[93] In one case in Leeds in 1901, the rabbi's contention that the marriage should be recognised because the husband 'had, during the ceremony, to take hold of the woman's garment, which ... made the marriage legal, as in the case of Boaz and Ruth' was countered by the husband, who pointed out that 'though, for argument's sake, the marriage might have been legal according to Jewish law, yet, for the purposes of obtaining an order in an English court of law it was not so, unless it had been properly notified to the Registrar'.[94] Those who held official standing within Anglo-Jewry were equally eager to disclaim these marriages; in another desertion case from 1904, an 'assessor' to the Chief Rabbi confirmed that '[t]here were several forms of ceremony which might be used, and yet be valid as civil marriages; but there must be registration'.[95] The terminology of notification and registration should not obscure the fact that what they were talking about was giving notice before the marriage, not registering it after it had taken place.

The status of marriages conducted according to Jewish rites without such prior notification was considered in a work by the Jewish barrister – and future President of the Board of Deputies – Henry Straus Quixano Henriques in 1909. It was his contention that the annulling provision of the Marriage Act 1836 did not apply to Jewish marriages at all, on the bases that the 1836 Act was 'an enabling and not a disabling Act', that it 'did not abolish or restrict any of the old forms', and that it did not

---

[92] [1917] 1 KB 634, at 645, per Darling J.

[93] See, e.g., 'Jewish Marriage Problem: An Interesting Imbroglio', *Birmingham Daily Post*, 4 August 1900, reporting a case in which the parties had married in a Jewish religious-only ceremony. The Manchester City Stipendiary Magistrate commented that he could make no order for maintenance if the parties were not married by English law. Attempts were made to reach an agreement rather than proceeding against the 'husband' for an affiliation order, which would have declared their child to be illegitimate.

[94] *Yorkshire Evening Post*, 3 May 1901. The case was adjourned for the attendance of the Superintendent Registrar for Leeds. The sequel (reported in the *Courier and Advertiser*, 11 July 1928) suggests that the marriage was recognised.

[95] 'Under the Canopy: Jewish Marriage Practices', *Derby Daily Telegraph*, 3 August 1904. This case involved two young immigrant Russians; the woman's case was that he had 'frightened her into consenting to go through a ceremony with him' and 'promised her a public wedding afterwards when they were better off'. The form they signed – printed in Hebrew – was apparently available for 3d from Jewish printers in the East End.

contain any words expressly declaring such marriages to be void.[96] By his reasoning, all that was needed for a Jewish marriage to be valid under English law was for it to be celebrated according to Jewish usages.[97] The drafting of the 1836 Act was sufficiently ambiguous to make this at least arguable,[98] although it was something of a stretch to argue that Jewish marriages came within the exemption for marriages solemnised under the earlier Marriage Act 1823,[99] which had expressly stated that it did not extend to them,[100] while simultaneously arguing that they were not solemnised under the provisions of the 1836 Act, which did.

Yet against the absence of any mention of Jews (or Quakers) in the annulling provision of the 1836 Act, there had to be set the fact that the provision allowing such marriages to be solemnised according to their usages implied that giving notice was a condition of validity.[101] If so, Jewish couples would be more at risk of their marriages being unrecognised if the annulling provision did *not* apply than if it did; after all, the annulling provision made it clear that only if the failure to give notice was 'knowing and wilful' would a marriage be void,[102] rather than this being an absolute precondition to recognition. The most natural reading of the

---

[96] H. S. Q. Henriques, *Jewish Marriages and the English Law* (Oxford: Hart, 1909), p. 27.

[97] Although, as he admitted, even if conformity with Jewish usages was the test of validity, 'great inconveniences' might still arise because of difficulties in proving that the requirements of Jewish law had been observed. This, after all, had resulted in the non-recognition of a number of Jewish religious-only marriage ceremonies before the 1836 Act, and the divisions within Anglo-Jewry that had emerged since then raised the difficult question of who would decide what the requirements of Jewish law were.

[98] While s. 42 made no explicit reference to Quaker and Jewish weddings, and not all of the failures listed were relevant to them, deficiencies such as marrying without giving notice, or in a place other than that specified in the notice, or without a certificate being duly issued, were clearly applicable to them. However, it also referred to those marrying 'under the provisions of this Act', which raised the question as to whether Quakers and Jews, explicitly allowed to 'continue to contract and solemnise marriages' according to their own usages (s. 2), were in fact marrying under the Act.

[99] The proviso that s. 42 would not 'extend to annul any marriage legally solemnized according to the provisions of the Marriage Act 1823' was obviously intended to protect Anglican weddings, which remained governed by the 1823 Act.

[100] Marriage Act 1823, s. 31. This was in the same terms as the original exemption from the Clandestine Marriages Act 1753, as set out in s. 18: 'nothing in this Act shall extend to . . . any marriages among the people called Quakers, or amongst the persons professing the Jewish religion, where both the parties to any such marriage shall be of the people called Quakers or persons professing the Jewish religion respectively'.

[101] Marriage Act 1836, s. 2 stipulated that marriages conducted according to Jewish or Quaker usages would be valid 'provided . . . that Notice to the Registrar shall have been given, and the Registrar's certificate shall have issued'.

[102] Marriage Act 1836, s. 42.

1836 Act was that the annulling provision did apply to Jewish and Quaker marriages,[103] and that such marriages would therefore be void if both parties had knowingly and wilfully failed to give notice, or married without a certificate being issued.[104]

That such fundamental issues were left unclear in the 1836 Act indicates how little thought had been given to how it would apply to the formerly exempted groups. The need for the scheme it had established to be reviewed as a whole was becoming increasingly pressing. In the meantime, however, Nonconformists had been making the unsatisfactory compromise of the Marriage Act 1898 work for them.

Cooperation, Conviction, Concealment, and Convenience

The Nonconformists of the twentieth century were less prone to division than their nineteenth-century forbears, with an increasing number of mergers instead of constant splits.[105] They were also a declining force. The percentage of weddings in Nonconformist places of worship closely tracked the percentage of the population who were members of Nonconformist churches; there was a small increase up to 1906, and a slow decline thereafter.[106] By 1919, the percentage of weddings being conducted in a registered place of worship was smaller than it had been before the Marriage Act 1898.

There had, however, been a significant change in how they were conducted. While only a quarter of registered places of worship had appointed their own authorised person, nearly half of all weddings in such places were celebrated in the presence of an authorised person.[107] The explanation for this disparity may lie in the extent of cooperation between different places of worship and even denominations. While each

---

[103] This was reinforced by the reference in s. 42 to a marriage being void if it was knowingly and wilfully celebrated 'in any place other than the church, chapel, registered building, or office or *other place* specified in the notice'. This had to refer to Jewish and Quaker weddings, since there were no other places that any other type of wedding could be solemnised. By contrast, s. 39, which made it a felony to solemnise a marriage in a place other than that specified in the notice, explicitly excluded Jewish and Quaker weddings and made no reference to any other place.

[104] This was also the interpretation adopted in *Nathan* v. *Woolf* (1899) 15 TLR 250; see further Chapter 5.

[105] In 1907, for example, the United Methodist Church was formed as a result of a merger between the Bible Christians, the Wesleyan New Connexion, and the United Methodist Free Church.

[106] Field, *Periodizing Secularisation*, p. 109; ONS, 'Marriages in England'.

[107] *Eighty-second Annual Report*, p. xxiv and Table XII.

authorised person was appointed by a specific place of worship, their ability to register marriages was not limited to that particular place, but extended to any registered place of worship in the same registration district.[108] The registers of various denominations provide evidence of how this worked in practice. The Mount Tabor Methodist New Connexion chapel in Stockport had appointed its own authorised person but a number of entries in its marriage register were signed by the authorised person for the nearby Portwood Chapel.[109] In the Northamptonshire town of Desborough, cooperation crossed denominational divisions: weddings in the Independent or Congregational church were variously attended by its own authorised person, those from the Baptist and Methodist churches elsewhere in the town, and those from Independent churches in other nearby towns. A similar degree of cooperation was evident from the marriage register of the Baptist church.[110]

All this goes to show that Nonconformists were making the 1898 Act work for them, even if it had not provided quite what they had wanted.[111] Some of the conditions against which they had protested – for example, the need for a registered place of worship to have its own iron safe in which registers could be stored before an authorised person could be appointed – were less of a burden if the cost could be shared between different buildings in the same district. It was also noticeable that the percentage of weddings celebrated in the presence of an authorised person increased once couples were no longer required to pay the displaced civil registrar a fee for *not* attending.[112] This reinforces the suggestion that the slow take-up of the 1898 Act was the result of the difficulties that faced those who wished to avail themselves of it, rather than any lack of demand.

---

[108] Marriage Act 1898, s. 6(3).

[109] *Manchester, England, Non-Conformist Marriages, 1758–1937* [Ancestry.com, database on-line].

[110] See further Rebecca Probert and Liz Harris, 'Crossing the denominational divide: authorised persons and the registration of weddings in Desborough's Nonconformist chapels' (2021) JGFH (forthcoming).

[111] On the protests against the requirements of the 1898 Act (and the accompanying regulations), see further Chapter 5.

[112] In 1910, the first full year when no such fees would have been payable, 34 per cent of weddings in registered places of worship were conducted in the presence of an authorised person, as compared to 30 per cent the previous year. In some districts fees would have ceased to be payable at an earlier date, as the obligation to remunerate the registrar only applied to those in post before the 1898 Act came into force: Marriage Act 1898, s. 17(3).

It was, however, weddings in the register office that saw the greatest increase in this period. Their number continued to climb slowly but steadily, accounting for over one-fifth of the total by 1913.[113] A new generation of left-leaning novelists depicted such weddings both more frequently and more positively than previous authors had done. In H.G. Wells' *Love and Mr Lewisham*, the decision to marry in a register office is motivated by practical considerations but the registrar is depicted as 'business-like but kindly', and his parting benediction to the couple to be 'kind to each other' is simple but touching.[114] Wells' heroine Ann Veronica, who flouted the conventions by living with her husband-to-be, also marries in a register office.[115] And Amber Reeves – Wells' inspiration for Ann Veronica – depicts a young woman choosing a register office for ideological reasons in her novel *A Lady and her Husband*: Rosemary, the socialist daughter of the titular pair, is convinced that the marriage ceremony is merely 'the ratifying by the State of a private contract' and refuses to let her parents attend the wedding.[116] Even the party after the ceremony she regards as 'barbarous'; one ought, she feels, 'to get married on a mountain, or a cliff by the sea, and smell the fresh wind instead of pink roses from a florist's shop'.[117]

Whether such convictions were shared by many of those who married in the register office is doubtful. There were certainly some who rejected religion; one London shoemaker, who married in the Kensington register office in 1909, told his family that the local church 'was on land stolen from the people'.[118] There were others who certainly did not, as evidenced by the fact that they had an additional religious ceremony before or after their register office wedding, or by their known adherence to a particularly strict religious denomination.[119]

Convenience may also have played a role in encouraging couples to marry in a register office. While figures were not published for 1915–1918, there are a number of factors that might suggest that there was a higher than average number of such weddings during wartime than across the decade as a whole. First, there was a noticeable jump in the

---

[113] This was an increase from 15.3 per cent in 1900: ONS, 'Marriages'.
[114] H. G. Wells, *Love and Mr Lewisham* (1900), ch 20.
[115] *Ann Veronica: A Modern Love Story* (1909). In this case Wells did not depict the wedding at all; it is merely alluded to as having taken place.
[116] Amber Reeves, *A Lady and her Husband* (1914; London: Persephone Books, 2016), pp. 216–7.
[117] *Ibid*, p. 227.
[118] Email from Tony Allen, 13 June 2020.
[119] Kathy Irvine, 'The Peculiar People – weddings and customs' (2021) JGFH (forthcoming).

percentage of register office weddings in 1914. Second, family historians provided a disproportionate number of examples of register office weddings for the period of the war. Speed seems to have been the main motivation; unlike during peacetime, the majority of these weddings took place on the basis of a superintendent registrar's licence rather than a certificate, for example, where the husband was in the army and had a weekend's leave.[120] Again, the trends provide a warning against assuming that a decision to marry in a register office reflects a belief *in* civil marriage, as opposed to convenience or the lack of other choices.

Conclusion

The idea that English law had a single and coherent conception of marriage was true insofar as a marriage that had been validly entered into in England and Wales had the same consequences however it had been formed. But it did not prevent different religious groups from holding, and acting upon, their own very different conceptions of marriage. Nor did it mean that all religious groups had the same ability to marry in accordance with their own religious rites. There were continuing differences between Christian and non-Christian religions, between Catholics and Nonconformists, and between Orthodox and Reform Jews versus ultra-Orthodox and Liberal Jews.

The competing conceptions of marriage that were discussed in this period were also to set the tone for future interactions between the state and other non-Christian religions. The insistence by the courts that English law recognised only Christian marriage was hardly inclusive, while judicial references to the variety of ways in which marriages could be formed rarely did justice to the full range of possibilities. And as Chapter 7 will show, the consolidation of the law in the Marriage Act 1949 served to reinforce the impression that marrying in the Anglican church was the norm, just as it was ceasing to be.

---

[120] There was also a rise in the percentage of Anglican weddings that were conducted on the basis of a common licence, from 4.2 per cent in 1913 to 20.8 per cent in 1919: *Eighty-second Annual Report*, p. xxiv. While an Anglican common licence was marginally quicker than its civil counterpart, it was also more expensive.

7

Consolidating Complexity, 1920–1949

In 1921, a journalist drew attention to the 'tangle of the marriage laws' that existed in England and Wales, noting that '[s]o many anomalies exist that it is thought possible Parliament through the Government may be asked to reconsider and recast many of the existing regulations'.[1] Almost three decades later the Marriage Act 1949 finally brought all of the laws regulating marriage and weddings together into a single statute – but did very little by way of recasting the terms in which the law was stated, even less by way of removing anomalies, and absolutely nothing by way of reconsideration.

That the 1949 Act consolidated the existing laws, rather than seeking to reform them, was a missed opportunity. If anything, the law had become even more tangled and full of anomalies in the intervening period, as this chapter will show. Some of the issues that arose were of long standing but acquired new relevance in the interwar years, as demonstrated by the misunderstandings about what it meant to be authorised to register marriages in a registered place of worship and the continuing controversy as to whether the growing number of Liberal Jews could be classified as 'persons professing the Jewish religion'. Others were new. While a perusal of the list of statutes might suggest that there was little change to the weddings law during this time,[2] there were numerous Church of England Measures that altered the rules governing its weddings and caused them to diverge from those applicable to the newly disestablished Church in Wales. In addition, changes to local government affected the structures within which registration officials operated. All of these various problems, amendments, and reorganisations serve to underline why the

---

[1] *Dundee Evening Telegraph and Post*, 23 August 1921.

[2] See e.g. Stephen Cretney, *Family Law in the Twentieth Century: A History* (Oxford: Oxford University Press, 2003), p. 21, noting that 'to judge by the statute book, the first half of the twentieth century must have been a period of almost universal content with the rules governing the formalities for marriage'.

consolidation of marriage law in 1949 was welcomed, but also why further reform was needed.

Quite apart from the sheer complexity of the law, there was also the fact that the turbulence of the interwar years – and the still greater disruption occasioned by the Second World War – had had a profound impact on marriage. There were wild fluctuations in the number of couples marrying each year. In 1920, the number of weddings was at an all-time high, reflecting both postponed weddings and remarriages. For the rest of the 1920s and 1930s marriage rates, and the age at which couples married, remained relatively stable. The outbreak of war in September 1939 then led to a new rush to marry, with over 100,000 more weddings taking place in 1940 as compared to 1938.[3] The gloomy prognostication of one onlooker that 'they are all so young that they will change their minds quickly and then it will be too late'[4] reflected a new awareness of the fragility of such marriages. It was among the younger age groups that the increase in weddings was primarily concentrated, causing the average age at marriage to drop sharply.[5] And the number of divorces, which had been climbing throughout the period, sky-rocketed once the war was over.[6]

Exactly what impact all this had on *how* couples married during this period is difficult to assess, since official statistics on this are only available for 1929 and 1934. All that can be said is that the figures suggest that there were small shifts in the number of Nonconformist, Catholic, and Jewish weddings, that most weddings were still celebrated according to Anglican rites (but only just), and that the number

---

[3] ONS, 'Marriages in England and Wales, 2017', Tables 3 and 4. See also Sally Sokoloff, '"How are they at home?" Community, state and servicemen's wives in England, 1939-45' (1999) 8(1) *Women's History Review* 27, pp. 29–30 on the high rate of marriage among young men serving in the armed forces.

[4] Simon Garfield, *We Are At War: The Remarkable Diaries of Five Ordinary People in Extraordinary Times* (Ebury Press, 2009), p. 22 (recorded in the diary of Pam Ashford, 2 September 1939).

[5] The average age at first marriage fell to 21.7 for women and 24.2 for men in 1940; 15 years earlier it had been 23.8 for women and 25.6 for men: Robert Schoen and Vladimir Canudas-Romo, 'Timing effects on first marriage: Twentieth-century experience in England and Wales and the USA' (2005) 59 *Population Studies* 135, table 1a.

[6] The causes of the increase are complex, combining the widening of the grounds for divorce in 1937, the stresses of wartime, and the advent of legal aid: see Griselda Rowntree and Norman H. Carrier, 'The Resort to Divorce in England and Wales, 1858–1957' (1958) 11 *Population Studies* 188. However, since the number of formal separations – along with petitions for nullity and prosecutions for bigamy – also increased, it was clearly not simply a matter of broken marriages finding a different legal outlet.

of register office weddings was continuing to grow.[7] The main story here is the shifting balance between Anglican and civil weddings, which is explored partly in relation to the church's growing reluctance to conduct the remarriages of the increasing number of divorced persons, and partly in relation to the implications of marrying in a register office in this period.

With those broader trends in mind, this chapter will trace the story of each different route into marriage separately, since each experienced different problems.[8] Disentangling the different legal rules also serves to set the scene for the passage of the Marriage Act 1949. As the final section will show, while the 1949 Act brought the laws together in one place, it not only preserved but in some respects exaggerated the differences between them.

Disestablishment, Divergence, and Divorce

He doubted whether a matter of that kind could be satisfactorily considered without going very deeply into the whole marriage law of the country[9]

On 31 March 1920, the Church of England was disestablished in Wales and Monmouthshire. The Welsh Church Act 1914 had originally enacted that the new Church in Wales would have the same right to conduct weddings as any other religious group – that is to say, that banns and licences would cease to be legal preliminaries and couples would have to give notice at the register office, all new Anglican churches and chapels would have to be registered as places of worship, all ceremonies therein would have to include the prescribed words, and that clergy would have to be appointed as authorised persons if they wished to conduct weddings

---

[7] For estimates as to patterns during the intervening years see John Haskey, 'Marriage Rites – Trends in Marriages by Manner of Solemnisation and Denomination in England and Wales, 1841-2012' in Joanna Miles, Perveez Mody, and Rebecca Probert (eds.), *Marriage Rites and Rights* (Oxford: Hart, 2015).

[8] Save for those conducted according to the usages of the Society of Friends, which attracted comment only for their simplicity and rarity: see e.g. *Bath Chronicle*, 12 April 1924, noting the first wedding at Friends' Meeting House in Bath in 17 years; 'First Quaker Wedding for 17 Years', *Derby Daily Telegraph*, 3 February 1932; 'First in Hull for Forty Years', *Hull Daily Mail*, 1 August 1934.

[9] The Archbishop of Canterbury, responding to a suggestion by the Bishop of Lincoln that the publication of banns in the parish of residence of each of the intending spouses should 'be sufficient to authorize the solemnization of marriage in any church in the country': 'Church Assembly: The Marriage Measure', *The Times*, 22 June 1929.

in the absence of a registrar.[10] But before it came into force this particular provision was repealed by further legislation which provided that Anglican weddings were to continue as before under the auspices of the new Church in Wales.[11] Weddings thus constituted one of the 'vestiges of establishment'.[12]

This did not, however, mean that the same rules continued to be applicable to both the Church of England and the Church in Wales. In 1919, the Church of England had been given the power to pass measures that, when confirmed by Parliament, had the force of law.[13] Since such measures could only change the law governing the Church of England, they instantly created a divergence between it and the Church in Wales. The passage of a number of Church of England measures applicable to weddings – unaccompanied by any equivalent legislative provision for the Church in Wales – added considerable complexity to the law in this period.

Some of these changes were occasioned by the way in which the Church of England was reorganising itself. With formerly separate parishes being grouped together as united benefices, decisions had to be made about whether banns could be called, and weddings celebrated, in the old parish church or the new one. The Union of Benefices Measure 1923 somewhat elliptically stated that parishioners of any newly enlarged or amalgamated parish would have the 'same rights' to be married in what was now the parish church as if it had always been the parish church.[14] The failure to make any provision for couples to be married in what had *formerly* been their parish church may have arisen because it was envisaged that many churches would simply cease to exist.[15] Where

---

[10] Welsh Church Act 1914, s. 23. Existing churches were to become registered buildings automatically, while existing incumbents were to be entitled to be appointed as authorised persons upon application to the Registrar-General. For the earlier proposals see Nicholas Roberts, 'The Historical Background to the Marriage (Wales) Act 2010' (2011) 13 *Ecclesiastical Law Journal* 39.

[11] Welsh Church (Temporalities) Act 1919, s. 6.

[12] Thomas Glyn Watkin, 'Vestiges of Establishment: The Ecclesiastical and Canon law of the Church in Wales' (1990) 2 *Ecclesiastical Law Journal* 110, p. 112.

[13] Church of England Assembly (Powers) Act 1919. On this see Canon Peter Boulton, 'Twentieth-Century Revision of Canon Law in the Church of England' (2000) 5 *Ecclesiastical Law Journal* 353, p. 354.

[14] Union of Benefices Measure 1923, s. 25(1).

[15] The preceding section of the 1923 Measure was rather depressingly entitled 'Pulling Down, Sale, and Appropriation of Churches'. For an example of the demolition of churches within united benefices see 'Churches: Privy Council Dismisses Appeals', *Church Times*, 29 January 1932.

the church survived, and couples continued to be married in it,[16] orders had to be passed validating such marriages.[17]

Further complex issues were raised by the failed attempts to produce a new official version of the 1662 Prayer Book. Discussions had already been going on for some time by 1920,[18] but following disestablishment the Church in Wales withdrew from the debates.[19] Throughout the 1920s there continued to be discussions about modernising the marriage service, and the revised version that formed part of the new Prayer Book approved by the Church Assembly in 1927[20] was distinctly different from its predecessor. The earthy references to 'men's carnal lusts and appetites', 'brute beasts that have no understanding', and marriage being ordained for the avoidance of 'fornication' among 'such persons as have not the gift of continency' were replaced by more delicate references to 'natural instincts and affections' or removed entirely.[21] The change that captured most attention, however, was the substitution of symmetrical vows, with brides no longer declaring that they would 'obey'.[22] Changes to the Prayer Book were not, however, a matter for the

[16] This might well occur where there was a quick turnover of clergy and the new incumbent was unaware of what had gone before. For example, under the Union of Benefices Act 1919, an Order in Council on 31 January 1922 set out the union of the parishes of Brignall and Rokeby, with the latter as the parish church. This scheme only came into effect upon the retirement of the incumbent of Brignall, which took place in 1929. The incumbent of Rokeby – himself newly appointed – who then became the rector of the joint parishes was presumably unaware that Brignall was not licensed for the solemnization of marriages, and marriages were solemnised there between 3 June 1929 and 14 October 1936 before the error was realised (*Church Times*, 15 March 1929; Brignall Church Order (Provisional Orders (Marriages) Confirmation Act 1937). A quick succession of appointments seems to have been responsible for a similar error at Stowell (*Church Times*, 19 August 1938, 4 November 1938, 30 December 1938; St Leonard Stowell Order, Provisional Order (Marriages) Confirmation Act 1941).

[17] For further examples see the Provisional Order (Marriages) Confirmation Acts passed in 1932 and 1936.

[18] See *The Times*, 8 July 1911, 16 February 1912.

[19] 'Position of the Church in Wales: Archbishop and the Prayer-Book', *The Times*, 4 October 1928.

[20] *The Times*, 7 July 1927, reporting the 'decisive majority' in favour of the Prayer Book Measure.

[21] On the changing symbolism of the Anglican liturgy, see Sarah Farrimond, 'Church of England Weddings and Ritual Symbolism' in *Marriage Rites and Rights*.

[22] For reports of the debates on this change see *The Times*, 6 July 1923, 15 June 1927. A survey of clergy suggested a strong preference for the status quo, with 70 per cent of the 9,706 responses to a questionnaire survey being against symmetrical vows: *The Times*, 9 July 1923.

Established Church alone to decide,[23] and Parliament's subsequent rejection of the Prayer Book Measure meant that the new service had no official status.

Despite this, there was a clear sense that couples could use it if they so wished, and their choices were seen as reflecting whether they valued equality or tradition.[24] But the use of the revised service raised questions about the status of the liturgy itself, what it meant to be married according to the rites of the Church of England, and how far other departures from the set form might be possible. Even before the church had approved the new form, one bishop had gone so far as to claim that 'there was not a single church in which the strict letter of the Prayer Book was carried out'.[25] Either there were hundreds of thousands of marriages that were invalid because they did not adhere to the exact words of the Prayer Book, or the precise words used did not actually matter, at least in legal terms, at all.

Exactly what should, or did, matter for validity remained a matter of some debate and uncertainty. In 1930, the long-standing principle that the wedding had to take place in the parish where at least one of them was resident was modified to allow couples in England[26] to marry in the church that was their usual place of worship.[27] The Archbishop of Canterbury described it as meeting a 'very general wish', suggesting that 'it continually happens that people are in the habit of worshipping at churches other than those in which they may be said to have only a geographical interest acquired by residence'.[28] There was perhaps an element of wishful thinking in this. While new forms of transport had made it easier to travel to a different church to worship on a Sunday morning, the evidence suggests that fewer people were attending any church.[29] In any case, the new measure was designed to cater for

---

[23] The Church in Wales, being disestablished, had the freedom to choose what service to use without this being approved by Parliament: see discussions in *The Times*, 2 May 1928.

[24] See Timothy Willem Jones, 'Love, Honour and Obey? Romance, Subordination and Marital Subjectivity in Interwar Britain', ch. 6 in Alana Harris and Timothy Willem Jones (eds.), *Love and Romance in Britain, 1918–1970* (Basingstoke: Palgrave Macmillan, 2014).

[25] 'Prayer-Book Revision: Bishops' Discussion', *The Times*, 17 April 1923.

[26] It was eventually extended to the Church in Wales by the Marriage (Wales and Monmouthshire) Act 1962: see further Chapter 8.

[27] Marriage Measure 1930. For the recommendations of the Banns of Marriage Committee see *The Times*, 15 June 1927; for the reports of debates by the Church Assembly and some of the proposals for wider reform see *The Times*, 17 November 1928 and 22 June 1929.

[28] *Hansard,* HL Deb., vol. 76, col. 928, 13 March 1930.

[29] Field, *Periodizing Secularization*, ch. 7.

committed members of the Church of England rather than occasional worshippers, since a person's usual place of worship was to be determined by whether they were included on its electoral roll.[30] Moreover, unless a licence was obtained, banns still had to be called in the parish where the bride and groom were resident,[31] adding to the legal complexity and expense of this option.

Two further measures – neither of which applied to marriages in the Church in Wales – were motivated by uncertainty as to the legal requirements. One of these related to who should publish the banns.[32] The post-First World War shortage of clergy[33] had led to lay persons being authorised to take services, and in the course of doing so reading the banns for couples.[34] The Archbishop of Canterbury introduced a measure to 'regularise' this practice, the legality of which he acknowledged might be regarded as 'doubtful'.[35] The second related to the licensing of chapels of ease under the Marriage Act 1836[36] and again had its origins in doubts as to the legality of certain practices that had developed.[37] The Archbishop of Canterbury's reassurance that the matter was not controversial could not quite disguise the fact that there was

---

[30] Marriage Measure 1930, s. 4. The number who were on the church's electoral roll was less than half the number of active church attenders: Field, *Periodizing Secularization*, table 9.2.

[31] Marriage Measure 1930, s. 3 (on the grant of a licence) and s. 1(2) (on the necessity of banns being published in the parish of residence).

[32] Banns of Marriage Measure 1934.

[33] Concerns about a shortage of clergy had been noted before the First World War but were more frequently voiced after 1920. See e.g. *The Times*, 9 June 1920 (report of the Additional Curates Society on how fewer individuals were being ordained), 19 November 1920 (reporting discussion at the National Assembly), 7 July 1922 ('Bishops on Dearth of Clergy', reporting debates in Convocation), 3 October 1924 ('Church Short of 3,000 Clergy', reporting discussion at the Church Congress).

[34] C.f. the advice offered by the incumbent of Helmdon in Northamptonshire, who advised couples to give notice at the register office instead on the basis that '[a] lay-reader cannot publish banns': 'Publication of Banns', *The Times*, 13 May 1924.

[35] *Hansard*, HL Deb., vol. 93 col. 1094, 25 July 1934. During the discussion in the House of Clergy the year before it had similarly been noted that the proposed measure 'would establish the legality of a great number of marriages which might otherwise be illegal': 'Banns of Marriage: Provision for Reading by Laymen', *The Times*, 14 November 1933.

[36] Marriage (Licensing of Chapels) Measure 1938.

[37] The Marriage Act 1836 had allowed a bishop to licence the solemnization of marriages in chapels of ease 'for Persons residing within a District the Limits whereof shall be specified in the Bishop's Licence' (s. 26). The Archbishop of Canterbury reported that it had become 'customary' for such licenses to include districts 'which did not wholly lie within the parish in which the chapel was situated', but that doubts had arisen as to the legality of such marriages: *Hansard*, HL Deb., vol. 108, col. 674, 13 April 1938.

clearly considerable uncertainty among bishops both as to the scope of their powers and as to how such powers had been exercised.[38]

Indeed, the complexities of the law governing weddings in the Church of England continued to require regular remedial action.[39] Of the 46 orders made validating marriages between 1920 and 1949, 28 involved questions about the status of Anglican churches. There were churches that had once been the parish church but had been replaced by a new church within the same parish,[40] new churches that had been consecrated but not formally substituted for the existing parish church,[41] and churches that had been built in addition to the parish church.[42] In the case of St John's Shotley, in Northumberland, the realisation of the necessity of licensing seems to have been particularly belated: the church had been consecrated on 30 August 1837 but was not licensed for weddings until 11 November 1936.[43]

During the Second World War, the complete destruction of a large number of churches – and the damage suffered by many more – led to a further rethinking of what provision was needed for the church's shrinking number of attendees.[44] Newly created Diocesan Reorganisation Committees were given the power to defer the restoration of churches damaged by bombing,[45] necessitating special provision to be made for the weddings that might otherwise have taken place there.[46]

---

[38] As the Archbishop explained, the Home Office had concluded that the matter could not be dealt with under the Marriages Validity (Provisional Orders) Act 1924 'because it would be far from easy to obtain exhaustive lists of the chapels affected' (*Hansard*, HL Deb., vol. 108, col. 675, 13 April 1938), which in itself raised questions about the quality of record-keeping within the church.

[39] It was somewhat ironic that in 1924 Parliament had to pass legislation to validate the validating legislation, having realised that the Provisional Order (Marriages) Act 1905 had not authorised the inclusion of certain clauses that had been a standard part of every order made under it: see *Hansard*, HL Deb., vol. 56, col. 1025, 25 March 1924.

[40] See the Provisional Orders (Marriages) Confirmation (No. 2) Act 1926, and the Acts passed in 1927, 1932, 1933, and 1935.

[41] Such orders appear in the Acts passed in 1925, 1928, 1929, and 1936.

[42] Such orders appear in the Acts passed in 1926, 1935, and 1945.

[43] St John, Shotley Order: Provisional Orders (Marriages) Confirmation Act 1937.

[44] For discussion of the extent of the destruction and the way in which decisions were made see Peter J. Larkham and Joe L. Nasr, 'Decision-making under duress: the treatment of churches in the City of London during and after World War II' (2012) 39 *Urban History* 285. On the decline in church attendance see Field, *Periodizing Secularization*, Table 9.2.

[45] Diocesan Reorganisation Committees Measure 1941, s. 3(1).

[46] Diocesan Reorganisation Committees Measure 1941, s. 3(3). Such provision was necessary because the existing legislation only addressed where banns could be called, and marriages solemnised, if there was no parish church (Marriage Act 1823, s. 12), or where the parish church had been 'demolished in order to be rebuilt', or was under repair (s. 13).

Further reorganisation was contemplated by the Reorganisation Areas
Measure 1944 and the Pastoral Reorganisation Measure 1949.[47]

Marrying in church remained the ideal for some,[48] and the default for
many more, whether they were churchgoers or not.[49] But while the official
statistics that are available suggest that the majority of weddings were still
celebrated in an Anglican church, it was fast becoming a very slim
majority.[50] The escalating complexity of the laws governing Anglican
weddings was driven at least in part by a desire to make it *easier* for
couples to marry according to Anglican rites. But it was the Anglican
church's attitude to divorce – or rather, the remarriage of the divorced –
that had a more significant impact on the numbers doing so. Cosmo Lang,
who had succeeded Davidson as Archbishop of Canterbury in 1928, took
an even stricter line than his predecessor.[51] In 1932, he had made it clear
that he did not wish a church wedding to be available to those who were
unbaptised,[52] those who were within the 'prohibited degrees' as set out
within the Prayer Book,[53] and those who were divorced.[54] He also issued

---

[47] See Martin Elengorn, 'Measure for Measure' (2001–2) 6 *Ecclesiastical Law Journal* 395.

[48] The romantic Linda in Nancy Mitford's *The Pursuit of Love* (1945) is described as always
having had 'a mental image of what her wedding would be like, that is, as much like
a wedding in a pantomime as possible, in a large church, with crowds both outside and in,
with photographers, arum lilies, tulle, bridesmaids, and an enormous choir singing her
favourite tune' (p. 75).

[49] A 1947 survey by Mass Observation found that although three-quarters of their female
respondents said their ideal wedding would be in church, 'half said they were not religious
and only one in five said they belonged to any particular church or sect': 'The State of
Matrimony' (1947), p. 12. While these comments did not specifically relate to Anglican
weddings, the divergence between the numbers who were members of the Anglican
church (as indicated by its electoral roll) and the numbers who married there was
particularly striking: see further Field, *Periodizing Secularization*, Table 9.2.

[50] See Haskey, 'Marriage Rites'.

[51] On Davidson's approach see Chapter 6, and see further Bruce S. Bennett, 'The Church of
England and the Law of Divorce since 1857: Marriage Discipline, Ecclesiastical Law and
the Establishment' (1994) 45 *Journal of Ecclesiastical History* 625.

[52] Refusing to marry the unbaptised was particularly controversial, since not only was there
no statutory exemption for clergy in such cases, but no canonical authority either. On the
subsequent attempts to introduce a canon that would prevent the marriage in church of
the unbaptised, see Boulton, 'Twentieth-Century Revision', p. 364.

[53] By 1932 the list of prohibited degrees as set out in the Prayer Book was even further
removed from the rules laid down by statute following the passage of the Deceased
Brother's Widow's Marriage Act 1921 and the Marriage (Prohibited Degrees of
Relationship) Act 1931. Both amended the Deceased Wife's Sister's Marriage Act 1907,
thereby extending its provision that such marriages were 'not to be void as a civil contract'
and the exemption for Anglican clergy: on which see further Chapter 6.

[54] The direction appeared in the *Canterbury Diocesan Gazette*: see *The Times*,
5 January 1932. For commentary see 'Primate and Church Marriages: Vows – or

a pastoral letter stating that the marriage service was 'intended for those who profess and call themselves Christians' and pointing out that those who did not feel able to take its 'tremendous vows' could marry in a register office.[55] When the grounds for divorce were finally widened in 1937,[56] the existing exemption for Anglican clergy was expanded. Henceforth they could refuse to marry *any* person whose former marriage had been dissolved on any ground and whose former spouse was still living, and could also refuse to permit the wedding taking place in their church or chapel.[57] With the increase in divorce that followed the 1937 Act – and the even greater increase in the wake of the Second World War – there were many remarriages that no longer took place in the Anglican church. This was to have an impact on weddings in other places of worship[58] and, more significantly, on those in the register office, to which we now turn.

Marriage in the Register Office

the sort of weddings that are better celebrated in register offices than in church can now be just as pleasant as church ceremonies[59]

In 1924, the opening of a new register office in Marylebone Town Hall attracted some attention. The *Daily Mail* described it as the finest in the country, detailing its sweeping marble staircase and richly panelled rooms.[60] Six years later, there was speculation that there would be 'keen competition' to be the first to marry in London's fifteenth-century Guildhall.[61] And in 1933 even greater fanfare surrounded the first weddings at Caxton Hall, Westminster's register office; there, it was

Register Office: The Glory Of Parenthood: Critics Of His New Orders', *Daily Mail*, 6 January 1932; 'Marriage of the Unbaptised: Free Church Replies to Primate: "Our Ceremony is as Sacred"', *Daily Mail*, 7 January 1932; *Church Times*, 8 January 1932, 15 January 1932, p. 55.

[55] 'The Pastoral Letter', *Church Times*, 8 January 1932, p. 46.

[56] Matrimonial Causes Act 1937. The new grounds were cruelty, desertion for three years, and incurable insanity.

[57] Matrimonial Causes Act 1937, s. 12. The *Church Times*, 30 July 1937, welcomed the 'complete immunity' of the clergy under the new legislation but somewhat grudgingly noted that it did not follow that the Church could 'treat such a marriage as ecclesiastically null and void'.

[58] See, e.g., Jenny Gordon, 'A remarriage according to the rites of the Methodist Church, 1940' (2021) JGFH (forthcoming).

[59] 'New Register Office Splendour', *Daily Mail*, 28 September 1933.

[60] 'New Register Office: Rush to be Married in It', *Daily Mail*, 4 October 1924.

[61] 'Guildhall Marriages', *Daily Mail*, 20 March 1930.

noted, couples could choose one of six rooms, depending on the scale of their wedding, with 'room for all of even a debutante's wedding guests', while 'service, catering and every suitable splendour' could be had 'for a fee'.[62]

The emergence of these attractive new venues was significant for both social and legal reasons. The 1920s saw an increasing number of reports of high-profile couples tying the knot in a register office.[63] Some were doing so because other options were closed to them in the light of the post-First World War surge in divorce and the hardening attitude of the Church of England towards remarriages in church.[64] Others were combining the register office wedding with a religious ceremony of their choosing.[65] Some, it was noted, had faced parental opposition;[66] other weddings were what earlier generations would have condemned as mésalliances.[67] There were also a few 'celebrity' weddings where the public profile of the bride or groom led them to marry in the register

[62] 'New Register Office Splendour: Floodlights for Brides', *Daily Mail*, 28 September 1933. The first brides who married there reflected the range of facilities that were available: the first arrived in a luxurious car, 'resplendent in sables and purple orchids', while the second, the 65-year-old bride of a railway porter, arrived on foot: 'Weddings De Luxe at New "Super" Register Office', *Daily Mail*, 3 October 1933. Later weddings included that of Cary Grant and Virginia Cherrill, en route to Hollywood: 'Film Stars' "Secret" Wedding', *Daily Mail*, 10 February 1934.

[63] See, e.g., 'French Prince Married', *Daily Mail*, 16 April 1928. In a niche 'economist and dancer' category, we have the marriage of John Maynard Keynes to a Russian ballerina: 'Mme. Lopokova Married: Crowds Greet Her Outside Register Office', *Daily Mail*, 5 August 1925.

[64] It was noted in 1920 that marriage in the register office was 'largely used by persons whose former marriage has been dissolved by reason of their unfaithfulness': Arthur S. May, *Marriage in Church, Chapel and Register Office: a Practical Handbook* (London: Longmans, Green & Co, 1920), p. 66. For accounts of post-divorce register office weddings, see 'Lady Dalmeny's Wedding: 8.30am ceremony: Walk Through Snow Cheered by Village Girls', *Daily Mail*, 17 March 1920; 'Duke of Westminster: Coming Marriage with Mrs Violet Rowley', *Daily Mail*, 26 November 1920; 'Major C.W. Lowther, M.P.', *Daily Mail*, 17 February 1921; 'Duchess Weds: Ceremony at London Register Office', *Daily Mail*, 5 July 1921; 'Viscount Glerawley To Marry Lady Kilconnel', *Daily Mail*, 13 July 1921; 'Almina Countess of Carnarvon To Marry Guards Colonel', *Daily Mail*, 19 December 1923.

[65] 'Tomorrow's civil marriage to Miss Schilizzi', *Daily Mail*, 13 September 1921, noting that the second ceremony would take place according to the rites of the Greek Orthodox Church; 'Married in a Mosque: British Bride's Two Weddings', *Daily Mail*, 16 October 1930.

[66] 'Miss M. McCormick: Secret Marriage to Former Riding-Master', *Daily Mail*, 16 April 1923; 'Royal Lovers on Way Here', *Daily Mail*, 22 February 1932.

[67] 'Miss Jose Collins: Marriage to Lord R. Innes-Ker: Secret Ceremony', *Daily Mail*, 2 November 1920.

office in the (often vain) hope of securing some privacy. It would be going too far to claim that register office weddings were becoming fashionable; rather, the glamour of many of these brides made the backdrop of the register office seem particularly drab. The Mayor of Westminster's statement welcoming the fact that register office weddings 'can now be just as pleasant as church ceremonies'[68] was also a reminder that this had not previously been the case.[69]

In the case of Caxton Hall, the timing of the change had particular significance. In 1930 responsibility for the registration system was transferred from the Poor Law authorities to new county, or county borough, councils.[70] Registration officers appointed by councils became salaried officers, rather than receiving fees for each marriage they registered.[71] So the fees paid by couples now went to the council; the more weddings it conducted, the more money it received. Moreover, while the same fee was payable whatever the size of the room or the number of guests, at Caxton Hall couples could also pay to hire rooms for the reception after the wedding.[72]

Of course, in areas that had fewer register office weddings, or which served a less wealthy clientele, there was less incentive to provide more attractive venues. Outside London, the impact of the reorganisation of the registration system was mainly administrative. Since the boundaries of registration districts were often not those of counties and county boroughs, the immediate effect of the transfer of powers was that many councils acquired jurisdiction over parts of neighbouring counties.[73] Over the course of the 1930s there was much rejigging of registration districts to try to align them with the new units of administration.

---

[68] 'New Register Office Splendour', *Daily Mail*, 28 September 1933.

[69] The gushing descriptions of Caxton Hall explicitly contrasted its clean, bright, and 'immaculately painted' rooms in which they were celebrated with the dingy, cobwebbed, and cramped offices they had replaced ('Weddings De Luxe'). Similarly, the claim that 'hundreds of engaged couples from all parts of the kingdom' had contacted the registrar to ask if they could be married in Marylebone Town Hall (*Daily Mail*, 4 October 1924) had rather suggested that other register offices were not quite as attractive.

[70] Local Government Act 1929, ss. 1, 21.

[71] Local Government Act 1929, s. 22. Those who had been appointed previously could apply to become salaried officers.

[72] 'New Register Office Splendour: Floodlights for Brides', *Daily Mail*, 28 September 1933.

[73] Local Government Act 1929, s. 21(1)(b) provided that where registration districts were not wholly comprised within one county or county borough, they would be allocated to whichever one was estimated by the Registrar-General to contain 'the larger or largest part of the population of the registration district'.

Far removed from the glamour of Caxton Hall, there was another 'sort' of wedding that was regarded as suitable for the register office and which tended not to be accompanied by much celebration. These were the weddings where the bride was pregnant or had already had a child outside marriage. Here it is necessary to tread cautiously for two reasons. The first is the difficulty in obtaining reliable estimates of the extent of premarital pregnancy. The publication of official statistics showing that in 1938 18 per cent of all brides had been pregnant on their wedding day[74] occasioned a considerable amount of debate but, as Mass Observation pointed out, was not necessarily evidence of a change in social values since 'no comparable data' had been collected previously.[75] The second is because the statistics that were published did not differentiate between different types of weddings. Commentators did nonetheless often associate the register office with bridal pregnancy.[76] In Walter Greenwood's 1933 novel *Love on the Dole*, the wedding of Harry Hardcastle and his pregnant girlfriend Helen Hawkins is marked by a sense of shame and dreary resignation: standing on the steps of the workhouse, where the register office is located, all Harry can muster is an unhappy 'Come on, 'Elen. Let's get it over with.'[77]

In the wake of the Second World War it was the rise in divorce, rather than premarital pregnancy, that prompted the Denning Committee to make recommendations as to the content of weddings in the register office.[78] In its view, 'the form of marriage in Register Offices should be revised so as to emphasise the solemnity of the occasion and clearly to

[74] *The Registrar-General's Statistical Review of England and Wales for the years 1938 and 1939* (London: HMSO, 1947), p. 193.

[75] Mass Observation, *The State of Matrimony* (1947), p. 4. Subsequent investigations into attitudes towards sex before marriage did however suggest a shift in such attitudes: see Moya Woodside, 'Health and Happiness in Marriage' (1946) 4 *Health Education* 146; Liz Stanley, *Sex Surveyed 1949–1994: From Mass Observation's 'Little Kinsey' to the National Survey and the Hite Reports* (London: Taylor & Francis, 1995).

[76] C. Stella Davies, *North Country Bred: A Working-Class Family Chronicle* (London: Routledge & Kegan Paul, 1963), p. 153.

[77] Walter Greenwood, *Love on the Dole* (Vintage, 1993, first published 1933), p. 233. For an equally downbeat example of a register office wedding where the couple had already had a child together see Jerry White, *The Worst Street in North London: Campbell Bunk, Islington, between the Wars* (London: Routledge and Kegan Paul, 1986), p. 176; the wife recalled that a neighbour was 'good enough to come with us' to act as a witness and that the reception consisted of 'a cheese sandwich'.

[78] For contemporary criticism of the lack of impressiveness in the ritual of the register office wedding, see Margaret Cole, *Marriage: Past and Present* (London: JM Dent & Sons, 1938), p. 130, noting that it consisted merely of the repetition of certain 'uncoloured' statements 'with sometimes a homily by the registrar thrown in'.

express the principle that marriage is the personal union, for better or for worse, of one man with one woman, exclusive of all others on either side so long as both shall live'.[79] This recommendation was explicitly modelled on the practices of churches, whose wedding services were, in the eyes of the Committee, 'a model of what the ceremony should be where the parties have a sound religious faith'.[80] Registrars were subsequently asked to remind couples that they were exchanging vows of a 'solemn and binding character' and that 'marriage, according to the law of this country, is the union of one man and one woman, voluntarily entered into, for life, to the exclusion of all others'.[81]

The recommendation did something to fill the hole that the prohibition on the inclusion of religious content almost a century earlier had left,[82] although it may not have been entirely welcomed by those couples who were tying the knot for the second time. It was the superintendent registrar, as the more senior official, who was given this task of addressing the couple. This gave these officers a specific role within the ceremony for the first time,[83] albeit one that was to remain undefined as a matter of law.

Of more immediate practical significance than the question of what a superintendent registrar was for was the issue of whether those conducting weddings in registered places of worship were actually authorised to do so.

Marriages in Registered Places of Worship

If parson didn't tie us up, registrar did – all legal – as right as ninepence[84]

In 1938, J. B. Priestley's play *When We Are Married* was first performed on the London stage.[85] Set in 1908, it depicted three highly respectable couples celebrating what they believed to be their 25th wedding anniversary, having all married on the same morning at the same chapel. They then learnt that the man who married them – new in his post, and straight

---

[79] *Final Report of the Committee on Procedure in Matrimonial Causes*, Cm 7024 (London: HMSO, 1947), p. 17.

[80] *Ibid.*, p. 33.

[81] Stephen Cretney, 'Relationship: Law Content and Form' in Judith Trowell and Carola Thorpe (eds.), *Re-Rooted Lives* (Bristol: Jordans, 2007), p. 166.

[82] On which see Chapter 4.

[83] The change was reflected in the way in which marriages were recorded, with the superintendent registrar now signing before the registrar.

[84] J. B. Priestley, *When We Are Married* (1938), Act Three.

[85] It opened at St Martin's Theatre in October 1938 and transferred to the larger Princes' Theatre in March 1939: see *The Times*, 12 October 1938, 28 March 1939.

out of college – was not actually authorised to do so. All of them immediately assumed that they were not married, leading one or two of them to wonder whether they actually wanted to be. Before any of them could pursue their dreams of a new life, they were reminded that 'in them days – twenty-five years since – chapel wedding – registrar had to be there an' all – to sign certificate'. Reassured as to the legitimacy of their marriages, the couples resume their interrupted celebrations.

When We Are Married was a hugely popular play. It was regularly performed on the stage,[86] was broadcast on the Home Service,[87] and was quickly adapted for the cinema. The hole in the plot is of course the claim by the unauthorised 'parson'[88] that he did not realise what he needed to do to be recorded 'as an authorised person'. Given that the concept of an authorised person was only created in 1898 and that prior to this the status of the person conducting the ceremony was irrelevant as long as the registrar was present, it was implausible that a Nonconformist minister would have spent a quarter of a century worrying about the validity of the marriages he had conducted in 1883, or have expressed his concerns using that terminology. But unless they were extremely well-versed in the evolution of the law regulating weddings, audiences would doubtless have missed this subtlety.

For couples getting married in a registered place of worship in 1938,[89] as opposed to in 1883, there would not be the convenient *deus ex machina* of the registrar if the person officiating at the wedding turned out not to be authorised, but the somewhat slower machinery of a provisional order sanctioned by Parliament.[90] Between 1920 and 1949, it proved necessary to make quite a few of these orders to validate ceremonies that had taken place in registered places of worship without either an authorised person

---

[86] There was a revival at the Vaudeville Theatre in 1941 (*The Times*, 3 March 1941), along with numerous regional productions (*Dover Express*, 1 September 1939; *Western Daily Press*, 1 December 1939; *Hull Daily Mail*, 24 February 1940; *Nottingham Evening Post*, 16 April 1940).

[87] *The Times*, 29 July 1940, 27 November 1948.

[88] The term is the one used by the characters in the play, although it would normally signify an Anglican clergyman.

[89] For a case which bears such a close resemblance to the plot of *When We Are Married* that it may well have been Priestley's inspiration, see 'Marriages by Unauthorized Minister', *The Times*, 20 March 1938 (a young Methodist minister with no previous experience, who was under the impression that he was authorised to register the marriages he had conducted, and who had solemnised nine marriages without a registrar being present).

[90] Admittedly, this would probably have made for a less successful play.

or a registrar being present.[91] By this period, many of the first authorised persons would have retired, and their successors would not have had the same awareness of the campaign that had led to the 1898 Act or the fact that authorisation was not automatic.[92] Once the register books had been issued, there was nothing to prevent an unauthorised successor from entering the details of any subsequent marriages there, and it might take some time for the mistake to be discovered.[93]

There were some illuminating discussions behind the scenes in 1940 when the Home Office wrote to the Registrar-General to check whether there had been any problematic cases that year, in the expectation that there probably would be.[94] The reply noted yet another minister who had not realised that he had to be appointed as an authorised person.[95] An order was duly drafted to confirm the validity of the marriages celebrated in each of the churches, and copies were sent to each to be displayed on their doors during August 1940 so that their congregations were made aware of what had happened, although given what else was going on it seems unlikely that they would have given the matter much thought.[96] While it was hoped that the publicity would make everyone more careful,

[91] See the Provisional Order (Marriages) Confirmation Acts passed in 1930, 1937, 1938, 1941, and 1947, and the Provisional Orders (Marriages) Confirmation (No. 2) Act 1932. The 1947 Act alone listed six different orders relating to different denominations.

[92] For an example of contemporary confusion see *Tamworth Herald*, 20 March 1937, noting the rejoicing of the Bolebridge Street Hall at being 'licensed for marriages for all time under an "authorised person"'. Advice that the presence of a registrar was 'not absolutely necessary at a marriage at a dissenting place of worship registered for marriages' was true but unhelpful without additional explanation: see, e.g., 'Answers to Correspondents', *Nottingham Evening Post*, 11 January 1926.

[93] While superintendent registrars were directed to check whether the place specified in the notice of marriage had an authorised person (Rules and Regulations under the Marriage Act 1898 (61 & 62 Vict c. 58) For the Guidance of Registration Officers 1899, SI 1899/78), they were clearly not always informed when the previous authorised person had left.

[94] Letter from HO to MR Shackle, noting that 'at this period of year we have generally had to frame a Bill covering orders made by the Secretary of State under the Marriages Validity (Provisional Orders) Act 1905 and 1924, and I just want to make sure we are not overlooking any': TNA, HO45/25042, 5 April 1940.

[95] The marriages in question had taken place at the Baptist church on Higham Hill Rd and at the Tabernacle, Greenleaf Road. The local superintendent registrar had not realised the minister's lack of authorisation, accepting his returns every quarter and issuing books of marriage certificates to him. The trustees had passed the necessary minute authorising him as soon as they realised the necessity of doing so.

[96] TNA, HO45/25042, letter postmarked 1 October 1940 noting that the church had suffered from air raids and that the whole district was suffering from difficulties because of this and the care of refugees from the East End.

for a time at least, it was accepted that there would always be some mistakes:

> The only way to prevent similar mistakes generally would be to ensure that every Church of England and Nonconformist minister in the country had so firm a grasp of the technicalities of the Marriage Acts that he would never in any circumstances make a mistake about when and where he could validly celebrate a marriage. Considering the many and various possibilities of error and the notorious Haziness of many ministers on legal matters, I fear this is utopian. There are not really very many invalid marriages: two or three cases in a year come to the notice of the Home Office on the average; they are usually due to some misunderstanding or neglect about the registration of a church for marriages, and it is impossible to say beforehand where the next one will turn up or exactly what the mistake will be. No warning circular could cover all the possible forms of error, and if such a circular were possible it would only confuse the recipient's minds.[97]

The conclusion was that the authorities would have to resign themselves to potential errors and use the machinery provided to put them right.

The question as to the status of a marriage conducted in the absence of an authorised person arose in a bigamy case in 1947. Patrick Sharkey was found not guilty of bigamy on the basis that his first marriage, conducted in a Catholic church which had not appointed an authorised person, had never existed at all 'in the eyes of the Law'.[98] The phrasing of the Marriage Act 1898 was somewhat ambiguous on this point, in that it did not make it clear whether a marriage was only void if it was 'knowingly and wilfully' celebrated in the absence of an authorised person or whether the presence of an authorised person was an absolute requirement.[99] In short,

---

[97] TNA, HO45/25042.

[98] 'Marriages 23 Years Ago May Not Be Valid', *Hull Daily Mail*, 5 March 1947. It should be noted that the criminal context did not make it more likely that the courts would find the first marriage to be void; in earlier bigamy trials judges had been willing to presume in favour of the validity of the first marriage on the basis that those officiating might otherwise find themselves accused of a criminal offence: see *R* v. *Henry Mainwaring* (1856) 1 D & B 132; 169 ER 948; *R* v. *Cresswell* (1876) 1 QBD 446.

[99] This ambiguity derived from the fact that the 1898 Act did not set out the grounds on which a marriage would be void, but merely how the 1836 Act was to be amended. As such, it provided that the provision of the 1836 Act invalidating marriages 'knowingly and wilfully' celebrated in the absence of a registrar was repealed 'in respect of any marriage authorised by and solemnised in accordance with this Act' (s. 15). This was clear enough so far as weddings in the presence of an authorised person went, but it left open what the result would be if the person officiating at the ceremony was not in fact authorised. On a literal interpretation of s. 15, if a ceremony had not been conducted by an authorised person in accordance with the 1898 Act, then the annulling provision of the 1836 Act still

there was a strong case that such marriages were void even if the parties had genuinely believed the person marrying them to be authorised.

The scope for problems to arise was mitigated to some extent by the fact that most weddings in registered places of worship were still conducted in the presence of a registrar. Even when the head of the Salvation Army officiated at his daughter's wedding in the Army's Regent Hall in London, it was noted that after the couple had exchanged their vows, they 'went to a side hall where they were married again by the registrar'.[100] Whether a wedding was attended by a registrar did, however, differ considerably between denominations;[101] Catholic weddings were still overwhelmingly conducted in the presence of a registrar,[102] whereas among Nonconformists only a minority were.[103]

There was, of course, still the question of whether any given place of worship had been registered for weddings in the first place. The interwar years saw the growth of a number of newer denominations. The fastest-growing denomination was the Elim Pentecostal church;[104] founded in 1915, it had no places of worship for weddings until 1930.[105] Other denominations that saw significant growth – such as the Christian Scientists and Jehovah's Witnesses – had no places of worship for weddings at all.[106] As before, couples from different denominations, or whose place of

applied, and in such cases it would be difficult to argue that the couple had not knowingly married in the absence of a registrar.

[100] *Exeter and Plymouth Gazette*, 4 June 1929.

[101] *The Registrar-General's Statistical Review of England and Wales for the Year 1929* (London: HMSO, 1930), pp. 62–3.

[102] In 1929, 95 per cent of weddings registered as taking place in a Catholic church had been conducted in the presence of a registrar: *Statistical Review for 1929*, p. 62. On occasion local factors might prompt the appointment of an authorised person: see, e.g., Jim Lancaster, 'Marriage – Catholic and Civil' (2020) 38(3) *Lancashire Family History & Heraldry Society* 24, p. 27, noting how a 'threatened work-to-rule' by registrars in Manchester in 1931 'prompted several Roman Catholic Parishes in Manchester to have an Authorised Person'.

[103] Overall, 58 per cent of weddings in Nonconformist places of worship were celebrated in the presence of an authorised person. Among Wesleyan Methodists it was 80 per cent: *Statistical Review for 1929*, pp. 62–63.

[104] Field, *Periodizing Secularization*, table 7.1.

[105] *London Gazette*, 24 June 1930, recording the registration of the Elim church in Bermondsey. As in earlier decades, individuals might marry in places of worship registered to other denominations: see, e.g., *Bath Chronicle*, 8 August 1931, recording the wedding of the minister of the Bath Elim Foursquare Gospel Church at the Morice Square Baptist Church in Plymouth. Ministers from both the Baptist and Elim churches were in attendance.

[106] On the ambivalence towards marriage within the Christian Science movement, see Rodney Stark, 'The Rise and Fall of Christian Science' (1998) 13(2) *Journal of Contemporary Religion* 189.

worship had not been registered for marriages, either found a registered place of worship that would accommodate them[107] or resorted to the register office and went on to have a religious blessing.[108]

Followers of non-Judeo-Christian religions still accounted for only a tiny minority of the population of England and Wales. The small Hindu community was more focused on raising awareness of their religion within the wider public than coming together for public worship. The Hindu Association of Europe, founded in London in 1935, built a centre for lectures instead of a temple.[109] The even smaller Sikh community still had only one gurdwara.[110] The somewhat larger (if fluctuating)[111] number of Muslims did, however, finally have a place of worship in which they could legally marry. In December 1920, the Woking mosque was registered for weddings,[112] although getting married there required a registrar to be in attendance and the recitation of the words prescribed by statute.[113] Perhaps because of these limitations, some couples still preferred to marry in a register office and then travel to Woking for a separate celebration in the mosque.[114] Of course, for the many Muslims living in the north-east or in the large settlement in Cardiff, marrying in the Woking mosque would not have been a realistic option.[115] Not until 1943 was a second

---

[107] See, e.g., Christine Brumbill, 'A Baptist wedding in a Methodist Chapel, 1946' (2021) JGFH (forthcoming).

[108] See, e.g., 'A Second Marriage Ceremony', *Daily Mail*, 24 July 1935, noting that the marriage of the Hon Elizabeth Scott-Ellis and Count Orloff-Davidoff at Caxton Hall would be followed by a religious ceremony at the Russian church of St Philip.

[109] Sumita Mukherjee, 'The Emergence of a British Hindu Identity between 1936 and 1937' in Lucy Delap and Sue Morgan (eds.), *Men, Masculinities and Religious Change in Twentieth-Century Britain* (Basingstoke: Palgrave Macmillan, 2013), p. 154.

[110] Field, *Periodizing Secularization*, p. 228, puts the Sikh community as numbering 'no more than 1,000 or 2,000' by 1945.

[111] J. E. Bugby, 'Moslems in London' (1938) 28 *The Muslim World* 76, p. 77; Humayun Ansari, *The Infidel Within: Muslims in Britain since 1800* (London: Hurst, 2004), p. 48.

[112] *London Gazette*, 24 December 1920.

[113] See further Chapter 6 on the interpretation of the Marriage Act 1898 that barred non-Christian places of worship from appointing their own authorised persons.

[114] See, e.g., *Western Daily Press*, 1 August 1929, reporting the marriage of Lord Headley, a convert to Islam and president of the British Muslim Society, at the register office in Fulham followed by a second ceremony at the mosque in Woking; see also 'Married in a Mosque: British Bride's Two Weddings', *Daily Mail*, 16 October 1930, reporting that the Sultan of Johore had married Mrs Helen Wilson at the Prince's-row register office and then 'motored to the mosque at Woking'.

[115] On the distribution of the Muslim population in this period, see Ansari, *The Infidel Within*, p. 48; Field, *Periodizing Secularization*, p. 228.

mosque registered, and this too was in the south-east.[116] There is evidence that many Muslims wed validly other than in their own place of worship – sometimes in a register office but often in a church or chapel – but as early as the 1930s at least some were choosing to marry according to their own rites.[117]

While 'organised irreligion' was in decline,[118] it was significant that one Ethical Society – that based at Conway Hall in London's Bloomsbury – was registered for weddings in this period.[119] The South Place Ethical Society had its origins in a religious organisation, and its former premises at Finsbury Chapel, South Place, had been one of the first places of worship to be registered for weddings under the 1836 Act. But it had abandoned prayer as early as 1869, and in 1887 had formally changed its name.[120] It is perhaps understandable that the Society did not cancel the Finsbury Chapel's registration, but for twenty of its members to certify that its new meeting place was their usual place of worship seventy-six years after the Society had abandoned prayer did require a rather elastic concept of worship, not to mention ethics. Nonetheless, registered it was, and the Society's journal recorded the weddings of various members there over the years.[121]

Jewish Marriages

Are we Liberals, for the purpose of the Act and in the eyes of the law, persons professing the Jewish religion, or are we not?[122]

The years between 1920 and 1949 saw more Jewish marriages being recorded by synagogues than ever before.[123] With mass migration from

---

[116] *London Gazette*, 16 February 1943, recording the registration of the East London mosque.

[117] Ansari, *The Infidel Within*, p. 148.

[118] Field, *Periodizing Secularization*, p. 191.

[119] *The Monthly Record of South Place Ethical Society*, 40(11) Nov 1935, p. 8. The *London Gazette*, 8 October 1935, simply recorded that it was 'A Separate Building, duly certified for religious worship, named CONWAY HALL'.

[120] *In re South Place Ethical Society* [1980] 1 WLR 1565.

[121] *The Monthly Record of South Place Ethical Society* 41(2) Feb 1936; 42(2) Feb 1937; 42(5) May 1937; 42(7) Jul 1937; 42(11) Nov 1937. For its deregistration, see Chapter 8.

[122] 'Impasse at the Deputies', *Jewish Chronicle*, 29 April 1949.

[123] This has to be carefully phrased, given that Jewish weddings did not have to be conducted *in* synagogues unless they were registered places of worship, and that some of the ceremonies recorded by synagogues were not the legal wedding. The statistics compiled by Jewish researchers were thus slightly different from those published by the

Eastern Europe having ceased upon the outbreak of the First World War, concerns about irregular marriages seemed largely to have faded away.[124] The lack of litigation over the consequences of such marriages reinforces the sense that these were no longer taking place on the same scale as before,[125] and proposals to make it a felony to conduct marriages according to Jewish usages without the necessary civil preliminaries were quietly shelved. Accounts of Jewish marriages in this period instead emphasised how they were 'still carried out much as they were in the days of the Scriptures, with much ceremonial and symbolic practice'.[126]

The status of Liberal Judaism remained a contentious issue, the key question being whether Liberal Jews[127] could be seen as 'persons professing the Jewish religion' and so capable of being brought under the auspices of the Board of Deputies. By 1925, the Movement for Liberal Judaism had moved into new and larger premises in St John's Wood, later to be described as its 'Cathedral Synagogue'.[128] With this and a number of other Liberal synagogues being registered,[129] by 1933 the number of weddings in Liberal synagogues exceeded those in Reform synagogues.[130] Attempts were made by the then Chief Rabbi, Dr Joseph Hertz, to bring Liberal synagogues within the fold. In 1934, he declared that the Liberal Jewish Synagogue 'was a body of persons professing the Jewish religion',[131] which meant that its secretary could be certified by the Board of Deputies and marriages would no longer have to be conducted in the presence of a registrar.[132] However, Hertz's successor, Israel Brodie, took a different view as to whether Liberal Synagogues could be

Registrar-General, but both saw an increase: S. J. Prais and Marlena Schmool, 'Statistics of Jewish Marriage in Great Britain: 1901-1965' (1967) 9 *Jewish Journal of Sociology* 151.

[124] David Englander, '*Stille Huppah* (Quiet Marriage) among Jewish Immigrants in Britain' (1992) 34 *Jewish Journal of Sociology* 85, at pp. 103–4.

[125] The few cases that came before the courts tended to turn on the question of what proof was needed of a Jewish wedding that had taken place overseas: see, e.g., *Goldstone v. Goldstone* (1922) 127 LT 32; *R v. Hammer* [1923] 2 KB 786.

[126] *Nottingham Evening Post*, 24 June 1932.

[127] From 1944 the Liberal movement adopted the name of the 'Union of Liberal and Progressive Synagogues'.

[128] Alderman, *Modern British Jewry*, p. 208; *Sixth Report*, Minutes and Proceedings, 7 July 1949, evidence from Colonel Louis Gluckstein.

[129] *London Gazette*, 22 September 1925 (St John's Wood synagogue); 23 April 1929 (North London synagogue).

[130] Prais and Schmool, 'Statistics of Jewish Marriage', Appendix 2, Table II.

[131] Alderman, *Modern British Jewry*, 355.

[132] Other newly formed Liberal Synagogues were still registered as places of worship – two in Birmingham, in 1936 and 1938 respectively, and another in Hove in 1948: *London Gazette*, 6 November 1939 (Liberal Jewish Synagogue, Wellington Passage, Bennetts Hill,

certified as 'persons professing the Jewish religion'. He objected to a proposed change to the constitution of the Board on the basis that it would give 'a wrongful and misleading impression that Liberal Congregations, in the performance of marriages, conform to authoritative Jewish law'.[133]

In 1949, there were impassioned debates at a special meeting of the Board of Deputies that had been called for the purpose of debating an amendment to its constitution to enable the President to certify the secretaries of Liberal Synagogues. The obstacle was the constitution of the Board rather than the phrasing of the law. The advice of the Registrar-General had been that while it would not be within the terms of the statute to add 'in the Liberal form' to the prescribed phrase 'professing the Jewish religion' on certificates given in the case of Liberal Synagogues, the GRO would not question whether the President was justified in issuing such a certificate as long as it was in accordance with the Act.[134] In other words, it was up to the President to decide who should be regarded as 'professing the Jewish religion' and up to the secretary he had certified to decide whether any given ceremony was in accordance with Jewish rites and ceremonies.

But the fact that this was merely an internal affair did not make the debates any less bitter, since they went to the heart of what constituted Judaism. As the President asked, '[d]oes Jewish religion mean *the* Jewish religion, or does it mean Jewish religion in the various forms in which Jews like to practise it?' For the Orthodox, the fact that a marriage conducted by a Liberal synagogue could be described as in accordance with Jewish rites and ceremonies – without it being made explicit that these were Liberal rites and ceremonies – was problematic, and the proposed amendment was rejected by seventy-eight votes to sixty. For the Liberals, on the other hand, it was also a fundamental question of religious recognition, and upon reference being made to the Liberal Synagogue as part of the Board of Deputies, 'the Liberal Jewish Deputies cried: "No more," and walked out in indignation'.[135]

Birmingham); 19 July 1938 (Liberal Jewish Synagogue, Sheepcote Street, Birmingham); 6 July 1948 (Brighton and Hove Liberal Jewish Synagogue, 6 Lansdowne Road, Hove).

[133] Quoted in 'Impasse at the Deputies', *Jewish Chronicle*, 29 April 1949.

[134] *Ibid*. Similarly, he advised that the requirement that the secretary must certify that the ceremony was conducted 'according to the rites and ceremonies of the Jewish religion' did not need the words 'in the Liberal form' to be added, since this wording was appropriate 'in any form of Jewish marriage'.

[135] *Ibid*.

The Marriage Act 1949

surprisingly short and simple[136]

In the light of the number of changes made during this period, and how they had been effected,[137] it was unsurprisingly deemed desirable to enact a consolidating statute for weddings law. The Marriage Act 1949, which achieved this end, was welcomed by commentators on the basis that practitioners would 'appreciate the advantage of having the law on this subject available in one concise statute'.[138] The schedule to the Act listed no fewer than thirty-eight enactments, covering a period of over 400 years, that it had repealed either in whole or in part.[139] Yet while bringing all of these provisions together made the law more accessible, it did not necessarily make it any more coherent. The new Act clarified certain points, but obscured others, failed to resolve some long-standing ambiguities, and did nothing to address some of the controversies that had arisen in the preceding decades.

Many of the limitations of the Marriage Act 1949 are due to it being consolidating rather than reforming legislation. Yet even within these constraints more could have been done. Legislation passed earlier in 1949 had introduced a new procedure for consolidating legislation,[140] which had for the first time allowed 'corrections and minor improvements' to be made. Any such corrections and improvements had to be made according to a set process,[141] and could not be approved if they would effect changes 'of such importance that they ought ... to be separately enacted by Parliament'.[142] Despite this caveat, the definition of what constituted a 'correction or minor improvement' was quite wide-ranging. It encompassed amendments that would resolve ambiguities, remove doubts, or bring 'obsolete provisions into conformity with modern practice'. It also permitted the removal of 'unnecessary provisions or anomalies which are not of substantial importance' and

---

[136] (1949) 99 NLJ 617.
[137] Measures passed by the Church of England did not directly amend primary legislation but had to be read alongside it.
[138] 'Marriage Bill (HL)' (1949) 207 *Law Times* 374.
[139] Marriage Act 1949, Sch. 5. The enactments in question ranged from the Marriage Act 1540 to the Pastoral Reorganisation Measure 1949.
[140] Consolidation of Enactments (Procedure) Act 1949.
[141] They had to be set out by the Lord Chancellor in a memorandum, duly publicised, and considered by a joint committee of both Houses of Parliament.
[142] Consolidation of Enactments (Procedure) Act 1949, s. 1.

'amendments designed to facilitate improvement in the form or manner in which the law is stated'.[143]

Looking at the structure of the 1949 Act, it is hard to escape the suspicion that reformers simply started with the oldest statute governing marriage and worked forwards from there.[144] The structural split between Part II ('marriages according to the rites of the Church of England') and Part III ('marriage under superintendent registrar's certificate') reflected the fact that the bulk of the law in each Part derived from the Marriage Acts of 1823 and 1836, respectively, with Part IV ('registration') being the successor to the Births and Deaths Registration Act 1836, and Part V containing the provisions of the relatively new Marriage (Naval, Military, and Air Force Chapels) Act 1932. Part VI, for those who made it that far, brought together the provisions relating to offences, thereby exposing how vastly different penalties were imposed for substantially very similar actions or inactions.[145]

Far from improving the manner in which the law was stated, this chronologically inspired structure served to overemphasise the distinction between Anglican and other marriages.[146] The heading of Part II referred to a religious rite; that of Part III to authorisation by a civil official. Given that Part III had to make provision for Anglican marriages in any case – since they could also take place on the basis of a superintendent registrar's certificate – it might have been more logical to start with the civil preliminaries and then move on to the different types of marriages. And even if it had made the Act longer, it might have been helpful for it to have differentiated between the laws applicable to the Church of England and those applicable to the Church in Wales. The reader had to persevere almost to the very end of the Act to find any reference to the Church in Wales at all, only to be told, somewhat unhelpfully, that it was encompassed by the earlier references to the Church of England 'unless the context otherwise requires'; in layman's

---

[143] Consolidation of Enactments (Procedure) Act, s. 2.

[144] The first section dealt with the prohibited degrees, which dated back to the Marriage Act 1540.

[145] Marriage Act 1949, s. 75(1). It did at least substitute imprisonment for 14 years for the possibility of Anglican clergy being transported, but since transportation had been abolished almost a hundred years earlier this was hardly a bold move.

[146] Stephen Borton, 'Marriage in the Church of England: The Immigration Act 2014 and Beyond?' (2015) *Ecclesiastical Law Journal* 331, p. 336, suggests that this placement was deliberate and 'reinforces the view that Church of England (and Church in Wales) marriage remained in the eyes of the law the norm for the citizens of England and Wales'.

terms, Church of England meant Church in Wales, except when it didn't.[147]

Nor did the 1949 Act attempt to reconcile any of the existing ambiguities in the law. This was particularly evident in the provisions relating to banns, which accounted for thirteen of its eighty sections. Some of these were necessary to make provision for specific situations, such as the calling of banns in neighbouring jurisdictions or on naval ships,[148] but there was also something of an overlap. The issue here was where banns should be published if the parish church was unavailable, different provisions having been added at different times. The Clandestine Marriages Act 1753 had originally allowed banns to be published in an adjoining parish if there was no parish church in which divine service could be celebrated.[149] This had duly been included in the Marriage Act 1823,[150] but so too had another, more specific, provision setting out different arrangements where the church was being rebuilt or repaired.[151] That this apparent overlap had occasioned some confusion among clergy was evident from the passage of yet another order validating marriages that it was thought had been wrongly celebrated in neighbouring parishes rather than in the place directed by the bishop.[152] Nonetheless, both of the provisions from the 1823 Act were carried over into the new legislation; moreover, rather than any attempt being made to reconcile them, they were unhelpfully separated by eleven other sections.[153]

There were also occasional omissions. In making provision for the banns to be called in a specified place where the church or chapel was being rebuilt or repaired, the Marriage Act 1823 had omitted to specify that the subsequent marriages could also be solemnised there, or to make

---

[147] Marriage Act 1949, s. 78(2). To find out when it didn't, it was necessary to read on to Sch. 6, which listed the provisions that did not apply in Wales and Monmouthshire, and then start back at the beginning to remind oneself exactly what ss. 6(4), 9, 10, 11(2), 15(1)(b), 16(1)(b), 19, 20(7), 23, 35(3), and 72 had said.

[148] Marriage Act 1949, ss. 13 and 14.

[149] Clandestine Marriages Act 1753, s. 5.

[150] Marriage Act 1823, s. 12.

[151] Marriage Act 1823, s. 13 laid down a strict order of priority, beginning with any building licensed by the bishop of the diocese for the performance of divine service during the disuse of the church or chapel, followed by any such consecrated chapel as he had directed, and only in the absence of either of these authorising the banns being called in the church or chapel of an adjoining parish.

[152] St Edyth Sea Mills Order, Provisional Order (Marriages) Confirmation Act 1931.

[153] Marriage Act 1949, ss. 6(3) and 18.

any provision for licences to be granted. Both omissions had speedily been remedied by the Marriage Act 1824, but when this was consolidated into the 1949 Act the point relating to the grant of licences was overlooked.[154] Since the 1949 Act repealed the 1824 Act, there was thus no authority for a licence to be granted for a marriage to take place in the building indicated by the bishop.

The new structure also continued to obscure how tightly regulated Quaker and Jewish marriages were, although it did at least clarify that they were subject to the same annulling provisions as applied to marriages in registered places of worship or register offices.[155] Those casting their eye down the list of headings in the statute might well conclude that such weddings were almost free from regulation. The single section headed 'Marriages according to usages of Society of Friends' merely set out who could marry in a Quaker ceremony.[156] The complex rules as to who was required to certify those who could register Quaker and Jewish marriages – which revealed the structures within which such marriages were to take place – appeared under the unilluminating heading 'Interpretation of Part IV'.[157]

The Joint Committee set up to consider the draft bill interpreted their powers narrowly. A few minor amendments were made to the rules governing Anglican weddings.[158] The reformulation of the law also clarified a number of points.[159] The main controversy was whether provision should be made for Liberal Judaism in the clauses setting out who was responsible for authorising secretaries to register Jewish marriages. The President of the St John's Wood synagogue, Colonel Gluckstein, suggested that the lack of any existing provision could be categorised as an 'anomaly' that was 'not of substantial importance' and attributable solely to the fact that Liberal Judaism had not existed in England and Wales in 1856 when provision was made for the West London synagogue to authorise its own secretaries and those of

---

[154] Marriage Act 1949, s. 15(2) simply copied over the provisions about licences being granted for weddings in some adjoining place.

[155] For the earlier debate on this, see Chapter 6.

[156] Marriage Act 1949, s. 47.

[157] Marriage Act 1949, s. 67.

[158] Bishops obtained greater powers to license chapels of ease in 'any district'; the point in the service at which banns were to be called was clarified; and provision was made for weddings in benefices held in plurality.

[159] For example, the circumstances in which Jewish and Quaker marriages might be void were clarified: Marriage Act 1949, s. 49. For the earlier discussion as to whether the annulling provisions of the 1836 Act applied to such marriages, see Chapter 6.

synagogues associated with it.[160] In response, Mr Ross, the representative of the General Register Office, noted that the matter was one of some controversy within the Jewish community, doubted the wisdom of following the piecemeal reform adopted in 1856, and conveyed a sense of reluctance to allow the existing privileges enjoyed by Jews and Quakers to be extended any further. The Committee accordingly took the view that the matter was of substantial importance and therefore not one that was suitable for a consolidation measure.[161]

During the course of these discussions the Joint Committee also became aware of the anomaly that Liberal synagogues could not even appoint their own authorised persons under the Marriage Act 1898. Mr Ross argued that the removal of this particular anomaly was of sufficient importance to require separate legislation rather than being revised as part of the process of consolidation. It would, however, have been difficult to continue this anomaly without openly discriminating against non-Christian groups. There was no longer any justification for making the right to appoint an authorised person contingent on whether a particular place of worship could have been registered for marriages under the 1836 Act, since this Act was about to be abolished. As a result, this particular piece of discrimination against non-Christian religions was abolished by default. In this respect at least, the process of consolidation brought some improvement to the law.

Conclusion

The passage of the Marriage Act 1949 made the law easier to find. It also made it easier to see how incoherent it was. It was not merely that different rules applied to different routes into marriage, but rather that the very basis of regulation differed. Anglican weddings had originally been celebrant-based, in that the presence of an ordained clergyman had been both necessary and sufficient to secure their validity; upon this had been engrafted a requirement that weddings should generally – unless exempted by special licence – take place in specific buildings. The regulation of Quaker and Jewish weddings was based on the authorisation of organisations, while the regulation of other religious weddings was based on the registration of buildings.

---

[160] *Sixth Report*, Minutes and Proceedings, 7 July 1949, representation from Colonel Louis Gluckstein.

[161] For the eventual resolution of this issue see Chapter 8.

The fact that most Anglican churches were automatically places in which marriages could be solemnised, by virtue of being the parish church, meant that it was all too easy to overlook the need for some to be licensed for the purpose. In the nineteenth century, it had been the expansion in the number of chapels that led to such mistakes being made and validating legislation being passed. In the twentieth century, it was the reorganisation necessitated by a changing population, and the ambiguity of some of the Church of England's own Measures, that generated an even larger number of validating orders. By contrast, almost all of the problematic cases involving marriages in registered places of worship were ones in which the person officiating was not authorised to do so. But both sets of problems ultimately came down to the regulation of the place of the marriage rather than the person conducting it. Nonconformist ministers and Catholic priests were misled into thinking that they had authority to conduct and register marriages simply because the building in which they did so was registered, and had its own registers. Had the validity of a marriage rested solely on the issue of compliance with the required preliminaries and the authorisation of the person conducting or registering it, the law would have been a lot simpler and fewer mistakes would have been made.

Whether couples were contented with the options that were available to them in terms of how they could marry is difficult to ascertain. Overall, it seems that the complexities of the laws regulating marriage were something to be negotiated rather than challenged. But the second half of the twentieth century was to bring a whole host of new challenges that the legislators of 1949 had not foreseen, and for which no provision had been made.

8

Convergence? 1950–1993

In the early 1980s, the bridal magazine *Wedding Day and First Home* campaigned for reform of the law. Drawing inspiration from Australia and New Zealand, it suggested that those who did not want a religious wedding should have a more meaningful alternative available to them than was provided by a short exchange in a register office.[1] One particularly heartfelt response to its question of 'Is the Marriage Act Obsolete?' came from a woman who had married her Muslim husband in a register office. The two of them had 'asked around desperately for a romantic, meaningful alternative' but, she reported, were 'amazed and rather disgusted' that the only alternative to a church ceremony was this 'short, impersonal, unromantic ceremony'. As she tartly noted, when 'the numbers marrying outside the church were so negligible it was obviously felt there was no need to cater for this insignificant minority and the curt, businesslike civil ceremony would do'.[2]

These comments reflected the huge changes that had taken place in the previous decades in how couples married. Graphs plotting the relative number of religious and civil weddings over the period showed two converging lines, with parity being achieved in the late 1970s.[3] As this chapter will show, behind the statistics lay a more complex story about the relationship between what people believed and how they married. There were plenty of people marrying in the register office

---

[1] 'Is The Marriage Act Obsolete? The Establishment Talks Back', *Wedding Day and First Home*, early spring 1981, p. 14. The Act referred to was the Marriage Act 1949.
[2] 'Is The Marriage Act Obsolete?', *Wedding Day and First Home*, spring 1981, p. 31.
[3] John Haskey, 'Trends in marriages: church, chapel and civil ceremonies' (1980) 22 *Population Trends* 19 and 'Marriage Rites – Trends in Marriages by Manner of Solemnisation and Denomination in England and Wales, 1841-2012' in Joanna Miles, Perveez Mody, and Rebecca Probert (eds.) *Marriage Rites and Rights* (Oxford: Hart, 2015).

8

who had strong religious beliefs and plenty who wed in church who had none. And there were also a growing number who felt that other options should be available. The correspondent's use of the term 'meaningful' encapsulated the growing sense that the register office did not match couples' expectations of their wedding day.

Her comments also highlighted the lack of change in the legal options that were available to couples planning to marry. Such legislative changes as did occur during this period were limited to very specific issues. There was some convergence in terms of the laws applicable to different types of weddings: as the second section will discuss, new laws gave Liberal Judaism the same status as Reform Judaism, modified some of the preconditions for places of worship to be registered for weddings, enabled Anglicans and other denominations to celebrate weddings in the same building, and provided all couples with an alternative to the Anglican special licence in specific situations. In addition, case law generated new definitions of marriage and of religious worship. But convergence was not the same as consistency; limited as it was to specific areas, it often reinforced existing differences and complexities rather than removing them.

Nor should the lack of more wide-ranging reform be seen as evidence of contentment with the status quo, as the final section will suggest. Reviewing the laws regulating weddings in 1971, a joint working party of the Law Commission and the Registrar-General had identified that they fell 'woefully short' of the ideal in almost every respect,[4] and their subsequent recommendations for reform envisaged a complete overhaul of the process.[5] Similarly, in the late 1980s, the government described much of the law as 'unnecessarily complex and restrictive' and set out a package of reforms intended to simplify it and give couples greater choice.[6] Even so, only the most minor of its proposals found its way on to the statute books within the period under consideration.

---

[4] Law Commission, *Solemnisation of Marriage in England and Wales*, WP No. 35 (London: HMSO, 1971), para. 5.

[5] Law Commission, *Family Law: Report on Solemnisation of Marriage in England and Wales*, Law Com. No. 53 (London: HMSO, 1973), Annex.

[6] *Registration: A modern service. Proposals to reform the system for registering births, marriages and deaths in England and Wales*, 1988/89 Cm 531, para. 3.2; see also *Registration: proposals for change. The government's recommendations for reform of the system for registering births, marriages and deaths in England and Wales*, 1989/90 Cm 939.

The Convergence between Religious and Civil Weddings

Such uncorrected visions end in church / Or registrar[7]

Marriage achieved unprecedented levels of popularity in the 1950s.[8] More couples were getting married, and at a younger age, than ever before.[9] And their weddings were increasingly following a similar pattern, with the 'full formalities, white wedding, reception and honeymoon' becoming increasingly popular 'in all social classes'.[10] There was a small rise in the number and percentage of weddings celebrated in church or chapel, with Anglican, Catholic, and Nonconformist weddings all seeing an increase.[11] Yet despite the brief revival of religiosity that followed the Second World War,[12] the use of the church for rites of passage did not necessarily indicate any deeper connection with it, or even any specific beliefs.[13]

The relationship between belief and how couples married was complicated still further by the obstacles that some couples faced in having a wedding according to their own (or any) religious rites. The number of weddings celebrated according to Jewish usages fell noticeably, despite a considerable increase in the Jewish population in England and Wales.[14] Mixed marriages were seen as one possible reason for this,[15] but it was also speculated that the high fees charged by synagogues for conducting weddings might be deterring young couples from marrying there.[16] Muslims, Sikhs, and Hindus were largely unable to marry in a way that combined legal recognition and religious rites: as late as 1961 the Registrar-General's list of certified places of worship included only

---

[7] Philip Larkin, 'Breadfruit' (1961).

[8] Rachel M. Pierce, 'Marriage in the Fifties' (1963) 11(2) *The Sociological Review* 215; David Kynaston, *Family Britain, 1951–57* (London: Bloomsbury, 2009), p. 558.

[9] Richard Leete, 'Marriage and Divorce' (1976) 3 *Population Trends* 3, Table 1.

[10] Pierce, 'Marriage in the Fifties', p. 219.

[11] Although this varied by denomination, see Haskey, 'Marriage Rites', p. 30.

[12] On which see Callum G. Brown, *The Death of Christian Britain: Understanding Secularism, 1800–2000* (London: Routledge, 2001), p. 172.

[13] Arthur Marwick, *British Society since 1945* (London: Penguin, 4th ed., 2003), p. 80, notes that only 11 per cent of women and 7 per cent of men were regular churchgoers, while 26 per cent of men and 18 per cent of women 'admitted to no religious affiliation at all'.

[14] The Jewish population of England and Wales is thought to have peaked at around 450,000 in the mid-1950s: Geoffrey Alderman, *Modern British Jewry* (Oxford: Clarendon Press, 1992, 1998), pp. 321–2.

[15] S.J. Prais and Marlena Schmool, 'Statistics of Jewish Marriage in Great Britain: 1901-1965' (1967) 9 *Jewish Journal of Sociology* 151.

[16] *Jewish Chronicle*, 16 February 1951.

seven mosques, three gurdwaras, and one mandir in England and Wales,[17] and of these only three of the mosques, and none of the other places of worship, were registered for weddings.[18] Some would have married in the register office and had a separate religious ceremony, although not necessarily in that order; others, however, went through a religious ceremony without realising that there were other formalities with which they needed to comply.[19]

Many committed Anglicans would also have (re)married in the register office. The Church of England showed little sign of softening its institutional line that those who had been divorced should not be able to remarry in church. Resolutions that marriage, at least in its 'true principle', was 'indissoluble save by death' and that remarriage after a divorce during the lifetime of a former spouse inevitably involved 'a departure from that principle' were enshrined in a formal Act of Convocation in 1957.[20] This did not directly ban clergy from conducting remarriages, but the Archbishop of Canterbury made it clear that those who did so would put themselves in 'spiritual peril'.[21] As a matter of law, it remained a matter for individual clergy to decide whether to conduct the wedding of a person who had been divorced,[22] but only a few were willing to risk their bishop's disapproval by doing so.[23] While

[17] Ceri Peach and Richard Gale, 'Muslims, Hindus and Sikhs in the New Religious Landscape of England' (2003) 93(4) *The Geographical Review* 469, p. 477.

[18] In addition to the Woking and East London mosques (discussed in Chapter 7), the London Central mosque had been registered in 1955.

[19] See e.g. the evidence given by Mrs Bath about her 1956 wedding at 79 Sinclair Road, the first gurdwara established in England. As she told the court, it was conducted by a Sikh priest, with around 50 guests present, and '[l]ike most other first wave immigrants, we had no knowledge of the law, were completely illiterate and led to believe, by our elders and peers, that we had followed the correct procedures': *Chief Adjudication Officer* v. *Bath* [2000] 1 FLR 8, at p. 13.

[20] 'Primate Defines Church's Ruling on Remarriage: Spiritual Authority versus the Law of the Land', *Church Times*, 4 October 1957.

[21] *Ibid.* For protests against this move see 'Challenge to Primate on Remarriage: 39 Clergy Oppose Statement', *The Times*, 19 October 1957; '39 Birmingham Priests Challenge Primate's Statement: They Resent Reference to "Spiritual Peril"', *Church Times*, 25 October 1957; 'Who Speaks for the Clergy? Nature and Status of Convocation', *The Times*, 26 October 1957.

[22] Matrimonial Causes Act 1937, s. 12.

[23] On the practical ways in which bishops might manifest their disapproval and thereby deter clergy, see O. R. McGregor, *Divorce in England: A Centenary Study* (London: Heinemann, 1957), p. 112. For a particularly controversial example of a remarriage – of a vicar to a divorcée – see 'Bishop Calls Meeting on Vicar's Marriage: Wife's Previous Union was Dissolved', *The Times*, 18 September 1957; 'Dr Fisher on Remarriage of the Divorced: "Clergy Disobey at their Spiritual Peril"', *The Times*, 2 October 1957; 'Primate

Nonconformist churches tended to be more willing to conduct remarriages,[24] overall only a very small minority of those who had been divorced remarried in any kind of religious ceremony.[25]

While marriage was no less popular in the 1960s – the number of marriages continued to climb, and the average age of those marrying for the first time reached an all-time low in the late 1960s[26] – there were some noticeable changes in how couples married. The number and percentage of weddings in the register office increased sharply. One factor was the increase in non-marital pregnancies in the mid-1960s.[27] The emerging idea that sexual compatibility needed to be tested before marriage was difficult to reconcile with the still limited access to contraception[28] and the continuing assumption that a pregnancy should be followed by a marriage.[29] Another was the increase in divorce.[30] And a third was a change in attitudes to religion: for an increasing number a register office wedding was a way of manifesting their *lack* of belief.[31] A survey of fifty couples marrying in the late 1960s illustrated all three trends: of the twenty weddings that took place in a register office, six involved at least one divorced partner, seven of the brides were pregnant, and the remaining seven cited cost, speed, contempt for ritual, and atheism.[32]

Discussions in bridal magazines focused on the positive reasons for marrying in a register office. Not only was it presented as attractively

---

    Defines Church's Ruling on Remarriage: Spiritual Authority versus the Law of the Land', *Church Times*, 4 October 1957.

[24] On the official line taken by other Protestant churches, see McGregor, *Divorce in England*, pp. 116–7.

[25] Haskey, 'Marriage Rites', pp. 40–1.

[26] Office of National Statistics, 'Marriages in England and Wales 2017' (14 April 2020), table 5.

[27] In 1967, 38 per cent of teenage brides were pregnant: 'Marriage and Divorce'.

[28] On the availability of contraception and changing attitudes to pre-marital sex see Rebecca Probert, *The Changing Legal Regulation of Cohabitation: From Fornicators to Family, 1600–2010* (Cambridge: Cambridge University Press, 2012), ch. 6.

[29] This was a theme in a number of novels of the time: see e.g. Stan Barstow, *A Kind of Loving* (1960), Nell Dunn, *Up the Junction* (1963) and *Poor Cow* (1967), Margaret Forster, *Georgy Girl* (1965).

[30] Office for National Statistics, 'Divorces in England and Wales' (17 November 2020), table 1.

[31] For expressions of this view see e.g. William Cooper, *Scenes from Married Life* (1961; London: Penguin, 1963), p. 112; 'The right age to marry', *Honey's Bride Guide*, Winter 1968, p. 81 (bride explaining their simple register office wedding on the basis that they were not Christians and so didn't want a church wedding).

[32] Diana Leonard, *Sex and Generation: A Study of Courtship and Weddings* (London: Tavistock Publications, 1980), p. 206. The weddings in question took place in Swansea in 1968–9.

simple,[33] but some of those choosing it invoked a new norm of sincerity. The bride who 'hated the idea of just *using* a church for weddings and christenings'[34] was taking a subtle swipe at her contemporaries who were doing just that. Another eloquently explained that since neither she nor her husband-to-be were church-goers, 'it seemed wrong to pretend on this most important day', that a long white dress and veil seemed 'like play acting' at a time when she 'wanted to be absolutely serious', and that her wish was simply for 'a simple but sincere ceremony in front of the handful of people I truly wanted there'.[35] Such thoughtful reflections illustrate how couples were no longer automatically marrying in church as the default option regardless of their beliefs but rather feeling that it would be hypocritical of them to use it as a venue.

Against this backdrop of a general decline in the number of weddings celebrated with religious rites,[36] there was a noticeable expansion in the types of places of worship in which it was possible to marry. A sudden increase in immigration from the Caribbean and the Indian subcontinent[37] changed not only the size but also the composition of the Muslim, Sikh, and Hindu communities in England and Wales; with the arrival of wives and children, there was a greater emphasis on religious observance and an expansion in the number of mosques, gurdwaras, and mandirs.[38] Sikh and Hindu places of worship were registered for weddings for the first time in the 1960s, including no fewer than three Sikh gurdwaras in 1961,[39] and the Hindu temple in

---

[33] 'Quiet wedding' and 'Short and sweet: Marrying in a Register Office', *Honey's Bride Guide,* Easter 1969, pp. 32 and 110; 'At the Register Office', *Honey's Bride Guide,* Easter 1971, p. 89 ('so long as you won't miss the trimmings, this is the no-fuss way to get married'); 'Dresses to Register In: Informal Wedding Styles', *Woman Bride and Home,* Midsummer 1971, p. 78.

[34] 'Their Kind of Wedding', *Honey's Bride Guide,* Midsummer 1971, p. 11.

[35] 'White Weddings – are they worth it?', *Woman Bride and Home,* Easter 1968, p. 122, although even this bride admitted that she would have agreed to a white wedding if her mother's heart had been set on it.

[36] Including a continuing decline in the number of weddings in synagogues: see S.J. Prais and Marlena Schmool, 'Synagogue Marriages in Great Britain: 1966-8' (1970) 12 *Jewish Journal of Sociology* 21.

[37] The increase was prompted by the fear of impending restrictions: see Dominic Sandbrook, *Never Had It So Good: A History of Britain from Suez to the Beatles* (2005; London: Abacus, 2006), p. 308.

[38] Peach and Gale, 'New Religious Landscape', p. 478.

[39] *London Gazette,* 21 February 1961 (Moss Side, Manchester); 30 June 1961 (Dasmais Sikh Temple, Cardiff); 28 August 1961 (Sikh Temple and Mission Centre, Chorlton-on-Medlock). A further 18 were added to the list over the next decade.

Newcastle-upon-Tyne in 1967.[40] An increasing number of mosques were also registered, particularly in the Midlands and the north of England.[41] Even so, the number of Muslim, Sikh, and Hindu places of worship in which it was possible to marry lagged well behind the growing population.[42] Moreover, since such places of worship were almost invariably modest converted houses rather than purpose-built places of worship,[43] they were particularly vulnerable to change of use, with some registrations being cancelled within a few years.[44] As before, the majority of Muslims, Sikhs, and Hindus would have married in the register office with a separate religious ceremony,[45] or according to their own rites and thus lacking, whether any of those involved knew it or not, full legal validity.[46]

The 1960s also saw an increasing number of couples living together because one or both of them were unable to obtain a divorce from an earlier spouse. In earlier decades this might well have been disguised through a bigamous remarriage, but convictions for such began to fall

[40] *London Gazette*, 30 November 1967.

[41] At least a dozen mosques were registered for weddings in the 1960s: *London Gazette*, 16 February 1962 (South Shields), 16 March 1963 (Bradford), 9 October 1964 (Middlesbrough), 15 June 1995 (Birmingham), 13 August 1965 (Sheffield), 27 May 1966 (Batley), 15 February 1966 (Manchester), 21 February 1967 (Blackburn), 29 April 1969 (Reading), 26 June 1969 (Bristol), 2 September 1969 (Sheffield), 8 December 1969 (Leicester).

[42] See Peach and Gale, 'New Religious Landscape', p. 479, estimating that by 1971 there was one gurdwara for every 2,182 Sikhs (33 for 72,000), one mosque for every 7,533 Muslims (30 for 226,000), and one mandir for every 69,000 Hindus (two for 138,000). See also 'Newlyweds have to wait for love', *Daily Mirror*, 14 October 1971 for the campaign for a Hindu temple in Walsall.

[43] Peach and Gale, 'New Religious Landscape'.

[44] The Guru Nanak Darbar Sikh Temple in Gravesend, for example, was located in a small terraced house: its registration was cancelled within six years: *London Gazette*, 9 January 1969. Two even more modest gurdwaras were registered for fewer than three years: that on Grove Road in Leicester had occupied the ground floor of an end-of-terrace house (*London Gazette*, 24 August 1965, 11 June 1968) while that on Wilford Grove in Nottingham was opened in a converted garage (ATV's *Midland News*, 12 August 1963; *London Gazette*, 23 August 1963, 18 June 1966).

[45] See, e.g., 'Colourful Indian wedding is first in York', *Yorkshire Evening Press*, July 1969, reporting how one couple had married at York register office before having their Hindu ceremony at a local social hall.

[46] For an example of the difficulties that might arise where the expectation that this would be followed by a civil ceremony were not fulfilled, see the breach of promise case brought by one Sikh bride: '£700 award to woman in Sikh wedding', *The Times*, 20 May 1969. However, religious-only marriage ceremonies were not identified as a major issue in this period: see e.g. the brief consideration of the issue in David Pearl, 'Muslim Marriages in English Law' (1972) 30 *Cambridge Law Journal* 120.

noticeably in the 1960s.[47] Open cohabitation was, however, more visible than bigamy, and the existence of these 'stable illicit unions' was a key factor in the reform of divorce law in 1969.[48]

Following the coming into force of the Divorce Reform Act 1969 on 1 January 1971, there was a sharp rise in the number of divorces, and 1972 saw the number of marriages reaching their highest level since 1940 as the newly divorced tied the knot for a second time.[49] Most did so in a register office, resulting in the biggest single-year increase in such ceremonies since 1837.[50]

By contrast, bridal pregnancy – that other long-standing reason for marrying in a register office – fell during the 1970s. This was not because fewer couples were having sex before their wedding but rather because of the increased use of contraception and the reduced likelihood of a pregnancy precipitating a wedding.[51] The average age at first marriage crept back upwards during the 1970s as an increasing number of couples sought to test their relationship before deciding whether to marry.[52] With questions being asked as to whether a white wedding in church was appropriate for those who were on the pill, had had a child outside marriage, or were cohabiting,[53] these trends may also have contributed to the rise in the number of civil marriages.

By the late 1970s, the number of civil weddings had, for the first time, finally overtaken those celebrated with religious rites.[54] A 1976 photo-spread in *Honey* magazine depicting eighteen of the couples marrying at Wandsworth Town Hall on a Saturday in December illustrated both the sheer variety of couples marrying in the register office and how

---

[47] Rebecca Probert, 'Double Trouble: The Rise and Fall of the Crime of Bigamy', Selden Society Lecture 2013.

[48] Probert, *The Changing Legal Regulation of Cohabitation*, ch. 6.

[49] Office of Population Censuses and Surveys, *Marriage and Divorce Statistics: Review of the Registrar General on Marriages and Divorces in England and Wales: Series FM2 No. 1* (London: HMSO, 1977), table 2.1; *The Registrar General's Statistical Review of England and Wales for the Year 1972* (London: HMSO, 1974), table H2.

[50] For the figures, see Haskey, 'Trends in marriages', table 1.

[51] Probert, *The Changing Legal Regulation of Cohabitation*, ch. 6.

[52] Audrey Brown and Kathleen Kiernan, 'Cohabitation in Great Britain: evidence from the General Household Survey' (1981) 25 *Population Trends* 4, table 8. Those who had experienced the termination of one marriage were particularly likely to cohabit with a new partner before entering into a second: Jacqueline Burgoyne and David Clark, *Making a Go of It: A Study of Stepfamilies in Sheffield* (London: Routledge & Kegan Paul, 1984), p. 88.

[53] See e.g. *Woman*, 24 July 1971, p. 61, 8 May 1976, p. 58; 'No white wedding for me', *Woman Bride and Home*, Easter 1972.

[54] Haskey, 'Trends in marriages'.

expectations of the occasion – as hinted at by what couples were wearing – had changed.[55] Two brides appeared in long white dresses and veils, while several more were wearing outfits that were unambiguously bridal in terms of their colour and style. But the main picture featured a woman in a gorgeous knee-length scarlet dress, and another two were in dark trouser suits and floppy black hats.[56] While bridal magazines were still referring to the 'controversy' about what should be worn to a register office wedding into the 1980s,[57] brides were clearly making up their own minds as to what was appropriate.

For many commentators, the most surprising aspect of weddings in this period was how many still took place in church or chapel.[58] The reasons for doing so were complex. Mansfield and Collard's study of couples getting married in church on the eve of the 1980s found that while few were regular attenders, their reasons for marrying there 'suggested a belief in the marriage service as offering some kind of symbolic affirmation of their undertaking, an acknowledgement of the serious import of the occasion' that they clearly felt a register office wedding would lack.[59] The three recent brides interviewed by *Wedding Day and First Home* in 1980 displayed a similar sense of a church wedding being different, with one commenting that she was 'not particularly religious' but had 'always wanted a church wedding', and adding that she would not have felt 'properly married' in a register office'.[60]

---

[55] Contrast the earlier advice that either a coloured dress or a suit 'should be chosen for a Registry Office wedding': B. Owen Williams, *Planning Your Wedding Day from A to Z* (London: W. Foulsham & Co Ltd, 1964).

[56] 'All on a Saturday morning', *Honey*, December 1976.

[57] 'Extremely Civil Weddings', *Wedding Day and First Home*, late autumn 1982, p. 2. See also 'Civil Brides', *Wedding Day and First Home*, autumn 1985, p. 70, advising brides to 'avoid anything too full and flouncy', and Susannah Moss, *Brides' Wedding Planner* (London: Octopus Books, 1985), p. 70, suggesting that a train and veil 'might look over-elaborate' and were best dispensed with.

[58] W.S.F. Pickering, 'The Persistence of Rites of Passage: Towards an Explanation' (1974) 25 (1) *The British Journal of Sociology* 63–78.

[59] Penny Mansfield and Jean Collard, *The Beginning of the Rest of Your Life? A Portrait of Newly-wed Marriage* (Basingstoke: Macmillan, 1988), p. 98. The preference for a church wedding was more strongly marked among brides; interviewed after the wedding, two-fifths of grooms said that they had only married in church because it was what their wife had wanted.

[60] *Wedding Day and First Home*, summer 1980, p. 15. A second commented how 'the formal atmosphere of the church made her concentrate more intently on the ceremony, and especially on her vows', while the third, an only child, felt she 'owed it' to her family, as well as wanting 'to make a special day of it' and carry on 'a tradition of successful marriages'.

While the 1980s saw a small resurgence in the percentage of weddings being celebrated with religious rites, this should be seen against the downward trend in the overall number of weddings. The numbers marrying in Christian churches continued to fall. The regular surveys carried out by one bridal magazine from the late 1980s[61] found that less than one-third of respondents[62] cited religious beliefs as their reason for marrying in church.[63] Slightly more invoked 'tradition' or their parents' wishes.[64] And a few spoke about the importance of feeling properly married or admitted that they simply wanted an attractive backdrop for their wedding.[65]

At the same time, the expectations of a register office wedding were changing. It was not simply a matter of getting married but of being able to celebrate the event with family and friends. The potential scale of register office weddings and their accompanying celebrations was reflected in the advice offered by *Wedding Day and First Home*: some register offices, it noted, had room for 'a hundred or more guests'; while a feature in 1982 told readers that a civil wedding could be anything from a low-key midweek ceremony with two witnesses 'to a lavish event with a plush reception for hundreds'.[66] Readers were warned, however, that

---

[61] *Wedding and Home*, 'Love, sex . . . and marriage', autumn 1988, p. 86; 'The power of love', autumn 1989, p. 79; 'A love story', Oct/Nov 1990, p. 76; 'Endless love', Oct/Nov 1991, p. 38.

[62] Over a thousand readers responded to the survey each year; while they were by definition a self-selecting sample, and, given that 90 per cent of them were marrying in church, clearly not representative of *all* brides, their answers nonetheless provide an insight into the motivations for doing so.

[63] In 1988 29 per cent chose to marry in church 'because of their faith'; in 1989 28 per cent did so on account of 'religious conviction'; in 1990 33 per cent listed 'religious beliefs'; and in 1991 32 per cent simply cited 'religion'.

[64] In 1988 30 per cent cited 'upbringing and tradition', while in 1989 35 per cent did so, plus another 15 per cent who cited '[t]he feelings of family, particularly parents'. The following year 27 per cent cited tradition, while only 7 per cent said their decisions were influenced by their parent's wishes, and in 1991 36 per cent cited tradition and 6 per cent had 'given in to parental pressure'.

[65] In 1988 9 per cent chose 'a church setting because it provides a romantic backdrop for a white wedding with all the pomp and ceremony'; in 1989 13 per cent admitted 'that sheer romance and the sense of occasion influenced their decision to choose the full pomp and ceremony of a church wedding'; in 1990 16 per cent cited the importance of feeling properly married; and in 1991 8 per cent wanted 'the romance of a white wedding' and 13 per cent regarded a religious ceremony as 'more special'.

[66] *Wedding Day and First Home*: 'You ask us', summer 1980, p. 13; 'Extremely Civil Weddings', late autumn 1982, p. 2. See also 'Civil Brides', autumn 1985, p. 70, noting that those who chose the more lavish option 'usually organized it along similar lines to a formal wedding'.

register offices 'vary considerably in size',[67] and one couple reported that they had reluctantly resorted to having a church wedding because their local register office could 'only hold a handful of people'.[68]

The fact that only a small number of marriages were reported as taking place in non-Christian places of worship reflected how many Muslim, Sikh, and Hindu couples were still having to have dual ceremonies to ensure that their marriages had legal recognition, whether on account of their local place of worship not being registered for marriages or not able to accommodate the numbers expected to attend the wedding. One bride, who held her Hindu wedding in a Methodist church hall with 500 guests after marrying at the register office, noted that the first ceremony 'was getting married in the eyes of the English law, whereas the other ceremony is marriage in the eyes of God'.[69] In addition, the ongoing rise in divorce was identified as one of the reasons for the continued decline in the number of marriages in synagogues: as the researchers noted, a woman could only remarry in a synagogue if a *get* had been granted, and the number of *gittim* did not match the number of civil divorces within the Jewish community.[70]

A further factor influencing marriage patterns was the rise of cohabitation.[71] *Wedding Day and First Home* dropped the 'first' from its title in 1986, presumably to reflect the fact that many of its readers were already established in their homes. Premarital cohabitation was no longer seen as a reason to marry in a register office.[72] At the same time, couples who might have chosen to marry in a register office in the 1960s and 1970s were increasingly not getting married at all.[73] Financial factors

[67] 'Civil Brides', *Wedding Day and First Home*, autumn 1985, p. 70. See also 'What are you doing the rest of your life?', *19*, May 1986, p. 38, which noted unpromisingly that '[t]here can be as many guests as there are chairs for them to sit down'.

[68] 'Is the Marriage Act obsolete?', *Wedding Day and First Home*, spring 1981, p. 31.

[69] 'It was a lovely wedding', *Honey*, January 1981, p. 64. The same report featured a Greek Orthodox ceremony, which had similarly been preceded by a wedding at the register office.

[70] Barry A. Kosmin and Stanley Waterman, 'Recent Trends in Anglo-Jewish Marriages' (1986) 28 *Jewish Journal of Sociology* 49, pp. 53, 56.

[71] Probert, *The Changing Legal Regulation of Cohabitation*, ch. 8.

[72] 'Real Life Weddings', *Wedding Day and First Home*, new year preview 1985/86, p. 132 (cohabiting couple marrying in church, the bride explaining that she had 'always wanted a big, old-fashioned white wedding'). See also *Wedding and Home*, autumn 1986, p. 122 (couple married after their child was born, the vicar helpfully suggesting that they could combine the wedding and the christening).

[73] On the emergence of cohabitation as an alternative, rather than simply a prelude to marriage, see Éva Beaujouan and Máire Ní Bhrolcháin, 'Cohabitation and marriage in Britain since the 1970s' (2011) 145 *Population Trends* 35.

were increasingly playing a part in the decision whether or not to marry. Getting married had always been linked to attaining a certain degree of economic security, and the widespread unemployment of the early 1980s made it seem unattainable for many. But a new factor was how much couples were choosing to spend on the wedding itself. With a couple's wedding day no longer marking the start of their life together, the wedding itself had to become more of an event. From an average reported cost of £1,791 in 1980, the amount rose steeply to £7,359 in 1990,[74] far outstripping inflation.[75]

By 1993, the number of marriages celebrated each year had fallen below 300,000 for the first time since the 1920s, the age of first marriage was at an all-time high, and the marriage rate was at an historic low.[76] Fewer than one-third of weddings were taking place according to Anglican rites. Those who had been divorced continued to be rebuffed, and the advice of the Church of England's Press Officer that while it was 'possible' for them to marry in church, couples should not 'automatically expect' that their vicar would be 'prepared' to officiate was hardly calculated to encourage them to ask.[77]

Yet this transformation in when, who, and how couples married was not accompanied by any real change in the nature of the legal options that were available to them.

Legal Convergence?

it is a very dangerous practice to seek to deal with an undoubted anomaly when
the whole of our marriage laws are replete with anomalies and contain
discrimination for and against wide groups of people[78]

The laws regulating weddings did not remain entirely static throughout the period, but such changes as took place made only the most marginal difference to how couples could marry, which is why they are considered

---

[74] 'The cost of getting married', *Wedding Day and First Home*, Spring 1981, p. 14; 'The cost of love', *Wedding Day and Home*, April/May 1991, p. 92. On the nature of the sample, see above.

[75] According to the Bank of England's calculator, £1,791 in 1980 would represent £3,378 in 1990 (and £7,737 today).

[76] Office of National Statistics, 'Marriages in England and Wales 2017' (14 April 2020), tables 1, 5, and 8.

[77] 'Second time around', *Wedding and Home*, Jun/Jul 1993, p. 93.

[78] Leo Abse MP, commenting on the provisions of the Marriage (Registrar General's Licence Bill) 1970: *Hansard*, HC Deb., vol. 795, col. 1614, 13 February 1970.

separately from the broad trends in marriage patterns. Their significance lies rather in how they illustrate a growing, if gradual, degree of convergence between different routes into marriage. Different changes reduced the differences between different Jewish groups, between Anglican and other Christian denominations, between Anglican and other forms of marriage, and between Christian and non-Christian religions.[79] Such changes did not eliminate those differences, and sometimes had the effect of creating new anomalies. But the overall trend was to acknowledge both that differences in treatment were often unjustified, and that England and Wales was home to a more diverse range of religious beliefs than hitherto. That diversity also generated questions about what it meant to solemnise a marriage, and what constituted a religion for the purposes of registering a place of worship.

Liberal and Reform Judaism

Following the decisions that the secretaries of Liberal synagogues could not be certified by the Board of Deputies as persons professing the Jewish religion, and that this was not an anomaly that could be addressed as part of the consolidation of the law in 1949,[80] Liberal synagogues had continued to be registered as places of worship.[81] By the late 1950s, the membership of the St John's Wood synagogue had reached almost 2,400, its fifteen affiliated congregations had an aggregate membership of about 10,000,[82] and there were more weddings in Liberal synagogues than in Reform ones.[83] Lord Cohen, introducing the Marriage (Secretaries of Synagogues) Bill in the Lords, outlined the history of how first Reform and then Liberal Judaism had emerged, how the West

---

[79] And indeed between Anglican and Anglican: the Marriage (Wales and Monmouthshire) Act 1962 finally extended a number of the changes that had initially been made by a Church of England Measure to the Church in Wales, thereby allowing couples to marry in their usual place of worship (Marriage Measure 1930, Marriage Act 1949, ss. 6(4), 11(2), 15(2), 16(1)(b), 35(3), 72) and permitting lay persons to call banns (Banns of Marriage Measure 1934, Marriage Act 1949, s. 9). On the original rationale for these changes see Chapter 7.

[80] See Chapter 7.

[81] Marriage Act 1949, s. 41; see *London Gazette*, 25 June 1954 (Ealing Liberal Synagogue); 12 February 1957 (Wembley and District Liberal Synagogue). See also *London Gazette*, 17 January 1956, providing for the registration of the North London Progressive Synagogue, 100 Amhurst Park, Stoke Newington in place of the now disused North London Progressive Synagogue at 30 Amhurst Park, Stamford Hill, Hackney.

[82] *Hansard*, HL Deb., vol. 214, col. 229, 12 February 1959.

[83] Prais and Schmool, 'Statistics of Jewish Marriage', Table 1.

London synagogue (Reform) had been recognised by statute in 1856, and the doubts as to whether Liberal Judaism could be recognised as a matter of religion by the orthodox Board of Deputies.[84] As he noted, 'it was finally felt by Jewish authorities, orthodox and Liberal alike, that the only satisfactory way out of the difficulty was to extend to the Liberal congregations similar facilities to those already accorded to the Reform congregations'.[85] The 1959 Act did so by putting the St John's Wood synagogue on exactly the same footing as the West London synagogue.[86]

While this specific example of convergence in the legal status of Liberal and Reform Judaism affected only a few hundred weddings each year, it had a far wider significance in that it illustrated how dealing with one specific anomaly might well overlook far greater ones. The focus on equality of treatment of different Jewish communities did not generate any wider debate as to why Jewish weddings were treated differently in the first place. The bill passed through all of its stages in the Commons without a single speech, while in the Lords the only other person to speak did so only to confirm the government's support. This lack of debate was understandable: after all, the law had only just been consolidated in the 1949 Act; the Jewish population of England and Wales still far outnumbered all other non-Christian faiths combined;[87] and the post-war period was an inappropriate time to start questioning their legal rights. Nonetheless, with hindsight it can be seen as a yet further step away from any coherent marriage law.

It was also somewhat ironic that Lord Cohen had spoken of the emergence of Liberal Judaism as an example of Anglo-Jewish history having repeated itself,[88] for within a very short period it was to repeat itself again. In 1964, a new breakaway group emerged when 300 members of the United Synagogue 'resolved to form an independent congregation ... to "work for the return of the United Synagogue to its own traditions of tolerance and the 'Progressive Conservatism' referred

---

[84] On these developments see Chapters 3, 4, 6 and 7.

[85] *Hansard*, HL Deb., vol. 214, col. 228, 12 February 1959. This belied the fact that it remained a matter of controversy within Jewish communities: see *Jewish Chronicle*, 19 December 1958.

[86] Marriage (Secretaries of Synagogues) Act 1959, s. 1, amending Marriage Act 1949, s. 67. This allowed the St John's Wood synagogue to certify its own secretary (on the application of 20 members) and that of any synagogue connected with it.

[87] Estimates of their respective numbers suggest that there were over four times as many Jews as there were Hindus, Muslims, and Sikhs combined: Alderman, *Modern British Jewry*, pp. 321–22; Peach and Gale, 'New Religious Landscape', p. 479.

[88] *Hansard*, HL Deb., vol. 214, col. 227, 12 February 1959.

to in the preamble to its Byelaws"'.[89] What was termed the New London synagogue was duly registered for weddings,[90] alongside the three Orthodox synagogues that had previously chosen not to be authorised by the Chief Rabbi. The issue underscored once again the inflexibility that resulted from naming a specific group in the legislation.

An Ecumenical Matter

The 1950s and 1960s also saw the removal of some of the restrictions that applied to registered places of worship, thereby bringing the rules governing marriages in such places marginally closer to Anglican marriages. What was particularly striking in the debates on these changes was the focus – whether implicit or explicit – on Christian denominations. The explicit mentions of Catholics in discussions of reform – in conspicuous contrast to the earlier tendency to refer only to Dissenters and Nonconformists – was a marker of the growth of Catholicism in post-war England and Wales,[91] and of the greater number of Catholic weddings being celebrated.[92] And the focus on Christians as a whole reflected the post-war hopes of Christian unity and the reunion of different churches.[93] It was, as one MP noted, 'an ecumenical age'. But the limits of this were clear. While only one of the reforms was explicitly limited to Christian denominations, there was equally no mention of any non-Judeo-Christian faiths during the course of the debates.

The lack of any such mention was particularly surprising when the reform under consideration explicitly broadened the scope of a particular provision beyond Christian denominations. The Marriage Act 1949 (Amendment) Bill 1954 was primarily aimed at making it easier for

---

[89] Alderman, *Modern British Jewry*, p. 363.

[90] *London Gazette*, 17 November 1964. By the mid 1980s it had become part of the Masorti Assembly of Synagogues. Its recognition by the Chief Rabbi in 1981 meant that its secretary could be certified by the Board of Deputies, but its status within Orthodox Judaism remained somewhat tentative: Alderman, *Modern British Jewry*, pp. 364, 370, 395.

[91] On which see Doreen Rosman, *The Evolution of the English Churches, 1500–2000* (Cambridge: Cambridge University Press, 2003), p. 306. More Catholic churches were built in the 1950s and 1960s than any previous decades: Historic England, *19th- and 20th-Century Roman Catholic Churches: Introductions to Heritage Assets* (Historic England, 2017), para. 1.4.

[92] Catholic weddings had in fact overtaken ones in Nonconformist chapels during the 1950s, accounting for 11.5 per cent of all weddings in 1957, rising to 12.3 per cent in 1962: ONS, 'Marriages in England and Wales'.

[93] Rosman, *The Evolution of the English Churches*, pp. 322–26.

couples to marry in their usual place of worship by removing the condition that it should be no more than two miles outside the boundary of the registration district.[94] No such condition applied if a couple were marrying in the Church of England church they usually attended.[95] Brought forward by a number of Welsh MPs,[96] the short discussion in Parliament revolved almost entirely around Nonconformity and the topography of Wales.[97] At Committee stage, however, the scope of the bill was widened to amend the provision making it possible to marry in another place of worship outside the registration district(s) in which the parties lived. To the requirement that the persons seeking to marry should have to declare that they desired the marriage to be solemnised according to 'a form, rite or ceremony of a body or denomination of Christians'[98] was added the alternative 'or other persons meeting for religious worship'.[99] But what was contemplated by this was not adherents of other faiths but 'humanists and ethicists and other religionists who cannot normally be termed Christians'.[100]

The reference to 'humanists' reflected the adoption of this label by a number of the local groups formed under the auspices of the Ethical Union at this time.[101] Whether any such groups had followed the lead of the South Place Ethical Society[102] and registered their meeting places for weddings did not appear from the debate; if Conway Hall *was* the only place in England and Wales where such ceremonies could be performed at this time,[103] it was of considerable importance that its catchment area was not limited to those resident in the district. In numerical terms, however, it is more likely that this addition primarily benefitted those

---

[94] Marriage Act 1949 (Amendment) Act 1954, s. 1, amending Marriage Act 1949, s. 35(2).

[95] The possibility of a couple marrying in their usual place of worship had been introduced by the Marriage Measure 1930 and consolidated in ss. 6(4) and 15(2) of the Marriage Act 1949. Those marrying according to the rites of the Church in Wales were still limited to doing so in the parish where at least one of them was resident until the Marriage (Wales and Monmouthshire) Act 1962, noted above.

[96] *Hansard*, HC Deb., vol. 520, col. 1732–33, 18 November 1953.

[97] *Hansard*, HC Deb., vol. 527, col. 2522, 21 May 1954 (Tudor Watkins); HL Deb., vol. 188, col. 433–44, 5 July 1954 (Lord Haden-Guest).

[98] On the origins of this particular provision, see further Chapter 7.

[99] Marriage Act 1949 (Amendment) Act 1954, s. 2, amending Marriage Act 1949, s. 35(1)(a).

[100] *Hansard*, HL Deb., vol. 188, col. 434, 5 July 1954 (Lord Haden-Guest).

[101] Colin Campbell, 'Humanism in Britain: the Formation of a Secular Value-Oriented Movement' in David Martin (ed.), *A Sociological Yearbook of Religion in Britain 2* (London: SCM Press Ltd, 1969), p. 158.

[102] See Chapter 7.

[103] On its subsequent deregistration, see below.

Muslims who lived at a distance from the few mosques to have been registered for weddings and were unable to show that it was their usual place of worship, and possibly also those Jews whose synagogues were so registered. Nonetheless, it was telling that nobody referred to this as a possibility.

During the course of the debates on the 1954 bill, reference had been made to the possibility of a couple living on a new housing estate without any place of worship for their denomination.[104] Four years later it was the construction of churches and chapels on such estates that prompted a further change.[105] With hundreds of new churches and chapels being built as part of the post-war reconstruction efforts, one long-standing difference in treatment between Anglican churches and the buildings of other denominations became suddenly more obvious, and more oppressive. While Anglican churches could be licensed for marriages immediately, other buildings had to have been used as a place of worship for at least a year before they could be registered for marriages.[106] The Marriage Acts Amendment Bill[107] simply proposed to remove this condition. The debates were brief, since no one seemed able to think of any reason for ever having had, let alone retaining, a waiting period.[108] They were nonetheless illuminating. Virtually everyone who spoke referred to Nonconformists and Catholics (in that order).[109] The diversity of denominations whose buildings were registered for marriage was acknowledged,[110] but any concerns that might have been voiced about the stability of the congregations under whose auspices weddings would be conducted were pre-empted by the inclusion of a provision that a registrar should be present during the first year of registration

---

[104] *Hansard*, HL Deb., vol. 188, col. 434, 5 July 1954 (Lord Haden-Guest).
[105] Marriage Acts Amendment Act 1958.
[106] Marriage Act 1949, s. 41(2).
[107] The bill was a Private Members' Bill introduced by Somerville Hastings.
[108] Hastings referred to the requirement as 'a small error' (*Hansard*, HC Deb., vol. 586, col. 587, 18 April 1958), while Lord Milner described it as 'curious' and thought that it 'seems to have no very good purpose' (*Hansard*, HL Deb., vol. 209, col. 471, 20 May 1958). For the origins of this particular requirement see Chapter 2.
[109] *Hansard*, HC Deb., vol. 581, col. 1578, 7 February 1958 (The Rev. Llywelyn Williams); vol. 586, col. 587, 18 April 1958 (Somerville Hastings); HL Deb., vol. 209, col. 471, 20 May 1958 (Lord Milner).
[110] As Hastings noted, there were 'no less than 500 different sects in this country which have places of worship, and some are better known than others': *Hansard*, HC Deb., vol. 581, col. 1577, 7 February 1958.

before an authorised person could be appointed.[111] The inclusion of the latter provision underlines how tentative a step towards convergence this was. While the need to remedy the 'disability'[112] suffered by Nonconformists and Catholics was premised on an implicit comparison between their position and that of the Established Church, there was no question of putting them on exactly the same footing.

A decade or so on, it was the superfluity of many churches that led to provision being made for different Christian denominations to enter into formal agreements to share their buildings, old or new.[113] The idea was warmly welcomed as a way of both fostering Christian unity and making best use of scarce financial resources.[114] Buildings were seen as an expensive luxury, with Michael Ramsey, the then Archbishop of Canterbury, expressing the hope that 'in the Christianity of the future we may see a good deal more of what existed in New Testament times; namely, a Christian religious fellowship that was not so much bothered about the formal buildings'.[115] Yet again, in making provision for marriages to take place in these shared buildings, the Sharing of Church Buildings Act 1969 made only the most minimal move towards convergence. In essence, the different rules for different types of buildings continued even where the physical building was shared. This meant a building had to be separately *licensed* for Anglican weddings[116] and *registered* for weddings according to other religious rites.[117] The sole tiny

---

[111] Marriage Acts Amendment Act 1958, s. 1(2). This was key in ensuring government support: see *Hansard*, HC Deb., vol. 581, col. 1578, 7 February 1958 (David Renton, Joint Under-Secretary of State for the Home Department); HL Deb., vol. 209, col. 472, 20 May 1958 (Lord Chesham).

[112] This was the term used by both Hastings and Lord Milner: *Hansard*, HC Deb., vol. 581, col. 1577, 7 February 1958; HL Deb., vol. 209, col. 471, 20 May 1958.

[113] For the history of sharing church buildings see *Under the Same Roof: Guidelines to the Sharing of Church Buildings Act 1969* (London: Council of Churches for Britain and Ireland, 1994), and for an earlier example see A.J.C. Paines, 'The Cippenham Shared Church Project' (1969) 23 *Quis Custodiet* 73.

[114] *Hansard*, HL Deb., vol. 298 col. 1296, 30 January 1969 (Lord Brooke of Cumnor), col. 1299 (Lord Wade); 'Church Sharing – Officially Approved!' (1970) 27 *Quis Custodiet* 44.

[115] *Ibid.*, col. 1318.

[116] Unless it was the parish church or (in England) a parish centre: Sharing of Church Buildings Act 1969, s. 6(2). On the provisions for the licensing of Anglican chapels, see Marriage Act 1949, s. 20. *Under the Same Roof*, p. viii, noted that a sharing agreement might be 'seen simply as a necessary step to enable non-Anglican weddings to take place in an Anglican church'.

[117] Sharing of Church Buildings Act 1969, s. 1. For examples of such registrations where buildings were shared by Anglicans and Methodists, see *London Gazette*, 14 August 1970, 13 April 1972, 15 May 1972, 13 June 1972, 6 July 1972. Registration

step towards convergence occurred where the building was shared by non-Anglican denominations; the provision that it did not have to be a *separate* building[118] extended the exemption that had first been accorded to Catholics in 1837.[119]

This new emphasis on Christian unity also served to underline the division between Christian and non-Christian. At one level, there was no reason why the 1969 Act should not have encompassed all religions; after all, there was nothing that required denominations sharing the same building to come together for worship. Hindus regularly hired church halls for their weddings after the necessary formalities had been completed at the register office.[120] And the paucity of mosques, gurdwaras, and mandirs registered for marriage meant that these sharing arrangements would have been particularly beneficial for Muslims, Sikhs, and Hindus. Instead, it was the consequences of conducting a marriage otherwise than in a registered place of worship that were the focus of policy concern, and to which we will now turn.

Marriages Other than in Registered Places of Worship

In 1961 a Sikh priest, named as Bhi Mehar Singh Pardesi, was fined £50 for conducting a ceremony in contravention of the 1949 Act. According to the report of the case, he had been charged with solemnising a marriage in a place other than 'a' registered building.[121] This, however, was not what the Act said. It was an offence to solemnise a marriage in any place other than 'the' – not 'a' – 'registered place of worship or office specified in the notice of marriage and certificate required under Part III of this Act'.[122] The use of the definite article here was important, since it limited the offence to cases where notice had been given and a certificate issued but the marriage went ahead in a location other than that specified. There was no general offence of solemnising a marriage otherwise than in accordance with the Marriage Act 1949.

---

by any one group would enable the other parties to the sharing agreement to conduct weddings there too, and any authorised person appointed by one could similarly register marriages conducted according to the rites of the other, although each denomination could appoint its own authorised person if it so wished: Sch. 1.

[118] Sharing of Church Buildings Act 1969, Sch. 1, para. 1.
[119] See Chapter 3.
[120] For examples see above.
[121] *R* v. *Pardesi* (1962) 26(2) *Journal of Criminal Law* 95.
[122] Marriage Act 1949, s. 75(2)(a)(ii).

This mattered both in terms of the rule of law and the basic principle that a legislative provision imposing criminal sanctions should be interpreted in accordance with its terms. That Singh did not seek to challenge his conviction on this point was, however, unsurprising in the light of earlier authorities. In *R* v. *Rahman (Abdul)*,[123] counsel for the defendant had quite rightly objected that the terms of the indictment did not follow the words of the Marriage Act 1949 but instead referred to solemnising a marriage in a place 'other than … a registered building or office in which a marriage may validly be solemnised'. The judge, however, took the view that the indictment was good even if it did not match what he termed the *ipsissima verba* of the statute[124] – in plain words, it did not matter what the statute said.

Singh's actual defence – that he was not 'solemnising' a marriage at all – failed. It was, however, a defence that had succeeded in another earlier case. Back in 1943, an imam named Ali Mohamed had performed a Muslim ceremony of marriage between Rahim Dadd and Keziah Randall. Since Dadd was at that time still married to another woman, Mohamed had made it clear in advance that the ceremony was 'valueless' in English law and would not confer the status of husband and wife upon them. The judge had held that there was no case to go to the jury on the basis that the offence contemplated a ceremony 'which prima facie will confer the status of husband and wife upon those two persons', and it would not be right to convict a person of having solemnised a marriage when he had 'said some form of words to people' while making it clear that such words did not make them husband and wife.[125]

Four years after Singh's unfair conviction, the prosecution of a Muslim religious leader for the same offence generated much discussion about the meaning of marriage and the legal consequences of religious-only ceremonies.[126] Usuf Arif Bham had conducted a *nikah* for a couple in a private house and had been prosecuted at the Gloucester City Quarter

---

[123] (1949) 33 Cr App R 121.

[124] *Ibid.*, at 122. The relevant provision was then the Marriage Act 1836, s. 39.

[125] *R* v. *Mohamed (Ali)* [1964] 2 QB 350 (Note), at p. 352. The fact that the charge again referred to 'a' rather than 'the' registered place of worship does not seem to have been raised.

[126] 'Islamic Marriages and their Issue' (1965) 109 *Solicitors' Journal* 562; 'Criminal Law: Marriage: Solemnisation: Potentially Polygamous Mohammedan Ceremony in England: Whether a "Marriage"' (1965) 109 *Solicitors' Journal* 573; 'What Is Marriage?' (1965) 8 *Quis Custodiet* 52; 'Unlawfully Solemnizing a Marriage: *R.* v. *Bham*' (1965) 38(12) *Police Journal* 599; 'No Unlawful Solemnisation Of "Marriage": *R.* v. *Bham*' (1966) 30(1) *Journal of Criminal Law* 31.

Sessions in 1965. Convicted of knowingly and wilfully solemnising a marriage contrary to the Marriage Act 1949, he appealed on the basis that the ceremony he had performed in accordance with Islamic law was potentially polygamous and was therefore not a 'marriage' within the meaning of the section. The Court of Criminal Appeal, having reviewed the conflicting authorities,[127] agreed, and Bham's conviction was quashed on the basis that what was contemplated by the 1949 Act 'was the performing in England of a ceremony in a form known to and recognised by our law as capable of producing, when there performed, a valid marriage'.[128]

Given the lack of any general offence of solemnising a marriage otherwise than in accordance with the Marriage Act 1949, it was the right result. But the focus on the potentially polygamous nature of the ceremony confused the issue.[129] It was left unclear whether the suggestion of the Court of Criminal Appeal that the Marriage Act 1949 had no relevance to a ceremony which 'does not purport to be a marriage of the kind allowed by English domestic law'[130] related to the informality of the ceremony or its potentially polygamous nature.[131]

There was, of course, nothing to prevent a couple from celebrating a *nikah* in a registered place of worship.[132] Such a marriage could no more be described as potentially polygamous than one conducted in a register office, and the courts had long made it clear that the fact that an individual's religion allowed polygamy did not affect the legal status of such a marriage. Other groups, by contrast, were unable even to meet the threshold for registering their buildings, as the next section will discuss.

---

[127] Chiefly *R* v. *Mohamed (Ali)* [1964] 2 QB 350 (Note) (which had been decided in 1943) and *R* v. *Rahman (Abdul)* (1949) 33 Cr App R 121.

[128] *R* v. *Bham* [1966] 1 QB 159, at 168.

[129] See e.g. the suggestion that the result might differ according to whether the person officiating had claimed to be performing a marriage under English law: T.C. Hartley, 'Polygamy and Social Policy' (1969) 32 *Modern Law Review* 155.

[130] *Bham*, at 168.

[131] The question of whether a ceremony 'purported' to be a marriage was to re-emerge in the case-law on the validity of marriages in the late 1990s: see further Chapter 9.

[132] The issue was dealt with indirectly and briefly in *Bham*, with the court commenting that counsel for the Crown had not submitted that there was any registered place of worship where a 'nichan' could have been solemnised under the Marriage Act 1949 but instead had 'acknowledged that wherever performed in England this ceremony of nichan could never have been more than what he described as a purported marriage' (at 166). This, however, was intended to convey the fact that a wedding in a registered mosque could not be polygamous, rather than to deny the possibility of it taking place.

Defining Religion

In the late 1960s, the question arose as to whether Scientology constituted a religion or not. The Church of Scientology, established in the United States in the early 1950s, had established its headquarters at East Grinstead in Sussex in 1959.[133] Michael Segerdal, a minister in the church, had applied for the chapel to be certified under the Places of Worship Registration Act 1855. The Registrar-General had refused to register it, and Segerdal, together with the Church of Scientology, accordingly sought an order of mandamus to compel him to do so. The order was refused, and the applicants appealed.

There were two issues before the Court of Appeal.[134] The first was whether the Registrar-General had any discretion to refuse an application for a building to be certified as a place of worship. As Lord Denning MR noted, the existence of this duty depended on the building in question being 'truly' a place of worship.[135] This then raised the second issue, whether the building in question was in fact used for religious worship. For Denning, a 'place of meeting for religious worship' connoted 'a place of which the principal use is as a place where people come together as a congregation or assembly to do reverence to God'.[136] In his view the creed of the Church of Scientology was 'more a *philosophy* of the existence of man or of life, rather than a *religion*'.[137] His fellow judges agreed, with Buckley LJ noting that he could find nothing in the wedding ceremonies conducted by the Church of Scientology 'which would not be appropriate to a purely civil and non-religious ceremony such as is conducted in a register office'.[138]

The case also highlighted the power of the Registrar-General to strike premises which had ceased to be used for religious worship *off* the register. Questions arose whether certain places that were registered for marriage should continue to be so registered. One place that came under scrutiny was Conway Hall, possibly because of an interview in the *Daily Mail* in which its general secretary described the 'humanist' weddings

---

[133] Donald Westbrook, *Among the Scientologists: History, Theology and Praxis* (Oxford: Oxford University Press, 2019), ch. 3.

[134] *R v. Registrar General, ex parte Segerdal* [1970] 2 QB 697.

[135] *Ibid.*, at 705.

[136] *Ibid.*, at 707.

[137] *Ibid.*, at 707 (emphasis in original).

[138] *Ibid.*, at 709. This by itself should not have mattered, given that there was no requirement in the Marriage Act 1949 for any religious ceremony to be performed in a registered place of worship.

being celebrated there and how although they were a 'religious organisation' they 'do not believe in a personal god'.[139] Despite the best efforts of
the South Place Ethical Society to argue that 'worship' should be interpreted in a wide sense that incorporated its practices,[140] the Hall's
registration was cancelled. At the time it was hoped that this would be
merely temporary, and that the Society would be able to celebrate marriages there in the future, but the subsequent assessment that its concept
of worship was not worship 'in the sense in which worship is an attribute
of religion' effectively ruled that out.[141]

A Limited Amendment of the Law

In 1970, there were vigorous arguments in favour of greater convergence
between Anglican and other forms of marriage. The issue at stake was the
right of the Archbishop of Canterbury to grant a special licence to enable
an Anglican marriage to take place anywhere, and the lack of any
equivalent for non-Anglican marriages. Such lack was seen as
a particular hardship in cases where a person was dying and physically
unable to go to a register office or registered place of worship to be
married, and this was the scenario that the eventual Marriage
(Registrar General's Licence) Act 1970 addressed.[142] A number of MPs
clearly took the view that more wide-ranging reform was needed to
remove anomalies within marriage law.[143] Leo Abse was particularly
acerbic when it came to the dispensations that could be granted in
relation to Anglican marriages by virtue of a common or special licence,
arguing that they were 'discredited just as they were in mediaeval times';
a factory worker in his constituency of Pontypool, he noted, might face
difficulties in marrying a girl from Swansea in Cardiff, but 'no such
difficulty stands in the way of the well-heeled and well-connected'.[144]

Almost all of the amendments proposed by MPs were opposed by the
government on the basis that any divergence from the 1949 Act should be

---

[139] 'Saying "I will" with a sonnet: For a few ... it's the alternative to church or a register
office', *Daily Mail*, 12 July 1975.

[140] *Ethical Record*, May 1977, p. 11.

[141] *In re South Place Ethical Society* [1980] 1 WLR 1565, at 1573.

[142] Its original title – the Licensing of Marriages on Unlicensed Premises Bill – was quickly
changed because of the potential confusion with pubs: HC Deb., vol. 795, col. 1609,
13 February 1970.

[143] Some of these went far beyond the issue of parity between Anglican and non-Anglican
marriages, and are considered further below.

[144] *Hansard*, HC Deb., vol. 795, col. 1616, 13 February 1970.

as limited as possible.[145] Unlike the 1949 Act, however, the 1970 Act made no provision for a marriage to be conducted in the presence of an authorised person; instead, as before 1899, any religious wedding (unless Anglican, Jewish, or Quaker) had to be conducted in the presence of a registrar.[146] Nor, reading the debates, would one find any indication that England and Wales were any more religiously diverse than they had been in 1899: while there were general references to 'non-Anglicans' and 'other faiths', the only groups mentioned by name as likely to benefit from the bill were Catholics and Methodists.[147]

Wedding law reform came back before Parliament in 1983, with the government bringing forward a bill to allow those who were house-bound or detained to be married at their place of residence or detention. The tenor of the debates was very different from in 1970: this 'limited amendment' was put forward as being necessary to comply with the government's obligations under the European Convention on Human Rights and no attempts were made to broaden its scope. Instead, the discussion focused on whether an individual prisoner would be able to get married outside the prison if he wished to do so[148] and, if not, whether the marriage certificate would specifically record the wedding location as the prison. While the changes effected by the Marriage Act 1983 were limited,[149] the debates did disclose a new awareness of the range of places in which marriages could take place, with at least some allusion being made to the possibility of marriage in church, synagogue, or mosque.[150]

---

[145] *Hansard*, HC Deb., vol. 800, cols. 811, 814, 818, 24 April 1970 (Brian O'Malley).

[146] Marriage (Registrar General's Licence) Act 1970, s. 10(2).

[147] *Hansard*, HC Deb., vol. 795, cols. 1603, 1631, 1648, 13 February 1970 (respectively, Victor Goodhew, in introducing the bill, Norman St John Stevas, in welcoming it, and Dr John Dunwoody, in noting the figures on weddings in registered places of worship); HL Deb., vol. 310, col. 1143, 20 May 1970 (Baroness Llewelyn-Davies).

[148] Prison authorities may have changed their minds about allowing prisoners out for the day after an ambush outside a register office led to one making his escape ('Gang grab prisoner from his wedding', *Daily Mail*, 21 January 1987). A number of weddings were also reported as taking place within the prison itself where there were particular security concerns: see e.g. 'Jail bride for bullion raid's "Mr Goldfinger"', *Daily Mail*, 3 June 1987; 'Rapist to marry a murderous babysitter in Broadmoor', *Daily Mail*, 9 September 1987; 'Killer weds', *Daily Mail*, 9 December 1987; 'New Mrs Kray drinks to absent husbands', *Daily Mail*, 7 November 1989.

[149] For discussion of the details see 'Marriage And The Immovable' (1983) 127 *Solicitors' Journal* 466.

[150] *Hansard*, HL Deb., vol. 439, col. 1112, 1 March 1983.

Proposals for Reform: Convergence and Divergence

There was a strong sense from at least 1970 that the laws regulating weddings were outdated and in need of a complete overhaul rather than just piecemeal reform. During the course of the debates on the Marriage (Registrar General's Licence) Bill in 1970, MPs had drawn attention to the oddity of some of the requirements for civil weddings[151] and, more vocally, to the inadequacy of the facilities provided for their celebration. Register offices were labelled as 'dismal', 'squalid', and (perhaps unfairly) 'sleazy'.[152] One MP described how the rooms allocated for weddings in his constituency measured 18 × 12 feet and 20 × 12 feet, respectively, and were 'divided by a stairway and a public lavatory'.[153] The solution, in the eyes of many, was to allow couples to marry in hotels and town halls.[154] One extolled the option of marrying at home – as was possible in many other parts of the world – on the basis that marriage was 'not only a matter of contract and ceremony and passion: it is a matter of domesticity, and the centre of domesticity is the home'.[155] Some favoured keeping certain restrictions on where weddings could take place, with a short but spirited debate unexpectedly developing on whether it should be possible to marry in a lion cage.[156] Others, however, thought that the choice should be left to the couple themselves: as Leo Abse perspicaciously pointed out, people in 1837 had 'regarded the idea of anybody wanting to marry anywhere other than in church as extraordinarily eccentric'.[157]

The government's response to the frequent attempts of MPs to widen the scope of the 1970 bill was to point out that the issue of reform was being considered by a joint working party of the Law Commission and the Registrar-General.[158] The report of that working party[159] envisaged

---

[151] Including the necessity for both a superintendent registrar and a registrar to be present: see further Chapter 10.

[152] *Hansard*, HC Deb., vol. 795, col. 1644, 13 February 1970 (Mark Carlisle), col. 1618 (Leo Abse), col. 1622 (Eric Lubbock).

[153] *Ibid.*, col. 1610 (John Fraser, MP for Lambeth Norwood).

[154] *Ibid.*, cols. 1623, 1644 (Eric Lubbock, David Weitzman, Mark Carlisle).

[155] *Ibid.*, col. 1628 (Will Howie).

[156] *Ibid.*, col. 1613.

[157] *Ibid.*, col. 1618.

[158] *Hansard*, HC Deb., vol. 795, col. 1646, 13 February 1970.

[159] The provisional proposals of the joint working party of the Law Commission and the Registrar-General had been published as part of the Law Commission's series of Working Papers in 1971 (*Solemnisation of Marriage*). Its subsequent Report was published as an Annex to the Law Commission's 1973 *Report on Solemnisation of Marriage*.

the convergence of the different routes into marriage, with (almost) universal civil preliminaries[160] and the minimisation of differences between different religious groups. The latter was to be achieved by requiring all weddings, including those of Jews and Quakers, to be solemnised in a prescribed place, in the presence of a prescribed person authorised to 'supervise the solemnization of the marriage and to see that it is duly registered'.[161] When it came to its own report, however, the Law Commission noted its regret that it had been unable to reach agreement on whether to support this proposal. While some Commissioners agreed with the working party that weddings should only be celebrated in prescribed places, others took the view that the law need only require the presence of a prescribed *person*, and that the actual place was 'unimportant'.[162] In the light of such disagreement, it made no recommendation on this point,[163] and its report, contrary to its custom, contained no draft bill. This may explain why this particular report was one of the few from this period that was not implemented.

Despite the criticisms voiced by MPs, the joint working party of the Law Commission and the Registrar-General had seen no need to expand the range of places in which civil marriages could be solemnised beyond the register office. Instead, it had suggested that the existing facilities should be improved,[164] and in the years that followed efforts continued to be made to this end. In response to the campaign by *Wedding Day and First Home* in 1981, the Deputy Registrar-General suggested that the GRO's campaign for better facilities had been 'pretty successful', although one registrar frankly admitted that while some register offices were attractive, 'the accommodation provided by some local authorities can at best be described as indifferent and at worst abysmal'.[165] Four

---

160 Annex, para. 24.
161 Annex, paras. 74, 84, 91. The 'prescribed places' comprised registered places of worship, Anglican parish churches and chapels licensed or authorised by the bishop, and register offices. The 'prescribed persons' comprised authorised persons, Anglican clergy, and registrars.
162 *Report on Solemnisation of Marriage*, para. 22.
163 Its recommendations on where weddings might take place were limited to the simplification of the process whereby places of worship were registered (*Report on Solemnisation of Marriage*, para. 28) and the possibility of the Registrar-General permitting a wedding at a place where it would not otherwise be possible to marry if the parties could not reasonably be expected to comply with the legal requirements and hardship would be caused if the dispensation were not granted (para. 24).
164 *Solemnisation of Marriage*, para. 76.
165 'Is The Marriage Act Obsolete? The Establishment Talks Back', *Wedding Day and First Home*, early spring 1981, p. 14.

years later the magazine noted the 'bad press' that register offices had received in the past and commented that in many places 'efforts have been made to make the atmosphere warmer, brighter and more personal'.[166] But it still warned readers that it was 'a matter of chance' whether their local register office was 'an attractive old house with a garden, or part of a modern municipal office block'.[167]

A decade and a half after the Law Commission's report, new proposals for reform were put forward by the Conservative government.[168] Since these proposals originated in and focused on reforms to the registration system, they did not envisage a wholesale reform of the law.[169] Indeed, what the government proposed in fact involved greater *divergence* between different routes into marriage. Having eschewed consideration of universal civil preliminaries in the light of likely opposition from the Church of England,[170] the proposals as to how the existing civil preliminaries might be improved set up the potential for them to diverge even further from their Anglican counterparts.[171] The proposal that

---

[166] 'Civil Brides', *Wedding Day and First Home*, autumn 1985, p. 70.

[167] *Ibid.* As it noted, those who did not want to leave it to chance could establish a real or fictitious residence in whichever district had the most 'appealing' register office.

[168] *Registration: a modern service. Proposals to reform the system for registering births, marriages and deaths in England and Wales*, 1988/89 Cm 531, para. 3.2. This was followed by a White Paper setting out its recommendations: *Registration: proposals for change. The government's recommendations for reform of the system for registering births, marriages and deaths in England and Wales*, 1989/90 Cm 939.

[169] *Registration: a modern service*, para. 3.1 ('The Government has no plans to review fundamental marriage law').

[170] The Report of a Working Party set up by the General Synod to consider marriage and divorce had rejected the idea of universal civil preliminaries, reiterating the objections it had made to the Law Commission's proposals a decade and a half earlier: *An Honourable Estate: The doctrine of Marriage according to English law and the obligation of the Church to marry all parishioners who are not divorced* (London: Church House Publishing, 1988), p. 73. *Registration: proposals for change*, paras. 3.2–3 noted that some responses had raised the issue of universal civil preliminaries on the basis that they 'would be seen to be equitable, would result in a better quality of registration and would allow for greater use of new technology' but took the view that it would not be appropriate to deal with such a fundamental change 'in the context of what is principally legislation concerning the registration service'.

[171] The reforms that it proposed included a requirement for each of the parties to give notice in person, the ability of registration officers to require supporting documentary evidence, a standard waiting period before the licence to marry was issued, the removal of the need for notices to be displayed during that time, and the licence to marry being valid for longer (*Registration: a modern service*, paras. 3.5, 3.8–3.11, 3.19). These were broadly welcomed (*Registration: proposals for change*, paras. 3.5, 3.10, 3.15) and were eventually enacted by the New Labour government as part of the Immigration and Asylum Act 1999: see Chapter 9.

authorised persons should be appointed by a religious body rather than the trustees of a particular building[172] went some way towards reducing the differences between marriages according to Jewish and Quaker usages and those in registered places of worship, by shifting the focus away from the building to the organisation, but there was no attempt to suggest that Jewish and Quaker weddings should only take place in certain buildings, or that they would have to include the prescribed words. Most fundamentally of all, the government proposed that there should be a greater choice of venues for civil marriages, and that couples should be able to marry in any such venue in England and Wales, rather than being limited to those in their district(s) of residence,[173] setting up the potential for divergence between civil and religious weddings.

In making recommendations for the content of weddings, it also laid more emphasis on the ability of the parties themselves to have some say as to the content of the ceremony itself. There had long been suggestions that more could be included in a civil ceremony, but largely in terms of what legislators and policymakers thought the content should be,[174] rather than what couples might want to include. The registrar who suggested that officials usually used the 'flexibility and discretion' available to them in their opening address to create 'a charming as well as dignified ceremony'[175] simply underlined the fact that it was they who got to choose what was said. In the White Paper, the government acknowledged that many of those who did not want to marry in a church 'nevertheless find the present civil marriage ceremony rather stark and lacking in character'.[176] Responding to requests from various religious denominations, it agreed that a modern alternative to the prescribed words would be provided.[177] It also indicated that it would permit additions such as poetry readings in civil ceremonies 'to help

---

[172] *Registration: a modern service*, para. 3.31; *Registration: proposals for change*, paras. 3.34–3.36.
[173] *Registration: a modern service*, paras. 3.13 and 3.15. The subsequent report noted that the latter suggestion had met with a positive response among members of the public, and that appropriate safeguards and limitations would be included to assuage any concerns about the types of places that might be licensed: *Registration: proposals for change*, paras. 3.16–3.20.
[174] See, e.g., *Hansard*, HL Deb., vol. 199, col. 998, 24 October 1956 (Archbishop of Canterbury).
[175] 'Is The Marriage Act Obsolete? The Establishment Talks Back', *Wedding Day and First Home*, early spring 1981, p. 14.
[176] *Registration: proposals for change*, para. 3.22.
[177] *Registration: proposals for change*, para. 3.24

organisations like the Humanists to have a marriage ceremony which goes some way to meeting their requirements and their particular beliefs'.[178] But it maintained the view that there had to be a clear distinction between civil and religious ceremonies.

Of the package of recommendations put forward by the government, just one was speedily enacted.[179] The condition that only a 'separate' place of worship could be registered for marriages had prevented the registration of those places of worship in newly built community centres that also included cafes, bookshops, offices, and games halls,[180] or which included schools and other facilities.[181] The removal of the condition of 'separateness' was welcomed on the basis that it would 'enable Christian and non-Christian people alike to marry in buildings where they regularly worship'.[182] The allusion to non-Christian faiths demonstrated the cultural shift that had taken place since the debates over the preconditions for registration in the 1950s, even if it defined them by reference to what they were not. In legal terms, however, the Marriage (Registration of Buildings) Act 1990 did no more than remove the difference between Catholic and other registered places of worship that had existed since 1837.[183]

Conclusion

Looking at this period as a whole brings into sharp relief the profound disjunction between the enormous changes in the social and legal

---

[178] *Registration: proposals for change*, para. 3.26. It emphasised, however, that any additions would have to be 'secular', that they should not 'detract from the dignity of the occasion' and would need to be agreed in advance.

[179] *Registration: a modern service*, para. 3.24, proposing that it should not be necessary for a place of worship to constitute a separate building in order for it to be registered for weddings. This had previously been recommended by the joint working party of the Law Commission and the Registrar-General: Annex, para. 79.

[180] It was noted by Viscount Brentford in moving the second reading of the bill in the Lords that 19 applications for registration had been rejected in the previous two years alone: *Hansard*, HL Deb., vol. 521, col. 75, 9 July 1990.

[181] See e.g. A. Bradney, *Religions, Rights and Laws* (Leicester: Leicester University Press, 1993), pp. 40–41, identifying the requirement of separateness as a particular problem for mosques and gurdwaras.

[182] *Hansard*, HL Deb., vol. 521, col. 75, 9 July 1990 (Viscount Brentford). The benefit of the bill to Christian and non-Christian groups was similarly emphasised by Lord Hampton (col 75) and Baroness Blatch (col 77).

[183] For the reasons why the requirement of separateness did not apply to Catholic chapels, see Chapter 3.

significance of marriage as an institution and the lack of change in how entry into marriage could be celebrated. The convergence between civil and religious weddings was not an indication that half of those marrying regarded marriage as a civil matter. While some of those marrying in a register office were motivated by their lack of religious belief, many more did so because they were unable to marry in accordance with their beliefs. For Anglicans, it was the restrictions placed by the church on the remarriage of those who had been divorced that was the key constraint. For other denominations and faiths, it was primarily the lack of places of worship in which weddings could legally take place. The changes made to the rules governing which places of worship could be registered did something to facilitate weddings. But removing the condition that weddings had to take place in a prescribed building would have done more. So too would the possibility of including religious content in a wedding in a register office, as had been possible before 1857.[184]

While there was to be no comprehensive new Marriage Act, the years after 1993 were to see the piecemeal implementation of a number of the government's proposals, including that allowing civil weddings to take place in a wider range of locations. As the next chapter will show, this was to have a profound effect on how weddings were celebrated.

[184] See further Chapter 4.

9

The Rise of the Wedding, 1994–2020

In the spring of 1994, the film *Four Weddings and a Funeral* became an unexpected hit. With all four weddings of the title being church ones,[1] at first sight it might have looked like an exercise in nostalgia. The only register office wedding was that of the kooky Scarlet, and was relegated to the closing montage. Yet the film also gently mocked the conventions it depicted. The most stable and committed relationship it portrayed was that of Gareth and Matthew, described as married 'for all intents and purposes', but with no means of formalising their relationship. The fragility of marriage was made clear, with one couple separating after only a few months, and as Charles and Carrie finally kissed in the rain in the final scenes, they vowed *not* to be married to each other.

As a celebration of marriage, and even of weddings, it was distinctly equivocal. But this is precisely why it serves as such a useful introduction to the period. In cultural terms, weddings were celebrated as never before, with a proliferation of films, TV series, and novels with some allusion to weddings in their title[2] and an increasing amount of time, money, and effort being spent by couples on their own weddings.[3] In demographic terms, however, never before had so few weddings been

---

[1] Angus and Laura marry in a country church in Somerset, Bernard and Lydia in a Catholic church, and Carrie and Hamish in a Scottish church, while Charles is due to marry Henrietta in a London church.

[2] See, e.g., films such as *Muriel's Wedding* (1995), *The Wedding Singer* (1998), *The Wedding Planner* (2001), *Wedding Crashers* (2005), *Bride Wars* (2009), *Bridesmaids* (2011); TV series such as *Don't Tell the Bride* (14 series and 164 episodes 2007–2020); *My Big Fat Gypsy Wedding* (2 series, 2010–12); *Marrying Mum and Dad* (7 series 2012–18); *Married at First Sight* (4 series, 2015–19); *Say Yes to the Dress* (2 series, 2016–17); and novels including Christina Jones, *An Enormously English Monsoon Wedding* (2013), Paige Toon, *Thirteen Weddings* (2014), Carole Matthews, *The Chocolate Lovers' Wedding* (2016), Wendy Holden, *Laura Lake and the Hipster Weddings* (2017), Debbie Johnson, *A Wedding at the Comfort Food Café* (2019).

[3] Sharon Boden, '"Superbrides": Wedding Consumer Culture and the Construction of Bridal Identity' (2001) 6(1) *Sociological Research Online*; Elizabeth van Acker, *Marriage and Values in Public Policy* (Abingdon: Routledge, 2017), ch. 3.

celebrated, with a continuing decline in the marriage rate.[4] With only a small proportion of couples not living together before they married, the wedding was becoming as much a celebration of an existing relationship as it was the first day of the rest of their lives.[5]

These trends were also linked to how couples married, which changed more dramatically during this period than at any point since 1837.[6] The Marriage Act 1994 introduced the possibility of marrying on 'approved premises', and this chapter looks first at the popularity of this option and the corresponding decline in weddings in both Anglican churches and register offices. The fact that couples were increasingly choosing a civil wedding did not, however, indicate that they were rejecting religion, and the second section explores the rise of 'celebratory ceremonies' held separately from the legal wedding where there were particular obstacles to couples marrying in accordance with their beliefs or wishes. Some couples, meanwhile, married according to religious rites alone, sometimes unaware that such ceremonies had no standing in the eyes of the law, and the third section analyses the evolving case law in this area and how official concerns focused in particular on Muslim marriage practices. The final section focuses on the dramatic events of 2020 and how the restrictions imposed by COVID-19 exposed many of the problems with the current law and brought out the distinction between the celebratory and legal aspects of getting married.

The Rise of the Wedding on Approved Premises

Those of us who believe in marriage want it to be celebrated in the style and manner that the couple choose[7]

On 15 June 1994, the MP Gyles Brandreth introduced a bill to amend the law governing weddings.[8] Invoking the success of *Four Weddings and*

---

[4] ONS, 'Marriages in England and Wales 2017' (14 April 2020), table 8.

[5] Rebecca Probert, 'From this Day Forward? Pre-Marital Cohabitation and the Rite of Marriage from the 1960s to the Present Day' in Joanna Miles, Perveez Mody, and Rebecca Probert (eds.), *Marriage Rites and Rights* (Oxford: Hart, 2015).

[6] There were also changes to the preliminaries required before all non-Anglican weddings as a result of the Immigration and Asylum Act 1999 and the Immigration Act 2014. Under the 1999 Act, each person had to give notice separately; and superintendent registrars were given a power to call for evidence of name, age, marital status, and nationality (s. 162); in addition, the possibility of paying extra to shorten the wait between giving notice and being able to marry was abolished, with a standard 15-day period being substituted. This was increased to 28 days by the 2014 Act.

[7] *Hansard*, HC Deb., vol. 246, col. 1327, 15 July 1994 (Gyles Brandreth).

[8] *Hansard*, HC Deb., vol. 244, col. 630, 15 June 1994.

a Funeral, he explained that his bill would give couples more choice as to where civil weddings could take place.[9] The two changes it made – removing the limitation that couples could only marry in their district of residence and allowing a wider range of places to be approved for weddings – had both been part of the package of reforms proposed a few years earlier,[10] and with government support the bill sailed through its stages in both Houses.

Despite the warmth of its welcome both inside and outside Parliament,[11] it was, as many pointed out, a very limited measure.[12] A number of MPs regretted that it did not allow for weddings in gardens or private homes.[13] In addition to the issue of choice, a deeper connection was made between the location of the wedding and the location of the marriage: as Harry Cohen MP suggested, a couple might 'wish to get married in the place where they will live out their vows'.[14] He also suggested that the same facilities should be extended to religious weddings, expressing his concern that some couples were effectively required to have two ceremonies – one civil and one religious – because the law did not effectively cater for them to marry in the way that they wished. Outside Parliament, too, commentators highlighted how some 'romantic choices of venue' had been ruled out.[15]

---

[9] *Hansard*, HC Deb., vol. 246, col. 1327, 15 July 1994.

[10] *Registration: a modern service. Proposals to reform the system for registering births, marriages and deaths in England and Wales*, 1988/89 Cm 531; *Registration: proposals for change. The government's recommendations for reform of the system for registering births, marriages and deaths in England and Wales*, 1989/90 Cm 939; see further Chapter 8.

[11] David Brindle, 'Law eases path to picturesque wedding venues', *Guardian*, 29 December 1994; Paul Wilkinson, 'Trawler weddings offer historic opportunity to become a fishwife', *The Times*, 6 January 1995; Carol Ramey, 'Get me to the castle (or pavilion, or boat . . . even Liverpool's Cavern Club) on time', *Daily Mail*, 18 March 1995.

[12] The Registrar-General was quick to dampen the expectations that might have been raised by some of the early newspaper reports, noting that it was 'premature' to say which premises might be licensed, but that the draft regulations 'would not allow marriages to take place in open spaces, or in many of the more exotic venues which have been mooted in media reports': 'Marriage locations', *The Times*, 19 January 1995.

[13] *Hansard*, HC Deb., vol. 246, col. 1333, 15 July 1994 (Mr Harry Cohen), cols. 1338–9 (Mr Michael Stern); HL Deb., vol. 557, cols. 562–3, 25 July 1994 (Baroness Jay).

[14] *Hansard*, HC Deb., vol. 246, col. 1333, 15 July 1994.

[15] Chris Barton, 'Get me to the submarine on time', *The Times*, 31 January 1995; Anthony Doran, 'Bang go hopes of bliss in a balloon', *Daily Mail*, 7 March 1995; David Brindle, 'Weddings remain a serious business under new site rules', *Guardian*, 7 March 1995; 'Where you may marry', *The Times*, 18 March 1995.

Once the necessary regulations had been made, the Marriage Act came into force early in 1995.[16] While take-up was initially modest, by the end of 1995 almost 800 places had been approved for weddings and by May 1998 this had swelled to over 2,000.[17] Most were hotels, pubs, and restaurants that could cater for the reception as well as the wedding, but there were also a number of stately homes and museums.[18] Reviewing the range of venues that had been approved, *The Times* noted that alongside Pinewood Studies and London Zoo, there were also 'small farmhouses, cottages, bed-and-breakfasts and country houses' catering for those who wanted a smaller ceremony.[19]

Even at such modest venues the new option was not a cheap one. Reviewing the cost of getting married in 1996, *Wedding and Home* suggested that the 'dramatic rise' in the fees for getting married might be accounted for by those charged by registrars at the new wedding venues.[20] In addition, the even sharper increase in the amount that readers reported spending on their reception venue – from £430 the previous year to £711 – suggests that weddings were increasingly being seen as a commercial opportunity.[21]

The concept of 'approved premises' might, however, have proved to be short-lived. In 2002, the government proposed to introduce a celebrant-based system, regulating who was to conduct the ceremony rather than where it took place.[22] The proposals were welcomed both inside and

---

[16] The provision allowing couples to marry in a register office outside their district(s) of residence came into force on 3 January 1995 and that allowing weddings on approved premises on 1 April.

[17] John Haskey, 'Marriages in "Approved Premises" in England and Wales: the impact of the 1994 Marriage Act' (1998) 93 *Population Trends* 38, 40. The fact that Gyles Brandreth was MP for the City of Chester may explain why 13 of the first 20 places to be approved were in Cheshire: as he had teasingly noted during the third reading of the bill, 'a constituency such as mine, which is rich in heritage and packed with historic buildings and the finest hotels, is ideal' (*Hansard*, HC Deb., vol. 246, col. 1328, 15 July 1994).

[18] Haskey, 'Marriages in "Approved Premises"', table 2. See also '15,000 wedding awaydays', *Daily Mail*, 13 March 1998, reporting on how a number of football grounds were 'now in the love match business'.

[19] Rachel Kelly, 'A quiet spot to tie the knot', *The Times*, 14 February 1996. There was also, she noted, 'a James Bond theme pub in Warwickshire called 007 and, naturally, licensed to wed'.

[20] 'The cost of love', *Wedding and Home*, Apr/May 1996, p. 108.

[21] For the figures for 1995, see 'What price love?', *Wedding and Home*, Apr/May 1995, p. 108.

[22] *Civil Registration: Vital Change; Birth, Marriage and Death Registration in the 21st Century* (2002) Cm 5355. For analysis, see Chris Barton, 'White Paper Weddings – the Beginnings, Muddles and Ends of Wedlock' [2002] *Family Law* 431.

outside Parliament;[23] as one MP argued, as long as the person 'standing before the couple on behalf of society' could conduct the wedding 'with due dignity', people 'should have the freedom to choose where they want to get married, whether on the stands of the Millennium stadium or the top of a mountain in the Rhondda'.[24] In the event, the government's hope that such a fundamental change could be achieved by delegated legislation, under the Regulatory Reform Act 2001, was not to be realised,[25] and the proposals were quietly shelved.

In the meantime, the number of weddings on approved premises continued to grow. Within a decade of the 1994 Act coming into force, such weddings accounted for half of all civil weddings.[26] Five years later, over half of *all* weddings were taking place in such venues, and by 2017 this had risen to almost 70 per cent.[27] The rough parity that had existed between civil and religious weddings since the 1970s had been replaced by an apparently overwhelming preference for the former.

Of course, a preference for a particular type of venue does not necessarily equate to a desire for a particular type of wedding. We shall see in due course how weddings on approved premises might be accompanied by a range of other rites; first, however, we should examine the impact of the Marriage Act 1994 on the numbers getting married in the Anglican church.

Welcoming Weddings: Getting Married in the Anglican Church

The popularity of approved premises led to a sharp drop in Anglican weddings. By 2004, they accounted for less than a quarter of all weddings, down from just under a third ten years earlier.[28] The precarious position of the Anglican church was further underlined by empirical research

---

[23] 'Beneath these goal posts, I thee wed', *Daily Mail*, 22 January 2002.

[24] *Hansard*, HC Deb., vol. 392, col. 119, 4 November 2002 (Chris Bryant, MP for Rhondda).

[25] A draft Regulatory Reform Order dealing with the registration of births and deaths was brought forward (Regulatory Reform (Registration of Births and Deaths) (England and Wales) Order 2004) but the Committees appointed to consider it concluded that the order-making powers conferred by the Regulatory Reform Act 2001 should not be used to effect such a change. It was subsequently announced that no Regulatory Reform Order would be brought forward to reform marriage law: 1 March 2005.

[26] Ben Wilson and Steve Smallwood, 'Understanding recent trends in marriage' (2007) 128 *Population Trends* 24.

[27] ONS, 'Marriages in England and Wales 2017', table 1.

[28] *Ibid.* See also Haskey, 'Marriages in "Approved Premises"', p. 51, calculating that around 42 per cent of those marrying on approved premises would previously have chosen to marry in a religious ceremony.

exploring the motivations of those couples who were still choosing to get married in church despite being – at best – irregular attenders. Few were motivated by any 'latent religiosity'; it was, rather, a sense of 'tradition', connotating a mix of gravitas, family expectations, and aesthetics.[29] Traditions, however, can emerge very quickly, and stately homes and castles had the advantage of being able to host the reception as well as the ceremony. It was telling that by 2006, when market researchers carried out an investigation into why couples did – or more importantly didn't – marry in church, hardly anyone said the main reason for marrying in church was its appearance.[30] The declining importance attached to aesthetic considerations in the later research may well have been because those who might otherwise have chosen the church as an attractive backdrop had gone elsewhere. There was still a hope within the church that those who referred to a church wedding as 'proper' or 'traditional' were expressing some sense of the transcendent.[31] But there was also an acceptance that for most the wedding would be their sole contact with the church.[32]

The ability of couples to marry in any register office or approved premises in England and Wales, irrespective of whether it was located in their district of residence, also shaped expectations of church weddings. Commenting on such changed expectations, a 2001 review of the laws governing marriage in the Church of England noted how a mistaken claim in one Sunday newspaper that parish boundaries were to be abolished had led to a number of clergy receiving 'pressing demands for marriage bookings' on the following morning.[33] While the review did

---

[29] John Walliss, "'Loved the Wedding, Invite Me To the Marriage": The Secularisation of Weddings in Contemporary Britain' (2002) 7(4) *Sociological Research Online*.

[30] Tamar Kasriel and Rachel Goodacre, *Understanding Marriage, Weddings, and Church Weddings: An exploration of the modern day wedding market among couples* (March 2007), fig. 13.

[31] Andrew Body, *Making the Most of Weddings: A Practical Guide for Churches* (London: Church House Publishing, 2007), p. 2; Stephen Lake, *Welcoming Marriage: A Practical and Pastoral Guide to the New Legislation* (London: Church House Publishing, 2009), pp. 32–33; Gillian Oliver, *The Church Weddings Handbook* (London: Church House Publishing, 2012), pp. 14–15.

[32] See, e.g., the discussion of 'aftercare', which presupposed that the couple would not be attending church: Oliver, *The Church Weddings Handbook*, p. 96.

[33] *Just Cause or Impediment? A report from the Review of Aspects of Marriage Law Working Group* (October 2001, GS1436), para. 15. The review had originally been prompted by discussions in the General Synod about devising an alternative to banns, but the government's mooted celebrant-based system meant that the residence requirements became its main focus.

not favour such a complete deregulation of where weddings could take place, it did propose that couples should be able to marry in an Anglican place of worship with which they had a 'demonstrable connection'.[34] A year later the Church of England's formal response to the then government's proposals for a celebrant-based system[35] not only supported this idea of couples being able to marry in places of worship with which they had such a connection but also suggested that 'the Church will wish to welcome the opportunity to extend its ministry in this area outside places of worship'.[36] While the latter possibility vanished when those particular proposals for reform were abandoned, the Church of England continued to develop the idea of widening the range of churches within which marriages could take place.[37] The Measure that eventually became law in 2008[38] set out eight new ways of establishing what was now termed a 'qualifying connection';[39] while most assumed past interactions with the parish or family links,[40] it was also possible to qualify by attending services at the church in question for at least six months.[41]

That this widening of the range of churches in which couples could marry did not result in any increase in the number of Anglican weddings may have been because couples had already been marrying where they wanted to by attending services for long enough to have their names on its electoral roll,[42] establishing residence in the parish for a brief period,

---

[34] *Just Cause or Impediment?*, para. 63. As it noted, a majority of those who had responded to its consultation favoured some relaxation in the preconditions for getting married in church (para. 62).

[35] *Civil Registration: Vital Change*, discussed above.

[36] *The Challenge to Change* (2002), paras. 9–11. It also favoured the abolition of banns as a legal preliminary, although it recommended that clergy would take couples' details and send them on to the registration services.

[37] For an account of the process of reform, see Lake, *Welcoming Marriage*, pp. 14–19.

[38] Church of England Marriage Measure 2008. The possibility was extended to the Church in Wales by the Marriage (Wales) Act 2010.

[39] As various writers noted, the term 'qualifying' was not the best choice, with its implications of 'pass or fail' (Lake, *Welcoming Marriage*, p. 9) and its potential to compound 'the sense of disqualification in couples' (Oliver, *The Church Weddings Handbook*, p. 21).

[40] Specifically, on account of having been baptised in the parish or entered in the register book of confirmation or having lived in the parish for six months at some point, a parent having lived in the parish for six months or having habitually attended public worship there for that period, or a parent or grandparent having married there: Church of England Marriage Measure 2008, s. 1(3); Marriage (Wales) Act 2010, s. 2.

[41] This was similar to the existing possibility of marrying in the church that was the usual place of worship of one or both of the couple but without the necessity of being on the church's electoral roll.

[42] Or possibly not even attending: the MP Chris Bryant noted that from his former days as a vicar he knew that 'many vicars who have pretty churches are happy to enable anyone to

giving the address of a parent, or simply pretending.[43] After all, unlike registration officials, clergy had no power to call for documentary evidence as proof. And while removing the incentive to establish a fictitious residence may have enabled couples to be more honest, it also made it necessary for the banns to be called in the couple's *actual* parish(es) of residence as well, leading to more work for clergy, more hassle for couples, and a greater likelihood of mistakes being made. The 2008 Measure may therefore have simply added an additional layer of complication.[44]

Couples may also have decided not to marry in church for other reasons.[45] The market researchers commissioned to investigate couples' motivations found that almost half ranked 'not religious enough' as a key reason for not getting married in church; some, they noted, would have liked to have done so but would have felt 'hypocritical'.[46] Others, as one clergyman noted, thought they could not marry in church if 'they don't go to church, or haven't been baptized, or are living together'.[47] It was telling that there was no reference within this list to those who had been divorced, those who were within the formerly prohibited degrees, and those who had undergone gender reassignment, for whom the possibility of marrying in church was not a matter of right but contingent on finding a member of the clergy willing to conduct the service.[48] And while the Church of England's official line on the remarriages of those whose first marriages had ended in divorce softened considerably in the

---

qualify to be on their electoral roll, regardless of their attendance at the church': *Hansard*, HC Deb., vol. 392, col. 120, 4 November 2002.

[43] Walliss, 'Loved the Wedding', para. 3.9, noted the 'common scenario' of couples 'metaphorically "parachuting-in" to (typically) small, traditional-looking village churches and then not being seen again afterwards'.

[44] A further layer of complication was added by the Mission and Pastoral Measure 2011, as a result of which a qualifying connection to one church in a benefice could be extended to other churches in the same benefice.

[45] See, e.g., Oliver, *The Church Weddings Handbook*, p. 17, discussing couples' own sense of hypocrisy and fear of rejection.

[46] Kasriel and Goodacre, *Understanding Marriage, Weddings, and Church Weddings*, fig. 15 and p. 32.

[47] Body, *Making the Most of Weddings*, p. 6. Some clergy may have contributed to a sense that baptism was a precondition by continuing to use a form that asked about it: Oliver, *The Church Weddings Handbook*, p. 50.

[48] Anglican clergy were specifically exempted from any obligation to conduct such marriages: see respectively Matrimonial Causes Act 1965, s. 8(2); Marriage Act 1949, ss. 5A and 5B.

twenty-first century,[49] the advent of same-sex marriage refocused attention on those weddings that the Anglican church would *not* permit.[50]

There was also a certain ambivalence within the church as to whether
weddings were welcome. Publications such as *Making the Most of
Weddings, Welcoming Marriage*, and *The Church Weddings Handbook:
the seven pastoral moments that matter* emphasised that they were. But
since their intended audience was those conducting weddings, rather than
couples themselves, they left a strong impression that some clergy were not
as welcoming as they might be, particularly if couples' wishes were not
expressed in a way that resonated with the church's own sense of what was
important.[51] Similarly, while each advocated allowing a degree of 'personalisation' of the marriage service,[52] suggestions that conversations about
hymns and readings needed to be couched in positive terms rather implied
that too many were not.[53] The optimism expressed in *The Church Weddings
Handbook* that the Anglican church 'could easily conduct double the
number of weddings by just marrying the people who thought that church
was the right place for it'[54] proved to be unwarranted. By 2017 only around
one-sixth of marriages were taking place in the Anglican church.[55]

Not Welcoming Weddings: The Disappearing Register Office Wedding

The statistics revealed an equally dramatic shift away from getting married in a register office. By 2017 just 8 per cent of civil weddings were

---

[49] *Marriage in Church after Divorce, A Report from the House of Bishops* (GS 1449,
      May 2002), para. 1, referred to the church's 'pastoral ministry to divorced persons who
      seek a further marriage in church'. The provisions of the 1957 Act of Convocation that
      restricted such marriages were rescinded by the General Synod with effect from
      14 November 2003: Mark Hill, *Ecclesiastical Law* (Oxford: Oxford University Press,
      2018), para. 5.48.
[50] See Giles Goddard, 'The Church of England and gay marriage: What went wrong?' in
      Nicola Barker and Daniel Monk (eds.) *From Civil Partnership to Same-Sex Marriage:
      Interdisciplinary Reflections* (Abingdon: Routledge, 2015).
[51] Body, *Making the Most of Weddings*, p. 6.
[52] Body, *Making the Most of Weddings*, p. 51; Lake, *Welcoming Marriage*, p. 101; Oliver, *The
      Church Weddings Handbook*, pp. 72–79.
[53] Lake, *Welcoming Marriage*, p. 70. See also Oliver, *The Church Weddings Handbook*, p. 77,
      giving the example of a vicar who told a couple that their chosen hymn – 'Jerusalem' – was
      inappropriate for a wedding. Given it is included in *Hymns Ancient and Modern* and is
      suffused with Biblical references, couples might well be baffled by such a refusal.
[54] Oliver, *The Church Weddings Handbook*, pp. 13–14. The basis for this was the finding that
      53 per cent of those surveyed still thought that church weddings were more 'proper':
      Kasriel and Goodacre, *Understanding Marriage, Weddings, and Church Weddings*, p. 2.
[55] ONS, 'Marriages in England and Wales 2017', table 1.

classified as taking place there.[56] The figures do, however, need to be interpreted with a degree of caution. After 1995 a number of register offices were reclassified as approved premises, either in part or in their entirety. The incentive for local authorities to do so was very clearly financial. A wedding in a register office was a statutory ceremony, and the fees that a local authority could charge were fixed by statute.[57] A wedding on approved premises was subject to no such restrictions, and the fees charged generally varied according to the number of guests, day of the week, and attractiveness of the venue.[58]

By 2020 there were entire counties that had only one actual register office,[59] although the extent of the change was obscured by the fact that many of the physical buildings in which approved premises were located were still described as a 'register office',[60] while others had adopted the subtly different term 'registration offices'. Almost all local authorities limited the times and days of the week when statutory ceremonies were available.[61] Their minimum obligation was to provide a slot for statutory ceremonies twice a month, and some did no more than this.

Some couples might not even have been aware that it was possible to marry in a register office for no more than £127. Reviewing local authorities' websites, information about the statutory ceremony was often very

---

[56] *Ibid.*

[57] The Registration of Births, Deaths and Marriages (Fees) (Amendment) Order 2014, SI 2014/1790, reg. 2; The Registration of Births, Deaths, Marriages and Civil Partnerships (Fees) (Amendment) and Multilingual Standard Forms Regulations 2018, SI 2018/1268, Sch. 1 para. 2. Such restrictions have not prevented some local authorities from adding additional booking fees: see Stephanie Pywell, '2 + 2 = £127, if you're lucky', *Law Society Gazette*, 3 March 2020.

[58] See eg https://www.devon.gov.uk/registrationservice/venues/registration-offices/exeter (different prices for different rooms, or for more guests in the same room).

[59] These include Buckinghamshire, Cambridgeshire, Cornwall, Cumbria, Derbyshire, Devon, Dorset, Essex, Herefordshire, Nottinghamshire, Oxfordshire, Shropshire, Staffordshire, Suffolk, Wiltshire, and Worcestershire. Cheshire, being split administratively, has two, in Cheshire East and Cheshire West and Chester.

[60] Birmingham, for example, invites couples to 'Book a ceremony at Birmingham Register Office', offering the option of a wedding in its 'ceremony suite' alongside the statutory ceremony: www.birmingham.gov.uk/info/20212/marriages_and_civil_partnerships/735/book_a_marriage_or_civil_partnership_ceremony_at_birmingham_register_office. The only hint that the three rooms within the suite are approved premises is that the cost of getting married there starts at £210 rather than £46.

[61] Stephanie Pywell, 'Availability of two-plus-two marriage ceremonies', *Law Society Gazette*, 31 March 2020.

hard to find, and the way in which many stressed the lack of any ceremonial element, the unattractive location of the ceremony, and the limitation of guests to the two witnesses seemed designed to discourage couples from choosing this option.[62] A number referred to it in terms of 'registration'[63] or 'administration', or made it explicit that this was for couples who 'wish to complete only the legal requirements with no ceremony included'.[64] Those who described it as 'basic'[65] or as taking place in a 'working office'[66] cannot have thought that this would be an enticement to choose this option.[67] And while the statutory ceremony is often dubbed a '2+2' ceremony to reflect the fact that in many cases only the couple and their two witnesses are allowed to attend in addition to the superintendent registrar and registrar, this is the legal minimum, not a maximum which cannot be exceeded.

The massive diminution in the number of register offices, and in the availability and accessibility of the statutory ceremony, meant that many couples who might have wished to marry with minimal ceremony and at the minimum cost simply did not have the option of doing so. This had implications not only for couples of limited means but also for those who saw the register office wedding as a formality that needed to be completed before or after their 'true' wedding. As the next section will show, some of the reasons for this separation of the legal and celebratory aspects of a wedding are familiar ones, but others illuminate the changing nature of belief in the twenty-first century.

---

[62] See. e.g., https://www.staffordshirewedding.info/statutory-ceremonies/.

[63] See, e.g., East Sussex, www.ceremoniesineastsussex.co.uk/crowborough-register-office-fees ('statutory registration of marriage'); West Sussex www.westsussex.gov.uk/births-ceremonies-and-deaths/marriages-and-civil-partnerships/ceremony-administration/ceremony-fees/ ('£57 fee covers administration and is non-refundable').

[64] www.cornwall.gov.uk/advice-and-benefits/weddings-in-cornwall/ceremony-type/wedding-ceremony-packages/.

[65] See, e.g., southwark.gov.uk/births-deaths-marriage-and-citizenship/marriage-and-civil-partnership/booking-a-venue?chapter=3.

[66] See, e.g., East Sussex (ceremoniesineastsussex.co.uk/crowborough-register-office-fees); Dorset (www.dorsetcouncil.gov.uk/births-deaths-marriages/weddings-marriages-and-civil-partnerships/dorset-weddings/dorchester-register-office.aspx); www.shropshire.gov.uk/births-and-marriages/our-fees/fees-for-2019-2022/.

[67] Some even detailed the office furniture: see, e.g., www.staffordshirewedding.info/statutory-ceremonies/ ('there will be a desk, chairs, cabinets') and www.northamptonshire.gov.uk/councilservices/births-deaths-ceremonies/weddings-and-ceremonies/weddings/Pages/default.aspx#expand-Amarriageorcivilpartnershipregistration ('computers and files are in situ').

The Rise of the Celebratory Ceremony

You want your day to be Special. Different. Unique[68]

In 1994, a journalist wrote about her difficulty in finding a way of getting married that would reflect her and her partner's belief in some 'overarching spirituality' without it taking place in a church. Describing herself as a 'lapsed Catholic' and her husband-to-be as 'a passionate agnostic', they rejected the atheistic ceremony offered by the Humanists and found an Anglican vicar willing to conduct a non-denominational blessing in a garden. Since this would be – in her words – 'illegal', she noted that they would 'still have to drop by at Camden Registry Office' for the 'admin' but would not be exchanging rings until the 'wedding'.[69] Her dilemma was shared by an increasing number of couples: by those whose place of worship was not registered for weddings or who wanted to include some religious elements in their wedding at a secular venue; by those same-sex couples who were unable to marry in their place of worship; and by the increasing number of couples wanting a more personalised ceremony. This section accordingly analyses the constraints that such couples faced, and the additional celebratory ceremonies they chose in default of legal options.

Religious Rites

As in previous decades, some couples were not able to have a legal wedding in the place where they worshipped, and so had to have a separate religious ceremony to reflect their beliefs. While the widening of the concept of 'religious worship' as a result of the decision of the Supreme Court in *R. (Hodkin & Anor) v. Registrar General of Births, Deaths and Marriages*[70] enabled the Church of Scientology to register its buildings and conduct legally recognised weddings,[71] it did not do anything to assist those

---

[68] Dianne Ffitch, *Planning a Non-traditional Wedding* (Ipswich: Teach Yourself Books, 2000), p. 1.

[69] 'True love challenged by sects before marriage', *Guardian*, 13 July 1994.

[70] [2013] UKSC 77, para. 57, describing religion as 'a spiritual or non-secular belief system, held by a group of adherents, which claims to explain mankind's place in the universe and relationship with the infinite, and to teach its adherents how they are to live their lives in conformity with the spiritual understanding associated with the belief system'. On this basis, the Supreme Court overruled *Ex p. Segerdal* [1970] 2 Q.B. 697, discussed in Chapter 8.

[71] Josh Halliday, 'Couple in UK's first Scientology church wedding', *The Guardian*, 23 February 2014, noting the wedding of Louisa Hodkin and Alessandro Calcioli.

religious groups that had no buildings to register, whether because they met in less formal settings[72] or chose to worship outdoors.[73]

Nor did the Marriage Act 1994 assist such couples. While it made it possible to have a civil wedding in a far wider range of buildings, the limits on what could be included as part of this were quickly made clear. In addition to the statutory prohibition on a ceremony including a religious 'service',[74] new regulations provided that any 'readings, music, words or performance' included in a ceremony on approved premises must be 'secular in nature'.[75] A circular issued to registration officers emphasised the need 'to ensure that any enhancements to a civil marriage ceremony do not amount to an alternative ceremony or quasi-religious ceremony';[76] that this was issued some months *after* weddings had begun to take place on approved premises suggests that couples marrying in such locations had different expectations as to what could be included and that registration officers had been faced with new types of requests.[77] The insistence that no reference to a god or deity, or to prayer or worship, could be included meant that E.M. Forster's 'only connect' passage from *Howard's End* was barred, as were readings from Khalil Gibran's *The Prophet*.[78]

A subsequent review of the requirements found widespread support for ceremonies being able to include readings, songs, or music containing 'an incidental reference to a god or deity in an essentially non-religious context'.[79] As the GRO's Handbook noted, this meant that Robbie

---

[72] On the rise of 'house churches' in the late twentieth century, see Doreen Rosman, *The Evolution of the English Churches, 1500–2000* (Cambridge: Cambridge University Press, 2003), pp. 343–8.

[73] On the rise of Paganism, see Ronald Hutton, *The Triumph of the Moon: A History of Modern Pagan Witchcraft* (Oxford: Oxford University Press, 1999). The number of individuals identifying themselves as Pagan grew significantly in the twenty-first century, from 42,000 in 2001 to 75,000 in 2011; see Edward Docx, 'Here come the druids', *Prospect*, September 2013, p. 52, noting that informal estimates 'are three times this number'.

[74] Marriage Act 1949, s. 46B(4).

[75] Marriage (Approved Premises) Regulations 1995 (SI 1995/510), Sch. 2, para. 11 (in force from 1 April 1995).

[76] Circular GRO No. 11/1995, [5.2].

[77] Stephanie Pywell and Rebecca Probert, 'Neither sacred nor profane: the permitted content of civil marriage ceremonies' [2018] 30 *Child and Family Law Quarterly* 415.

[78] *Ibid. The Prophet* was apparently a popular choice at Humanist weddings, indicating that the bar also affected couples who wanted a *non-*religious ceremony: 'True love challenged by sects before marriage', *Guardian*, 13 July 1994.

[79] GRO, *Content of Civil Marriage Ceremonies: A consultation document on proposed changes to regulation and guidance to registration officers: Outcome of Consultation* (November 2005), para. 21. The review was instigated following a refusal to permit the reading of Elizabeth Barrett Browning's poem 'How do I love thee?': GRO, *Content of Civil Marriage Ceremonies: A consultation document on proposed changes to regulation and guidance to registration officers* (June 2005), paras. 11, 14.

Williams' 'Angels' or Aretha Franklin's 'I Say A Little Prayer' could be included in a civil wedding. But the revised regulations still prohibited content that was 'religious in nature' and specified that weddings on approved premises could not include extracts from religious marriage services or sacred religious texts, be led by a minister of religion or religious leader, involve one or more religious rituals, or include hymns or religious chants or any form of worship.[80] In practice, these prohibitions were not necessarily interpreted consistently or indeed sensibly, with considerable variation in practice and religious significance even being attributed to periods of silence.[81]

As a matter of law, there was nothing to prevent couples from having the ceremony of their choice at the same venue once the legal part had been completed and the registration officials had departed.[82] After all, the types of venues that were approved for civil weddings and partnerships by their very nature usually served multiple functions. Nonetheless, on occasion registration officials made difficulties about conducting a civil wedding on the same day and at the same venue as a religious ceremony.[83] Guidance issued by the GRO confirmed that the two could be performed on the same day and in the same place, but should be separated by a clear break. It also stipulated that it should be made clear that any 'additional blessing or commemorative event' does not have any legal standing, and stressed that it would be 'best practice' for the religious ceremony to follow the civil ceremony.[84] That it did not say

---

[80] The Marriages and Civil Partnerships (Approved Premises) Regulations 2005, SI 2005/3168, Sch. 2, para. 11(2). This was in addition to the statutory prohibition on a ceremony including a religious 'service': Marriage Act 1949, s. 46B(4).

[81] Pywell and Probert, 'Neither sacred nor profane'; Law Commission, *Getting Married: A Consultation Paper on Weddings Law*, CP No. 247 (3 September 2020), para. 6.87. On the challenges in determining the boundaries between religious and non-religious content, see also Peter W. Edge and Dominic Corrywright, 'Including Religion: Reflections on Legal, Religious, and Social Implications of the Developing Ceremonial Law of Marriage and Civil Partnership' (2011) 26(1) *Journal of Contemporary Religion* 19.

[82] For a fictional account of such a wedding, see Christina Jones, *An Enormously English Monsoon Wedding* (2013), in which the couple set up a *mandap* in the grounds outside the approved premises and bring various Hindu traditions into their celebrations before and after the legal event. As the groom's parents commented, while they understood that the service itself would have to be 'boringly civil and fairly British', there was 'no need for the reception to follow the same trend' (p. 163). For a real-life example, see 'My Big Fat Asian Wedding', C4, first broadcast 14 April 2015, which depicted a couple having a Hindu ceremony on approved premises; the priest pronounced them husband and wife, and the couple then had their civil wedding before registration officials shortly afterwards.

[83] See Rebecca Probert and Shabana Saleem, 'The legal treatment of Islamic marriage ceremonies' (2018) 7(1) *Oxford Journal of Law and Religion* 376.

[84] General Registrar Guidance Handbook, March 2017, para. 34.

that this was a legal requirement calls into question whether the provision in the Marriage Act 1949 allowing a religious ceremony to take place after a civil wedding has any purpose.[85]

Same-Sex Commitment Ceremonies and Blessings

To focus on same-sex commitment ceremonies and blessings rather than civil partnership and same-sex marriage is not to ignore the important changes that have taken place enabling same-sex couples to obtain formal legal recognition.[86] But in providing a history of the period it is worth remembering how recent such formal recognition is. During the 1990s same-sex couples only had the option of a commitment ceremony.[87] Moreover, even when it became possible to enter into a civil partnership in December 2005, its pared-down requirements emphasised that it was not the same as a marriage. Requiring only the signing of the register and no spoken avowal of commitment,[88] it signalled a conceptual distinction between the legal act of becoming a civil partner and any accompanying ceremony.[89]

The Civil Partnerships Act 2004 had originally envisaged an entirely civil process, allowing civil partnerships to be conducted in register offices and on approved premises but nowhere else. When the Equality Act 2010 provided that religious groups could (but would not be obliged to) host civil partnership ceremonies, it was on the basis that their buildings were approved premises for this purpose. While this meant that the standard prohibition that the proceedings could not be 'religious

---

[85] Marriage Act 1949, s. 46. This re-enacted s. 12 of the Marriage and Registration Act 1856; on the confused origins and interpretation of this particular provision, see further Chapters 4 and 5.

[86] See further Chapter 1.

[87] On these earlier commitment ceremonies, see e.g. Beccy Shipman and Carol Smart, '"It's Made a Huge Difference": Recognition, Rights and the Personal Significance of Civil Partnership' (2006) 12(1) *Sociological Research Online*; Victoria Clarke, Carole Burgoyne and Maree Burns, 'Unscripted and Improvised: Public and Private Celebrations of Same-Sex Relationships' (2013) 9(4) *Journal of GLBT Family Studies* 393.

[88] Stephen Cretney, 'Relationship: Law Content and Form' in J Trowell and C Thorpe (eds.) *Re-Rooted Lives* (Bristol: Jordans, 2007), p. 169.

[89] For discussion of the significance of this, see Paul Johnson and Robert M. Vanderbeck, 'Sacred Spaces, Sacred Words: Religion and Same-Sex Marriage in England and Wales' (2017) 44(2) *Journal of Law and Society* 228, p. 237. See also Clarke, Burgoyne and Burns, 'Unscripted and Improvised' for discussion of the different choices made by couples about whether to have a celebration as well as a civil partnership, and Carol Smart, '"Can I Be Bridesmaid?" Combining the Personal and Political in Same-Sex Weddings' (2008) 11 *Sexualities* 761 on the different types of 'personal-political style' in the ceremonies.

in nature' applied, this did not preclude a religious service being used before or after, or even during any 'interval' in the proceedings.[90] Similarly, while the Marriage (Same Sex Couples) Act 2013 made provision for religious groups to conduct same-sex weddings if they so wished, a 'triple lock' meant that no religious group or minister could be compelled to do so,[91] while an additional lock explicitly provided that it would not be possible for same-sex marriages to be conducted according to Anglican rites.[92] The Society of Friends, who had been celebrating same-sex partnerships since the 1990s and were at the forefront of pressing for religious groups to have the option to conduct same-sex marriages, were among those who opted in.[93] Only a few others did so,[94] and the number of same-sex marriages celebrated with religious rites remained tiny.[95] But a far larger number of religious *blessings* took place, including ones conducted by Anglican clergy.[96]

The Rise of the Personalised Ceremony

The biggest change over the period was without a doubt the rise of the 'personalised' ceremony. Not only were couples marrying on approved premises able to incorporate readings and music of their choice into their weddings (subject to the approval of the registration officials conducting them) but there were also an increasing number of additional ceremonies being carried out.

A number of these additional ceremonies were explicitly Humanist ones. As the British Humanist Association's wedding booklet noted in 1996, non-religious ceremonies had been a 'rarity' in 1988, when the

---

[90] Marriage and Civil Partnerships (Approved Premises) (Amendment) Regulations 2011, Sch. 3, para. 15.

[91] The three components of the 'triple lock' were the provisions that (a) religious groups had to make a conscious effort to opt in; (b) a failure to do so would not contravene equality law; and (c) even if a religious group had opted in, no individual member of that group could be compelled to take part in that service: Marriage (Same Sex Couples) Act 2013, s. 2.

[92] Marriage (Same Sex Couples) Act 2013, s.1(2).

[93] Frank Cranmer, 'Quakers and the Campaign for Same-Sex Marriage', in Russell Sandberg (ed.), *Religion and Legal Pluralism* (Abingdon: Routledge, 2016).

[94] Paul Johnson, Robert M. Vanderbeck, and Silvia Falcetta, *Religious Marriage of Same-Sex Couples: A Report on Places of Worship in England and Wales Registered for the Solemnization of Same-Sex Marriage* (University of York and University of Leeds, 2017) found that as of 2015 just 139 places of worship had opted in.

[95] ONS, 'Marriages in England and Wales 2017', table 1.

[96] See Goddard, 'The Church of England and gay marriage'.

booklet was first issued, but had since 'taken off'.[97] In 2004, it was still performing fewer than 300 ceremonies, but the number was growing and in 2018 the newly renamed Humanists UK[98] proudly announced that the number 'topped 1,000 in 2016'.[99]

One reason for this increase may have been a greater awareness of Humanist ceremonies on account of the increasingly high-profile campaign for them to be given legal recognition.[100] In 2013, an amendment to the Marriage (Same Sex Couples) Bill required a review to be carried out as to whether an order should be made 'permitting marriages according to the usages of belief organisations to be solemnized'.[101] That review found widespread support for non-religious belief organisations to be able to conduct legally recognised weddings, but also highlighted the difficulties in devising a scheme to achieve this within the framework of the existing law.[102] The matter was referred to the Law Commission, which similarly concluded that wider reform was needed.[103] In 2020, six couples challenged the law on the basis that their inability to marry in a Humanist ceremony constituted unlawful discrimination; the court

[97] Jane Wynne Willson, *Sharing the Future: A Practical Guide to Non-religious Wedding Ceremonies* (London: British Humanist Association, 1996), p. 1.

[98] 'BHA becomes Humanists UK', 22 May 2017, https://humanism.org.uk/2017/05/22/bha-becomes-humanists-uk/.

[99] 'Revealed: How many marriages each religious group and Humanists UK do', 9 May 2018, https://humanism.org.uk/2018/05/09/revealed-how-many-marriages-each-religious-group-and-humanists-uk-do/. There was a particularly sharp jump after 2012, when 496 ceremonies were performed, to 635 in 2013, 732 in 2014, and 975 in 2015: https://docs.google.com/spreadsheets/d/1DxfMf_wRUJFg-SWyxoKHYbFB6J9U1T5o-NafAA29r2U/edit#gid=1699515432.

[100] On the earlier stages of this campaign, see: *Registration: proposals for change*, para. 3.25, noting the case put forward by the BHA 'for the law to allow those who do not want a strictly civil ceremony or a religious one to have one which accords with their beliefs'; All-Party Parliamentary Humanist Group, *'Any Lawful Impediment?' A report of the All-Party Parliamentary Humanist Group's inquiry into the legal recognition of humanist marriage in England and Wales* (2018), p. 12, noting the 'strong case' made for Humanist celebrants to be included when the move to a celebrant-based system was mooted in the early 2000s and the scheme of recognition proposed in the Marriage (Approved Organisations) Bill 2012-13. On the way in which the debate subsequently evolved, see Russell Sandberg, *Religion and Marriage Law: The Need for Reform* (Bristol: Bristol University Press, 2021), ch. 5.

[101] Marriage (Same Sex Couples) Act, s. 14(1)(a). These were defined as organisations 'whose principal or sole purpose is the advancement of a system of non-religious beliefs which relate to morality or ethics' (s. 14(7)).

[102] Ministry of Justice, *Marriages by Non-Religious Belief Organisations* (26 June 2014); *Marriages by Non-Religious Belief Organisations: Summary of Written Responses to the Consultation and Government Response* (18 December 2014).

[103] Law Commission, *Getting Married: A Scoping Paper* (17 December 2015).

agreed that there was a difference in treatment but held that it was legitimate for this to be addressed as part of a wholesale reform of the law.[104]

The All-Party Parliamentary Humanist Group that reviewed the law in 2018 suggested that a Humanist ceremony was 'distinct from other forms of wedding in a number of ways', including a 'bespoke' script reflecting the humanist beliefs of the couple, the fact that those beliefs were shared with the celebrant, and the location of the ceremony in the venue 'most meaningful to them'.[105] There was, however, no shortage of independent celebrants and organisations offering similarly bespoke ceremonies that reflected the beliefs of the couple and were held at a location chosen by them. Just before the 1994 Act was passed, a company called Garlands began to offer what it described as 'wedding ceremonies with a difference'. These were personalised ceremonies conducted by celebrants in the location of the couple's choice.[106] Another company, Civil Ceremonies Ltd, founded in 2002, provided training for would-be celebrants as well as a range of ceremonies.[107] Over the next few years a number of other organisations sprang up to represent and train the growing number of celebrants.[108] By 2020, there were over 2,000 celebrants conducting perhaps as many as 10,000 bespoke ceremonies each year in a wide range of locations and often incorporating elements from different religious traditions and beliefs.[109]

Popular TV programmes such as *Don't Tell the Bride* also ensured the cultural visibility of personalised ceremonies. The premise of the show, which started in 2007, was that the groom has just three weeks to organise the wedding but can have no contact with the bride during that time. The early series depicted hapless grooms struggling to make

---

[104] *Harrison* v. *Secretary of State for Justice* [2020] EWHC 2096 (Admin).

[105] 'Any Lawful Impediment?', p. 9.

[106] David Brindle, 'Law eases path to picturesque wedding venues', *Guardian*, 29 December 1994. See also 'Your Place or Mine?', *Wedding and Home*, December 1994/January 1995, p. 120 noting that a survey carried out by Garlands had found that 60 per cent of British couples 'weren't able to marry in their ideal location' on account of the restrictions then in place.

[107] www.civilceremonies.co.uk/about-us.

[108] These included the Association of Independent Celebrants, the Fellowship of Professional Celebrants, the Fellowship of Independent Celebrants, the UK Society of Celebrants, and the Institute of Professional Celebrants.

[109] Stephanie Pywell, 'The day of their dreams: celebrant-led wedding celebration ceremonies' [2020] *Child and Family Law Quarterly* 177 and 'Beyond beliefs: a proposal to give couples in England and Wales a real choice of marriage officiants' [2020] *Child and Family Law Quarterly* 215.

the necessary arrangements for a wedding within the time (and budget) available.[110] By series six, in 2012, a few grooms were planning ceremonies that could not be conducted within the constraints of the current law – one outdoors at Brighton Pavilion's ice rink, another underwater[111] – requiring the legal wedding to be organised separately. By series nine, three years later, the majority of ceremonies were non-legally binding ones.[112] From March 2015, the change in the period of notice required[113] made organising any actual wedding other than an Anglican one impossible. The decision of the programme-makers not to extend the time available to the grooms was an indication of how its focus had already shifted to organising a celebratory ceremony rather than getting married.

Some local authorities also began to offer purely celebratory ceremonies as part of tailored packages for couples.[114] That such ceremonies were not subject to the same constraints as legal weddings was reflected in the fact that a number of local authorities offered to conduct them anywhere couples might choose – whether outdoors,[115] 'under the stars',[116] or aboard a canal boat or hot air balloon[117] – although almost all included caveats about risk assessments and insurance.[118] Several

---

[110] In the first episode, broadcast on BBC3 on 8 November 2007, the groom booked Ragley Hall – an approved venue – for the wedding and reception, and the only quirky element was his Moulin Rouge theme.

[111] Series six, episodes 14 and 9 respectively.

[112] Locations included a nightclub (episode one), Snowdon (episode two), a roller hockey arena (episode three), the SS *Great Britain* (episode four), a grassed square in the East End with an *EastEnders* actor presiding (episode five), Wookey Hole (episode six), a derelict hospital (episode ten), a shopping centre (episode eleven), and a car rally (episode twelve).

[113] Under the Immigration Act 2014, 28 days' notice, rather than 15, has to be given before every non-Anglican wedding.

[114] Such ceremonies are sometimes described as 'duo' or 'combination' ceremonies (see Norfolk 'Any Place Duo', *Marry in Norfolk*, p. 11; Wiltshire, 'Combination Ceremonies'), reflecting the fact that the package includes a legal ceremony. Others emphasise the absence of the usual legal controls over place and content by referring to them as 'freedom' or 'celebration' ceremonies (see e.g. Redcar and Cleveland's 'Freedom Ceremonies Guide'; *Your Ceremony, Your Choice, Your Cheshire*, p. 32).

[115] See, e.g., *Celebrate in Hampshire*, p. 6 ('outdoors, on the beach'); Cumbria, *Say 'I Do'*; *Your Cheshire: Wedding Venues Guide*, p. 4; *Ceremonies in East Sussex*, p. 38; *Oxfordshire: The Place to Celebrate*, p. 21; *Weddings and Ceremonies in West Sussex*, p. 12; *Civil ceremonies in Worcestershire*, p. 12 ('by a lake, in the woods').

[116] Northamptonshire, 'Your day, your way'.

[117] Wiltshire, 'Combination Ceremonies'.

[118] *Ceremonies in East Sussex*, p. 38; Cumbria, *'Say 'I Do'*; *Civil ceremonies in Worcestershire*, p. 12.

specifically mentioned the possibility of a celebratory ceremony taking place in the couple's own home (or back garden), or in that of a friend or member of their family.[119] Wherever they were celebrated, the hallmark of these ceremonies was the opportunity for personalisation.[120] Some local authorities even offered to include spiritual or religious rituals, which they would have been prohibited from including if the wedding were in a register office or on approved premises.[121]

Those local authorities offering such packages were quick to point out their unique ability to combine the celebratory and the legal, contrasting this with the non-legally binding ceremonies conducted by independent celebrants.[122] And all made it very clear that the celebratory ceremony was not legally binding by itself. Yet not all insisted on the legal ceremony taking place first,[123] and a few were willing to offer a celebratory ceremony independently of any other ceremony.[124]

Where couples marked their commitment to each other by a personalised, Humanist, or Pagan ceremony, this was seen as a matter of individual choice even if they did not go through a legal wedding as well. There was, however, a growing concern over religious-only marriage ceremonies, as the next section will discuss.

---

[119] Weddings at home (whether inside or in the garden) are mentioned by *Weddings and Ceremonies in West Sussex*, p. 12 ('at home in your garden'); *Your Ceremony in Hertfordshire*, p. 42 ('a marquee in your garden at home'); Wiltshire, 'Combination Ceremonies' ('family garden'); *Celebrate in Hampshire*, p. 6. The frequent references to marquees suggest that officials are envisaging quite sizeable gardens: see, e.g., Northamptonshire, 'Your day, your way'; *Oxfordshire: The Place to Celebrate*, p. 33.

[120] See e.g. Cumbria, *Say 'I Do'* ('Our bespoke packages enable you to have the ceremony you want, where you want'); Northamptonshire, 'Your day, your way', ('the celebration is where you want it and how you want it'); *Civil Ceremonies in Worcestershire*, p. 3 ('We offer more options to personalise your day than anywhere else').

[121] See, e.g., *Ceremonies in East Sussex*, p. 11, which invites couples to consider including hymns, handfastings, and prayers; Wiltshire, 'Combination Ceremonies', which depicts 'hand tying' and a 'unity candle'; *Civil ceremonies in Worcestershire*, p. 12, which offers a celebration 'in any style you please, even including a religious element if you wished.'

[122] See, e.g., *Weddings and Ceremonies in West Sussex*, p. 14; *Oxfordshire: The Place to Celebrate*, p. 33.

[123] North Yorkshire, Northamptonshire, Norfolk, and Suffolk all offer the possibility of the celebratory ceremony taking place before the legal ceremony.

[124] Suffolk, West Sussex, and Worcestershire offer a 'Commitment Ceremony' that is independent of any legal formalities: 'Renewal of vows and commitment ceremonies; *Weddings and Ceremonies in West Sussex*, p. 13 ('Not sure that a legal marriage ceremony is for you, but you still want to mark and celebrate your commitment to one another?'); *Civil ceremonies in Worcestershire*, p. 6.

The Concern over Religious-Only Marriage Ceremonies

*The answer to the question of whether a person is recognised by the state as
being validly married should be capable of being easily ascertained*[125]

In 2000, the Court of Appeal was called upon to decide on the validity of
a marriage ceremony conducted in a Sikh temple some forty-four years
earlier. Kirpal Kaur Bath had been denied a widow's pension on the basis
that the ceremony she had gone through with Zora Singh Bath in 1956
had not created a valid marriage. Her appeal had been dismissed by
a Social Security Appeals Tribunal on the basis that the temple had not
been registered for marriages. A Social Security Commissioner had then
allowed her appeal; relying on the fact that the couple had lived together
as husband and wife for thirty-seven years until Mr Bath's death, he held
'that "marriage" is validated by the common law presumption from long
cohabitation'. When the Department of Social Security then challenged
that decision, the sympathies of the court were clear; as Evans LJ commented, '[r]arely can it have been necessary for counsel . . . to seek to
justify such an unattractive case'.[126]

   He, along with his fellow judges, dismissed the appeal. Unfortunately it
was not clear whether this was because the Baths were presumed to have
complied with the requirements for a valid ceremony or because their
lengthy relationship justified the court in disregarding the fact that they
had not. This lack of clarity was partly to do with the way in which the
case was argued and partly because of the way that the judges agreed with
each other while saying different things. The single submission before the
court was that any presumption in favour of the validity of the marriage
had been rebutted by the finding of the Tribunal that the temple was not
registered for marriages. The problem with this argument, as Evans LJ
pointed out, was that there was nothing in the Marriage Act invalidating
a marriage on the basis that the place of worship in which it had been
celebrated was not registered.[127] He also went on to hold that in any case
the presumption in favour of the validity of the marriage had not been
rebutted, explicitly presuming that the celebrant had been an authorised
person and indicating that he would also have been willing to presume
that the temple had been registered.[128] By contrast, Robert Walker LJ

---

[125] *AG v. Akhter* [2020] EWCA Civ 122, para. 10.
[126] *CAO v. Bath* [2000] 1 FLR 8, at p. 11.
[127] *Bath*, p. 16.
[128] *Bath*, p. 18. The first, of course, was not possible without the second: if the temple was not
       registered it could not have appointed an authorised person and any authorised person

(with whom Schiemann LJ agreed[129]) spoke of presuming in favour of the validity of 'an irregular ceremony . . . followed by long cohabitation', which seemed to imply that he thought the presumption could validate a ceremony that was known to be invalid; however, the fact that he then concluded by agreeing with Evans LJ that there was insufficient evidence to rebut the presumption could be taken as implying that he thought that non-compliance had *not* been proved.[130]

The difference mattered enormously. It was the difference between presuming compliance with the law where the contrary had not been shown, and holding as valid a ceremony that was known not to have complied with the law just because the parties had lived together for a long time.[131] In the wake of *Bath* the only cases in which the presumption in favour of marriage was successfully invoked were those in which the ceremony had taken place overseas.[132] Faced with ceremonies that were known not to have complied with any of the requirements for a valid marriage, judges tended to sidestep *Bath* on the basis that the couples in question had not lived together long enough for the presumption to arise.[133]

That meant that they then had to decide how such a ceremony should be classified. It was at this time that the controversial term 'non-marriage' emerged.[134] By itself, the lack of recognition accorded to a religious-only marriage was nothing new.[135] Nor was the idea that there might be

---

attending from a different registered building in the same district would have been committing a criminal offence. It should be noted that the temple in question was the gurdwara at 79 Sinclair Road in Shepherd's Bush that had been established in 1911. It had not in fact been registered by the time of the Bath marriage in 1956: see Chapters 6, 7, and 8.

[129] On the basis that, as a 'relative stranger in the area of matrimonial law', he preferred the latter's 'narrower grounds'.

[130] *Bath*, pp. 23-24.

[131] On this, see further Rebecca Probert, 'The Presumptions in Favour of Marriage' (2018) 77(2) *Cambridge Law Journal* 375.

[132] See, e.g., *A-M* v. *A-M* [2001] 2 FLR 6; *Pazpena de Vire* v. *Pazpena de Vire* [2001] 1 FLR 460; *Asaad* v. *Kurter* [2013] EWHC 3852 (Fam); *Hayatleh* v. *Modfy* [2017] EWCA Civ 70.

[133] See, e.g., *AAA* v. *ASH* [2009] EWHC 636, para. [70]; *Dukali* v. *Lamrani* [2012] EWHC 1748 (Fam), para. 33; *MA* v. *JA* [2012] EWHC 2219 (Fam); c.f. *Hayatleh* v. *Modfy* [2017] EWCA Civ 70.

[134] For discussion of the evolution of the term and the concept, see further Rebecca Probert, 'The evolving concept of non-marriage' [2013] *Child and Family Law Quarterly* 314.

[135] See Chapter 3 on the non-recognition of Catholic religious-only weddings in the 1850s, Chapters 4, 5, and 6 on Jewish *stille huppah* from the 1860s to the early twentieth century, and Chapter 8 on Sikh marriages in the 1960s.

a category of marriages that was not even void.[136] What had changed was the implications of holding a marriage to be void. By this time the courts could only grant a decree of nullity in relation to a void marriage – rather than declaring the marriage to be void – and doing so enabled them to exercise the same extensive powers to award financial relief as when granting a decree of divorce.[137] Where the void marriage had ended in death rather than separation, the courts similarly had a discretion to make provision for the surviving spouse if they had entered into it in good faith.[138]

It was therefore necessary for the courts to make explicit the difference between a marriage that was void (but to which certain legal consequences might still attach) and one that was no marriage at all. Exactly where the dividing line was to be drawn between the two was a matter of some uncertainty.[139] There were some situations that everyone agreed should be classified as non-marriages,[140] but these by their very nature were not the ones that came before the courts. With a few exceptions,[141] judges did not engage closely with the terms of the Marriage Act but applied vaguer tests such as whether the ceremony 'purported' to be a marriage, or had the 'hallmarks' of one.[142]

A greater degree of clarity was brought by the decision in *AG* v. *Akhter* in 2020.[143] The case concerned the status of an Islamic ceremony of

---

[136] See, e.g., Joseph Jackson, *The Formation and Annulment of Marriage* (London: Butterworths, 2nd edn, 1969), p. 86, noting that 'where a marriage requires a declaration before a registrar or priest, a private and secret declaration of consent does not create any kind of marriage, not even a void one'.

[137] The stakes were raised still further by the expansion of the range of orders than could be made in the early 1970s.

[138] Inheritance (Provision for Family and Dependants) Act 1975, s. 25(4).

[139] For analysis of the case-law, see Rebecca Probert, 'When are we married? Void, non-existent and presumed marriages' (2002) 22 *Legal Studies* 398 and 'The evolving concept of non-marriage'.

[140] The standard examples are a wedding in a play or children playing: see, e.g., *Akhter* v. *Khan* [2018] EWFC 54, para. 81.

[141] See, e.g., the judgment of Moylan J in *MA* v. *JA* [2012] EWHC 2219 (Fam).

[142] See, e.g., *Gereis* v. *Yagoub* [1997] 1 FLR 854 (ceremony 'gave all the appearance of and had the hallmarks of a marriage'); *A-M* v. *A-M* (the wedding 'in no sense purported to be effected according to the Marriage Acts, which provide for the only way of marrying in England'; *Hudson* v. *Leigh (Status of Non-Marriage)* [2009] EWHC 1306 (Fam), para. 79 (incorporating both tests into a new four-part test that also asked about the beliefs and intentions of the parties and the officiant and 'the reasonable perceptions, understandings and beliefs of those in attendance'). *R* v. *Bham* was regularly cited, despite the fact that the validity of the marriage had not been the issue before the court in that case: see Chapter 8.

[143] [2020] EWCA Civ 122.

marriage that had taken place in a restaurant in 1998; the understanding had been that it would be followed by a legal one, but the husband had subsequently proved reluctant to honour this. At first instance Williams J had held the marriage to be void, on the basis that a more flexible interpretation of the law was required as a matter of human rights law.[144] The Court of Appeal, however, allowed the appeal. Paying close attention to the words of the statute, it highlighted how the statutory list of circumstances in which a non-Anglican marriage would be void was prefaced by the words '[i]f any persons knowingly and wilfully inter-marry under the provisions of this Part of this Act'.[145] This, it confirmed, meant that there was a threshold that had to be crossed before a marriage could be either valid or void; in other words, that there had to have been *some* engagement with the Marriage Act.[146] The ceremony in that case was accordingly held to be a 'non-qualifying' one.[147]

Amongst the ceremonies that were found to be non-qualifying, or to have resulted in a non-marriage, it was striking that none of them were celebrated in a place of worship,[148] or indeed in any place where weddings of that type could legally have been celebrated at the time.[149] There was the occasional case where the couple had genuinely, and with good justification, believed that they could legally marry at the place in question.[150] In others one of the parties was already married, and the informal nature of the ceremony – at home, in a restaurant, or in a hotel –

---

[144] *Akhter* v. *Khan* [2018] EWFC 54. For criticism of the reasoning in the case, see Chris Barton and Rebecca Probert, '*Akhter* v. *Khan* and the status of a religious-only marriage: valid, void or "non"?' [2018] *Family Law* 1540.

[145] Marriage Act 1949, s. 49.

[146] [2020] EWCA Civ 122, paras. 44-45.

[147] For commentary, see Russell Sandberg, 'Unregistered Religious Marriages are Neither Valid Nor Void' [2020] 79(2) *Cambridge Law Journal* 237, noting that the Court of Appeal had 'rightly rejected' the 'well-meaning but flawed judicial creativity' of Williams J.

[148] Contrast *Gereis* v. *Yagoub* (ceremony in a Coptic Orthodox church held to be void; couple knew that they should have given notice, as well as being aware of the non-registration of the church and the lack of authorisation of the priest conducting the ceremony); *MA* v. *JA* (marriage in a mosque that had been registered for marriages and in the presence of an authorised person held to be valid; couple had not given notice but had not realised that they needed to do so).

[149] With the exception of *Galloway* v. *Goldstein* [2012] EWHC 60 (Fam); the finding of non-marriage in this case was based on the fact that the couple were already married to each other, and the ceremony could therefore effect no change in their legal status.

[150] See, e.g., *Dukali* v. *Lamrani* [2012] EWHC 1748 (Fam) (Islamic ceremony in the Moroccan consulate, conducted on the assumption that marriages there were governed by Moroccan law).

may have been intended to avoid the risk of prosecution for bigamy.[151] Some individuals knew that their religious ceremony did not constitute a marriage but believed that it would be followed by a legally binding marriage which in the event never materialised.[152] And some cases involved one party even denying the other's claim that a ceremony had taken place.[153]

It was also striking that most of these cases involved Muslim ceremonies and that religious-only ceremonies were not reported as occurring within other religious groups on anything like the same scale.[154] A new narrative began to emerge about the non-engagement of Muslim couples with the required formalities and about the non-recognition of Muslim marriages by English law, with claims that as many as 80 per cent of Muslim marriage ceremonies were taking place outside the legal framework.[155] This marked a distinct change; scholars writing in the 1980s and 1990s had emphasised how Muslims generally complied with the law by marrying in one of the mosques that had been registered for marriages or by having a separate legal wedding where necessary.[156]

The reasons for the change in marriage patterns were complex, and the extent to which they reflected the genuine choice of both parties was contested.[157] Some couples were simply unaware that their religious-only ceremony would not be legally recognised. For others, a religious-only ceremony was a means of avoiding the risk of the male partner being prosecuted for bigamy if he took a second 'spouse', allowing forms of Islamic divorce to be used in the event of breakdown, and ensuring that the financial consequences would be determined by courts applying

[151] *A-M* v. *A-M* (1980 ceremony at the couple's home); *Gandhi* v. *Patel* (1989 ceremony at a restaurant); *Sharbatly* v. *Shagroon* (1994 ceremony at a hotel).

[152] *Hudson* v. *Leigh* (Christian ceremony in South Africa in 2004; couple split up before their planned civil ceremony); *Akhter* v. *Khan* [2018] EWFC 54.

[153] *Al-Saedy* v. *Musawi* [2010] EWHC 3293 (Fam); *El Gamal* v. *Al Maktoum* [2011] EWHC 3763 (Fam).

[154] Although the ceremony in *Gandhi* v. *Patel* had been conducted by a Brahmin priest and that in *Hudson* v. *Leigh* by a Christian minister.

[155] For discussion of the various estimates, see Dame Louise Casey, *The Casey Review: A Review into Opportunity and Integration* (Department for Communities and Local Government, 2016), para. 8.42; Patrick Nash, 'Sharia in England: The Marriage Law Solution' (2017) 6 *Oxford Journal of Law and Religion* 523, p. 526.

[156] See, e.g., David Pearl and Werner Menski, *Muslim Family Law* (London: Sweet & Maxwell, 3rd ed 1998), p. 169, suggesting that most Muslim couples married legally before having a *nikah*.

[157] The literature is also vast: for an introduction, see Rajnaara C. Akhtar, Patrick Nash and Rebecca Probert (eds.), *Cohabitation and Religious Marriage: Status, Similarities and Solutions* (Bristol: Bristol University Press, 2020).

Islamic law rather than the law of England and Wales.[158] And for others a simple *nikah* ceremony was a way of achieving the freedom to have a sexual relationship that their religion would otherwise regard as sinful.[159]

At least some individuals, then, were actively choosing a religious-only ceremony. That said, the celebrant-based system mooted in the early 2000s would certainly have made it easier for members of religious groups to marry according to their own rites. The then government proposed removing the restrictions on where religious weddings could take place and what they had to include,[160] as well as changing how they were to be registered.[161] One flaw in the proposals was that they gave no indication of how the validity of marriages would be tested if the parties had not given notice or the celebrant turned out not to be authorised.[162] Other proposed reforms, while not addressing the status of religious-only marriage ceremonies directly, would have conferred a remedy on those who were financially disadvantaged by the subsequent relationship.[163]

In the absence of such reforms, the focus of some policy-makers switched to deterrence. Baroness Cox was particularly active in arguing that it should be an offence to solemnise a religious-only marriage ceremony, variously proposing amendments to general legislation,[164]

---

[158] The point here is that since the English courts have no jurisdiction to grant a divorce or order financial provision in relation to a non-qualifying ceremony, they equally have no power to restrain a sharia court from doing so. For discussion, see Islam Uddin, 'Nikah-only Marriages: Causes, Motivations, and Their Impact on Dispute Resolution and Islamic Divorce Proceedings in England and Wales' (2018) 7(3) *Oxford Journal of Law and Religion* 401.

[159] Rajnaara C. Akhtar, 'Modern Traditions in Muslim Marriage Practices, Exploring English Narratives' (2018) 7(3) *Oxford Journal of Law and Religion* 427.

[160] Rather than prescribed words being said, the only requirement would have been for the parties to make a declaration (in whatever form and language they wished) that they accepted one another as husband and wife.

[161] The proposals envisaged weddings being conducted by a celebrant nominated by a religious body; this was defined as 'an organised group of people meeting regularly for common religious worship' (para 3.4.29), which in turn was defined as 'the worship of a supreme god or deity' (3.4.10). The marriage would then be recorded on the schedule issued by the registration authorities rather than in a register book.

[162] Rebecca Probert, 'Lord Hardwicke's Marriage Act 250 years on: vital change?' [2004] *Family Law* 583.

[163] Law Commission, *Cohabitation: The Financial Consequences of Relationship Breakdown: A Consultation Paper* (CP No. 179, 2006); Law Commission, *Cohabitation: The Financial Consequences of Relationship Breakdown* (Law Com No. 179, 2007).

[164] See her proposed amendment to the Anti-Social Behaviour, Crime and Policing Bill 2013 seeking to make it an offence to solemnise a marriage according to the rites of any religion or belief if it was not also solemnised as a legal marriage *and* either party wrongly

bringing forward specific bills to this end,[165] and pressing the government to act.[166] Her Marriage Act 1949 (Amendment) Bill 2017, for example, proposed imposing the obligation to register on 'the priest or a similar person principally responsible for the solemnisation of the marriage according to those rites and usages'. For this to work, however, there would also have needed to be changes to the system of registration to permit the person celebrating the wedding to register it without any prior engagement with the law, rather than authorising the individual responsible for registration in advance.[167]

The *Independent Review into the Application of Sharia Law in England and Wales* similarly recommended that the Marriage Act 1949 should be amended to make it an offence for 'the celebrant of specified marriages, including Islamic marriage' to fail to ensure that the marriage was 'civilly registered'.[168] From the *Review*'s sparse discussion it was not clear whether this meant that a celebrant would be required to check that the parties were already legally married before conducting a ceremony, or whether it misunderstood the scope of the existing offences or the role of registration in the making of a valid marriage.[169] The government's subsequent *Integrated Communities Strategy Green Paper* assumed the former, a requirement which it indicated that it supported 'in

believed that they were legally married on account of the religious ceremony (*Hansard*, HL Deb., vol. 749, col. 676, 12 November 2013) and a further proposed amendment to the Policing and Crime Bill 2016 requiring the 'celebrant' of a religious marriage to ensure that it was also legally registered or face a potential penalty of three years in prison (*Hansard*, HL Deb., vol. 776, col. 1475).

[165] Marriage Act 1949 (Amendment) Bill 2017; Marriage Act 1949 (Amendment) Bill 2020.

[166] *Hansard*, HL Deb., vol. 796, col. 298, 28 February 2019.

[167] On this, see further Rebecca Probert, 'Criminalising non-compliance with marriage formalities?' [2018] *Fam Law* 702.

[168] *Independent Review into the Application of Sharia Law in England and Wales* (Home Office, February 2018), p. 17. While the Parliamentary Assembly of the Council of Europe called for them to be implemented ('Resolution 2253: Sharia, the Cairo Declaration and the European Convention on Human Rights' (22 January 2019), para. 14), the Advocate-General for Scotland, Lord Keen of Elie, rightly pointed out that 'some of what has been said by the Council of Europe ... does not reflect the true position of marriage law in England and Wales' and described the reference to 'civilly registering' a marriage as 'inept'.

[169] Any person who is able to register a marriage is already under an obligation to do so and commits a criminal offence if they do not: Marriage Act 1949, s. 76(1) expressly states that '[a]ny person who refuses or without reasonable cause omits to register any marriage *which he is required by this Act to register* ... shall be liable on summary conviction to a fine' (emphasis added).

principle',[170] but its follow-up plan focused on awareness-raising rather than making specific proposals for any new offence.[171]

For some, the solution lay in the recognition of a religious marriage ceremony as a legal marriage.[172] That effectively brings us full circle, to the debates prior to the passage of the 1836 Act. It is worth recollecting that the law does not recognise *any* religious marriage ceremonies in and of themselves, in that the recognition of Anglican, Jewish, and Quaker weddings, as well as those in registered places of worship, takes place within a framework of formalities and, in particular, certain preliminaries intended to detect (and thereby deter) sham or forced marriages or those that would be void because the parties are not eligible to marry. In the absence of those formalities, the question arises as to whether the status of a ceremony would be tested by reference to whether it accorded with what that particular religion regarded as essential; if that were the case, then the case law on the recognition (or rather the non-recognition) of Jewish ceremonies before the 1836 Act provides a warning that the result will not always be a valid marriage.[173] If it is not to be determined by adherence to particular religious rites, then it would presumably rest on a simple exchange of consent by the parties, and non-recognition might still be the result if one chose to deny that such an exchange had taken place.[174] As Lord Keen of Elie noted in one recent debate '[i]t is not possible simply to say that we will acknowledge all religious ceremonies of marriage, of any kind, as legally enforceable'.[175]

That particular debate took place at a time when virtually no legal weddings were taking place at all on account of the restrictions imposed by the government to try to curb the spread of COVID-19. As the next section will show, the impact of those restrictions differed depending on how couples had been planning to marry.

---

[170] *Integrated Communities Strategy Green Paper* (March 2018), p. 58. It did at least draw attention to the fact that it was possible for couples 'from faith communities' to 'enter a legally recognised marriage through a religious ceremony if the requirements of the law are met', something which the *Review* had failed to do.

[171] Ministry of Housing, Communities & Local Government, *Integrated Communities Strategy Green Paper: Summary of consultation response and Government response* and *Integrated Communities Action Plan* (MHCLG, February 2019).

[172] See, e.g., Prakash Shah, 'Judging Muslims' in Griffith-Jones, *Islam and English Law*, p. 150 ('we should seriously consider whether a nikah itself should suffice').

[173] See further Chapters 5 and 6.

[174] See Rebecca Probert, *Marriage Law and Practice in the Long Eighteenth Century: A Reassessment* (Cambridge: Cambridge University Press, 2009), ch. 2.

[175] *Hansard*, HL Deb., vol. 804, col. 557, 30 June 2020.

Love in the Time of COVID-19

It was like everything else was stripped back and it felt really pure and special[176]

In March 2020, rumours of an impending lockdown spurred a few couples into bringing the date of their wedding forward to marry before the full restrictions took effect. The media reported a number of weddings that had taken place on 22 and 23 March.[177] Just a few hours after these weddings had taken place, on the evening of 23 March 2020, the Prime Minister announced a raft of measures aimed at stopping the spread of COVID-19. He declared that the government would 'stop all social events, including weddings, baptisms and other ceremonies'.[178]

While the new regulations did not specifically ban weddings from taking place, the restrictions that they imposed meant that in practice it was not possible for a wedding (or civil partnership) to take place. Places of worship were required to close except when conducting funerals or broadcasting an act of worship.[179] The vast majority of approved premises were also required to close as a result of the pandemic.[180] Most fundamentally of all, the restrictions on movement and on gatherings of more than two people posed an obvious obstacle to a wedding or civil partnership ceremony taking place,[181] even if the number attending had been reduced to the legal minimum.

It is perhaps unsurprising that making provision for people to formalise their relationships was not a priority at this time of crisis. At the time the measures were introduced it was unclear how long the restrictions

---

[176] The Reverend Turnbull, commenting on the wedding he conducted at 4pm on Monday 23 March: 'Joe and Alana said "I do" with two hours' notice before lockdown!', *Stoke Sentinel*, 4 April 2020.

[177] *Ibid.*, see also 'Couple married on Anglesey with no guests', BBC News, 24 March 2020, www.bbc.co.uk/news/uk-wales-52018518 (civil wedding in a hotel on Sunday 22 March, with two members of staff at the hotel acting as witnesses); 'Couple who married just HOURS before the nation's lockdown reveal they had just five days to prepare for their fast-track wedding – and only had four guests present' *Daily Mail Online*, 30 March 2020, www.dailymail.co.uk/femail/article-8169063/Couple-married-just-HOURS-nations-lockdown.html, (civil wedding at 1pm on Monday 23 March).

[178] www.gov.uk/government/speeches/pm-address-to-the-nation-on-coronavirus-23-march-2020.

[179] The Health Protection (Coronavirus, Restrictions) (England) Regulations 2020, SI 2020/350, reg. 5(5) and (6).

[180] The Health Protection (Coronavirus, Business Closure) (England) Regulations 2020, SI 2020/327; The Health Protection (Coronavirus, Restrictions) (England) Regulations 2020, SI 2020/350, reg. 5(3).

[181] The Health Protection (Coronavirus, Restrictions) (England) Regulations 2020, SI 2020/350, regs 6(1) and 7.

would need to be in place.[182] And given the near-ubiquity of pre-marital cohabitation, it may simply have been assumed that the postponement of a wedding or civil partnership ceremony would not have had any effect on couples' relationships or day-to-day life. But for some couples, the inability to have a wedding meant that they were unable or unwilling to begin living together or start a family.[183]

Over the months of lockdown, in the absence of any possibility of marrying legally, some couples devised various inventive ways of signalling their commitment to each other in a purely celebratory ceremony. On 31 March, Slough Baptist Church conducted a virtual wedding: a couple exchanged vows in their home, with the pastor appearing on a YouTube live stream in the background.[184] A few days later, another couple videoed themselves exchanging rings on what would have been their wedding day.[185] And the friends of one couple who had had to cancel their wedding arranged a surprise (virtual) wedding party for them, described by one attendee as the '[f]irst Zoom wedding ever'.[186]

The restrictions imposed by the pandemic also highlighted some of the more systemic problems with the law of marriage. It underlined how the facilities for death-bed and emergency weddings varied between Anglican and non-Anglican weddings and the advantage (for Anglicans) of having a single body responsible for authorising emergency weddings.[187] The Church of England's Faculty Office was impressively swift to act in response to the crisis, provided clear and helpful information on its website, and put special measures in place to facilitate the issue of special licences. Those wishing to marry in a non-Anglican ceremony faced more of a challenge in tracking down the necessary information. Application for a Registrar-General's licence had to be made to the superintendent registrar for the district in which the person seeking the

---

[182] Provision was made for the restrictions to be reviewed every 21 days, but to end only when the Secretary of State published a direction to that effect: The Health Protection (Coronavirus, Restrictions) (England) Regulations 2020, SI 2020/350, reg. 3.

[183] See Rebecca Probert and Stephanie Pywell, 'Love in the time of COVID-19: a case-study of the complex law governing weddings' (2021) *Legal Studies* (forthcoming).

[184] www.youtube.com/watch?v=baCaqwNlDYo.

[185] Harriet Johnson, 'Couple with 25-year age gap celebrate lockdown wedding as they exchange vows in their living room surrounded by Harry Potter trinkets and listening to Elvis music', 8 April 2020, www.dailymail.co.uk/femail/article-8199497/Couple-forced-lockdown-wedding-tie-knot-living-room.html.

[186] 'Doctors surprised with virtual wedding party', www.bbc.co.uk/news/av/uk-52192390/coronavirus-virtual-wedding-surprise-celebration-for-doctors. See also Channel 4, *Hitched at Home: Our Lockdown Wedding*, first broadcast 1 June 2020.

[187] Probert and Pywell, 'Love in the time of COVID-19'.

licence was resident. A survey of 169 websites conducted on 2 April, shortly after lockdown had begun, found that the vast majority of local authorities were simply stating that they were not conducting wedding ceremonies because of COVID-19,[188] and one explicitly stated that it would not be issuing Registrar-General's licences at all.[189]

While lockdown restrictions were still in place, a petition on Parliament's website asked for weddings to be able to go ahead with only five persons present – the couple, two witnesses, and the registrar.[190] For religious weddings, this would have meant simply amending the restrictions in the emergency regulations on the number of persons who could meet. For civil weddings, by contrast, this would have required amendments to primary legislation about how weddings are conducted, since such weddings require the presence of both a superintendent registrar *and* a registrar in addition to the parties and their witnesses.[191]

The announcement that weddings would be able to go ahead from 4 July highlighted a further anomalous distinction between Anglican and other ceremonies, this time to the detriment of the former. Couples who had been planning to marry in the Anglican church between late March and mid-June might already have had their banns called, or obtained a common licence. Since each of these is only valid for three months from when they are completed or issued,[192] the lapse of time between the start of lockdown and the opening up of places of worship for weddings meant that the authority to marry would be void, and the couple would need to go through the process again. By contrast, those who had already given notice of their intention to marry in a non-Anglican ceremony would in all likelihood have been able to marry as soon as the wedding could be rearranged after restrictions were lifted, since a superintendent registrar's certificate is valid for a full year.[193]

The fact that, even after 4 July, weddings could only go ahead with a limited number of guests – and, at some points, without any subsequent reception – also brought into sharp focus the question of whether couples attached value to getting married independently of any accompanying

---

[188] Rebecca Probert, 'Love in a COVID-19 climate', *Law and Religion UK*, https://lawandre ligionuk.com/2020/05/05/love-in-a-covid-19-climate/.

[189] https://en.powys.gov.uk/article/8818/Coronavirus-COVID-19-Registrars.

[190] https://petition.parliament.uk/petitions/315627.

[191] Marriage (Registrar General's Licence) Act 1970, s. 10(2).

[192] Marriage Act 1949, ss. 12(2) and 16(3).

[193] Marriage Act 1949, s. 33.

celebration. Some married the very minute that it was legally possible, with the first couple tying the knot under the Peace Garden Pergola at Runcorn Town Hall register office at one minute past midnight.[194] But for others getting married was not enough. Many could not envisage marrying without their friends – and more particularly their families – being present. Others had spent two or three years planning the event and were not willing to sacrifice their efforts.[195] As a result, even when it was possible to marry, some couples continued to postpone their weddings in the hope of being able to have the day of their dreams at a later date.[196]

Conclusion

Virtually all of the problems discussed in this chapter could have been avoided had the New Labour government persevered with its proposed introduction of a celebrant-based system. By removing the need for a wedding to take place in a specified location, it would have given couples who did not want to marry in a religious ceremony a genuine alternative to either commercial (and expensive) approved premises or a register office. It would also have given those who did want a religious ceremony more choice. While such couples may still have wanted to get married where they worshipped, they would not have been precluded from doing so by a lack of registration. The reforms would therefore have enabled those religious groups without a formal place of worship to conduct weddings where they met, allowed those marrying on approved premises to include religious rites, and facilitated weddings at home. While nothing in the White Paper suggested that any thought had been given to the complex law on nullity and non-marriage, such matters would have to have been addressed had reform been enacted. Incorporating Humanist and independent celebrants into such a framework would also have been far simpler than under the existing buildings-based scheme. And although some restrictions would inevitably have to have been placed on the size of any celebration during the COVID-19

---

[194] 'Coronavirus: Widnes couple say "I do" after clock strikes midnight', BBC News, 4 July 2020, www.bbc.co.uk/news/uk-england-merseyside-53281391.

[195] 'Here's what a post-lockdown wedding looks like. Has Coronavirus made us rethink the OTT celebration?', *Glamour Magazine* (online edition) 17 May 2020.

[196] Probert and Pywell, 'Love in the time of COVID-19'.

pandemic, a celebrant-based scheme would have enabled weddings to take place more safely outside, as was the case in Northern Ireland.

Of course, similar proposals for reform have been made both before and since. And it is to the legacies of the past and the lessons for the future that we shall now turn to consider in the final chapter.

10

The Legacy of the Past and Lessons for the Future

a law so intricate and, indeed, bizarre, that only the (often chance) factors of the
legislative process can explain it[1]

So much of the current law regulating weddings has come about by chance. Legislators have responded to specific problems and situations by making what might seem to be minor amendments to the legislation but which at best create new anomalies and at worst change the options available to couples entirely. Examining how and why particular provisions were included reveals how many were stopgap measures that were never intended to be permanent, or were introduced as afterthoughts, without full consideration of their implications, or were intended to serve an entirely different purpose from that which is now attributed to them. And the resulting confusion has made the law difficult to understand. In this concluding chapter I reflect on the legacy of the past, drawing together the strands from the preceding chapters to show how decisions made in the nineteenth century continue to have an impact on how couples marry in the twenty-first, and drawing out the implications for future reform.[2]

Two hundred years ago, the Unitarians campaigned to be relieved from the necessity of marrying according to Anglican rites. Had that campaign been framed differently, then the legislative process might have taken a very different turn. By focusing on what they did *not* want, they missed the opportunity to provide reassurance about their own ministers and places of worship. By putting forward a range of alternatives – suggesting, for example, that they could continue to marry in the Anglican church but

---

[1] John Eekelaar and David Feldman, 'Stephen Cretney' (2020) 19 *Biographical Memoirs of Fellows of the British Academy* 309, p. 332, paying tribute to Stephen's mastery of the intricacies of marriage law.

[2] See the proposals for reform set out by the Law Commission, *Getting Married: A Consultation Paper on Weddings Law*, CP No. 247 (3 September 2020).

be allowed to omit references to the Trinity, or that they could be married by Justices of the Peace – they sent the message that any alternative to compulsory conformity would do. In that sense the Marriage Act 1836 gave them, and other Dissenters, exactly what they had been asking for. Under its provisions, no one would be compelled to marry in a way that offended their conscience. But that was not the same as giving religious groups the right to conduct weddings.[3]

Herein lie both the success of the 1836 Act and its fundamental weakness. On one level, the fact that the scheme it established has lasted so long justifies it being seen as a success. The reason *why* it has lasted so long is its flexibility. Had any of the earlier denomination-specific bills become law – that is to say, those focused exclusively on the Unitarians or alternatively on Catholic weddings – then there would have needed to be a whole succession of later amendments as other groups campaigned to be included. By opening up the possibility of marrying in *any* certified place of worship – even if that was subject to it being registered for weddings – the 1836 Act ensured its own longevity. This flexibility provided a means of recognising the sheer diversity of dissent in nine-teenth-century England and Wales. And after changes to the require-ments for certification were made in 1855, removing the restriction that only Christian places of worship could be certified as such, the scheme was capable of accommodating the far greater religious diversity of the twentieth and twenty-first centuries.

Reforms elsewhere, by contrast, often conferred the right to conduct marriages on named religious groups.[4] A comparison with the position in Scotland – generally held up as having a far more flexible approach to getting married – is instructive. Under Scottish law, a regular marriage was defined as one conducted by ministers of certain denominations.[5] This limitation did not matter so much when it was possible to marry by exchanging consent in private, but this form of irregular marriage was abolished in 1940.[6] From that date, the only recognised weddings were those conducted by registrars and ministers of specified Christian

---

[3] See Chapter 2.

[4] On the position in Ireland, see Maebh Harding, *From Catholic Outlook to Modern State Regulation: Developing Legal Understandings of Marriage in Ireland* (Intersentia, forth-coming). For a comparative overview, see Rebecca Probert, 'State and Law' in Paul Puschmann (ed.), *A Cultural History of Marriage in the Age of Empire* (London: Bloomsbury Academic, 2020).

[5] See Rebecca Probert, Maebh Harding, and Brian Dempsey, 'A Uniform Law of Marriage? The 1868 Royal Commission Reconsidered' [2018] *Child and Family Law Quarterly* 217.

[6] Marriage (Scotland) Act 1939.

denominations. In 1966, a conference held by the Campaign against Racial Discrimination heard how Sikhs in Glasgow were travelling to Birmingham to be married in the nearest temple to be registered for weddings, in an ironic inversion of nineteenth-century couples eloping to Gretna Green to escape the constraints of English law.[7] Only in 1977 was it possible for those of other faiths to be recognised as celebrants and conduct weddings.[8] In other words, not naming specific religious groups meant that English law was able to accommodate non-Christian religions much earlier than Scottish law, with the first mosque being registered for weddings over half a century before it was possible to have a Muslim wedding in Scotland.

That, however, brings us on to one of the key weaknesses of the 1836 Act – its explicit mention of Jewish regulating bodies and of the Society of Friends. The non-recognition of Reform Judaism by the Board of Deputies prevented the West London synagogue from conducting marriages for over a decade, while Liberal Jews had to wait more than five decades before the legislation was changed to make explicit reference to them. The experience within Judaism underlines the importance of not naming particular groups in legislation. That the Society of Friends did not experience the same problems was a reflection not only of its cohesion but also of the fact that breakaway groups simply registered their buildings for weddings.

More fundamentally, the explicit mention of these two groups paved the way for confusion about the scope of the 1836 Act. Later commentators interpreted the absence of any mention of other groups as an absence of provision for other religions.[9] And their criticisms do have some force. While the constraints that apply to Quaker and Jewish marriages should not be underestimated,[10] there are many other religious groups who would welcome the same freedom to marry where they choose, and without having to say the prescribed words.

The fact that it has been *possible* to marry in a registered place of worship since 1837 does not mean that all couples have been able to marry in accordance with their beliefs. The requirement that marriages

---

[7] Celia Haddon, 'When Birmingham is Gretna Green', *Daily Mail*, 10 October 1966.
[8] Marriage (Scotland) Act 1977.
[9] This is implicit in Bradney's comment that 'the policy objections to ... further widening the range of religions that can combine both a religious marriage ceremony and one that is recognised by the state are obscure': A Bradney, *Law and Faith in a Sceptical Age* (Abingdon: Routledge, 2009), p. 108.
[10] See Chapters 3, 4, and 7 for discussion of these constraints.

take place in a specific building registered for the purpose has posed problems ever since it was introduced. It was a limitation which affected many of the smaller Nonconformist congregations in the nineteenth century[11] and which delayed the legal celebration of marriages by other faiths in the twentieth.[12] It has resulted in a wide variety of religious groups having dual ceremonies.[13] In the nineteenth century these included Christians of all different denominations whose own places of worship had not been registered for marriages, Reformist Jews who were not recognised by the Jewish authorities, and Muslims whose ceremonies were held at the Liverpool mosque in the 1890s.[14] Its impact is felt today, not just by those religious groups who do not worship in a particular building, or who do not wish to marry there, but also by couples who wish to marry in a Humanist or Pagan ceremony or in one that combines traditions from different religions.[15]

In terms of reshaping the law for the future, it is worth reflecting on what purpose requiring weddings to take place in specific buildings actually serves. Jewish weddings have long been celebrated in private homes as well as inside (and outside) synagogues. Similarly, the Archbishop of Canterbury's special licence can, in principle, be used to permit a wedding to take place anywhere. The hypocrisy of legislators who argued against the loosening of restrictions was the subject of a powerful speech by George Canning, then Prime Minister, in 1827, when one of the unsuccessful predecessors to the Marriage Act 1836 was being debated in Parliament. Pointing out that he, and probably most of those listening to him, had been married in their own homes by virtue of a special licence, he expressed his astonishment that opponents of the bill were essentially arguing that 'the rich, who were able to purchase the right to marry, were at liberty to do so, while those who, not being rich, contracted marriage in any other place than a church, were unworthy of the protection of the legislature'.[16]

In a similar vein, the fact that Catholic places of worship were exempted from the limitation that only 'separate' buildings could be registered for weddings meant that weddings could take place in the

---

[11] See Chapter 3 for examples.
[12] See Chapters 7 and 8 on the registration of Muslim, Hindu, and Sikh places of worship.
[13] See Chapter 3.
[14] See Chapters 3 and 5.
[15] See Chapter 9.
[16] Parl. Deb., ser. 2, vol. 17, col. 1345, 19 June 1827.

private chapels of wealthy Catholics.[17] And the subsequent removal of the requirement of 'separateness' has enabled many more modest places of worship to be registered for weddings. At present at least 440 of the approximately 22,500 registered places of worship consist of just part of a building and sometimes just a single room.[18] While weddings in such registered places of worship are technically required to be celebrated 'with open doors', the force of this is blunted somewhat if the place of worship is on the third floor of a building and not visible to passers-by. The key points here are, first, that the requirement of registering buildings has prevented some couples from being able to marry in accordance with their beliefs, and second, that the types of places that have been registered cover the entire spectrum from the most impressive purpose-built churches, mosques, and temples, to single rooms in what might appear to be private houses. When combined with the long history of ceremonies taking place in buildings that have not been registered, necessitating the passage of validating legislation,[19] and the deficiencies in the official register of places of worship,[20] the clear lesson is that any future law should not be based on the licensing of buildings.

In assessing whether any given couple have been able to marry in accordance with their beliefs, it should also be noted that those who have married in a registered place of worship have been required to repeat certain words prescribed by law. How that was experienced will have varied according to whether those words were seamlessly integrated into the marriage service, or whether they had to be repeated separately before a civil registrar (or, after 1898, an authorised person). This was a particular issue for Catholics in the nineteenth century and remains an issue for many Hindus, Muslims, and Sikhs today.[21] It reinforces the

---

[17] See Chapter 3.

[18] This was calculated by searching for the term 'floor' in the GRO's list: 'Places of Worship Registered for Marriage' (September 2020), www.gov.uk/government/publications/places-of-worship-registered-for-marriage.

[19] Nor have Anglican places of worship been immune from problems, as the long list of Acts validating weddings in unlicensed chapels of ease and other churches demonstrates.

[20] As I have detailed elsewhere, some of the buildings listed are no longer used as places of worship. Even where a formal notice cancelling the registration of the building has appeared in the *London Gazette*, this has not always been followed by the removal of the building from the official list. And some places of worship have kept the same name, but moved to a different location, raising questions about the status of any ceremonies of marriage that they conduct. For further details, see Rebecca Probert, 'A Uniform Marriage Law for England and Wales?' [2018] *Child and Family Law Quarterly* 259.

[21] See further Chapters 5 and 9.

impression that the religious rites of groups other than Anglicans, Jews, and Quakers are afforded no legal recognition.

The fact that the 1836 Act did not otherwise regulate the rites that would form the wedding was a strength that turned into a weakness. Under the original terms of the Act, couples were able to marry in a form of their choosing, subject only to the inclusion of the prescribed words. There was no stipulation that a wedding in a registered place of worship had to be conducted according to religious rites, still less that those rites should be those of the denomination that had registered the building. Instead, the Act expressly permitted a wedding to take place according to 'such Form and Ceremony' as the couple getting married 'may see fit to adopt'.[22] This formulation was wide enough to encompass the essentially secular ceremony that the Shilohite Bradleys of Birmingham had devised in 1834.[23] As long as the requisite preliminaries had been completed, the registrar was present, and the prescribed words were said, this was a marriage in the eyes of the law. The Act drew no distinction between 'civil' and 'religious', recognising that many religious groups regarded marriage as a civil contract but did not believe that this precluded it being celebrated with religious rites.

After 1856, however, the ability of every couple to marry as they chose was lost. The provision in the Marriage and Registration Act 1856 that a couple had to obtain consent from the relevant authorities before they could marry in a registered place of worship placed more weight on the rights of religious groups to control access to their buildings than to the choices of individual couples. It was, of course, still open to the minister or trustees of any registered building to allow couples holding different beliefs to marry there, as has happened in some cases. Indeed, in 1996 the then British Humanist Association described how some Humanist weddings had taken place in registered places of worship.[24] It was fitting that these should be Unitarian ones, given their own earlier campaign to be relieved from compulsory conformity. But under the original terms of the Act, Humanists would not have been dependent on the permission of individual religious groups.

A similar loss of flexibility occurred in relation to register office weddings. As we have seen, the 1836 Act contained no prohibition on the inclusion of religious content, and many who married in a register

---

[22] Marriage Act 1836, s. 20.

[23] See Chapter 2.

[24] Jane Wynne Willson, *Sharing the Future: A Practical Guide to Non-religious Wedding Ceremonies* (London: British Humanist Association, 1996), p. 4.

office in the first twenty years of its operation were able to incorporate prayers, hymns, and bible readings into the ceremony.[25] This was entirely consistent with its origins. It was intended as an option for Dissenters who regarded marriage as a civil contract. This was a theological view with a long lineage,[26] and one that was perfectly compatible with the inclusion of religious rites. The General Register Office was clearly unaware of this history when it claimed that it had been a 'fundamental principle' ever since 1837 'that civil marriage should be clearly separated from religious marriage'.[27] Nor was the 1856 prohibition on the inclusion of a religious service motivated by any policy decision to make a sharp separation between the sacred and the secular; rather, it seems to have come about almost by accident, as a by-product of the overreaction of the authorities to a handful of clergy conducting Anglican ceremonies after a legal wedding had already taken place.[28]

The consequence of the prohibition was to deprive couples who were unable to marry in the place of their choosing of the religious dimension that many wanted. Had it not been for that prohibition, then couples would have had a far wider range of options available to them. Couples would have had no cause to complain about the register office wedding being 'curt' and 'businesslike',[29] or felt the need to have a separate ceremony that reflected their beliefs, since they would have been able to personalise it as they chose. And there would have been no need for registrars to determine the dividing line between the secular and the sacred. From this perspective, enabling a wider range of content to be included in registrar-led ceremonies would not be a move away from a fundamental principle of English marriage law, but a return to it. It would, as Stephen Cretney put it, enable 'those who feel the need for some "numinous" element to mark what is on any basis a hugely important rite of passage' to incorporate material that is meaningful to them.[30]

In political terms, the achievements of the Marriage Act 1836 went beyond devising alternative routes into marriage, as it was also used to justify the implementation of the New Poor Law across the entirety of

---

[25] See Chapter 3.

[26] See Rebecca Probert, 'Secular or sacred? The ambiguity of register office weddings in England and Wales, 1836-56' (in preparation).

[27] GRO, *Content of Civil Marriage Ceremonies: A consultation document on proposed changes to regulation and guidance to registration officers* (June 2005), para. 4.

[28] See Chapter 4.

[29] See Chapter 8.

[30] Stephen Cretney, 'Relationship: Law Content and Form' in Judith Trowell and Carola Thorpe (eds.), *Re-Rooted Lives* (Bristol: Jordans, 2007), p. 164.

England and Wales. The Unions created by the Poor Law Amendment Act 1834 formed the basis of a new system of local government, replacing the former parish-based system of relief and all the variability that that had entailed. Around 10,000 parishes were amalgamated into 600 or so Unions. It was not a matter of devolving decision-making to the local level, but rather creating larger units of administration better equipped to meet the administrative needs of the nineteenth century. That such local administration has survived into the twenty-first century is somewhat surprising. The local authorities of today are the direct descendants of the Unions of the 1830s, and while they operate on a different scale, and take a number of different forms,[31] they are still making decisions as to how the law should operate at a local level. Different local authorities make different choices about what can be included in a 'civil' wedding, where such weddings can take place, and when statutory ceremonies will be made available.[32] That such local variation should still exist is baffling, both as a matter of principle and, one suspects, to anyone trying to find out what their options for getting married are in any given locality. While there will always be a need for officers to interpret the legal requirements, there should at the very least be a standard template for the provision of information about weddings, and in particular about the nature and availability of statutory ceremonies.

The fact that the Marriage Act 1836 was linked to the implementation of the New Poor Law also meant that those responsible for its administration were given a key role in overseeing the process of getting married. It was written into the legislation that the clerk of the Union had to be offered the post of superintendent registrar. Such clerks were local appointees, and it was the superintendent registrar who then appointed the registrar of marriages. But their duties and responsibilities were set by statute, and it was the Registrar-General who directed how such duties and responsibilities should be carried out. Even in 1837 it was suggested that a more sensible approach would be for such officials to be appointed directly by the Registrar-General. Over 150 years later, a review of the

---

[31] At the time of writing there are 27 counties, 33 London boroughs, 37 Metropolitan boroughs, 56 English unitary authorities, and 22 Welsh unitary authorities.

[32] Stephanie Pywell and Rebecca Probert, 'Neither sacred nor profane: the permitted content of civil marriage ceremonies' [2018] 30 *Child and Family Law Quarterly* 415; Probert, 'A Uniform Marriage Law for England and Wales?'; Stephanie Pywell, '2 + 2 = £127, if you're lucky', *Law Society Gazette*, 3 March 2020, and 'Availability of two-plus-two marriage ceremonies', *Law Society Gazette*, 31 March 2020.

operation of the registration services highlighted how the status of registration officers was 'confused', in that they were 'appointed by the local authority but ... carry out their work on the instructions of the Registrar General'.[33] It is a confusion that has yet to be resolved.

Had the campaign for reform of the laws regulating weddings not been taking place at the same time as campaigns for the introduction of civil registration, then any new law would probably have been designed around who was responsible for conducting the wedding, rather than being designed backwards from who was responsible for registering it. Authority would in all likelihood have been conferred on ministers of religion and (for those who regarded marriage as a civil matter) Justices of the Peace,[34] and there would have been no need to create the new roles of superintendent registrar and registrar.

In evaluating these roles, it is important to bear in mind that nine-teenth-century legislators rightly expected that only a few weddings would be taking place in register offices.[35] It is also worth noting that the role of the superintendent registrar was a somewhat ambiguous one. They had important administrative functions, being tasked with receiving notices of marriage and with ensuring that copies of registers were duly dispatched to the General Register Office to be centrally registered. They were not, however, given any specific role in celebrating weddings. The provision that they had to be present at any wedding in a register office may have been dictated by purely practical considerations. After all, the register office was *their* office. Given that many of the early superintendent registrars were solicitors and operated out of their professional offices rather than a purpose-built civic building, it would have been odd to provide for a wedding to take place in their office without them being present.[36] The provision requiring their presence may also have been a tactical move to head off potential objections to the requirement that a registrar be present at a wedding in a registered place of worship, since it sent the message that the presence of a registrar alone

---

[33] *Registration: a modern service* (HMSO, 1988), para. 1.34

[34] See Chapter 2 for proposals to this effect.

[35] See Chapter 3 on the low take-up.

[36] It is also worth noting how modest many of these early register offices were. To take just one example, the superintendent registrar's office for Stoke Damerel was at 20 Fore Street in Devonport, the workplace and home of Joseph Elms, who combined his role as superintendent registrar with his day job as a watchmaker and auctioneer: Rebecca Probert and Liam D'Arcy-Brown, 'Workhouse weddings? A case study of register office ceremonies in Devon, 1837–1856' (in preparation).

was not sufficient to create a valid marriage, and that his role was simply to register it.

For over a hundred years the role of the superintendent registrar seems to have been an essentially passive one. Their secondary role was underlined by the fact that they signed the marriage register *after* the registrar. Only after World War Two, when the Denning Committee recommended that couples marrying in the register office be reminded of the solemn nature of the commitment they were undertaking, did superintendent registrars, as the more senior officer of the two, begin to take on a more active role. From then on, their names appeared first on the certificate.[37] Yet when questions arose in Parliament as to why it was necessary for both a superintendent registrar and a registrar to be present at a civil ceremony, no one was able to come up with any good reason. A somewhat harried Parliamentary Under-Secretary of State admitted that he could only describe, rather than explain, the law, and the best he could come up with was that a superintendent registrar was needed 'to give legal validity to the ceremony'.[38] As one MP noted, it was 'extraordinary' that two officials had to be present – one to register the marriage and one whose function seemed simply to hear the prescribed words being said – and he expressed the hope that the requirement would be reviewed 'so that these valuable officials ... can possibly find more useful things to do with their time'.[39]

Since then, the time that registrars and superintendent registrars spend on weddings has expanded enormously, not just because the number of civil weddings has increased but because such weddings now mostly take place on approved premises. Registration officials thus have to spend time travelling to venues, where the weddings they conduct tend to be far longer and require more organisation and coordination than the utterance of the prescribed words in a register office. Some are now even marketing themselves as 'celebrants' and offering a range of additional celebratory ceremonies.[40] While this may provide a useful additional

---

[37] See Chapter 7.

[38] *Hansard*, HC Deb., vol. 800, col. 818, 24 April 1970 (Brian O'Malley). He did later ask 'who would perform the civil marriage ... if it were not the superintendent registrar' (col. 820), but there was nothing in the Marriage Act 1949 to say that this was what the superintendent registrar did.

[39] *Ibid*, col. 819 (Will Howie). Similarly, when reform of the registration services was being considered, the government was similarly unable to think of any good reason for both registration officials to be present and proposed that it should be sufficient for just one to be present: *Registration: a modern service*, para. 3.18.

[40] See Chapter 9.

revenue stream for local authorities, it is not clear why the state should be in the business of providing commitment ceremonies or vow renewals.

The role of registrars would seem to be more defined, in that they are specifically tasked with the registration of the marriage. Where they are working with a superintendent registrar in a register office or on approved premises, that is clearly their role. Where the wedding takes place in a registered place of worship, however, the role of the registrar becomes more ambiguous. First, their presence at a religious service is yet a further example of how the 1836 Act drew no clear distinction between the sacred and the secular. Second, in those situations where the pre-scribed words are not incorporated within the religious service but repeated separately before the registrar, it is ambiguous whether they are registering a marriage that has been conducted according to religious rites or conducting a separate wedding.

In the early years of the 1836 Act, the 'civil' role of the registrar was blurred still further by the appointment of registrars who shared the same beliefs as those whose marriages they were registering.[41] This went some way to mitigating the resentment felt by religious groups at having to have a registrar at their weddings. Of course, since 1899 it has in principle been open to the trustees of any registered place of worship to appoint their own authorised person.[42] That many were slow to take up the option does not mean that there was no desire to dispense with the presence of the registrar. Even within the Wesleyan Methodists, who had campaigned the hardest for change, only a minority of ministers became authorised. The reason would seem to be that a number of last-minute changes to the 1898 Act made the role of the authorised person an essentially passive one, and the regulations issued by the GRO the following year made it a distinctly unattractive one. Again, the legacy of this continues to the present day. Only around half of all registered places of worship have appointed an authorised person, and the reasons given by imams today for not becoming authorised are almost identical to those expressed by Nonconformist ministers in the nineteenth century.[43] If the focus of regulation is to switch to the person officiating at the ceremony, then care needs to be taken to ensure that the terms of any new scheme do not deter individuals from taking on this role. While

---

[41] See Chapter 3.
[42] See Chapter 5.
[43] Rebecca Probert, Rajnaara Akhtar, Vishal Vora, Sharon Blake, and Tania Barton, 'The importance of being authorised: the genesis, limitations, and legacy of the Marriage Act 1898' (in preparation).

there needs to be a degree of regulation, there also needs to be reassurance that minor mistakes are unlikely to result in either the invalidation of marriages or criminal sanctions being imposed.

That brings us on to the issue of religious-only marriage ceremonies. In the light of current policy debates,[44] it is vital to underline the fact that these are by no means an exclusively modern phenomenon, or one exclusively linked to non-Christian religious beliefs. There are examples of Catholic priests conducting marriages outside the legal framework in the 1840s, of Greek Orthodox marriages taking place in private homes in the 1850s, and of Jewish immigrants from Eastern Europe being married by their own rabbis from the 1860s.[45] At the same time, looking back at the history of Muslim ceremonies of marriage in England and Wales, it does not appear that the requirement to marry in a particular building is one that is intrinsically problematic for Muslim couples. After all, ceremonies took place at the Liverpool Institute and at the Woking mosque when neither were registered for weddings,[46] suggesting that those couples who went through a ceremony there did so out of choice rather than necessity. That is not to say that weddings should have to take place in specific buildings, merely that we need to look deeper into the reasons why religious-only marriage ceremonies are taking place in order to ensure that any future law makes suitable accommodations for all religious faiths.

It should also be noted that the modern concept of the non-qualifying ceremony is not as new as it might seem. There have long been cases in which the courts have refused to recognise ceremonies that had been conducted according to religious rites but not necessarily in accordance with English law, leaving the parties without legal rights or recognition.[47] Moreover, the differentiation between a marriage that was void and one that was no marriage at all has long been implicit. Ever since the early nineteenth century the law had made it very difficult to invalidate a marriage on the basis of non-compliance with the required formalities. The Marriage Acts of 1823 and 1836 both stipulated that a marriage would only be void if both parties knowingly and wilfully failed to comply with certain specified requirements. At the same time, when religious-only

---

[44] See Chapter 9.
[45] See further Chapters, 3, 4, and 5.
[46] See Chapters 5 and 6.
[47] See for example the issues with Catholic religious-only marriage ceremonies in the 1850s and Jewish *stille huppah* from the 1860s to the early twentieth century, discussed in Chapters 3, 5, and 6.

marriage ceremonies came before the courts, their consequences seem to have been resolved solely by reference to whether the parties had complied with the law, rather than by taking into account whether their non-compliance had been deliberate. The non-recognition of ceremonies that had been conducted entirely outside the legal framework suggests that even in the nineteenth century there was a category of ceremonies to which the 'knowing and wilful' test did not apply.[48] Only after it became possible to make financial orders upon a decree of nullity, and only when it was determined that such a decree (as compared to a declaratory order) could be made in relation to a void marriage, was there a need to make a formal differentiation between a marriage that was void and a ceremony that was no marriage at all.[49] Again, that is not intended to justify the current law, simply to point out that it has evolved without any real evaluation of what is the minimum needed to create a marriage in the eyes of the law, and to stress the importance of any revised scheme providing clarity on this point.

The laws regulating how and where couples can get married are now widely recognised as overly complex, restrictive, outdated, and in desperate need of reform. And such reform needs to be informed by the situation in the twenty-first century, rather than by the legacy of the nineteenth. That the structures established by the Marriage Act 1836 do not work for all faiths today is hardly surprising given that some faiths had no opportunity to shape them.

Looking at how past proposals for reform were received can also provide reassurance as to the likely impact of future change. Practically every single amendment to the law regulating weddings that has been proposed over the past 180 years has generated some resistance. The more wide-ranging the reform, the wilder the predictions as to the consequences that would follow. One writer warned about fake religions and the commercialisation of marriage, claiming that any building could be 'registered by any fanatic or impostor for any form of belief, however extravagant'; such 'marriage-houses', he argued, would compete for trade with 'glitter, and lights', with the ceremonial being 'followed by a dance, a concert, a lottery, a *fete*, or scenes of still more startling festivity'. The idea of being able to marry in a register office attracted an even more dramatic prediction: in that same writer's view '[i]f, in the vengeance of Heaven, this rash, odious, and insulting proposition should ever pass into

---

[48] See Chapters 5 and 6.

[49] The stakes were raised still further by the expansion of the range of orders that could be made in the early 1970s: Matrimonial Proceedings and Property Act 1970; Matrimonial Causes Act 1973.

the statute book there is an end of the morals of England'.[50] The proposed
bill that was the subject of his ire was what became the Marriage Act 1836.
Happily, these dire prognostications did not prevent the bill from becoming law, and in the event they proved very wide of the mark.

Writing this final chapter at the end of 2020, under the shadow of
another lockdown and with the likelihood of future restrictions being
imposed on weddings, it is perhaps not the best time to be making
predictions about the future. Instead, I close with the hope that it will
once again be possible for families and friends to come together, that
those who have had or chose to postpone their weddings will be able to
celebrate them, and that this time recommendations for reform will be
implemented. The law should reflect how twenty-first-century couples
wish to marry, rather than how nineteenth-century lawmakers thought
they should.

---

[50] *Blackwoods Magazine*, 1836, reprinted in the *Morning Post*, 11 May 1836.

INDEX

Lightning Source UK Ltd.
Milton Keynes UK
UKHW020847120921
390429UK00003B/43